KT-376-995

AND SO OUR STORY BEGINS...

The Age of Industry has come to Albion.

Though some call it the Age of Oppression.

When freedom is nothing but a dream, it's time to make a stand.

To lead a rebellion. To be a Hero.

Welcome to the city of the downtrodden, where those who dare to speak out are punished.

And those who dare to hope, find nothing to hope for.

True rebels fight against all odds. True rebels never give up.

Yet they cannot triumph alone.

The uprising has begun, but who will lead the revolution?

USING THIS GUIDE

Fable III is a special game that requires a unique approach when organizing a strategy guide. You'll find all of the expansive content you've come to expect from BradyGames, but in a slightly different format. This strategy guide is primarily divided into three sections. The largest of these, titled "The Road to Rule", provides a guide to each of the dozens of quests contained in the game. This section is divided into individual chapters that coincide with the major objectives in the main story campaign. Each of the optional side-quests contained in the game is covered within these chapters, right when they first become available during the story. *Fable III's* glowing trail and ability to fast travel make it possible to follow along with the story and receive tactics for each of the quests in a streamlined fashion without having to wade through pages of maps and information on collectables and other superfluous information. This section is for those who want assistance on a particular objective or quest.

The next major section is what we call the "Albion Atlas." This sizable chapter is a compendium of information for each and every area within the game. This is where you'll find maps to each of the areas, complete with callouts for every bit of treasure and collectable item in the game. This section also includes a listing of shops and jobs in each area as well as strategy regarding Demon Doors, Gold Doors, finding the Gold Keys, as well as tips for unlocking secret side areas within each region. This portion of the guide is for those players who love the treasure hunting aspect of *Fable* games. Whether you're searching for the missing Brightwall Books, dirty-mouthed Gnomes, or the last of the Gold Keys, this section will help you find it.

The third major section of the book is really a collection of chapters and data that lifts the hood on the game and lets you see its inner workings. Here you'll find a wealth of data along with advanced strategies for topics including the weapons and magic system, earning money through real estate and jobs, relationship building, battling enemies, and so much more. These chapters are guaranteed to provide you with the knowledge needed to become a ruthlessly efficient ruler who will not only have little trouble slaying foes and maximizing riches, but one with a clear path to unlocking every Achievement in the game.

FABLE III

CAST OF CHARACTERS

You are the star of *Fable III* but what form your character takes is entirely up to you. Will you be male or female? Will your actions and gestures give you the reputation of a benevolent hero or a tyrannical ruler? Will you stroll about town in a comically unattractive chicken suit or will you mind your appearance and be considered dapper and well-coifed? Each of the choices you make will affect your appearance to some degree. Consult the "Hero's Way" and "Items and Clothing" chapters of this book for full details on how your decisions can affect your outward appearance—and how easily you may change that appearance on a whim. In the meantime, continue reading to learn about some of the characters you will meet along the way to becoming ruler of Albion.

YOUR ROYAL FAMILY

KING LOGAN

Logan, your elder brother, is the unpopular King of Albion and your only surviving blood relative. He inherited the throne following your parents' deaths and was not only charged with ruling the land of Albion, but being your legal guardian as well. A man of few words, Logan shares little with the public. His subjects perceive him to be a ruthless and selfish leader, completely unlike the former ruler. His policies, taxes, and lack of compassion have given rise to an underground resistance.

SIR WALTER BECK

He received his knighthood while leading the Albion army under your father's rule and has known you since birth. He has been your mentor, your confidant, and is your most trusted friend. Walter's sense of duty is unmatched and he would not hesitate to lay his life down in order to protect Albion. While his peers concern themselves with advancing their careers and appeasing the crown, Walter acts of his own accord and is not afraid to speak his mind when it benefits the nation he loves. Walter has been growing weary of King Logan's rulings and has realized that as long as he continues to serve the King of Albion, he cannot serve its people.

JASPER

Jasper is your personal attendant and, like Walter, is every bit the family member Logan is. Jasper has been there to raise you since the days of your youth and isn't about to abandon you now. After leaving the castle, Jasper assumes stewardship of the Hero's Sanctuary, where he is always on hand to offer a compliment, a witty remark, or even help alert you to some important news. Your father has left a book for Jasper that contains all there is to know about being a Hero. Jasper will happily spend his days mastering the book's subject matter so that you may get the most out of the Sanctuary. After all, Jasper sees you not as his employer, but his child. He wants nothing more than to see you succeed in your efforts. He will forever be on hand to help you any way he can.

SABINE

Sabine is the aging leader of the Dwellers who reside in a small caravan camp in the snow-covered mountains of Mistpeak. The Dwellers eke out a simple existence, preferring to live in harmony with their natural surroundings rather than move to a city. They are accustomed to a harder life, but Logan's policies have pushed them to the brink of starvation. Whereas the former Ruler granted them a measure of autonomy within the kingdom, Logan has increasingly targeted their lands for exploitation and resource harvesting and has given the Dwellers no say in the measure. The Dwellers are in dire need of assistance, yet who is in a position to help?

BEN FINN

Lieutenant Ben Finn is a charismatic friend of Walter's stationed at Mourningwood Fort, the least desirable of all military outposts in Albion. Ben Finn is a seasoned traveler, writer, and soldier whose memoirs have been scattered throughout the pubs of Bowerstone. They provide enjoyable reading for all who scan their pages. A self-fashioned ladies' man, Ben Finn puts few things above his pursuit of happiness—and female companionship. Though his demeanor may cast him as someone who can't be relied upon, his devotion to Major Swift and Sir Walter Beck is complete. Ben Finn will not let these men down. He is an invaluable ally and combatant.

PAGE

Page is the leader of the Bowerstone Resistance, an underground organization plotting to overthrow King Logan. She and her members live in the sewers beneath Bowerstone Industrial, free from prying eyes and looser lips. Her headquarters are safe from Logan's soldiers, at least for now. But Page has seen firsthand the hunger, homelessness, and suffering that Logan's policies have brought the commoners and she is willing to die to bring about the change the city's poor require to survive. Page is reluctant to trust anyone and will not hesitate to kill those who threaten her operation—a policy that has kept her alive for this long—but she is as compassionate as they come. Page is the guardian that Bowerstone's lower class so desperately needs.

KALIN

Across the sea is a forgotten land of sand and rock, home to a dying people known as the Aurorans. Kalin is the leader of those who remain, having inherited the role from her deceased father. Unspeakable horror threatens the city they call Aurora. Many have died and Kalin, along with just a handful of other Aurorans, has been forced to live as a prisoner within her own city, afraid to venture out into the desert for fear of certain death. Yet, despite their predicament, Kalin and her people will not hesitate to help those who need their care. Kalin knows that her city cannot survive without Albion's protection, but she is limited in what she can do to convince its ruler to deem Aurora worth saving.

REAVER

For every King there is an unscrupulous advisor whispering in his ear. In Albion, that man goes by the name of Reaver. The millionaire head of Reaver Industries has been granted complete control of Bowerstone Industrial and enjoys a monopoly on ruthless profiteering. Reaver cares not for the environment and even less for his fellow man. He proudly employs children in sweatshop conditions and treats his adult employees like slaves. A brutally efficient businessman, Reaver will not hesitate to kill anyone who dares protest. Those who deafly ignore his suggestions do so at their own peril.

THERESA

Theresa is the seer who resides in the Tattered Spire, far off the coast of Albion. Theresa played an important role in your father's defeat of Lucien and subsequent rise to power. Her motives are unknown, as are her true powers and identity. Theresa will escort you along the Road to Rule and be there to cast judgment when the time comes.

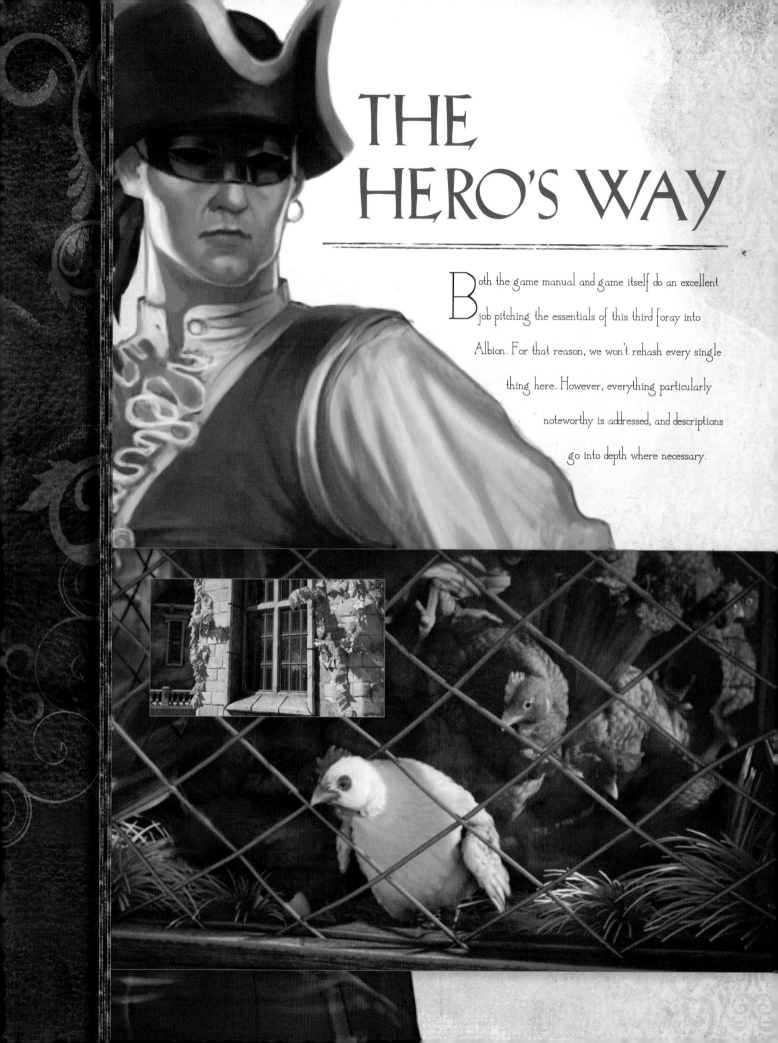

THE HERO'S WAY

Both the game manual and game itself do an excellent job pitching the essentials of this third foray into Albion. For that reason, we won't rehash every single thing here. However, everything particularly noteworthy is addressed, and descriptions go into depth where necessary.

GENDER BIAS

Upon starting *Fable III*, you'll have to select the gender of your Hero. The main thrust of the game is the same either way, so the choice comes down mostly to aesthetics. Do you prefer male or female voice acting for the lead protagonist? Would you rather fuss over the wardrobe of a woman, or a man? For most major aspects of gameplay, though, gender doesn't matter. The Hero, whether man or woman, will become a titan in combat, and ultimately a legend to the people of Albion—whether that's as a benevolent savior, or as yet another ghastly cog in the machine of ongoing political corruption, is up to you.

Do you want to follow the path of the prince, or the princess?

LEFT TRIGGER 9   10   8 **RIGHT TRIGGER**

1 **Movement**. The left analog stick controls your movement. While not available right at the beginning, sprinting for extra speed can be accomplished soon enough by holding Ⓐ while moving with 🕹.

2 **Camera Control**. The right analog stick controls the movement of the camera. Camera controls can be inverted if desired under the **Options** panel, in the **Hero's Sanctuary**.

3 The D-Pad can occasionally be used for extra, context-sensitive commands. During battle, the D-Pad handles using healing items and magic potions. Outside of combat, the D-Pad may point your attention to spending points on the **Road to Rule**, or to checking in with your family or with pressing objectives via the **World Map Table**. Contextual commands on the D-Pad can also be used to move between rooms in the Hero's Sanctuary more quickly.

D-PAD DIRECTION	POSSIBLE COMMANDS
Up	World Map, Road to Rule, Slow Time potion, Train your Dog, Apologize for a Crime you Commit
Down	Safety On/Off, Summon Creatures potion
Left	Food item
Right	Health potion

4 **Melee attack** or **Evil Expression**.

5 **Ranged attack** or **Silly Expression**.

6 **Magic attack** or **cancel**.

7 **Interact, good expression, sprint,** or **roll**.

8 Holding 🎮 centers the camera behind you. If citizens of Albion are in view, symbols appear above their heads indicating the status of their relationship with you. Also, occasional points of interest prompt the holding of 🎮 to zoom in on something important.

9 🎮 comes into play when mingling with villagers. When facing a citizen of Albion, press 🎮 to hold hands with them. They follow you thereafter, until you press 🎮 again to release your grasp. Holding 🎮 also uses over-the-shoulder aiming while wielding a firearm.

10 Tap 🎮 to center the camera behind you, or hold 🎮 to enter first-person view. This is ideal for getting your bearings, taking in the beautiful scenery, or scouting out a pesky garden gnome.

11 **The Hero's Sanctuary.** This is a secret space you can visit almost anytime that represents your menu, essentially. You can peruse your weapons and outfits, scope out the **World Map Table**, or even go stand on your accumulated money and swell with pride.

THE ROAD TO RULE

The aged seer Theresa leads you along the Road to Rule. This mystical path represents the struggle for Albion's throne. As you close in on the magical facsimile of Bowerstone Castle set on the edge of the Road to Rule, so too will you be closing in on the actual castle, with its actual throne. Various important followers you've brought over to your cause are also represented along the Road to Rule, and the appearance of your Hero at the time is immortalized as you pass each new gate along the way. Also spread across the Road to Rule are special treasure chests, which require the spending of Guild Seals in order to open. The first Guild Seal is obtained at the beginning of the game, while escaping from Bowerstone Castle. You'll accumulate hundreds of Guild Seals throughout your travels by gathering followers to your cause, which you can accomplish through valor in combat, quests, and interactions with the citizenry of Albion.

■ The Road to Rule is where the Hero learns new abilities and spells.

All told, you'll be pulled into the Road to Rule by Theresa at ten distinct points in the adventure, generally after major accomplishments. She will bring you up to speed on your progress toward usurping Logan, and then you'll have an opportunity to gain new abilities from chests you couldn't access before. If you lack the Guild Seals to open a chest you want, or if you simply decline to spend Guild Seals, you can always return to the Road to Rule later by entering it from the glowing blue seal in the Hero's Sanctuary.

■ Here's something interesting: while being in the Hero's Sanctuary freezes time, standing on the Road to Rule does not!

ROAD TO RULE 1: AFTER GUILD SEAL

CHEST CONTENTS	GUILD SEAL COST	EFFECT
Fireball Spell	1	New Spell Gauntlet

ROAD TO RULE 2: AFTER MUSIC BOX

CHEST CONTENTS	GUILD SEAL COST	EFFECT
Dye Pack I	2	Red, blue, grey, green dyes available.
Friend Expression Pack	2	Whistle, Hero Pose, and Chat expressions available.
Landlord Pack	2	Can buy, rent, and decorate houses.
Melee Level 1	20	Do more damage with all melee weapons.
Ranged Level 1	20	Do more damage with all guns.
Magic Level 1	20	Do more damage with all spells.
Shock Spell	40	New Spell Gauntlet

ROAD TO RULE 3: AFTER SAKER

CHEST CONTENTS	GUILD SEAL COST	EFFECT
Lover Expression Pack	5	Dance, Hug, and Kiss expressions available.
Family Pack	5	Can now get married, buy homes, have kids, and adopt. (Lover Expression Pack also unlocked)
Upgrade Blacksmith to Level 2	5	Make more money smithing.
Upgrade Pie Making Level 2	5	Make more money baking.
Upgrade Lute to Level 2	5	Make more money strumming.
Melee Level 2	40	Do more damage with all melee weapons.
Ranged Level 2	40	Do more damage with all guns.
Magic Level 2	40	Do more damage with all spells.

ROAD TO RULE 4: SABINE PROMISE

CHEST CONTENTS	GUILD SEAL COST	EFFECT
Joker Expression Pack	5	Tickle, Pat-A-Cake, and Chicken Dance expressions available.
Dye Pack II	5	Khaki, purple, orange, and pink dyes available.
Upgrade Blacksmith to Level 3	10	Make more money smithing.
Upgrade to Pie Making Level 3	10	Make more money baking.
Upgrade Lute to Level 3	10	Make more money strumming.
Ice Storm Spell	40	New Spell Gauntlet.

ROAD TO RULE 5: AFTER THE HOLE

CHEST CONTENTS	GUILD SEAL COST	EFFECT
Dye Pack III	5	White, lime, yellow, and brown dyes available.
Entrepreneur Pack	5	Can now haggle and own shops.
Vortex Spell	40	New Spell Gauntlet.
Spell Weaving	50	Can now wear two different spell gauntlets simultaneously.

ROAD TO RULE 6: SWIFT PROMISE

CHEST CONTENTS	GUILD SEAL COST	EFFECT
Bully Expression Pack	5	Insult, Point and Laugh, and Threaten expressions available.
Theft Pack	5	Can now steal from private property.
Upgrade Blacksmith to Level 4	25	Make more money smithing.
Upgrade Pie Making Level 4	25	Make more money baking.
Upgrade Lute to Level 4	25	Make more money strumming.
Melee Level 3	60	Do more damage with all melee weapons.
Ranged Level 3	60	Do more damage with all guns.
Magic Level 3	60	Do more damage with all spells.

ROAD TO RULE 7: PAGE MEETING

CHEST CONTENTS	GUILD SEAL COST	EFFECT
Good Parenting Pack	5	Tickle Child, Pick Up and Hug Child, and Cuddle Baby expressions available.
Hooligan Expression Pack	5	Rodeo, Fart on Villager, and Vulgar Thrust expressions available.
Upgrade Blacksmith to Level 5	60	Make more money smithing.
Upgrade Pie Making Level 5	60	Make more money baking.
Upgrade Lute to Level 5	60	Make more money strumming.
Force Push Spell	40	New Spell Gauntlet.

ROAD TO RULE 8: PAGE PROMISE

CHEST CONTENTS	GUILD SEAL COST	EFFECT
Scary Expression Pack	5	Growl, Scary Laugh, and Bloodlust Roar expressions now available.
Force Push Spell	40	New Spell Gauntlet.
Melee Level 4	80	Do more damage with all melee weapons.
Ranged Level 4	80	Do more damage with all guns.
Magic Level 4	80	Do more damage with all spells.

ROAD TO RULE 9: KALIN PROMISE

CHEST CONTENTS	GUILD SEAL COST	EFFECT
Blades Spell	40	New Spell Gauntlet.

ROAD TO RULE 10

CHEST CONTENTS	GUILD SEAL COST	EFFECT
Melee Level 5	100	Do more damage with all melee weapons.
Ranged Level 5	100	Do more damage with all guns.
Magic Level 5	100	Do more damage with all spells.

Opening every treasure chest along the Road to Rule requires a hoard of Guild Seals—1570, to be exact. There is, naturally, an Xbox LIVE Achievement available if you snag every chest. If you don't care about the Achievement, or if you'd like to focus on the story before going for a 100% completion rate, you can lower the Guild Seal burden by focusing your upgrades. Specializing in weapons, for example, is a good way to limit the amount of Guild Seals spent. You can easily get away with focusing on only one weapon type to fully upgrade. Or, consider being selective with your jobs. There are three hands-on occupations for direct money-earning, but you can save Guild Seals by figuring out which job you enjoy most, then just upgrading that one. If a spell doesn't sound particularly interesting to you, you don't have to open the chest for it. Additionally, if you know you'd like to focus on making your Hero either naughty or nice, you can avoid purchasing expression packs for expressions you won't need. You can always go back and open any chests you passed up at first, once you have more Guild Seals.

STAYING UP-TO-DATE ON GUILD SEALS

ROAD TO RULE VISIT	GUILD SEALS REQUIRED	CUMULATIVE TOTAL
1	1	1
2	104	105
3	145	250
4	80	330
5	100	430
6	265	695
7	250	945
8	285	1230
9	40	1270
10	300	1570

Don't worry, at first, about opening every single chest on the Road to Rule. Open chests for things you think you'll use, then come back for chests you skipped later on, whenever you have a surplus of Guild Seals.

WEAPONS THAT CAN SPEED UP EARNING GUILD SEALS IN COMBAT

WEAPON NAME		LEGENDARY BONUS	OBJECTIVE	REWARD
SWORD	The Splade	Scrounger	Dig up 30 items.	Earn Guild Seals Faster in Combat.
	Slimquick	Shopping Spree	Spend 8,000 of your personal gold.	Earn Guild Seals Faster in Combat.
	Wolfsbane	Overkill	Kill 50 enemies with flourishes.	Earn Guild Seals Faster in Combat.
	The Casanova	Charmer	Become friends with 30 villagers.	Earn Guild Seals Faster in Combat.
	The Channeler	Researcher	Spend 8,000 of your personal gold.	Earn Guild Seals Faster in Combat.
	Beadle's Cutlass	Dayripper	Kill 300 enemies in the daytime.	Earn Guild Seals Faster in Combat.
	Souldrinker	Blackguard	Decrease your moral standing.	Earn Guild Seals Faster in Combat.
	Really Sharp Pair of Scissors	Despot	Earn Guild Seals from evil expressions.	Earn Guild Seals Faster in Combat.
	Thunderblade	Show-off	Kill 200 enemies with flourishes.	Earn Guild Seals Faster in Combat.
	Thunderblade	Hero	Complete 30 quests.	Earn Guild Seals Faster in Combat
HAMMER	Sorrow's Fist	Loose Morals	Have an orgy with 4 other people.	Earn Guild Seals Faster in Combat
	The Absolver	Party Animal	Become friends with 30 villagers.	Earn Guild Seals Faster in Combat
	The Champion	Heartbreaker	Make 5 villagers love you.	Earn Guild Seals Faster in Combat
	Scythe's Warhammer	Legendary	Complete 30 quests.	Earn Guild Seals Faster in Combat
	The TYPO	Popular	Make 5 villagers love you.	Earn Guild Seals Faster in Combat
	The TYPO	Thwack!	Kill 100 enemies with flourishes.	Earn Guild Seals Faster in Combat
	The Tenderiser	Fiend	Earn Guild Seals from evil expressions.	Earn Guild Seals Faster in Combat
PISTOL	Holy Vengeance	Paragon	Increase your moral standing.	Earn Guild Seals Faster in Combat
	Reaver Industries Perforator	Retail Therapy	Spend 10,000 of your personal gold.	Earn Guild Seals Faster in Combat
	Briar's Blaster	Heroine	Complete 30 quests.	Earn Guild Seals Faster in Combat
	Bloodcraver	Blood Drinker	Kill 20 villagers who love you.	Earn Guild Seals Faster in Combat
	Dragonstomper .48	Revolutionist	Kill 50 nobles.	Earn Guild Seals Faster in Combat
	Defender of the Faith	Settled	Get married.	Earn Guild Seals Faster in Combat
	Ol' Malice	Hooligan	Smash 50 crates.	Earn Guild Seals Faster in Combat
	Ol' Malice	Featherbrained	Kick 100 chickens.	Earn Guild Seals Faster in Combat
RIFLE	The Hero's Companion	Family	Have 2 children.	Earn Guild Seals Faster in Combat
	Facemelter	Unholy	Decrease your moral standing.	Earn Guild Seals Faster in Combat
	Swift Irregular	Loyalty	Kill 300 mercenaries.	Earn Guild Seals Faster in Combat
	Arkwright's Flintlock	Socialite	Become friends with 30 villagers.	Earn Guild Seals Faster in Combat
	Arkwright's Flintlock	Spendthrift	Spend 10,000 of your personal gold.	Earn Guild Seals Faster in Combat
	The Shrieking Pilgrim	Saintly	Make 5 villagers love you.	Earn Guild Seals Faster in Combat

THE HERO'S SANCTUARY

The Guild Seal, a token passed down from your forebear, allows the stepping out of time to a safe haven. Jasper serves dutifully here, always ready with instruction, praise, and carefully-measured criticism. When you first cross through the Guild Seal to discover the Hero's Sanctuary, its rooms and functions are limited. As Jasper cleans up and explores this place of reprieve further, he'll gradually open new rooms and functions.

Acquiring the Guild Seal, and thus the Hero's Sanctuary, is the first step on the road to ruling Albion.

WORLD MAP TABLE

The World Map Table is a tremendous locus of power. From here, you can monitor all of Albion—the landscape can be surveyed, properties can be purchased/sold, and quests can be reviewed. You can even instantaneously fast travel to previously-visited locations.

You can survey the entire kingdom from this table

FAST TRAVEL

Fast travel is accomplished by pressing ❌ while viewing the desired destination. Sometimes, due to circumstance or a critical quest, fast travel is unavailable. Fast travel is a wonderful boon when you'd like to cut down on time spent hoofing it between locales. You do miss out on opportunities for dig spots, keys, treasure chests, gnomes, and combat experience, however.

Fast travel saves time and streamlines questing, but you never know what you might miss!

QUESTS

There's the Hero's main quest, of course, the focus of *Fable III*: the struggle with King Logan for the preservation of Albion. This is always in the foreground, but meanwhile, and much of the time, you're free to engage in various other worthwhile and profitable adventures. Through completion of these quests you engage further with the populace of Albion, earning Guild Seals, treasure, and gold along the way.

Citizens of Albion, along with a few other entities, indicate they offer a quest with a floating exclamation point (this is also true outside of the Hero's Sanctuary, away from the World Map Table). By hovering over them with the magnifying glass and pressing Ⓐ you can review their quest, make it the active one if desired, and even fast travel to the nearest possible location.

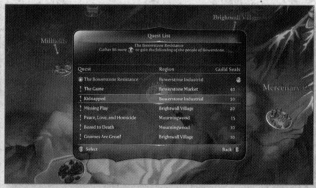

Though not immediately available, the quest list can eventually be accessed by pressing **Y** while viewing the World Map Table. Only one quest is active at a time, and the glowing trail traces its path. To direct the glowing trail elsewhere, make another quest the active one by selecting it from the quest list with **A**.

WEAPONS TO WEAR WHILE COMPLETING QUESTS

WEAPON NAME		LEGENDARY BONUS	OBJECTIVE	REWARD
SWORD	The Channeler	Quester	Complete 30 quests.	+ Shock Damage
	Beadle's Cutlass	Braggadocio	Complete 30 quests.	+30% Damage vs Human Enemies
	Thunderblade	Hero	Complete 30 quests.	Earn Guild Seals Faster in Combat
HAMMER	Faerie Hammer of the Moon King	Adventurer	Complete 30 quests.	+10 Extra Damage
	The Champion	Adventurer	Complete 30 quests.	+15 Extra Damage
	Scythe's Warhammer	Legendary	Complete 30 quests.	Earn Guild Seals Faster in Combat
PISTOL	Briar's Blaster	Heroine	Complete 30 quests.	Earn Guild Seals Faster in Combat
	Chickenbane	Swashbuckler	Complete 30 quests.	+12 Extra Damage
RIFLE	The Hero's Companion	Saviour	Complete 30 quests.	+20% Damage in Multiplayer
	The Sandgoose	Adventurous	Complete 20 quests.	+25 Extra Damage

AN ENTREPRENEUR IN ALBION

Our Hero isn't able to trade in real estate at first…apparently it takes a while for even children-of-state to get a license under King Logan's reign. Eventually domiciles can be purchased, then lived in or rented out. Owned rental properties naturally generate rent. Businesses can also be acquired, with a profit kicking back to the owner. As the owner of business and rental properties, you can set the rate of rent and price of goods along a full spectrum—all the way from heartless profiteering, to literally giving things away. How you act as a real estate owner in a given town goes an enormous way toward determining what people in that town think of you. For more on real estate, visit our "Real Estate Magnate" chapter.

Frou Frou Frocks (Clothing)
Owner: bradygames02
Price (Best Offer): 35655
Profits: 2376
Clothes Sale 40% off all items!

Select **A**
Back **B**
Fast Travel

Profits from rent and goods, as well as any familial upkeep, are calculated about every five minutes. No one will know if you idle in a safe place and take a nap. No one but you…

ARMORY

Stored in the armory is the Hero's vast arsenal. This formidable array of weaponry starts with the Hero weapons passed on from Albion's former Hero, and is bolstered by Legendary weapons and magical spell gauntlets found throughout the ongoing struggle. No single player will be able to get every Legendary weapon on his or her own—only so many Legendary weapons are available to a given Gamertag, and those you can't find on your own, you'll have to trade for with other players on Xbox LIVE. The Hero's combat prowess in general increases the more combat he or she sees, and upgrades for each weapon type can also be purchased on the Road to Rule with Guild Seals. Also, Legendary weapons have bonuses that can be unlocked by fulfilling certain requirements. Press **Y** when examining a weapon, whether in the armory or in a shop, to see more details on it, including these bonuses. For much more on combat and weapons in Albion, check out the "Weapons of Yore" chapter.

Melee attacks are performed with **X**. Melee weapons include agile swords and enormous hammers.

Ranged attacks are performed with **Y**. Spew a fusillade from afar with pistols and rifles. Isn't technology grand?

Magical spells are activated with **B**. The magic used is determined by the spell gauntlets worn.

THE ART OF FIGHTING

The Warrior

If you want to get up close and personal, this is your path. Inflicting damage and killing enemies with both swords and hammers contributes to the strength stat. The higher your strength, the stronger your stabs and swings[md]you'll look buffer, too. Flourish attacks help immensely. Any time you have an opening, charge up a flourish by pointing the left analog stick at the desired target while holding **X**. Once charged, simply release **X** to unleash the gathered strike. If the enemy is out of range, simply wait for him to foolishly step forward. Flourishes can hit more than one foe at a time and knock down most enemies, creating a perfect chance to rush over and finish them off with a downed attack. Your dog might take care of that for you, too. Focus your Guild Seals on treasure chests with melee-focused rewards along the Road to Rule. This increases damage for all swords and hammers, changes their appearance slightly, and increases the probability of flashy finishing moves in combat. For defense, practice rolling away from attacks by moving the left analog stick while pressing **A**, or enter a guard stance which blocks most incoming blows by holding **X**. If you need a serious boost in combat, break out a Slow Time potion (found occasionally throughout your adventure, and available from stores which sell potions). This potion, predictably, slows down all enemies. In effect, giving you blazing speed, so put this to good use by romping on foes with your melee weapon while they're rendered too sloth-like to retaliate. As a secondary option, both firearms and spells work well to support the melee-focused warrior. Go for firearms if you'd like to pepper enemies while they close to melee range, or spells if you would like to rely on area-of-effect magic to get you out of a bind in a hurry. Whichever secondary option you choose also comes in handy against bosses and enemy leaders, who often make it dangerous to stay close for very long.

The Highwayman

Rifles and pistols are available for those who prefer more discretionary altercations. Firearms, as you might expect, allow you to attack from distance. This forces enemies to fight on your terms, with the significant benefit that you'll usually be too far away for them to strike back. Pistols are a little faster and have one more round per reload, while rifles are slower and pack a heavier punch. Beware enemies of Albion who can also strike from afar. Some foes wield guns and magic, too. Gunplay increases your stature stat, which influences both strength of gunfire and your height. Along the Road to Rule, you'll want to focus on opening just the chests that increase the power of guns. Opening gun chests not only increases the power of your firearms, but also enhances their appearances, adds more rounds to each reload, and ups the frequency of flashy finishing moves in combat. Firearms have a flourish attack that charges by holding down **Y**. Release **Y** after a second to unload the powered-up shell, resulting in an extra-strong firearm salvo that deals extra damage and can knock foes down. While guns are great, you cannot guard while wielding one. All of your defense must come from evasion, which is normally fine. If you roll over and over against most enemies, they may never hit you, but you can't fire either. Against huge groups of enemies you may find yourself rolling more or less constantly, unable to get a word in edgewise with your firearm of choice. Consider making either melee attacks or magic a part-time fallback

THE ART OF FIGHTING (CONT.)

solution for when you are overrun and boxed in. Cut your way out with a sword, bash your way out with a hammer, or use a charged-up area-of-effect spell to hit everything around you at once. Even a small opening can leave you clear of the group again, and then it's back to circling the fringes while spraying gunfire.

The Wizard

Prefer a more arcane approach? That avenue is certainly open to you, through spell gauntlets. These special gloves allow you to cast an unlimited amount of offensive magic. Hold **B** to charge a spell, and release it to cast. Press the left analog stick toward the desired target for more powerful focused magic, or don't touch the left analog stick while releasing **B** for an area-of-effect cast centered on you. The addition of spell weaving allows the creation of entirely new spell effects, by combining any two spells into one potent cast. Using spells to damage and destroy enemies increases your magical aura stat. The higher this stat, the more powerful your magic. Higher levels of magical aura also cause you to glow with energy when charging up flourish attacks or more powerful spells! Some of our favorite spell weaving combinations include Fireball plus Blades for pure damage, Fireball plus Vortex for a great combination of instant offense and defense, and Vortex plus Ice Storm for personal, area-of-effect defense! Open magic-centric treasure chests along the Road to Rule to power up your magic, and note that increases magical ability also boosts the effectiveness of the Slow Time and Summon Creatures potions! A properly-timed Summon Creatures potion can change the complexion of any battle, no matter how hopeless it might seem, as every enemy becomes disinterested in you in favor of your ethereal shadow creature reinforcements.

DRESSING ROOM

The Hero's wardrobe is within these walls. There are custom slots for favorite outfits, and areas to select between garments, makeup, hair, tattoos, and dyes. At a few points in the game you'll be forced to wear a particular outfit, but generally you have complete control over your appearance. Different outfits generate different reactions from people. They'll find you more or less attractive or frightening, which has an effect on what they think of you. Pieces of various outfits are found throughout the game, in treasure chests, from dig spots, from dive spots, on bookshelves, in cabinets…wait, the Hero of Albion is wearing things the dog found in the dirt? Nevermind. Clothing, tattoos, and hairstyles can also be purchased in stores. Additional dyes are unlocked along the Road to Rule. For more on clothing, visit our Items and Clothing chapter.

Picking a starting outfit is practically the first thing you'll do. Further costume changes are made in the dressing room.

TROPHY ROOM

In this room lies ample proof of your spoils. Achievements and trophies are cataloged here, lining the walls of the hallway leading to the treasure storeroom and ledger. Here your fortune is piled, as bountiful or meager as you can manage. The ledger contains a history of the most recent transactions. Gold can be both earned and spent in myriad ways. You'll find it in dig spots, dive spots, treasure chests, bookshelves, just about everywhere. You'll get it from selling unneeded items or trade goods to pawnbrokers. You'll earn it in rent and profits from houses you rent out and businesses you own. But you'll also spend it on properties, weapons and outfits, general goods, and upkeep for families and houses. Eventually, money becomes a matter of importance way beyond just keeping you in nice duds—you're going to need an *abundant* supply of it, and you're going to have to work hard if you want to stay on the moral and ethical high ground while also making enough money to avoid disaster. Although for every ethical stand you bend on, a little, or a lot, you can stand to lessen the burden.

WEAPONS THAT CAN HELP AMASS WEALTH

WEAPON NAME		LEGENDARY BONUS	OBJECTIVE	REWARD
SWORD	Shardborne	Heartless	Drag 8 villagers to work.	Gain Money per Hit
	The Inquisitor	Extort	Earn Guild Seals from evil expressions.	Gain Money per Hit
HAMMER	Faerie Hammer of the Moon King	Assassin	Kill 100 enemies with flourishes.	+1 Gold per Hit
	The TYPO	Chum	Become friends with 30 villagers.	Gain Money with Each Hit
PISTOL	The Barnumificator	Hard Worker	Earn 10,000 gold from jobs.	+1 Gold per Hit
	The Barnumificator	Philanthropist	Give gifts to 20 players over Xbox LIVE.	Gain Money with Each Hit.
	Tee Killer Shooter	Accumulator	Spend 10,000 of your personal gold.	Gain Money with Each Hit
RIFLE	The Sandgoose	Aggressive	Earn Guild Seals from evil expressions.	+1 Gold per Hit
	The Sandgoose	Popularity	Become friends with 30 villagers.	Gain Money with Each Hit

There are extra spoils for Heroes who sock away enough gold. 6,000,000 ought to do it…

LIVE ROOM

This mysterious room, as Jasper explains haltingly, would seem to allow you to commune with other versions of the Hero, in other versions of Albion! Quantum physics in Albion, it would seem, hold to the Everett interpretation. Everything online is handled in this room. You can check available downloadable content, adjust online preferences and settings, and invite friends to your world. Overall statistics for your Hero are shown here, too.

Online play has many advantages. You can trade with friends to get weapons and outfits you can't find, and earn both Guild Seals and gold at accelerated rates.

WEAPONS THAT CAN BOOST MULTIPLAYER DAMAGE

WEAPON NAME		LEGENDARY BONUS	OBJECTIVE	REWARD
SWORD	The Merchant's Bodyguard	Big Spender	Spend 8,000 of your personal gold.	+20% Damage in Multiplayer
RIFLE	Scattershot	Donor	Give gifts to 20 players over Xbox LIVE.	+20% Damage in Multiplayer
	The Hero's Companion	Benefactor	Give gifts to 20 players over Xbox LIVE.	+12 Extra Damage

WEAPONS TO GIVE GIFTS WITH OVER XBOX LIVE

WEAPON NAME		LEGENDARY BONUS	OBJECTIVE	REWARD
SWORD	The Merchant's Bodyguard	Trader	Give gifts to 20 players over Xbox LIVE.	Gain Money with Each Hit.
PISTOL	The Barnumificator	Philanthropist	Give gifts to 20 players over Xbox LIVE.	Gain Money with Each Hit.
RIFLE	Scattershot	Donor	Give gifts to 20 players over Xbox LIVE.	+20% Damage in Multiplayer
	The Hero's Companion	Benefactor	Give gifts to 20 players over Xbox LIVE.	+12 Extra Damage

HERO STATUS PANEL

Shown here are the Hero's stats. While this paints a general portrait of the Hero's ability, there is more going on behind-the-scenes than is ever made transparent to the player.

COMBAT STATS AND HERO LEVEL

These attributes start at 0% experience and scale up to 100% slowly, through dealing damage and scoring kills with a particular type of attack. At certain points along this progression, the star rating shown to the player here changes, though not perfectly—some stars are worth more than others. And even though stars might all be filled up, implying mastery, you still might not be done capping experience for that attack type. Together, these combat stats go toward a hidden stat: Hero Level. Hero Level starts at 1 and eventually goes all the way to 10. Your Hero Level determines enemy difficulty and random loot quality.

STAT	INCREASED BY USING	INFLUENCES
Strength	Swords and hammers	Hero Level, melee attack power, and brawn
Stature	Pistols and rifles	Hero Level, firearm attack power, and height
Magical Aura	Spell gauntlets	Hero Level, spell power, and glow

EXPERIENCE LEVEL	COMBAT MULTIPLIER	STAR RATING
0~17%	0x~1.17x	0
18~33%	1.18x~1.33x	★
34~50%	1.34x~1.5x	★★
51~71%	1.51x~1.71x	★★★
72~83%	1.72x~1.83x	★★★★
84~100%	1.84x~2x	★★★★★

MORALITY: GOOD AND EVIL

This game is full of choice. You choose your gender, you choose what to wear, you choose how to arm yourself, and you choose whether to be kind or dastardly to citizens on an individual level. But you'll also make choices that influence the kingdom at large, impacting, for better or worse, huge swaths of the populace at a time. The journey to the seat of power in Bowerstone Castle is long and difficult, and you won't make it there without followers to back you up. Securing these followers in the first place comes by way of making **promises** to them—inducements assuring that Albion will be better under your care than under that of Logan. And so here is the problem politicians run into about promises— eventually, one might be expected to keep them. Keeping an old promise made when you seemed weak and powerless is noble, but your priorities may have shifted since, and your resources may be strained. The decisions you make—whether you honor your promises—is the primary force shaping whether you walk a path of virture, or malice.

Morality
Attractiveness
Weight

Morality scales from a max of 1000 to a low of -1000. The Hero begins the game at 0, or neutral, morality.

WEAPONS TO WEAR WHILE INCREASING MORAL STANDING

WEAPON NAME		LEGENDARY BONUS	OBJECTIVE	REWARD
SWORD	Avo's Lamentation	Righteous	Increase your moral standing.	+20% Damage vs Evil Enemies
HAMMER	The Champion	Wrath	Increase your moral standing.	+ Flame Damage
PISTOL	Holy Vengeance	Paragon	Increase your moral standing.	Earn Guild Seals Faster in Combat
RIFLE	The Shrieking Pilgrim	Righteous	Increase your moral standing.	+20% Damage vs Evil Human Enemies

POSITIVE MORALITY

REQUIREMENT	EFFECT
Show charity to a beggar	+1 morality
Eat tofu or carrot	+1 morality
Eat celery	+2 morality
Catch criminal	+10 morality
Various story decisions	+25~+175 morality

NEGATIVE MORALITY

REQUIREMENT	EFFECT
Threaten expression	-1 morality
Assault	-5 morality
Vandalism	-5 morality
Eat crunchy chick	-5 morality
Force a citizen to work	-10 morality
Kill soldier or villager	-15 morality
Various story decisions	-25~-175 morality

WEAPONS TO WEAR WHILE LOWERING MORAL STANDING

WEAPON NAME		LEGENDARY BONUS	OBJECTIVE	REWARD
SWORD	Mr Stabby	Assassin	Decrease your moral standing.	Gain Money and Evil with Each Hit
	Shardborne	Unholy	Decrease your moral standing.	+5 Extra Damage, +30% vs Non-Evil Enemies
	Souldrinker	Blackguard	Decrease your moral standing.	Earn Guild Seals Faster in Combat.
PISTOL	Reaver Industries Perforator	Fiend	Decrease your moral standing.	+7 Extra Damage, +30% vs Non-Evil Enemies
	Facemelter	Unholy	Decrease your moral standing.	Earn Guild Seals Faster in Combat
RIFLE	Skorm's Justice	Demon	Decrease your moral standing.	+10 Extra Damage, +30% vs Non-Evil Enemies
	The Sandgoose	Popularity	Become friends with 30 villagers.	Gain Money with Each Hit

CAREER OF EVIL

Eventually you will be able to donate to or embezzle from the kingdom's treasury. Donating money is viewed as a good act, while embezzling into your own coffers is viewed as evil. It's not a zero-sum exchange, though; donating then embezzling the same amount of money results in a net loss of morality. This means that once you have access to the treasury, you can easily max out evil any time you like. The most you can donate or remove at once is 1,000,000 🪙. This donation of one million grants +200 morality. Then, immediately taking that million back grants -300. So, even from totally virtuous, maxed-out morality (1000), you can go all the way to infernal evil (-1000) in only 20 swaps of the same one million gold! Sadly, there is no way to game the banking system for an equally quick and painless trip in the other alignment direction, although donating to the treasury in large quantities is also the fastest way to gain morality. Like many good moral decisions, it just costs a lot more.

It's not terribly hard to be evil anyway, but this is the easiest way to max out either alignment. This is also a method that allows you to easily achieve totally evil morality without ever harming a single citizen or making a single evil decision, should you so desire.

The consequences of morality are reflected in your renown; complete strangers will have opinions of you based on things you did. As a kind hero of the people you'll garner grateful hoots, hollers, and claps throughout the land, and some especially appreciative citizens will present you with gifts (these gifts pile up inside the Hero's Sanctuary, where opening them reveals items). As a scourge who attends only to your own selfishness, you'll draw scorn and derision from many citizens—at least, from those who aren't too frightened to do naught but tremble in your presence, and there will be many of them, too.

REQUIREMENT	EFFECT
Donate 100 🪙 to treasury	+0.02 morality
Donate 1,000,000 🪙 to treasury	+200 morality
Remove 100 🪙 from treasury	-0.03 morality
Remove 1,000,000 🪙 from treasury	-300 morality

WEAPONS THAT CAN HELP YOU BE EVIL (AND RICH!)

WEAPON NAME		LEGENDARY BONUS	OBJECTIVE	REWARD
SWORD	Mr Stabby	Assassin	Decrease your moral standing.	Gain Money and Evil with Each Hit
	Mr Stabby	Taskmaster	Drag 8 villagers to work.	Gain Money and Evil with Each Hit

Morality also alters appearance. The faces of the virtuous take on a luminous, joyful cast, while the faces of the wretched purse into a permanent, threatening sneer. In the end, the wholly good or evil will find themselves adorned like an angel or demon.

CRIME AND PUNISHMENT

Many activities that have a negative moral value are also considered illegal. These acts include theft, assault, vandalism, and murder. Witnesses to these acts usually flee and look for a guard. The current bounty cost and duration are displayed, and alerted guards chase you down and demand your surrender. You'll have three options. You can either pay a fine or perform community service, with higher penalties incurred for more egregious offenses. Or, you can resist arrest. The guards will draw their weapons at this point, and you'll now have to run, fight, or apologize and surrender.

This icon's appearance indicates you've been witnessed committing a crime. You can hold up on ○ to apologize, which sometimes absolves you of guilt if the onlooker forgives you.

If you have job expertise leveled up all the way along the Road to Rule, even the steepest fines are easy to work off through community service, making a life of crime totally manageable. While using community service to pay off a debt to society, you are considered on parole—if you add to your bounty again at this point it bears an extra penalty for parole violation!

PURITY AND CORRUPTION

Morality deals with good and evil, and is a stat you can see. There's another behavior scale you can't see, though, that deals more with questions of consideration and selfishness than virtue. This is the purity and corruption scale. You begin the game at 0, or fully pure. Through inconsiderate, selfish actions, this value can increase to become as high as 1000. Like morality and attractiveness, this value effects what the populace thinks of you. Here, it's manifested mostly as gossip—the snippets of dialog you'll hear about yourself as you wander among the people.

Setting prices on properties all the way up or down is the most potent way to continually and automatically influence purity and corruption.

Most activities that change purity and corruption only adjust this value a slight amount. One activity can change this stat in a meaningful way, though—real estate management. How you set the prices for rent and goods in your buildings has such a profound and frequent effect on purity and corruption that the decision to deviate from normal prices on properties renders all other purity and corruption considerations moot. Once you own a sizeable empire of businesses in every settlement, simply picking a pricing extreme (either maxed prices, or completely free) changes this rating by triple-digit amounts every five minutes, capping the stat in either direction in less than an hour! Of course, this assumes you high-or-lowball uniformly across all your properties. If you have a balance of overpriced and underpriced properties, the net impact on purity and corruption each cycle may be much less, and harder to predict or discern.

REDUCE CORRUPTION

REQUIREMENT	EFFECT
Cuddle expression	-1 corruption
Tickle expression	-1 corruption
Dance expression	-1 corruption
Pat-a-cake expression	-1 corruption
Whistle expression	-1 corruption
Hero pose expression	-1 corruption
Shake hands expression	-1 corruption
Pet dog	-1 corruption
Fetch with dog	-1 corruption
Eat vegetables or tofu	-1~-5 corruption
Set prices on rental properties and shops to low or free	-tons of corruption

CORRUPTION NEUTRAL

CHICKEN EXPRESSION

Kick chicken
Drink wine
Set prices to normal on rental properties and shops

WEAPONS THAT CAN HELP WITH WEIGHT LOSS AND CORRUPTION

WEAPON NAME		LEGENDARY BONUS	OBJECTIVE	REWARD
HAMMER	The Tenderiser	Soul Burner	Kill 3 spouses.	Lose Weight and Gain Purity with Each Hit.

ATTRACTIVENESS

Attractiveness is what it sounds like—a measure of the physical appeal of the Hero. This is influenced by weight and by dress, from different clothes, to tattoos, to makeup and hairstyles. Check out our chapter on Items and Clothing for more.

INCREASE CORRUPTION

REQUIREMENT	EFFECT
Vulgar thrust expression	+1 corruption
Belch expression	+1 corruption
Roar expression	+1 corruption
Scary laugh expression	+1 corruption
Growl expression	+1 corruption
Fart expression	+1 corruption
Rodeo expression	+1 corruption
Insult expression	+1 corruption
Point and laugh expression	+1 corruption
Tell off dog	+1 corruption
Drink spirits	+1 corruption
Eat crunchy chick	+2 corruption
Drink beer	+2 corruption
Set prices on rental properties and shops to high or very high	+tons of corruption

WEAPONS THAT CAN BOOST ATTRACTIVENESS

WEAPON NAME		LEGENDARY BONUS	OBJECTIVE	REWARD
SWORD	The Love Sword	Phwoar	Make 5 villagers love you.	+25% Attractiveness, Immunity to Scarring
	The Casanova	Beloved	Make 5 villagers love you.	+25% Attractiveness, Immunity to Scarring
PISTOL	Reaver Industries Perforator	Player	Have an orgy with 4 other people.	+25% Attractiveness, Immunity to Scarring

WEIGHT

You are what you eat in Albion. Weight rises or falls depending on the types of foods you ingest to regain health in combat (or the food you eat just for the heck of it, which is also possible). Produce, juices, and tofu reduce weight (along with reducing corruption), while meats, sweets, and alcoholic drinks increase weight (while also usually increasing corruption). Heavier weight effects attractiveness adversely.

WEAPONS TO WEAR WHEN GAINING WEIGHT

WEAPON NAME		LEGENDARY BONUS	OBJECTIVE	REWARD
SWORD	Slimquick	Slimmer	Make yourself fatter.	Lose Weight with Each Hit
HAMMER	The Absolver	Big Hearted	Make yourself fatter.	+15 Extra Damage
RIFLE	Simmon's Shotgun	Gulliver	Make yourself fatter.	+30% Damage vs Humans

WEAPONS THAT CAN HELP WITH WEIGHT LOSS

WEAPON NAME		LEGENDARY BONUS	OBJECTIVE	REWARD
SWORD	Slimquick	Slimmer	Make yourself fatter.	Lose Weight with Each Hit
PISTOL	Miriam's Mutilator	Beloved	Make 10 villagers love you.	Lose Weight with Each Hit

Sorrow's Fist	★★★★★
The Bonesmasher	★★★★★
Vortex Spell	★★★★★
Fireball Spell Gauntlet	★★★★★

CURRENT WEAPON LEVELS

Here you'll see which weapons are currently equipped, along with the current **Road to Rule** unlock level. Weapons for a particular type are all strengthened across the board by opening special chests for that weapon type on the **Road to Rule**. For more on weapons and combat, see our "Weapons of Yore" chapter.

OPTIONS PANEL

While the game loads automatically, and autosaves pretty frequently, you can manually save or load here. You can also tweak various settings related to presentation, from graphic brightness to audio volume and quality. You can also alter settings for the glowing trail.

> The game isn't really paused in the Hero's Sanctuary; the Hero is just taking a breather and reviewing his or her approach. (Albion time does come to a stop while in the Hero's Sanctuary, but NOT while on the Road to Rule) To truly pause the game, visit the options panel (alternately, press the XBOX guide button).

Life in the Castle
Choose an outfit.

THE GLOWING TRAIL

Our Hero, the player's character, *you*: a Hero has a true sense of where to go to get the job done. The glowing trail points the way toward the current, active quest. If you'd like to point the glowing trail to a new target, then change the active quest at the **World Map Table.** If you'd like to adjust the trail's brightness, or remove it altogether, visit the **Options** panel in the **Hero's Sanctuary.**

Without the people, a nation is just a piece of land. It was the people who cordoned off the land and made it sovereign in the first place, after all. So too is the kingdom of Albion its people. Citizens of Albion are nobles, soldiers, shopkeepers, blacksmiths, cooks, husbands, wives, children, criminals, beggars, whores, lovers, and friends—pretty much the full gamut of the human experience.

PROMISES, DECISIONS, AND JUDGMENTS

This being a game in the *Fable* series, you'll have to make many choices that affect your Hero, the general citizenry, and Albion at large. These choices come in the form of promises, decisions, and judgments.

PROMISES

There it is, right at the beginning of the game: the huddled masses entreat you, as prince or princess, to make a commitment to eliminate poverty in Albion by adding your John Hancock (wait…they probably don't know who that is) to their petition. Here you can choose whether to agree and sign, or whether to decline in a fashion most insulting. Many more promises will follow, and while occasionally you will have a choice whether or not to commit your services, often you will not—in the course of amassing followers to challenge the throne, you will *have to* make promises. Welcome to politics in Albion!

Promise to help the poor, or laugh in their faces at the gall they have to beg for aid in the first place.

DECISIONS

Of course, the problem with promises is that people remember them, and expect you to adhere to what you said before. Now, here's an interesting thing: you don't have to keep your promises! Now, naturally this will turn trust to hate in the people you misled, and your morality takes a hit as a result. However, there may be benefits to breaking a promise that outweighs the psychic cost. Keeping promises is often costly, while breaking them may even generate money and new opportunities. It's up to you to choose how you honor your accords.

It doesn't follow-up a promise, but early in the game you can decide whether to give an encouraging pep talk to King Logan's beleaguered staff, or to deride them for their insolence. It's not hard to figure which of these choices follows a moral path, and which skews towards selfishness and evil.

JUDGMENTS

More cut-and-dried than promises and decisions, judgments occasionally occur on the spur of the moment, and usually have to do with whether you execute or spare a wrongdoer. Here again, you'll have to weigh the balance…execution is a hard-line stance that suggests a lack of forgiveness and incurs a concurrent drop in morality. Sparing a life, on the other hand, is a benevolent, morality-boosting gesture. It's up to you.

An agonizing, impossible decision! Later judgments will be less paradoxical. A master logician and humanitarian King Logan is not.

THE GRASSROOTS APPROACH

You can interact one-on-one with nearly everyone in Albion.

The villages and towns of Albion, from the vibrant mansions of Millfields to the grinding poverty of Bowerstone Industrial, are overflowing with people. Just a few guards and citizens excepted, you can foster a personal relationship with each and every soul. By using expressions to build personal relationships, you'll earn lots of Guild Seals. More expressions and relationship possibilities are unlocked along the Road to Rule. Building up relationships can eventually lead to having best friends, spouses, and children. On the other hand you can also torpedo relationships, causing people to hate or even fear you. And keep in mind that your reputation can and will precede you…if something you did devastated an area, or if you raise prices in shops and rental properties you own, then affected residents won't like you before you've even met. For more on expressions and relationships, visit our "Albion Love Connection" chapter.

Hold [RT] while interacting with a villager to learn important details about their personality.

FILLING THE COFFERS

Money is the motive for much of *Fable III*. Revolution doesn't come cheap, so you'll need to invest at least a little time into making money in Albion.

JOBS

Taking on manual labor is the most direct means of making money. Other money-making solutions, like property ownership and skillful bartering of trade goods, are more efficient financial paths, but they are longer-term. Jobs are for when you need money right now.

Jobs are all performed in public. Performing well at a job, especially lute hero, makes nearby villagers like you more, while poor performance causes them to heckle with disdain.

Each job is a rhythmic minigame that requires you to press either Ⓐ, Ⓧ, or Ⓨ in time with onscreen prompts. By successfully stringing together inputs without mistakes, you'll build up a multiplier that increases how much money you make. As the multiplier rises, the rhythm gets faster and the margin for error smaller. String together nine perfect rounds in a row and you'll be at the highest possible multiplier, earning ten times the normal amount of money for each perfect round after. Make a mistake anytime, though, and your multiplier returns to one.

Job expertise can be increased by opening up chests along the Road to Rule. This makes the jobs a little bit harder (eventually adding in an extra button to lute hero and pie making), but also increases how much you earn for your talents. Truthfully, jobs aren't great money…that is, until you hit Level 5 expertise in a given job, and can consistently get a 10x multiplier going. At that point, jobs provide *fantastic* opportunities to make money.

If you commit a crime, get caught, and opt for community service, you'll pay off your debt working. If you plan on a life of crime, it's worth upgrading job skills even if you don't plan on working voluntarily—even huge fines for scores of atrocities committed are easy to pay off with high-level job expertise!

JOB LEVEL	GUILD SEAL COST	AVAILABILITY
Lv1	0	Available initially
Lv2 Jobs	5 each	Road to Rule 3: After Saker
Lv3 Jobs	10 each	Road to Rule 4: Sabine Promise
Lv4 Jobs	25 each	Road to Rule 6: Swift Promise
Lv5 Jobs	60 each	Road to Rule 7: Page Meeting

WEAPONS TO USE WHILE WORKING

WEAPON NAME		LEGENDARY BONUS	OBJECTIVE	REWARD
PISTOL	The Barnumificator	Hard Worker	Earn 10,000 gold from jobs.	+1 Gold per Hit
	Briar's Blaster	Blaster	Earn 10,000 gold from jobs.	+ Shotgun Spray
	Dragonstomper .48	Workaholic	Earn 10,000 gold from jobs.	+18 Extra Damage

PIE MAKING

Only in Brightwall Village and Bowerstone Market can our Hero put him or herself to the noble task of manufacturing baked sweets. Here, you must press Ⓐ or Ⓧ in time to the rolling of the pie dough. Like with lute hero, at higher levels of aptitude Ⓨ is added to the equation, making the game slightly harder.

JOB LEVEL	LV1	LV2	LV3	LV4	LV5
🪙 per successful roll	2	4	8	16	48
Rolls per round	3	4	5	6	7
🪙 per perfect round	6	16	40	96	336
🪙 per perfect round with 10x multiplier	60	160	400	960	3360
Buttons used	Ⓐ Ⓧ	Ⓐ Ⓧ	Ⓐ Ⓧ	Ⓐ Ⓧ Ⓨ	Ⓐ Ⓧ Ⓨ

LUTE HERO

Lute hero is the most widely available job. You can pluck the heartstrings of Albion in Dweller Camp, Brightwall Village, Bowerstone Market, or Aurora. You'll have to strum in time with Ⓐ and Ⓧ, and eventually Ⓨ too at higher levels. Lute hero much more than the other jobs encourages a crowd to gather, and they will be free with their evaluations of your musicianship. Lute hero ultimately has the highest potential payout per round of the jobs, but it also takes the longest, too.

JOB LEVEL	LV1	LV2	LV3	LV4	LV5
🪙 per successful strum	1	2	2-5	7~9	29~30
Strums per round	8	9	10	11	12
🪙 per perfect round	8	18	50	110	360
🪙 per perfect round with 10x multiplier	80	180	500	1110	3600
Buttons used	Ⓐ Ⓧ	Ⓐ Ⓧ	Ⓐ Ⓧ Ⓨ	Ⓐ Ⓧ Ⓨ	Ⓐ Ⓧ Ⓨ

BLACKSMITHING

Blacksmithing can be performed in Mourningwood Village, Bowerstone Market, and Aurora. You must press Ⓐ and Ⓧ to temper hot steel in time with the prompts onscreen. Unlike lute hero and pie making, blacksmithing doesn't add in another button to worry about at higher difficulties. The rounds for smithing are quicker than with other jobs, too. For these reasons, blacksmithing tends to be the most efficient job for making money.

JOB LEVEL	LV1	LV2	LV3	LV4	LV5
🪙 per successful strike	1	3	6	12	36
Strikes per round	5	6	7	8	9
🪙 per perfect round	5	18	42	96	324
🪙 per perfect round with 10x multiplier	50	180	420	960	3240
Buttons used	Ⓐ Ⓧ	Ⓐ Ⓧ	Ⓐ Ⓧ	Ⓐ Ⓧ	Ⓐ Ⓧ

COMMERCE IN ALBION

You'll engage in business with shopkeepers in Albion. Blacksmiths run weapon stores, tailors sell clothing, market kiosks offer all kinds of items, and there are even tattoo parlors and barber shops. At all of these establishments you can buy things. Weapons, outfits, and items you will use. Books help you teach your dog new tricks. Many items serve solely as gifts, given to fulfill the requests of children, friends, or lovers. And trade items provide an investment opportunity: they have no function save being bought and sold. Now, shops will only sell you items, and pawnbrokers only buy things you no longer want. So, if you can first catch shop items on sale or haggle the price down, then wait and sell when pawnbrokers are offering extra during shortages, you stand to make a pretty penny, and for no effort other than paying attention. What shops offer for prices, and what pawnbrokers offer in payment, is variable. There will be sales in shops, with reduced prices, and shortages for pawnbrokers, so they offer more than usual. Haggling is also possible, once it's unlocked on the Road to Rule. Romancing a pawnbroker or shopkeep, or striking fear in their hearts, can also skew prices in your favor. Finally, you also receive a discount on purchases, or markup on sales, from any establishment you own!

You'll find the same items in the majority of shops, however, weapon shop inventories are randomly generated.

Don't worry if you clean a vendor out of a particular item; come back later and they'll have restocked.

PAWNBROKER INVENTORY

Pawnbrokers aren't just useful for selling undesirables or trade items. While you can view all your weapons, dyes, hairstyles, tattoos, and outfits in the Hero's Sanctuary, there is no place in the Sanctuary to view items. The only place you can scan your potion, item, gift, trade item, and furniture inventories is at a pawnbroker.

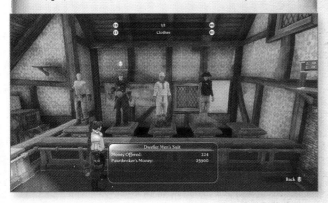

WEAPONS TO SPEND 🪙 WITH

WEAPON NAME		LEGENDARY BONUS	OBJECTIVE	REWARD
SWORD	The Merchant's Bodyguard	🛡 Big Spender	Spend 8,000 of your personal gold.	+20% Damage in Multiplayer
	Slimquick	🛒 Shopping Spree	Spend 8,000 of your personal gold.	Earn Guild Seals Faster in Combat.
	The Channeler	🔍 Researcher	Spend 8,000 of your personal gold.	Earn Guild Seals Faster in Combat.
	The Inquisitor	💎 Extravagant	Spend 3000 of your personal gold.	+15 Extra Damage
PISTOL	Reaver Industries Perforator	🛍 Retail Therapy	Spend 10,000 of your personal gold.	Earn Guild Seals Faster in Combat.
	Tea Killer Shooter	💰 Accumulator	Spend 10,000 of your personal gold.	Gain Money with Each Hit
RIFLE	Arkwright's Flintlock	💸 Spendthrift	Spend 10,000 of your personal gold.	Earn Guild Seals Faster in Combat.

DAY AND NIGHT

Albion cycles through a full day, from dusk to sun-up to sunset and twilight, in about 20 minutes. Towns are bustling during the day, and most shops close at night. Keep this in mind when planning your commerce.

To get to a desired time of day quickly, find a bed where it's safe to rest until then.

WEAPONS TO USE DURING THE DAYTIME

WEAPON NAME		LEGENDARY BONUS	OBJECTIVE	REWARD
SWORD	Beadle's Cutlass	Dayripper	Kill 300 enemies in the daytime.	Earn Guild Seals Faster in Combat.
PISTOL	The Bonesmasher	Solar	Kill 250 enemies in the daytime.	+30% Damage to Enemies in Daytime
	Desert Fury	Sunblasted	Kill 400 enemies in the daytime.	+30% Damage to Enemies in Daytime
RIFLE	Defender of the Faith	Sunblessed	Kill 400 enemies in the daytime.	+30% Damage to Enemies in Daytime

WEAPONS THAT CAN DO MORE DAMAGE DURING THE DAYTIME

WEAPON NAME		LEGENDARY BONUS	OBJECTIVE	REWARD
PISTOL	The Barnumificator	Solar	Kill 250 enemies in the daytime.	+30% Damage to Enemies in Daytime
	The Barnumificator	Sunblasted	Kill 400 enemies in the daytime.	+30% Damage to Enemies in Daytime
RIFLE	The Sandgoose	Sunblessed	Kill 400 enemies in the daytime.	+30% Damage to Enemies in Daytime

WEAPONS TO USE AT NIGHT

WEAPON NAME		LEGENDARY BONUS	OBJECTIVE	REWARD
SWORD	Wolfsbane	Moonglow	Kill 50 enemies at night.	+40% Damage at Night
	Shardborne	Darkness	Kill 200 enemies at night.	+15 Extra Damage
HAMMER	Lunarium Pounder	Night Watchman	Kill 200 enemies at night.	Extra Knockdown vs All Enemies
PISTOL	Tee Killer Shooter	Nightowl	Kill 200 enemies at night.	+40% Damage at Night
RIFLE	The Equaliser	Night Watchman	Kill 200 enemies at night.	+40% Damage to Enemies at Night

WEAPONS THAT CAN DO MORE DAMAGE DURING THE NIGHT

WEAPON NAME		LEGENDARY BONUS	OBJECTIVE	REWARD
PISTOL	Tee Killer Shooter	Nightowl	Kill 200 enemies at night.	+40% Damage at Night
RIFLE	The Equaliser	Night Watchman	Kill 200 enemies at night.	+40% Damage to Enemies at Night

OTHER INCOME SOURCES

As is covered in-depth in our "Real Estate Magnate" chapter, land ownership is potentially the most potent way to make money. Unless you decide to give out rental properties and goods for free, which is actually a thing you can do, you'll have some money coming in roughly every five minutes of play. Brick-and-mortar stores offer you the most bang for your buck, but the initial investment to buy is highest. Merchant kiosks are much less expensive, so while you won't make near as much per shop, you can make up for that somewhat by buying small shops en masse. Building up money to purchase property on a whim becomes much simpler once you have your favorite job maxed out. At that point, even if a desired property is 50,000 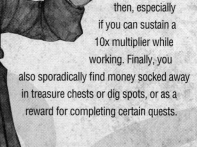 or more, it really doesn't take that long to grind the money out right then, especially if you can sustain a 10x multiplier while working. Finally, you also sporadically find money socked away in treasure chests or dig spots, or as a reward for completing certain quests.

HERO'S BEST FRIEND

You have a trusty four-legged best friend right from the start in *Fable III*. Your dog stays by your side for the full breadth of the adventure. He sniffs out dig spots, eyeballs carefully hidden treasure chests, and helps finish off enemies you've knocked down. During exploration, if you hear a bark or growl from your dog, pay attention. He's constantly on a vigilant watch for enemies or treasure.

You can check your dog's stats, and change his name, in the Hero's Sanctuary.

Your dog's abilities increase as you learn new methods to teach him from books. Dog training books are found occasionally in treasure chests and shop kiosks. You'll find books on dog aggression, exploration, and charisma, all pertaining to a particular stat. Each stat starts at 1, and has a max level of 5.

It's possible to skip levels when training your pooch—if the only training book you ever find is Level 5, well, then that's the only book you ever needed to find. Aggression relates to how quickly your dog goes after downed foes, and how much damage he'll do. Exploration determines how easy it is for your dog to find dig spots and treasure. At higher exploration levels, he'll find treasure more quickly, and even unearth dig spots he overlooked before. Charisma relates to how sociable he is in town. Everyone loves a good dog, so cultivating his behavior makes it easier to make friends.

 Indicates when your dog has discovered treasure.

 Indicates when your dog has sniffed out a dig spot.

DIG SPOTS

Pay attention to your trusty pooch, and you'll find dig spots to be the most plentiful repository of hidden loot in Albion. Goodies are buried just under the surface all over the place, from the midst of the most weathered battlegrounds to the back-alleys of bustling towns. If enemies are nearby, your dog won't sniff out the spots until the threat is dispatched. With a higher exploration stat, earned from dog training books, your dog will find more and better dig spots.

WEAPONS TO DIG UP ITEMS WITHE

WEAPON NAME		LEGENDARY BONUS	OBJECTIVE	REWARD
SWORD	The Splade	Scrounger	Dig up 30 items.	Earn Guild Seals Faster in Combat.
PISTOL	Chickenbane	Scratcher	Dig up 30 items.	+12 Extra Damage
RIFLE	Simmon's Shotgun	Exhumation	Dig up 30 items.	+ Shotgun Spray

LOOT AND COLLECTIBLES

Apart from dig spots found by your dog, there are several more ways for goods and money to come to hand in Albion.

DIVE SPOTS

Dive spots are places you can plunge underwater in order to haul treasure to the surface. Dive spots are to water what dig spots are to land, except that you're not dependent on your dog to find dive spots; just keep an eye out for foamy, swirling water.

■ Like with dig spots, results for dive spots are determined by Hero Level.

TREASURE CHESTS

Scattered about the landscape, usually tucked away *just* off the beaten path, treasure chests contain all sorts of things. While just a handful of treasure chests have fixed content that is always the same (for example, the Bonesmasher pistol found in a treasure chest alongside the road during the first visit to Mourningwood), most treasure chests in fact have random contents. The possibilities for chest spoils are determined by your hidden Hero Level. A higher Hero Level means better potential loot from any random source of treasure.

SEARCHING AND STEALING

Inside houses and businesses you'll find lots of furniture (like cupboards, dressers, and stoves) which can be searched for items. If you own the house, no problem—no one will bust you for going through your own property. However, if you're in someone else's house, or a business, searching property is stealing. Stealing lowers morality by -5, and can be considered illegal. How is it considered illegal? Only if someone sees you!

■ Unless it's your house, use discretion when rifling through furniture. And remember that the morality ding is significant even if no one sees you.

 ■ Hold **A** to search while watching the eye icon. Closed means no one is watching!

 ■ An open eye means you are attempting to steal in plain sight, with someone eyeing you.

SILVER KEYS FOR SILVER KEY CHESTS

There are 50 hidden silver keys spread throughout Albion. Hidden also across the land are several silver key chests. Upon each is engraved a number—this is the number of silver keys required to access the chest. Silver keys are not expended upon use, so don't worry about having to make choices on chests. Your dog will assist quite a bit in the seeking of these keys, as he'll sniff them out just like dig spots or treasure chests. What you or your dog miss, we can make up for in the Albion Atlas.

◼ *The map table lets you know how many silver keys are squirreled away in each area.*

SILVER CHEST LOCATION	SILVER KEYS REQUIRED	SILVER CHEST LOCATION	SILVER KEYS REQUIRED
The Reliquary	1	Shifting Sands	10
Dweller Camp	5	Chillbreath Cavern	15
Mistpeak Valley	5	Bowerstone Market	15
Bowerstone Industrial	5	Mill Fields	20
Brightwall Village	10	Aurora	20
Mourningwood	10	Bowerstone Castle	50
Bowerstone Industrial	10		

GOLD KEYS FOR GOLDEN DOORS

Four golden doors can be found in Albion. Four corresponding gold keys open these doors, leading to huge treasures and riches. Like silver keys, their quantities per location are also listed on the World Map Table, but gold keys aren't all found on the world map…

◼ *Albion's rarest treasures are found beyond golden doors.*

EVIL GARDEN GNOMES

Poor Brian in Brightwall Village has a quest for you. He needs your assistance rounding up 50 garden gnomes gone wayward. These once-innocuous lawn ornaments have become foul fountains of bile-filled insults. It's from the verbal harpoons they hurl that you'll know a gnome is about. If you can hear a gnome needlessly berating you or your dog, search the area carefully using first-person view. It can sometimes be easiest to find gnomes by using manual aim with a gun, as the gun will auto-target the gnome and highlight it if you aim close enough. And once you find the gnome, you're just one gunshot away from blessed silence.

Gnomes are quite crafty tucking away their loathsome selves. Be prepared to look in every nook and cranny.

Guns highlight targets when manually aimed. This can help spot gnomes if you pan over them without realizing it.

GNOMES

ANCIENT TOMES

A librarian in the Brightwall Academy wants you to collect 30 missing, ancient books for the library. These books are hidden in plain sight everywhere: in bookshelves, on desks, even on the floor. For every five you collect and donate, the librarian will have one specific rare book he'll send you after, usually in the midst of a fair amount of baddies.

It can be hard to tell what is just a background element and what is a book that can be inspected, so ere toward checking any leafy-looking bound thing lying about.

AURORAN FLOWERS

In the faraway, sun-blasted land of Aurora, flowers still find a way to bloom in the parched desert heat. There are 30 total to collect, with an Achievement unlocked for finding every one.

Field the flora and fauna across the sea.

41

LIFE IN THE CASTLE

Morning has come to Albion and with it, so too arrives your faithful butler, Jasper, to stir you from your slumber. You are King Logan's only sibling, the youngest child of a beloved Hero credited for saving this land from an unthinkable horror some 50 years ago. The people of Albion know little about you and you're definitely not the talk of the town. Your brother does not garner the same description. They call him a tyrant, an unjust ruler, and they are starting to protest his reign in public. Yes, another morning has come to Albion, but the air is ripe with tension. This day will be like no other in your life. This day will set Albion on a new track. How it turns out in the long-term is up to you...

BOWERSTONE CASTLE

CHOOSE AN OUTFIT

It's time to rise and shine to a beautiful sunny day in Bowerstone. Jasper has taken the liberty of arranging two outfits for you in preparation for your meeting with Lady Elise (or Elliot if playing as the Princess) in the garden. Choose between the Practical Outfit and Elegant Outfit by approaching the stand and holding the A button. Slip into whichever attire suits your mood, but try both of them on to get additional credit towards the **Fashion Victim** Achievement. Wearing the pajamas and both outfits, even if only for a moment, will count for 12 of the 106 articles of clothing needed for the Achievement. Each outfit consists of pants, shirt, shoes, and gloves.

*Time to dress for the day. Each outfit counts as four pieces of clothing towards the **Fashion Victim** Achievement so try them both on.*

FIND ELISE/ELLIOT

▌ Follow the glowing trail through the garden and enjoy the pleasantries showered upon you by the castle's servants and nobles.

Your royal quarters reside on the second floor of the castle's rear, overlooking the garden. Exit the room via the stone walkway outside and descend the steps to the formal gardens below. The glowing trail leads the way through the garden to your meeting point. Quest objectives and key destinations are encircled by a ring of light resembling the glowing trail. Step inside the circle to trigger the next objective.

THE GLOWING TRAIL

Fable III contains a glowing trail that guides you to your next objective. This handy feature prevents you from getting lost and works quite well in lieu of an onscreen map and waypoint system. You can adjust the brightness of the glowing trail within the Options menu, or even turn it off completely if so inclined. Though we don't recommend disabling the feature, we do recommend veering away from the trail to explore on your own. The only way to uncover the myriad treasures and collectibles hidden throughout the kingdom is to deviate from the glowing trail and explore each area fully. Once satisfied with your off-trail exploits, simply resume following the glowing trail where it leads.

One of the key elements of *Fable III* is the idea of physical contact between people. In other words, *touching*. Continue your courtship of Elise by either hugging or kissing her when prompted—she'll respond positively to either. Elise tells you of problems in the city and a growing anger towards your brother, King Logan. She wants to accompany you to the castle so that you may help ease the tension building amongst the citizens.

HELLO MOTHER, HELLO FATHER

To make descriptions of the previous ruler less ambiguous regarding gender, this walkthrough is written with the assumption that your father was a King of Albion. Of course, the ending of *Fable II* could easily have had your Hero reigning as Queen of Albion.

LEAD ELISE TO THE CASTLE KITCHEN

HAND IN HAND	5 Points

This Achievement unlocks the first time you hold hands with someone. Whenever you need to bring someone along with you, you do so by holding their hand. This can be a romantic gesture—as it is with Elise in the garden—as a means of escorting a villager, or it can be far more sinister, such as dragging a person away to sell them to a factory. Press the Left Trigger while standing next to someone to hold their hand. Press the Left Trigger again to let go.

Stand next to Elise and press the Left Trigger to take her by the hand and guide her back through the garden towards the castle's back entrance. Ascend the few steps and enter the kitchen through the door to the right, directly beneath your royal bedroom.

■ *Elise won't have any trouble keeping up. Hold the A button to make the couple run if you wish.*

ADDRESS THE STAFF

CHOICE	GOLD	GUILD SEALS	MORALITY
GOOD: Give an encouraging speech.	-	-	+25
EVIL: Give a harsh speech.	-	-	-25

The servants are spreading rumors about the execution that took place at the factory this morning. They're clearly bothered by the living conditions in the city. The chef has gotten their attention so you may speak. Choose the appropriate button as prompted to give either an encouraging speech or a harsh one. This is the first of many moral choices you'll have to make throughout *Fable III*. Whether you decide to always do the right thing or be a complete tyrant—or something in between—is up to you. As you will eventually see, both paths have their difficulties.

■ *Little decisions like how you speak to the staff add up to say plenty about your morality over time.*

FOLLOW WALTER

Sir Walter Beck, your mentor and dear friend, has come to the kitchen in time to hear your speech. His reaction differs according to the tone you took with the staff, but know that Walter is a good man with a pure heart. Nevertheless, Walter has come to see to it that you are on time for your next training session. Follow him out of the kitchen towards the combat room.

SIGN THE PETITION

CHOICE	GOLD	GUILD SEALS	MORALITY
GOOD: Sign the petition.	-	-	+25
EVIL: Insult the petitioners.	-	-	-25

Your walk to the combat room takes you through the main entrance to the castle, where a group of petitioners is waiting to meet with the King. You are asked to sign the petition and lend your support to their fight against poverty in Albion, in hopes that the King may take the matter more seriously if your signature is among the others. Your choice in this matter has no long-standing effects other than the change to your moral standing, although you are likely to see Laszlo the petitioner again.

Walter defers to you when asked to sign the petition. Sign it or wipe your bum with it, the choice is yours.

COMBAT TRAINING

Grab the sword from the rack on the left-hand side of the combat room and prepare to fight Walter. He doesn't want you to hold anything back so treat this battle as if it were to the death. Attack with the X button in a rapid succession of two or three swings, then roll away by pushing the Left Thumbstick to the side or back and press the A button. This is a great way to evade attacks. It's also possible to block incoming attacks by using a defensive stance. This is done by holding the X button.

The training concludes once you perform your first successful flourish attack. Continue fighting Walter until you land several successful hits and the lesson advances to flourish attacks. Push the Left Thumbstick towards Walter while holding the X button to charge a flourish attack. Release the button to attack with a stylish, overpowering attack that cannot be blocked.

Hold a defensive stance to bait your opponent into attacking, then quickly counterattack!

FOLLOW ELISE

Elise bursts into the combat room and implores you and Walter to come with her to see the commotion outside. Follow her down the hall to the window to watch the protesters. Walter immediately turns and heads upstairs to the war room to speak with Logan. Elise wants the two of you to sneak upstairs and listen in to see how Logan is planning to handle the situation. Follow her to the door outside the war room where you can eavesdrop through the keyholes.

CHOOSE WHO MUST DIE

CHOICE		GOLD	GUILD SEALS	MORALITY
![good]	GOOD: N/A	-	-	-
![evil]	EVIL: N/A	-	-	-

The mob of protesters outside the castle clearly underestimates their king's ruthlessness.

Your efforts to stop Logan from executing the mob are seen by your brother as a betrayal. As punishment, he forces you to decide between executing Elise or the protesters. He'll have them all killed if you don't choose, so indecisiveness is not an option. There is no right or wrong choice here, and neither selection affects your moral standing in any way. Sacrificing Elise may save the larger number of lives, but the protesters chose to risk their lives in protest of the King. They had to have known the repercussions could be severe. Make your decision by pressing the corresponding button.

WHAT IF ELISE LIVES?

Choosing to execute the protesters instead of Elise/Elliot does have one small effect on later gameplay: if you decide to sacrifice the mob to save your friend, he or she will appear in a later quest. You can still complete this later quest regardless of the decision you make here in the throne room. The only difference will be the presence of Elise/Elliot (and with that the option to marry him/her) in place of an unfamiliar NPC.

ESCAPE THE CASTLE WITH WALTER AND JASPER

Can you sacrifice someone you love to save the lives of three complete strangers?

You'll be away from the castle for quite a while, but Jasper, Walter, and your dog will be with you every step of the way.

Walter comes to your room to lead an escape. He speaks of a revolution, a new King, and of a Hero. He wants to see if you are ready to be that Hero. Follow Walter and Jasper outside and across the garden to the cupola near where you met Elise earlier. Descend the steps to the Catacombs and open the door. It is time to leave the castle.

LEAVING THE CASTLE

Your brother's handling of the protests was the final straw. Something must be done and the time to act is now. Walter has devoted his life to being an honorable military man and defender of Albion's throne, but his love for his nation far outweighs any duty he feels to King Logan. He knows Albion is in dire trouble and the time to act is now. He has not mentored you all these years out of obligation, but in hopes that one day you would be ready to heed your true calling. It's time to learn whether or not Walter's investment in you was for naught.

THE CATACOMBS

PICK UP THE GUILD SEAL

Walter has led the party into the Catacombs not just to escape quietly in the night, but so you may obtain your father's most coveted item, the **Guild Seal**. The Guild Seal reacts in the hands of those who have what it takes to become legendary, to become a Hero. Walter has long suspected that you may one day fill your father's shoes and lead Albion to a bright new day. Take the item, feel its power, and enjoy your first trip to the Road to Rule.

■ Step between the sarcophagi of your parents and take hold of the Guild Seal to become Albion's next Hero.

 THE GUILD SEAL   10 Points

This is the first of the story progression Achievements and unlocks as soon as the Guild Seal reacts to your touch. Follow Walter and Jasper into the Catacombs and watch as Walter triggers the secret switch that reveals the sacred item. Pick it up to unlock this Achievement and make your first journey to the Road to Rule.

ROAD TO RULE

You have awoken the power of the Guild Seal and gained your first followers, Jasper and Walter. Though you only have one Guild Seal to spend, the first segment along the Road to Rule contains just a single inexpensive chest. Purchase this first ability to gain what is sure to be your most often-used magical attack, the Fireball Spell.

CHESTS NOW AVAILABLE

CHEST	TYPE	GUILD SEALS	DESCRIPTION
Fireball Spell	Gauntlet	1	Fireball burns your targets and blasts them back a step.

THE ROAD TO RULE, EXPLAINED

The Road to Rule is a mystical road divided into a number of segments by portals and gates. You will return to the Road to Rule and be granted access to a new segment every time you gain a critical follower in your quest to become the new ruler of Albion. Jasper and Walter are your first followers, but subsequent followers will require far more convincing on your part. But it's worth it! Each segment along the Road to Rule contains a number of chests. Spend the Guild Seals you acquire (through combat, making friends, and completing quests) to open these chests in order to gain powerful abilities. This is how you gain new expressions, increase your combat ratings, earn new spells, and even unlock the ability to buy property and start a family. As you will soon see, you can return to the Road to Rule to spend accumulated Guild Seals at any time, but you can only advance along the Road to Rule by growing an army of allies willing to follow you into rebellion.

Stand on the circular platform and use your newfound Fireball spell to open a secret entrance beneath the floor. Cast magic attacks by pressing the B button. You can either direct an attack at a specific target with the Left Thumbstick or unleash a circular area-of-effect attack by pressing the B button with the Left Thumbstick in the neutral position. Perform the latter here.

Even your Level 0 Fireball spell is strong enough to open the entrance to the underground tunnels.

ESCAPE THE CASTLE THROUGH THE UNDER-GROUND TUNNELS

Descend the stairs into the lower level of the Catacombs and follow the glowing trail through the narrow confines of the tunnel to the overlook in the distance. Practice casting targeted magical attacks by lighting the two extinguished braziers aflame with the Fireball spell. Enjoy the view and continue along the path to the left. Locate a **Silver Key** near the collapsed column to the left of the torches. There are 50 Silver Keys and 4 Gold Keys scattered across Albion—find them all to unlock the **I Am the Keymaster** Achievement. Silver Keys are used to unlock special chests that contain valuable treasures, while gold keys open special doors.

Follow Walter across the natural bridge and around the bend in the trail. A flock of bats attacks as you proceed. Move in front of the bats and rapidly cast the Fireball spell. Don't bother trying to target individual bats at first. Just cast area-of-effect spells to engulf the flock of bats in a small ring of fire. Switch to targeted casting to take down any stray bats that escape your initial attacks. With each bat you kill, you earn a small amount of points towards your next Guild Seal. The Guild Seal indicator on the left-hand side of the screen gradually fills with each enemy you slay in battle.

Continue along the rocky ledge and down the stairs towards the shallow stream within the cave. Additional flocks of bats attack, so be ready. Continue to use Fireball against them to rapidly accumulate a bevy of magical kills. The **Wizard's Revenge** Achievement can be unlocked by killing 500 enemies with magical attacks—using Fireball against the bats in this area nets you your first 100 kills and sets you well on your way to unlocking that Achievement in no time. You'll likely earn five Guild Seals from the battles as well.

Make your way into the sewers at the end of the Catacombs and scramble through the crack in the wall to the platform containing the Cullis Gate. Stand atop the circle and cast Fireball to activate the ancient transportation device. This whisks the party away to the Hero's Sanctuary.

*Move in front of the bats and cast Fireball over and over to set them aflame. This is an extremely efficient way of accumulating kills towards the **Wizard's Revenge** Achievement.*

The Cullis Gate is your way out of the Catacombs. There is more to see within this cave, but that's for another time.

INTERACT WITH MAP TABLE

THE HERO'S SANCTUARY

The Hero's Sanctuary is essentially an interactive menu screen. Pressing the Start button at any time will bring you to the map room of the Sanctuary where Jasper awaits. There are many other rooms radiating outward from this central room, each of which serves the purpose of a traditional menu screen. With time you will use the Sanctuary to equip different weapons, view your trophies and riches, customize your appearance, make use of the game's Xbox LIVE integration, and save your progress.

The Sanctuary was created by your father to aid him in his quests. Now the Sanctuary belongs to you, though it is in pretty sad shape. Fortunately, your father left a book detailing everything one needs to know about being a Hero and using the Hero's Sanctuary. Jasper remains behind to read the book and prepare the Sanctuary. After all, he's much better suited for domestic duties than he is combat. In the meantime, approach the map table and highlight the Dweller Camp with the magnifying glass. Press the X button to fast travel to that location.

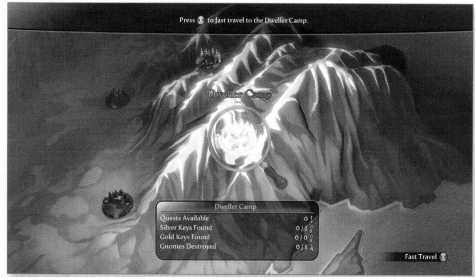

The map table not only allows you the ability to fast travel, but it keeps track of how many collectibles you've acquired in each area too!

FAST TRAVELLING THE WORLD

The ability to fast travel to anywhere in Albion (provided you've discovered it previously on foot) is an amazing power known only to Heroes like yourself. Though there is no harm in using this ability as often as you'd like, we strongly suggest exploring each area thoroughly. There are many caves and smaller areas of countryside off the beaten path that will not become accessible if you don't first travel there on foot—and many of these do not appear on the map table. Always search the perimeter of an area before moving on to avoid missing a valuable piece of treasure, or even an entirely new area.

A NEW HERO

If a revolution is to be successful, it must have the support of those who have been most impacted by the current rulers. Logan has made many enemies in his years as King, but perhaps none more than the mountain-loving gypsies of the Dweller Camp. Walter is going to introduce you to Sabine, the leader of the Dwellers, in hopes that you can prove that a last name is all you share in common with King Logan. Sabine will only risk the lives of his men in a rebellion if he truly believes it will yield a better life for his people. This is what you must prove to him.

DWELLER CAMP

FOLLOW WALTER

Descend the hillside from the Cullis Gate to the fire-lit ring of gypsy caravans in the distance. Follow Walter through the camp and up the path on the far side of the central ring of wagons towards the gate. The Dwellers will beg for money and food, but you need not interact with them just yet. There will be plenty of time for that soon enough.

Follow Walter through the encampment to the guarded gate in the distance. You are eventually able to buy these wagons and rent them to the Dwellers.

BUY MORE APPROPRIATE CLOTHES

Sabine, the leader of the Dweller Camp, isn't going to take kindly to royal visitors after the way King Logan has treated his people, so Walter gives you 500 gold to buy a proper Dweller outfit with. Return down the hill to the ring of wagons and locate the clothing shop to the right. The Dweller Suit costs 301 gold. Purchase the entire suit, then press the Start button to return to the Sanctuary. It's time to visit your dressing room.

Jasper unlocks the entrance to the dressing room within the Sanctuary. The Dweller Suit you purchased was immediately transferred to the Sanctuary, where Jasper set it up on a mannequin. Approach the mannequin and press the A button to select it, then choose which pieces of the outfit you wish to wear. For the purposes of fitting in amongst the Dwellers, go ahead and put on the entire suit.

The Dweller Suit is the only item available at the only shop that is currently being staffed in Dweller Camp.

TALK TO WALTER

Buying the Dweller Suit leaves you with 199 gold. You can effectively improve your moral standing and earn additional Guild Seals by giving some of the gold to the villagers in the camp. Interact with one of the people you see and press the Right Bumper to give them 10 gold. Simply shaking their hands can also earn a Guild Seal as well as help you earn the **Touched by a Hero** Achievement. Make your way back up the path to Walter once you're ready to meet with Sabine. He'll be waiting by the gate.

EARNING GUILD SEALS FROM STRANGERS

Approach one of the villagers and press the A button to interact with them. A meter appears on the bottom of the screen that shows how this person feels about you. Hold the Right Trigger to see how many Guild Seals can be earned from this villager if you satisfy their desires. You can perform a fun or nasty expression by pressing and holding the A button or Y button, respectively, or you can simply press the Right Bumper to give him or her 10 gold. Giving away gold is a quick and easy way to increase your moral standing and also earn a Guild Seal. It also improves the relationship with the person. Expressions and relationships are covered in great detail within the "Albion Love Connection" chapter of this book.

TALK TO SABINE

Sabine is every bit as ornery as Walter suggested. He and his people have been brutally oppressed by King Logan, and he's going to need convincing that you are not like your brother. He'll only lend his support to your cause if you manage to prove that you're a Hero, that you are skilled in combat, and that you possess the skills of a leader. Do this by accomplishing the following three tasks:

- Survive the trials of a dungeon beneath Brightwall and retrieve an ancient relic hidden there.

- Slay the mercenaries who plague Mistpeak Valley.

- Persuade the people of Brightwall to share their food with the Dwellers.

Exit Sabine's inner camp and follow Walter back through the camp to the gate leading to Mistpeak Valley. He's going to try to dig up some info on the mercenaries in the adjacent valley while you make your way through the mountains to the base of Mistpeak Valley, and then to Brightwall Village. Walter will meet you in Brightwall when he's formulated a plan.

Sabine drives a pretty hard bargain, but having him on your side is essential to the rebellion's success.

MISTPEAK VALLEY

FIND THE LIBRARIAN IN BRIGHTWALL

The path from the Dweller Camp leads to the northwest corner of Mistpeak Valley, high in the snow-covered mountains. Descend the trail to the signpost pointing the way farther down the mountain to Brightwall Village. The path to the right leads up to a nearby peak where a Silver Chest requiring five Silver Keys is located. Save it for another time and continue the descent.

LISTEN FOR THE BARKS

Always pay attention to the pitch of your dog's bark, as it is a great indication if treasure is nearby. The dog growls at enemies, but has a higher pitched bark if he senses treasure. The dog is capable of locating chests, Silver Keys, and dig spots among other collectibles you soon discover. Follow the dog off the trail to see what has drawn his attention.

A pack of wolves attacks beyond the bridge. Stand back and use targeted Fireball spells to destroy them. Hold the B button to charge up each spell while using the Left Thumbstick to target the nearest wolf. Your dog will attack any wolf you knock down but do not kill. Continue across the second bridge to find another small pack of wolves. Charge the Fireball spell and let them have it!

Wolves can't survive more than one or two Fireball attacks. Charge up the spell to take them down with a single blast!

Descend out of the snow, then immediately turn to the right and start running back uphill to reach Brightwall Village.

Zigzag back across the river canyon over the third bridge to reach the valley floor. Walter is going to learn more about the in the area, so don't go off exploring on your own just yet. Defeat the four wolves near the ruins and follow the sign around to the right to continue south towards Brightwall. Your dog will likely lead you to a chest and dig spot along the way.

BRIGHTWALL VILLAGE

FIND THE LIBRARIAN IN BRIGHTWALL (Cont'd)

Follow the path to the large stone bridge leading to the village proper. Continue past the bridge to a house in the distance to locate a chest and Silver Key, then return to the bridge and cross into the town. Take a moment to soak in the hustle and bustle of the village, and to inspect the traders' wares. The weapons shop is currently closed, but there is a chest in a room on the second floor, accessible via the stairs on the side—this is precisely the type of exploration you should be doing as you follow the glowing trail to the next objective. Cross the small stone bridge over the creek and head up the hill to the Academy.

Enter the library, formally known as Brightwall Academy, and speak to the caretaker at the front desk. He'll try to run you off for fear of attracting King Logan's wrath, but it only takes one look at the Guild Seal for him to know what to do. Follow him through the rear of the Academy to the door leading to the Reliquary.

LITERARY GOLD

The bookshelves within Brightwall Academy are an excellent source of gold. A surprising number of the library's bookshelves contain small amounts of gold (typically 3 gold per bookcase). Search each bookcase to yield a small fortune in gold as you make your way through the library.

There are many vendors in Brightwall looking to sell some food items. Don't feel compelled to buy anything just yet; you'll need your gold for larger purchases soon enough.

Show the librarian the Guild Seal, then use it to open the door to the Reliquary. Only a Hero can gain access to the cavern beneath the Academy.

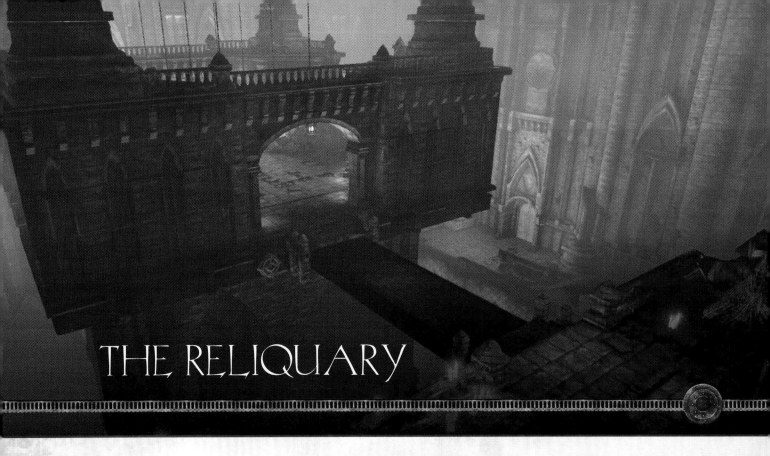

THE RELIQUARY

FIND YOUR FATHER'S TREASURE FOR SABINE

Descend the steps into the Reliquary and immediately set to searching the aisles that flank the central walkway. Search the bookshelves for gold and use the Silver Key you've found to open the chest in the aisle on the left. Whistle for your dog and press Up on the D-Pad to teach him from the Dog Combat Training 2 book you find. This upgrades his fighting ability and makes him more vicious in combat.

Continue past the books to the crumbling walkway that overlooks a large void. Open the chest on the left, then follow the glowing trail around the corner and down the stairs to the right. The door there is sealed shut, but a flit switch is present. This flit switch requires a melee weapon strike (note the switch's blue color corresponds to the X button on the controller) and it just so happens that Jasper has found two of your father's old weapons. Return to the Sanctuary and follow Jasper into the Armoury. Equip either the Hero Hammer or Hero Sword, then return to the Reliquary and strike the switch to extend a bridge.

Equip a melee weapon at the Sanctuary, then use it to strike the flit switch. Cross the bridge and prepare for battle!

The twinkling blue lights you see in the air are your signal that an attack by hollow men is imminent. Use your Fireball spell together with your newfound melee weapon to bash them to pieces. Each of these hollow men attacks with melee weapons; avoid all forms of danger by keeping your distance. Target individual enemies with the Fireball spell to knock them back, then move in for the kill with the sword or hammer. Cross the second bridge that extends and continue through the door that opens.

Use area-of-effect spells to knock the hollow men back if a group of them gets too close.

Step out onto the ledge and target the red flit switch that appears with your Fireball spell. This causes a staircase to rise up out of the abyss. Step on the floor switch atop the stairs to make another panel rise up within reach. You must use this and the subsequent blocks to cross the void. Step on the blue-lit arrow on the side of the panel corresponding to the direction you wish to travel. Cross to the left to reach the chest there, then double back and head across the gap to the other chests.

Step on the blue arrows to cross the chasm while collecting the contents of each chest. Don't let the hollow men scare you off!

Causing a panel to rise up beneath one of the lanterns glowing blue with hollow-men spirits triggers a short battle against a half-dozen or so enemies. Stick to the center of the platform and use your area-of-effect Fireball spell to knock them back. Descend the stairs that appear next to the final panel and head left. Leap down to the lower level, then step out onto the broken bridge and dive into the water far below. Search the dive spot for treasure and climb out of the water near the large circular door. Stand on the seal and target the door with a Fireball spell to open the vault beyond. Hold the B button to charge the spell and push forward on the Left Thumbstick to target the door, then release the button to hit it with the directed spell.

The Reliquary was built so only Heroes could explore its depths. Don't hesitate to cast a magic spell whenever you see a seal such as the one on the floor here.

The path continues beyond the door to a large rectangular area that towers several stories upwards in height. Proceed in a serpentine direction around the large pillars in the center to a hole in the wall on the far side of the area. Ascend the rocky ledge past the waves of hollow men to where the path leads back into the main area of the Reliquary.

LIGHT THE LAMPS

The path leads past a locked door at the end of a walkway lined with six extinguished braziers. Use the Fireball spell to ignite each of the metal lanterns to open the door. Collect the **Silver Key** then leap off the ledge to find a wooden chest. Circle around the area in a clockwise direction to return to where you were moments ago.

Follow your dog's barking to the chest around the corner to the right. Take a side-trip up the path here to the area overlooking the rising panels you crossed upon earlier. Throw the lever to trigger a fight against a large wave of hollow men, one or two of which may have rifles. Defeating the hollow men triggers a staircase to rise up from a ledge across the cavern—explore this area on a return trip.

Return to the main path leading upwards to the top of the Reliquary to encounter a yellow flit switch. Return to the Sanctuary to equip either the Hero Rifle or Hero Pistol that Jasper has found and use whichever you choose to shoot the flit switch. Ascend the ramp that extends while firing at the hollow men to reduce them to bones long before you get within range of their cleavers and sickles.

TOTAL WARRIOR	10 Points

This Achievement unlocks as soon as you have killed enemies with all three attack styles—magic, melee, and ranged attacks—in combat. You won't have gotten this far without using the Fireball spell a number of times already. You've likely already gotten quite comfortable using either the Hero Sword or Hero Hammer. Now all you need to do is use your newly equipped Hero Rifle or Hero Pistol to blast a hollow man.

The path ascends on a series of self-extending bridges that connect a number of small square landings. Hollow men wait in droves to attack you as you make your way up the path. Hang back and use the ranged weapons and targeted Fireball spells to weaken them while staying out of reach of their melee weapons. The hollow men get more numerous and better equipped the higher you go up. Consider using one of the Summon Creatures potions you've likely collected from the chests in the area—magical creatures appear and attack and distract the enemies, allowing you to pick them off from afar.

The final landing has the largest enemy force yet. Use Fireball and melee strikes to beat them back, then open fire with your ranged weapon.

PICK UP THE MUSIC BOX

CHOICE	GOLD	GUILD SEALS	MORALITY
GOOD: Pick up the Music Box.	-	50	-
EVIL: N/A	-	-	-

Ascend the stairs to the lofty door and enter the final room in the Reliquary. Here is where your father left a most prized possession, the **Music Box**. Taking this item into your hands is sure to prove to Sabine that you are indeed a Hero.

Only a true Hero could make it this far. And only a descendant of Albion's famed savior and King could understand how special this relic is.

ROAD TO RULE

Locating the Music Box is all the proof anyone could ever need of your being a Hero, but your future tests will not be so easy. Follow Theresa's instructions and use the Music Box to witness Logan's true intentions. This should eliminate any doubts you may have felt regarding the need for a revolution. You've earned 50 additional Guild Seals and access to the next segment of the Road to Rule. Open the gate and inspect the chests.

Upgrade Strategy: The most important thing early in the game is to increase your Magic Level and to gain a second magical gauntlet. It's possible in *Fable III* to "spell weave" two magical attacks at once by wearing two gauntlets. Purchase the Shock Spell and Magic Level 1 upgrade. Use extra Guild Seals to purchase the Landlord Pack so you can begin building your personal wealth by renting out properties. Purchase the Melee Level 1 upgrade if you still have 20 or more Guild Seals.

CHESTS NOW AVAILABLE

CHEST	TYPE	GUILD SEALS	DESCRIPTION
Melee Level 1	Skill Upgrade	20	Do more damage with any melee weapon you use.
Ranged Level 1	Skill Upgrade	20	Do more damage with any gun you use.
Magic Level 1	Skill Upgrade	20	Do more damage with any spell you cast.
Shock Spell	Gauntlet	40	Shock electrocutes opponents, damaging and momentarily stunning them.
Dye Pack 1	Dye Colors	2	Inject some color into your Hero's wardrobe by learning how to dye your clothes or hair red, blue, grey, and green.
Friend Expression Pack	Expressions	2	Learn Whistle, Hero Pose, and Chat expressions in order to become friends with the people of Albion.
Landlord Pack	Property Ownership	2	Become Albion's greatest land baron by learning how to buy, rent, and decorate houses.

IN WOLF'S CLOTHING

Walter has learned that the mercenaries that terrorize the Dwellers maintain a well-fortified camp on the edge of Mistpeak Valley. You're not going to be able to saunter up to the gate and gain access dressed as a Dweller—and certainly not dressed as the prince either—but Walter has a plan. It's a risky proposition, even for a Hero, but you're going to have to sneak into the Mercenary Camp and beat them into submission in order to prevent future attacks on the Dwellers. This is the only way to lay to rest Sabine's concerns over your combat ability.

BRIGHTWALL VILLAGE

MEET WALTER IN THE PUB

Samuel is thrilled to see you return from the Reliquary in good health and has word that Walter has gained some valuable info about the mercenaries. Head to the pub in Brightwall Village to meet with Walter. The pub is near the main entrance to the village, by the bridge leading to Mistpeak Valley.

PLAY THAT FUNKY MUSIC

There are plenty of opportunities to earn some extra money in Brightwall by playing the lute or by making pies. Between the two, playing the lute brings in more money. Approach one of the "Lute Hero" signposts near the tree in the upper village and begin playing. You'll earn 1 gold coin for each correct note you strum. Strum all eight notes in each tune (by pressing the X and A buttons in time with the needle) to increase the gold multiplier to a max of 10x. You can earn up to 80 gold per tune as a Level 1 lute player. Learn more about each of the jobs in the "Hero's Way" chapter.

Walter is waiting outside the pub. Follow him upstairs to the room above the bar to find one of the mercenaries passed out drunk. Follow Walter's advice and take the guy's clothes, then visit the Sanctuary to put on the Mercenary Suit. This is an important part of the costume, but you're going to need more than clothes to sneak into the Mercenary Camp.

Walter made sure Jimmy drank too much to stir. Take his clothes off him before he wakes up.

BUY THE MERCENARY TATTOO

Return to Brightwall and head across the bridge to the stylist. Purchase the Mercenary Right Arm Tattoo and Mercenary Beard for 500 gold each. There are plenty of ways to make money in Brightwall if you don't have enough. Working as a lute player or pie maker earns you as much gold as you feel fit to make. Another option is to stop by the pawnbroker's shop and sell the various gems and other gift items you've likely found so far. Return to the Sanctuary's dressing room and finish the costume by applying the tattoo and beard.

THE BEARDED LADY

Even if you're playing a female Hero, you will need to wear the mercenary beard. It's a slightly nontraditional look for a lady, but it will fool the dimwitted mercenaries.

MERCENARY CAMP

FIND CAPTAIN SAKER

There are several dig spots and dive spots around the perimeter of the lake. Collect the treasure, then approach the stockade wall to gain entrance to the camp.

Saker is the leader of the mercenaries and he's holed up at the Mercenary Camp in Mistpeak Valley. Cross the bridge to exit Brightwall Village and head down the hill in Mistpeak Valley towards the lake. You'll encounter numerous packs of wolves in Mistpeak, but they're nothing you can't handle at this point—just fire two quick shots with your gun, then blast away with the Fireball spell. Swim the length of the lake to find the two dive spots then exit the water near the guard post to enter Mercenary Camp. The guard will think you're Jimmy and open the gate without delay.

Open the chest beneath the watchtower on the right, then head over to the two mercenaries calling your name. One of the guys goads you into showing the other, Stilts, "that thing you do." Approach Stilts to interact with him and either press the A button to kiss him or the X button to fart on him. The choice is yours; you can even shoot the explosive barrel next to them to kill both of them if you'd like.

THE LOST JEWELRY

Take a quick detour up the wooden steps to the right of the caged wolves and continue past the mercenary searching in the grass. Locate the jewelry a few steps beyond him and pick it up. Locate the chest and dig spot at the end of the path, then return the way you came. You'll have an opportunity to give the jewelry to the man who's apparently searching for it. Giving the jewelry to the mercenary earns you +5 Morality. Keeping it will not tilt you towards an evil rating, which is good since the jewelry may not even be his anyway!

Continue to the second checkpoint and enter the main area of the camp as soon as the gate is raised. Ignore the two guys fighting in the center and take a moment to search the perimeter for loot (you can find a complete set of Mercenary Tattoos throughout the Mercenary Camp) before approaching the two mercenaries near the next gate. Though your costume is a dead ringer for a mercenary, the guys at the gate notice your eyes are the wrong color and attack. Fire two quick shots with your weapon, then roll away and attack with a Fireball spell. The gate opens as soon as the first four have been dispatched. Stand facing the gate and quickly fire at the barrels beyond it to defeat the two enemies standing near the explosives.

Your disguise, however perfect, won't get you past the two sharp-eyed mercenaries near this next gate. Be ready for battle!

Approach the open gate and target the barrel in the distance with the rifle. You can auto-aim by pointing the Left Thumbstick in the direction you wish to fire and pressing the Y button to fire—the weapon automatically targets the nearest target in that direction. Pressing and holding the Left Trigger while targeting an enemy locks on to the foe. Just tap the Y button to shoot, or hold Y down to execute a flourish shot. Another half-dozen foes attack from the left, so be ready. The path zigzags up the hill from here towards the fortified circle atop the hill where Saker is hiding out.

Distance is your best friend! Roll away from enemies to stay out of range of their melee weapons, then rely on guns and magic to dispatch them safely.

MERCENARY TATTOOS

You were able to purchase the Mercenary Right Arm Tattoo in Brightwall, but you can find the rest of the set at the Mercenary Camp. Locate the chests and dig spots (Level 1) in the area to find matching tattoos for the left arm, chest, left leg, and face.

Fight your way up the hill to the left, past the next watchtower to where three enemies approach on foot. Hold your ground, dispatch these foes, then shoulder the Hero Rifle and take aim at the explosives near the enemies in the distance. If you haven't already equipped the Hero Rifle, this is a prime time to do so, as its superior range makes the final push to Saker much easier. Slay the wolves that are released from their cage, then grab the Silver Key and ascend the watchtower.

There are three groups of mercenaries in the distance. They have taken cover behind sandbags, but they weren't smart enough to get clear of the explosive barrels they're hiding alongside. Use the Hero Rifle to snipe each of the barrels. The resulting explosions will eliminate any of the enemies standing nearby. This is a great spot to make some progress on the **Barrel of Laughs** Achievement, which requires 25 kills via explosive barrels. It typically takes two shots with the Hero Rifle to dispatch an enemy, but one shot to a barrel can eliminate multiple enemies at once!

Hold the Left Trigger to aim the reticle at one of the red barrels, then press the Y button to fire.

Descend to the ground and resume the push towards Saker's inner sanctum. Continue to make use of the Hero Rifle's outstanding range by sniping the distant enemies long before they can get close enough to be a bother.

DEFEAT CAPTAIN SAKER

CHOICE	GOLD	GUILD SEALS	MORALITY
GOOD: Spare Captain Saker's life.	-	50	+175
EVIL: Kill Captain Saker.	-	50	-75

Captain Saker leaps down off the wall that circles the inner area of the Mercenary Camp and attacks at once by lobbing Molotov cocktails. This is his only ranged attack, but it's an effective one. To avoid being engulfed in flame, point the Left Thumbstick in a direction and tap the A button to roll. Move gradually closer to Saker to take away his ability to attack with the explosive bottles.

Slash twice at Saker with your Hero Sword, then roll away before his counterattack. It's rare to be able to actually land three sword strikes on Saker without the last being blocked or your being hit, so stop at two. Saker has several melee attacks up his cut-off sleeves. First among those is a double-fisted jab that he'll deliver if you stand directly in front of him. Another is his leaping ground-pound attack that sends shockwaves outwards in all directions. Both of these attacks can knock you back and inflict moderate damage.

Continue dashing around the arena while pelting Saker with Fireballs and moving in and out of range for melee strikes. Several of his cronies eventually leap into the ring to lend a hand. Stay on the move to avoid Saker's Molotov cocktails and use the Hero Rifle and Shock or Fireball spells to dispatch the lesser foes as quickly as possible. Saker is immune to Shock, but it momentarily incapacitates his minions. Fireball just blasts everyone. Your choice! Consider using a Summon Creatures potion to even up the sides and distract both Saker and his men. This grants you the freedom to take your shots at Saker without risk of retaliation.

Two more batches of enemies enter the arena to assist Captain Saker. Stay on the move and use your ranged attacks against the lesser foes while mixing in attacks against Saker when possible. Roll away from the enemies twice, take a couple of quick shots with the Hero Rifle, cast a Fireball spell, then roll again. Saker gradually shifts to a boxer's style of fighting and tends to not throw his Molotov cocktails when his own men are in the ring. Stay out of range of his uppercuts and jabs and use Fireball spells and guns to knock him to his knees.

Saker accepts his fate like a good soldier and you're free to do with him as you please. You'll earn 50 Guild Seals regardless of whether you choose to spare his life or kill him, but the impact to your morality is severe. The choice you make regarding the fate of Captain Saker has greater impact on your morality than any other choice you make throughout the game. That said, it is hard to lead a rebellion if you ruthlessly kill those who may be of help to you in the future. We recommend sparing Saker. You receive **Saker's Flag** regardless of your choice.

ROAD TO RULE

By defeating Saker and his men and winning security for the Dwellers, you've successfully proven yourself in combat. Sabine will no doubt be impressed. Saker's image joins that of Jasper and Walter along the Road to Rule if you decided to spare him. Though the gate to the next round of upgrades opens regardless of your decision, you have one less follower by your side if you decided to kill Saker.

Upgrade Strategy: Continue the trend you set upon earlier and purchase the Magic Level 2 upgrade. This allows you to charge your magic spells even faster and greatly expands the area-of-effect for magic casting. Return to the previous segment of the Road to Rule and use your remaining Guild Seals to purchase the Ranged or Melee Level 1 upgrade that you likely had to skip last time. Consider purchasing either the Lute or Blacksmith Level 2 upgrade to aid in your gold earning. Lastly, purchasing the Family Pack can help you start your family and make it possible to bring a child of your own to the Demon Door in Brightwall Village, resulting in a very valuable reward.

CHESTS NOW AVAILABLE

CHEST	TYPE	GUILD SEALS	DESCRIPTION
Melee Level 2	Skill Upgrade	40	Do more damage with any melee weapon you use.
Ranged Level 2	Skill Upgrade	40	Do more damage with any gun you use.
Magic Level 2	Skill Upgrade	40	Do more damage with any spell you cast.
Lover Expression Pack	Expressions	5	Take your relationships to the next level by learning Dance, Hug, and Kiss in order to become best friends or even lovers with the people of Albion.
Family Pack	Family Abilities	10	Want to start a family? Unlock Marriage, House Buying, Having Children, and Adoption. (Also unlocks the Lover Expression Pack)
Blacksmith Level 2	Job Skill Upgrade	5	Become a better blacksmith and earn more money striking that steel.
Pie Maker Level 2	Job Skill Upgrade	5	Improve your cooking skills and earn more money making pies.
Lute Level 2	Job Skill Upgrade	5	Improve your lute playing skills and earn more money performing.

LEADERS AND FOLLOWERS

You've proven yourself a Hero and a skilled fighter. Now you must prove yourself a leader by winning over the hearts and minds of the people of Brightwall. The villagers who reside here are a generous lot, but they don't have much to spare. You must meet with Walter and Samuel in the pub to learn a way to ease the charity out of this village. Show the people of Brightwall that you are there for them, and they just might return the favor.

BRIGHTWALL VILLAGE

MEET SIR WALTER IN BRIGHTWALL

Climb the stairs to the room above the bar inside the pub to meet with Walter and Samuel. Walter has been trying to talk Samuel into lending some supplies to the Dweller Camp, but the people of Brightwall have very little to spare. Samuel believes that if you were to spread some cheer around the village and help people out, that those same villagers would then turn their gratitude into charity and send supplies to the Dwellers.

Walter and Samuel are enjoying a not-so-frosty mug at Ye Quill and Quandary. Climb the stairs to see what they have in mind for you.

GATHER 30 MORE GUILD SEALS TO GAIN THE FOLLOWING OF THE PEOPLE OF BRIGHTWALL

SIDE-QUESTING

Visit the Sanctuary to study the map table with Jasper. He's found a way to use the map to highlight those villagers who can benefit from your assistance. These quest givers are marked with an "!" above their heads and can be selected with the magnifying glass. You can also see a brief description of the quest and the number of Guild Seals you stand to earn for completing the quest.

There are currently four quests available: **Chicken Chaser**, **Missing Play**, **Missing Child**, and **Gnomes are Great!** You won't need to complete all of these quests in order to fulfill Samuel's requirement of 30 new Guild Seals, but the more side-quests you participate in, the more Guild Seals you'll have to spend along the Road to Rule. Lastly, we strongly recommend completing **Gnomes are Great!** and beginning the follow-up **Gnomes are Evil!** quest since it's quite lengthy and involves traveling throughout all of Albion—best to start it sooner rather than later.

MISSING PLAY

Lambert and Pinch need help putting on their plays in Brightwall.

AVAILABILITY: This quest becomes available after defeating Saker and returning to Brightwall.

UNLOCKS: N/A

REWARD: 20 Guild Seals & The Complete Works of Philipth Morley

MORALITY: N/A

Speak to the two thespians outside the Academy to learn of the missing play. The first step in finding the play is to find a man named Ransom Locke. Enter the Academy and continue straight past the front desk to the door that slams shut in the distance. Ignore the warnings and open the door to proceed deeper into the Academy. Continue through the second shut door to enter the study at the rear of the building. The missing play is in the far corner of the room.

Thumbing through the pages of the play triggers the arrival of Philipth Morley's ghost, who then sucks you into the world of *The Lost Works*. Ransom Locke is there to chaperone you to safety. Follow along with Ransom Locke as he leads you to three different sets from three of Morley's most celebrated works.

Approach the mannequin and put on the first costume, the lady's dress. You'll get the chance to either declare your love or abuse your suitor, Oliver. The play calls for you to express your love to Oliver, but the choice is yours. The next play requires you to perform as a jester in

 a chicken suit. Put on the costume and make the king laugh by tickling him (or risk his wrath and express your love instead).

HE'S A WOMAN. SHE'S A MAN. | 5 Points

This Achievement requires you to experiment with cross-dressing. Completing this quest requires you to wear both male and female costumes, so you will unlock this Achievement regardless of whether you're playing as the Prince or Princess of Albion. It may only be 5 Gamer Points, but it's an easy Achievement to complete.

The final play requires you to dress as a man named Titus and battle a gang of gladiators led by a character named Ace. Though the script calls for you to fall in battle, it's certainly worth putting on a good show. Not only will this be all the more convincing to the ghostly audience, but you'll earn additional Guild Seals through combat. Keep the fight going for a while to earn a Guild Seal or two. Ace eventually summons a larger group of his men to attack. Ready a Fireball spell for them and keep up the fight! There isn't any penalty for dying, so don't use any potions. Just keep fighting until the end. Win or lose, completing the scene is all that matters.

Collect the script to **The Ham Sandwich** from Morley to escape *The Lost Works*. Once outside the Academy, give the script to Lambert and Pinch, who immediately—and unfortunately—set about performing the play on the steps of the Academy. The audience may not like the play, but you'll still be rewarded with **The Complete Works of Philipth Morley** for your trophy wall.

TRAGICAL-COMICAL-HISTORICAL. | 10 Points

Complete the quest **The Missing Play** to unlock this Achievement. Don the three outfits, participate in the witty dialogue, and battle Ace's men to the death.

GNOMES ARE GREAT!

Brian in Brightwall wants your help retrieving a very special package.

AVAILABILITY: This quest becomes available after defeating Saker and returning to Brightwall.

UNLOCKS: Return the Gargoyle statue to unlock the "Gnomes are Evil!" quest.

REWARD: 10 Guild Seals

MORALITY: N/A

Speak to Brian in the area with the massive frog statues, to the east of the Academy. Brian has what some might say is a rather unhealthy affection for gnomes, and today is his favorite gnome Jonathan's birthday. The package Brian ordered has gone missing in Mistpeak Valley, and he believes the delivery coach may have lost a wheel. He needs you to head to Mistpeak Valley and retrieve the gift he ordered for Jonathan the gnome.

Follow the glowing path out of Brightwall Village, across the bridge, and down into Mistpeak Valley. Descend away from the snow-covered peaks on the left and continue along the trail as it winds its way along the ridge to the right. The wagon bearing Brian's package has indeed lost a wheel, but it's also been attacked by mercenaries! You'll likely only spot four of the mercenaries at first, but there are a total of seven of them hiding amongst the rocks. Use charged magic attacks to soften them up as they approach, then roll away and open fire with your gun. Use flourish attacks to finish the mercenaries off as they get close then unleash a final charged magic attack to clear the area.

LISTEN AND LEARN

If you rush the mercenary squad immediately, the bloodthirsty lot will attack as they're inclined to do. However, do yourself a favor; hang back unobserved to watch them and be treated to a brief discussion of philosophy among mercenaries.

Locate the missing package behind the wagon, a **Gargoyle**, and pick it up. Return the Gargoyle to Brian in Brightwall Village and place it on the pedestal beside him. You'll just have to watch and see what happens next, but do understand that this will unlock the **Gnomes are Evil!** quest. Consult the Quest List feature on the map table to see when it becomes available then head to Brian to initiate it.

CHICKEN CHASER

Bernard and Patsy's chickens have run amuck.

AVAILABILITY: This quest becomes available after defeating Saker and returning to Brightwall.

UNLOCKS: Complete this quest to unlock "A Day at the (Chicken) Races."

REWARD: 10 Guild Seals & Chicken Trophy

MORALITY: Save the chickens to earn +50 Morality. Kill the chickens to earn -50 Morality.

Locate the chicken farm on the west side of Brightwall Village and speak to Bernard, the panicked farmer. To his horror, someone has left the gate to his pen open and the chickens have escaped. They've split into groups of three, and he wants you to lure them back to his farm. Put on the Chicken Suit he gives you and set out to find the chickens. Press the A button when in range to flap your wings and get the chickens to follow you. Your dog barks when he gets near a set of chickens, and a quest indictor appears over his head to let you know the chickens are near.

The first group of chickens isn't hard to find; they're right under the arch in the wall near the farmhouse. Run up to them, flap your wings, then slowly lead them back inside the pen. Descend the path towards the small stone bridge and turn to the right. The second set of chickens is hiding near the houses up the path on the northwest side of the creek. The final group of chickens are in the town square, near the statue in front of the pub.

Bernard and Patsy don't agree on how to tend for the chickens going forward. Bernard would like to kill them, and Patsy wants to save them. They leave the decision up to you. Regardless of your decision, events unfold to allow you to bet on the chicken races later on. You probably won't win much money betting on the races, but it's worth sparing the chickens just to hear the narrator describe the chickens. You will earn the **Chicken Trophy** for your efforts regardless of the choice you make concerning their feathery fate.

A DAY AT THE (CHICKEN) RACES

Returning the chickens unlocks this betting game. Return to the chicken farm in Brightwall Village whenever you wish to lay some gold down on the chickens. There are five chickens in the race, each with their own unique name and odds. Approach the table near the house to place your bets. Bet on as few or as many chickens as you'd like, but know that the results are random. Even the long shot wins every so often.

MISSING CHILD

Search Mistpeak Valley's caverns for a lost little girl.

AVAILABILITY: This quest becomes available after defeating Saker and returning to Brightwall.

UNLOCKS: N/A

REWARD: 5 Guild Seals

MORALITY: N/A

Cross the bridge leading out of Brightwall Village and speak to the woman on the far side of the gorge. Her little girl has gone missing somewhere in Mistpeak Valley and she needs you to search for her. Mistpeak Valley has three entrances to an area known as Chillbreath Caverns. Descend the hill from Brightwall Village and turn left at the ruins, then head up into the snowy heights, via the bridge. Cross the snowy plains to a large cleft in the mountain and head inside. This is the entrance to Chillbreath Caverns you need in order to find the girl.

Chillbreath Caverns has three distinct routes within it that are not connected. Though the caverns are quite large, the trail you're following to the missing child is both short and straightforward. Follow the glowing trail into the caverns and round the corner to the left when you get to the ledge. Locate the dig spot and wooden chest just off the main path on your way to the girl, Eve, at the end of the trail.

Take Eve by the hand and guide her back the way you came to the exit of the cave. Several packs of wolves attack along the way. These packs usually consist of just two or three wolves each and don't pose much of a threat. Release Eve's hand, shoot the wolves, then continue escorting her to the exit. Lead her back through Mistpeak Valley (where more wolves attack) to Brightwall, where her mother waits patiently by the bridge, to complete the quest.

GNOMES ARE EVIL!

Brian in Brightwall brought his gnomes to life with your help, but now they're causing him problems. He needs you to find them and help him put them right. Return to Brian to give him any gnomes you find.

AVAILABILITY: Must first complete the Gnomes are Great! quest.

UNLOCKS: N/A

REWARD: 40 Guild Seals, the Gnomewrecker weapon, & Gnome Trophy

MORALITY: N/A

Return to the gnome garden area and speak with the visibly upset Brian about his gnomes. It seems that all 50 of the gnomes have gone missing, and he only knows where one of them can be found. That one, the gnome he calls Lionel, is inside Brian's house. Head up the path above the garden to his house and go inside. The gnome is on the wall opposite the chest. You'll hear its Gnomish trash talk as soon as you enter the house. Draw your gun and shoot the gnome to send it back to Brian.

FILTHY-MOUTHED BUGGERS

Those who played *Fable II* will no doubt be at home with gnome hunting, as it is indeed similar to the gargoyle quest from the previous game. One big difference here is that the gnomes are actually quite a bit meaner than the gargoyles ever were. You'll know you're near a gnome when you suddenly find yourself—or your dog—being insulted by a rather high-pitched voice. Move towards the voice to find the gnome (it becomes louder the closer you get), then draw your ranged weapon and shoot it. We suspect not even fans of garden gnomes will have a problem shooting these trash-talking little statues.

Return to Brian to see that Lionel magically reappeared in the garden once he was shot. Brian wants you to search all of Albion for the other 49 gnomes. Return to Brian to receive 10 Guild Seals for every 10 gnomes you recover (through the first 40 gnomes). Find all 50 gnomes to receive the Gnomewrecker weapon and to unlock the **Gnome Invasion** Achievement. Consult the "Albion Atlas" portion of the guide for details on all 50 gnome locations.

RETURN TO SAMUEL

Make your way to the front gate near the pub as soon as you have earned the 30 Guild Seals needed to win the support of Brightwall's villagers. Samuel is ready to shower you with praises and send plenty of supplies to the Dweller Camp, but not without first asking one more favor. He needs you to promise to reopen Brightwall Academy once the revolution is over and you become the new king of Albion. You have no choice in the matter; you must promise Samuel and give the people of Brightwall your word as Prince that you will one day reopen Brightwall Academy. Agree to the promise and earn 50 Guild Seals for completing this quest.

"I hereby promise that I shall reopen the Brightwall Academy."

GO TO THE DWELLER CAMP

You've completed all three tasks Sabine has set out for you; it's time to return to the Dweller Camp and see if he has been fittingly impressed by your efforts. Use the map table to fast travel to the Dweller Camp to meet with Sabine. As was the case with Samuel, Sabine is most impressed with your performance, but has one more request before he'll agree to join your revolution. You must first promise to him that you'll restore the mountains to their natural splendor and grant the Dwellers full custody of them. Agree to the promise to gain a most important ally, earn 50 Guild Seals, and unlock the **And So It Begins** Achievement.

"I hereby promise to restore the lands of Mistpeak and return them to the Dwellers."

ROAD TO RULE

You've gained a crucial ally in Sabine, but have had to make promises you may find difficult to keep later on. This is the cost of being a leader. Nevertheless, there is much work to be done before you can ever be in a position to make good on these promises. You must first gain additional allies. Logan has an entire army and all you have is Walter and a few Dwellers. You will need far more than that if you're to overthrow your brother.

Upgrade Strategy: Depending on how many of the available quests you completed, you may have more than 180 Guild Seals to spend. You certainly have at least 130. Return to the previous segment of the Road to Rule and purchase any additional combat skill upgrades you haven't yet acquired. Now upgrade your job skills. Focus on blacksmithing if you're simply going for the most direct path to maximum earnings. Purchase all three job skill upgrades if you plan on completing most of the quests and want to really make the most out of your time in Albion. The Ice Storm spell is a fine ability to add to your repertoire, but should only be purchased at this time by those setting out to earn the maximum Guild Seals possible. Those taking a more streamlined approach and not necessarily completing every optional quest should conserve some of their Guild Seals to spend along the next segment of the Road to Rule.

CHESTS NOW AVAILABLE

CHEST	TYPE	GUILD SEALS	DESCRIPTION
Ice Storm Spell	Magical Gauntlet	40	Ice Storm summons frozen shards that rain down destruction on your foes.
Joker Expression Pack	Expressions	5	Become a comedian by learning the Tickle, Pat a Cake, and Chicken Dance expressions.
Dye Pack II	Clothing Dyes	5	Tired of your appearance? Learn how to dye your clothes or hair khaki, purple, orange, and pink.
Blacksmith Level 3	Job Skill Upgrade	10	Become a better blacksmith and earn more money striking that steel.
Pie Maker Level 3	Job Skill Upgrade	10	Improve your cooking skills and earn more money making pies.
Lute Level 3	Job Skill Upgrade	10	Improve your lute playing skills and earn more money performing.

THE MISTPEAK MONORAIL

Sabine and the Dwellers will be of great service during the revolution, but you need more than just them to battle Logan and his men. Fortunately, Walter has given a great deal of thought to this planned rebellion and has several more contacts he wants you to meet. The next suitable ally is located in Mourningwood. Not one for parties, Walter has already left for the Mistpeak Monorail Station and left you in the Dweller Camp to enjoy your newfound celebrity. Take as much or as little time as needed before going to meet him—he won't leave without you.

DWELLER CAMP

Walter is waiting at the monorail station in Mistpeak Valley to kick off the next leg of your army-building adventure. Don't rush off just yet! This is a great time to complete additional side-quests and purchase some houses to begin amassing your riches (you can't purchase any shops or stalls right now, but you will soon). The "Real Estate Magnate" portion of this book provides complete listings of house and shop prices for all of Albion, along with strategies on how to get the most bang for your buck. If you're low on funds right now, then stick to buying just one or two caravans at the Dweller Camp. You'll receive rent every five minutes spent playing the game in real-time. The more expensive houses and shops offer the biggest return on your investment, but even little purchases like Dweller caravans can yield sizable returns over time.

Repair the caravan to ensure the tenants pay rent. Caravans only yield about 45 gold each in rent, but collecting 45 gold every five minutes adds up to thousands of gold over time.

RENTAL UPKEEP AND RATES

Buying a shop or a really high-priced house is the most effective way to earn the highest return on your investment, but they cost a lot! Build your early fortune by purchasing a few caravans or small houses and renting them out. Make any necessary repairs to the structure, otherwise the renters will stop paying their rent. Decorating a house automatically increases the rent you can charge, but you can adjust the rent manually too. Raising or lowering the rent is an effective way to shift your Morality rating towards the good (low rent) or evil (high rent) end of the spectrum. We suggest keeping it at the default setting unless you're already a millionaire or trying to be completely evil.

SIDE-QUEST DWELLER CAMP

SPECIAL DELIVERY

Mrs. Tibbins has found something interesting in her backyard.

AVAILABILITY: This quest becomes available after making the promise to Sabine.

UNLOCKS: Deliver the package to Saul to unlock **An Ancient Key** quest.

REWARD: 5 Guild Seals

MORALITY: N/A

Mrs. Tibbins lives in the caravan in the center of the Dweller Camp, within the fence. She needs someone to deliver a package to her cousin Saul at the Brightwall Academy. You can reach Brightwall by descending the mountainside on foot to Mistpeak Valley and then journeying through the pass to the village. Alternatively, you can use the map table at the Sanctuary to fast travel there—the choice is yours. The latter is obviously much faster, but you'll gain more Guild Seals by going on foot and battling any wolves or mercenaries you encounter. Either way, head over to Brightwall Academy and give Saul the package. He's in the room to the left of the front desk.

 SIDE-QUEST BRIGHTWALL VILLAGE

AN ANCIENT KEY

Saul has the key to an ancient secret, but he needs some help.

AVAILABILITY: Complete **Special Delivery** to unlock this quest.

UNLOCKS: An Evil Presence

REWARD: 5 Guild Seals

MORALITY: N/A

Exit Brightwall Village to allow some time to pass, then return to the Brightwall Academy and meet Saul in the room with the suits of armor by the entrance to The Reliquary. Accept the **Key of Forbidden Knowledge** from him and lead him by the hand down the stairs into The Reliquary. The glowing trail leads through the aisles of books to the cavernous portion of the old repository. Descend the stairs on the right and prepare for battle. A number of hollow men will attack at three points along your journey to use the key. Release Saul's hand and prepare a fully charged Fireball spell to shatter their bones. Cross the bridge that

you extended on your first visit to reach a second battle, then continue down the stairs to the right.

Use the key to unlock the door and head up the stairs inside the hallway where the third set of hollow men attack. Use the key once again atop the stairs to bring Saul to a long-forgotten room containing hundreds of ancient tomes. This is the best treasure Saul could have hoped for!

ABOUT THAT FLIT SWITCH

Shooting the flit switch on the wall inside the room you brought Saul to reveals the first step in a lengthy process needed to reach the golden door at the base of The Reliquary. Shoot the flit switch three times to open the door and gain access to another flit switch. Slash at this one as it moves from one position to the next to activate a series of stairs and platforms that spiral downwards around the central tower to reach the golden door. You can read more about this golden door in the **Albion Atlas** portion of the book.

MERCENARY CUSTOMS

Escort a wandering trader to Brightwall.

AVAILABILITY: This quest becomes available upon entering Mistpeak Valley after making the promise to Sabine.

UNLOCKS: N/A

REWARD: 5 Guild Seals

MORALITY: N/A

Billy the wandering trader is patiently waiting outside the Mistpeak Monorail Station for someone brave enough to escort him to Brightwall Village. He's terrified about being killed and robbed, or was that robbed and killed? Either way, he needs some help. Take him by the hand and lead him back along the path leading into the hills above the lake to Brightwall Village.

Several bands of mercenaries will attack along the way. When this happens, release Billy's hand and use your ever-sharpening combat abilities to destroy them. The mercenaries often drop from trees or leap out from behind rocks. Immediately prepare a Level 2 magic spell and unleash it just as they draw within the circle marking the spell's area of effect. Finish them off with melee and gun attacks. Guide Billy by the hand over the bridge into Brightwall Village.

MEET SIR WALTER AT THE MISTPEAK MONORAIL STATION

Partake in as much side-questing as you want (available side-quests are detailed prior to this section), then travel across Mistpeak Valley to the monorail station near the lake. It's on the opposite side of the lake from the Mercenary Camp. The station is crowded with travelers, but it's not that large. Ascend the stairs to learn about some friends of Sir Walter's that he wants to recruit for the revolution.

Walter is sitting on a bench on the upper platform. Continue through the hustle and bustle to meet him.

The sudden collapse of the monorail car sends Walter into action. Follow him to the main platform where he will pry open the gate leading to the maintenance lifts. Proceed down the walkway and board the lift atop the first set of stairs on the right. The lift lowers you to the floor of the cave.

THE HOLE

FIND THE MONORAIL WRECKAGE

Exit the lift and descend the path alongside the cart tracks to the ruined monorail car. Walter was hoping to find survivors, but the only things alive in the area are several hobbes. These squat, troll-like creatures are both weak and extremely flammable, so prime your Fireball spell and let them have it! Hobbes come in many varieties—you'll encounter much tougher ones later—but this first encounter takes place against the weakest of them all. After the fight, continue across the wooden bridge.

Use your gun to pick off the first few hobbes, then ready the Fireball spell for the larger group that approaches later.

EXIT THE CAVE

The path ahead is crawling with hobbes, many of which are taking cover behind walls of sandbags or inside the barrels. Unfortunately for these dimwitted cave dwellers, they don't realize they're standing near explosive barrels. Use a rifle and shoot the barrels from afar as soon as you see them. The hobbes will charge up the hill towards your position, so just keep firing—Walter will cut down any that get too close!

TECHNICIAN'S KEY REQUIRED

It takes a special key to open the locked gate to the left of the racks of barrels. You'll find this key later on, so remember to return to this place (via the Monorail Station lift) to unlock it and explore the area fully. Consult the **Albion Atlas** portion of this book for maps and additional information about The Hole.

Follow the trail to the north, past the small pools of water, and up the slope to the narrow ledge located across from the hobbes in the distance. The hobbes have built themselves an impressive set of wooden walkways and structures across the chasm, but they've loaded it up with a number of explosive barrels. Shoulder your rifle and snipe the barrels as Walter charges ahead along the path to get a closer shot with his pistol. You can eliminate the majority of the hobbes in the area by detonating each barrel with the rifle.

Use a rifle to snipe the red explosive barrels across the chasm. The resulting explosions will engulf the hobbes in flames.

Keep firing on the hobbes until there is no more movement, then continue around the U-shaped bend in the cave. Another large group of hobbes is waiting in the distance and they won't hesitate to charge your position. Shoot at the barrel on the left-hand side of the path just as the hobbes run past it, then prepare your magic and melee attacks for a more intimate battle. These hobbes only have access to melee weapons, so try to stay a couple steps away to avoid taking damage.

Beware the hobbes in the red military uniforms! These elite hobbes carry large axes and muskets, plus they can withstand a lot more abuse than lesser hobbes!

FIND A WAY TO THE SUMMONER HOBBE

Eliminate the last of the hobbes, then open the wooden chest on the left and continue through the cave. Splash through the shallow pool of water and climb up the slope to where a summoner hobbe seals off the opening

in the rocks. There's no way past its magical barrier, so you must find another way around.

The summoner hobbe won't be safe for long. Head down the path to the right to loop around and attack from behind!

Leave Walter near the barrier to distract the hobbes and head down the path on the right to the water. Swim through the tunnel in a counterclockwise direction to reach the hobbes behind the barrier and then take aim at the summoner hobbe with your gun. You only need to distract him momentarily to lower the barrier and allow Walter through. The summoner hobbe can call upon fallen hobbes and cast fireballs, so focus your attacks on him first, then deal with the others later.

Run and somersault past the hobbes with the cleavers and muskets to attack the summoner hobbe first. This makes dealing with the others easier.

Continue down the path to a ledge looking across a bottomless pit to a series of ruins. Cross the rickety bridge near the collapsed columns and head up the hill to enter the Hobbe Arena.

DEFEAT THE HOBBES

The hobbes have converted an ancient temple into a gladiatorial arena, complete with a ring of drummers banging out a tribal beat to complement the combat. Three summoner hobbes appear on a central dais and beckon a dozen skeletal hobbes. The unarmored skeletal hobbes are the weakest of all the hobbes and can be shattered with a single Fireball spell (Level 2

or higher). The armored ones can withstand a bit more punishment, but fall to Fireball spells as well.

Use high-powered magic spells to decimate the hobbe skeletons that are summoned. The faster you clear out the summoned hobbes, the sooner you can reach the summoner hobbes.

The magical barrier surrounding the summoner hobbes gets dispelled as soon as the first wave of summoned hobbes is destroyed. Take aim at one of the summoner hobbes with your gun (or use spells) and blast it off the dais and away from the others to separate it from the group. The others will summon another small wave of hobbes. Let Walter take care of them and charge after the one you isolated from the group. Use magic and melee attacks to defeat the summoner hobbe, then focus on defeating the others in the same manner. Clear the arena of hobbes to earn 50 Guild Seals and another trip to the Road to Rule.

Attempt to isolate the summoner hobbes by knocking them off the platform one at a time with rifle shots. Focus on the summoner hobbes to minimize the number of other hobbes that join the fray.

READING HOBBE BODY LANGUAGE

Watch for the hobbe to slowly raise and pull his empty hand backwards as if to suck power from the air. This motion indicates that it is preparing to throw its own version of the Fireball spell. When this occurs, quickly dodge to the side to avoid the incoming magical projectile. Don't roll forwards or backwards, or else you'll get hit; always roll to the side!

ROAD TO RULE

Defeating the hobbes proves that you can overcome sudden, unexpected challenges. Theresa is confident that your conquests in The Hole will be told for ages throughout the lands of Albion. Your experience as a Hero continues to build and new abilities await. This next segment of the Road to Rule contains one of the most important powers that you can earn—enjoy this victory. You deserve it!

Upgrade Strategy: The 50 Guild Seals earned for surviving the Hobbe Arena are just enough to purchase the Spell Weaving ability. If you only purchase one chest during this trip along the Road to Rule, then this is the one! You may have more than 90 Guild Seals remaining if you did each of the available side-quests and used your Silver Keys to unlock the chest in Mistpeak Valley. If so, purchase the Vortex Spell and the Entrepreneur Pack along with any chests from previous road segments that you skipped on previous visits. Unlocking Spell Weaving and the Vortex Spell are among the most important purchases to make along the Road to Rule. Visit the Sanctuary and combine Vortex with Fireball for an absolutely devastating combination!

CHESTS NOW AVAILABLE

CHEST	TYPE	GUILD SEALS	DESCRIPTION
Vortex Spell	Magical Gauntlet	40	Vortex creates a windstorm that picks up enemies and hurls them around, preventing them from attacking and potentially knocking them into objects.
Spell Weaving	Magic Ability	50	Gain the ability to combine two spells together by wearing two gauntlets.
Dye Pack III	Clothing Dyes	5	Experiment with more colors by learning how to dye your clothes or hair white, lime, yellow, and brown.
Entrepreneur Pack	Shop Buying Ability	5	Learn how to haggle and own shops and you'll soon be running your own business empire.

Spell Gauntlet 4 / 4

Vortex Spell

EXIT THE CAVE (CONTINUED)

Walter will create an exit from the arena and you're not far from the cave's exit. Just go straight across the wooden bridge and up the hill to reach the exit. Pay attention to your dog in this area as there are several dig spots worth checking out. You emerge from The Hole in Mourningwood.

FIND THE TECHNICIAN'S KEY

There's more to The Hole than what you just experienced, but you'll have to find a special key to explore it further. Cross the wooden bridge and venture down the narrow path to the left of the flaming cauldrons. There is a chest at the end of this path that contains the **Technician's Key**. Use it on a return trip to explore the area beyond the locked gate not far from the monorail wreckage.

THE HOLLOW LEGION

Men like Walter don't advance to the upper echelon of the royal army without making plenty of friends along the way. Some of his old war buddies are currently stationed at Mourningwood Fort, just beyond the swamp in the northeast corner of Mourningwood. Walter has a feeling that Major Swift and his men have been wavering in their allegiance to King Logan with each passing day that they've been stationed at this forsaken outpost. Perhaps there's a way you could help the men and win their support in the coming revolution?

MOURNINGWOOD

FIND ALLIES IN MOURNINGWOOD

You emerge from The Hole amongst the moss-draped trees in the dank swamp of Mourningwood. Splash your way south through the marshland to a stone bridge. The path spirals downward into the narrow valley below. Explore the area just beyond the bridge with your dog to find some treasure and note the location of the Silver Key Chest—you'll probably have to come back to open it at another time, as it requires 10 Silver Keys. Descend to the wooden walkway below and locate the chest ahead, on the left. Immediately visit the Sanctuary's weapon room and equip **The Bonesmasher** pistol found here.

The Mourningwood Fort is just up ahead. Walter knows the men stationed here quite well, and believes Major Swift and the soldiers under his charge will join the revolution. Follow Walter around the fort as he introduces you to Major Swift and Ben Finn. Major Swift then asks for your assistance in manning the mortar.

Take a moment to purchase any potions you might need from the supply table in the corner, then follow Ben Finn onto the wall above the front gate. Follow Jammy's instructions on using the mortar and destroy the left and middle scarecrows that he's set up in the distance. Position the targeting reticle on the target, then press the A button to fire the mortar.

Most wooden chests yield random treasures, but this one always contains The Bonesmasher. This pistol is devastating against hollow men, which are in abundance throughout this area.

Major Swift and Ben Finn are part of Logan's royal army, but they're not exactly fans of the king. Help them battle the undead to garner their support.

DESTROY THE HOLLOW LEGION

Dozens of hollow men spawn in groups of four to six all across the area outside the fort's main gate, and it's up to you to keep them at bay. The mortar can fire a shell roughly every 3 seconds and has a broad enough impact area to destroy six or more hollow men with a single blast, so long as they are tightly grouped. The hollow men primarily appear in six different areas: along the three angled roads to the left and on the three horizontal roads to the right. Look for the blue glow that precedes the appearance of a hollow man and wait for multiple hollow men to spawn before firing the shell. Individual hollow men are no threat to the fort, so focus on the groups just as they appear, before they scatter.

Target large groups of spawning hollow men near the ruins to get the most out of each shell. The more hollow men you kill, the more Guild Seals you'll earn!

ACCESS THE SILVER KEY

The shockwave from each mortar impact can set off the nearby explosive barrels. Fire the mortar as far and to the right as you can to detonate the barrels near the boarded-up bunker in the corner. The explosion destroys the wooden barricade and grants access to the Silver Key after you leave the fort. You can also smash the barricade with a melee attack, but where's the fun in that?

The battle rages for several minutes with wave after wave of hollow men lumbering towards the middle of the approach. Some stand near a barrel or behind a piece of fortification to fire their weapons, but most remain on the move. Continue to pan around the area with the targeting reticle in a semicircular pattern. Sweep from the upper-left down across the bottom to the upper-right then back the other way. It also helps to listen for Jammy's directions, as he does an admirable job of calling out fresh hollow men targets.

Don't worry about being shot by the stray hollow men that split from the groups. Most congregate along the central paths on the left and right, so be ready to hit them where it counts!

DEFEND THE REAR GATE

The hollow men may be undead, but they're not stupid. It only takes a few minutes for them to change plans. Leap off the balcony to lend support on the floor of the fort against the hollow men set to smash through the rear gate. Draw the Bonesmasher pistol and begin firing on the hollow men as soon as they breach the fort's defenses. The Bonesmasher is perfectly suited for shattering hollow men and can destroy most of them in just one or two shots, depending on your ranged attack level.

Stand back and open fire with the Bonesmasher to decimate the hollow men from afar. Killing 300 hollow men with the Bonesmasher earns a hefty attack bonus—this battle gets you off to a good start.

Blast away at the hollow men that appear near the gate, then turn around to take on those that attack near the stairs. There are nearly a hundred hollow men that attack during this battle so fire rapidly, stay on the move, and don't be afraid to use your magical and melee attacks if surrounded.

SPELLWEAVER | 5 Points

This battle is likely to be the first chance you get to cast a magical attack while wearing two gauntlets, assuming you purchased the Spell Weaving ability at the Road to Rule as you left The Hole. Access the Sanctuary's weapon room and select a combination of Gauntlets to wear (we recommend Fireball + Vortex) and let loose with a dual-threat attack!

The stairs leading to the balcony have been blocked off, so you must do your fighting on the ground. The hollow men essentially attack from four areas within the fort: 1) near the rear gate, 2) by the stairs, 3) near the window beyond the stairs, and 4) near the burial plots on the opposite wall. You'll earn experience towards additional Guild Seals even when Walter, Ben Finn, and the other soldiers kill a hollow man, so don't feel like you need to slay them all by yourself. Stay on the move to keep your distance and continue relying heavily on the Bonesmasher pistol, even if your character has a higher magical attack rating.

The combination of casting Fireball and Vortex causes the hollow men to fly around in a fiery whirlwind. Shoot them with the pistol as they sail past.

DEFEAT LIEUTENANT SIMMONS

Nobody follows to orders anymore: Major Swift told Lieutenant Simmons to stay dead, but does he listen? Absolutely not! It's up to you to send Lieutenant Simmons back to the grave once and for all. Lieutenant Simmons is the largest of all the hollow men that attack the fort and he not only has the ability to summon a number of other hollow men into the fray, but he can employ magical attacks as well.

Ready a Level 3 spell as soon as the battle begins and unleash it as soon as the hollow men spawn. It damages Lieutenant Simmons, but more importantly destroys many of the lesser hollow men.

Lieutenant Simmons attacks primarily by swinging his twin swords downward in an overhand swing. Move towards him to bait him into attacking, then quickly roll to the side, get up, and counterattack. He attacks with one sword at a time when standing still but swings both at once after taking a few running steps. You can sometimes sneak a third strike in against him, but it's best to strike twice and then roll away to avoid being hit. Additional hollow men spawn around Lieutenant Simmons in an effort to aid him. Unleash rapid area-of-effect magic attacks or open fire with the Bonesmasher, but don't spend too much time fighting them. It's more important to thin them out quickly, then focus on Lieutenant Simmons.

Be ready to dodge Lt. Simmons's massive sword swings. Lure him into a running attack, roll to the side, then get up and counterattack!

The biggest threats you face from Lieutenant Simmons are his magical attacks—Blades and Shock to be exact. Watch for the cavity in his chest to suddenly glow either blue or red. This is your cue that he's about to unleash a powerful magic spell. A blue glow in his chest precedes an area-of-effect electric Shock spell, whereas the red glow typically indicates a targeted Blades attack. Neither of these spells is particularly powerful, but they can inflict moderate damage if they make a direct hit.

Fire away at Lieutenant Simmons when not close enough to strike him with a melee weapon. He eventually vanishes and reappears across the fort, where he summons a fresh batch of hollow men to renew the attack. Continue crushing him with melee strikes and blasts from the Bonesmasher to inflict extra damage. You have to force him to relocate three times before you can finally defeat him. Use a health potion if you are struck by his magic attacks or hit by too many sword swings. It's best to play it safe with so many enemies in close proximity.

Defeating Lieutenant Simmons goes a long way toward convincing Major Swift to support your cause. He just needs you to promise to restore the old guard once you become king. Making this promise unlocks the **Swift Justice** Achievement and earns you 50 Guild Seals along with the **Simmons's Head** trophy.

Roll to the side as soon the Blades spell appears over Lt. Simmons's head. These Blades move fast and can home in on your position easily.

"I hereby promise to appoint Major Swift as leader of the royal army."

ROAD TO RULE

Your battle against the Hollow Legion didn't just save the lives of the men stationed at Mourningwood Fort; you've won the support of Major Swift and Ben Finn as well. Having them on your side certainly makes any conflict against Logan's army much more even. Still, you need additional followers in order to rule the kingdom. And for that, you'll need even more powerful abilities.

Upgrade Strategy: Don't hesitate to purchase the Magic Level 3 upgrade. Level 3 magic represents the "sweet spot" of magic casting, as the reduced time it takes to cast more powerful spells makes it worth charging up to the higher damage levels. This is also a great time to purchase the Blacksmith Level 4 upgrade as you're soon going to have an excellent opportunity to build your wealth and purchase a number of shops and houses. Working as a Level 4 blacksmith provides you with an avenue to quickly get the money needed to make those higher-priced purchases. Purchasing the other abilities on this segment of the Road to Rule is completely optional. Unless trying to shift your character's morality to completely evil, we advise staying away from the Bully Expression Pack and Theft Pack for now. Save your Guild Seals for more valuable chests farther along the road. You can always buy these other ones later on.

CHESTS NOW AVAILABLE

CHEST	TYPE	GUILD SEALS	DESCRIPTION
Melee Level 3	Skill Upgrade	60	Do more damage with any melee weapon you use.
Ranged Level 3	Skill Upgrade	60	Do more damage with any gun you use.
Magic Level 3	Skill Upgrade	60	Do more damage with any spell you cast.
Bully Expression Pack	Expressions	5	Learn to coerce people and bend them to your will with the Insult, Point and Laugh, and Threaten expressions.
Theft Pack	Thievery Ability	5	Become a master thief by learning how to steal. Just don't get caught.
Blacksmith Level 4	Job Skill Upgrade	25	Become a better blacksmith and earn more money striking that steel.
Pie Maker Level 4	Job Skill Upgrade	25	Improve your cooking skills and earn more money making pies.
Lute Level 4	Job Skill Upgrade	25	Improve your lute playing skills and earn more money performing.

MEET WALTER IN BOWERSTONE INDUSTRIAL

Exit the Mourningwood Fort via the south entrance and take a moment to collect the Silver Key up the path to the right and to locate the wooden chest inside the crypt to the left. Walter is going to continue on ahead to Bowerstone Industrial while you have a look around Mourningwood. The branching paths south of the fort lead to a main path that loops through Mourningwood in a clockwise direction. Advance along this main path, past the enemies that attack, to where the road forks near the entrance to Sunset House. Make a quick detour to the Sunset House so that you can access it via the map table at a later point. Return at once to Mourningwood and continue north.

The western half of Mourningwood is crisscrossed with numerous trenches dug into the hillside. Explore the network of paths for dig spots and a chest en route to the marshy lowland to the northwest. Keep the Bonesmasher on hand to deal with the hollow men that appear. The swamp is crawling with hollow men; hurry through the water to a wooden walkway leading to the relative safety of a small village.

The northwest corner of Mourningwood is home to a band of eco warriors who eke out their existence among the trees they hug so dearly. Interact with some of the villagers to gain some quick and easy Guild Seals, then locate the chest on the storage platform to the north. There are two large sewer tunnels just beyond the village. The ground has collapsed upon the right-hand one, leaving only a wooden chest and a nearby gnome to find. The left-hand one leads to Bowerstone Industrial.

THE FIERY BARRIER

What evil lies beyond this barrier? There's no way to know for sure—at least not at the moment—but you can bet that a fiery magical barrier wouldn't be here without a reason. Better come back later (or check the "Albion Atlas" if you don't mind a little spoiler).

Look behind the trees and around the ruins for wooden chests and other treasure.

There are plenty of people to meet and interact with in this corner of Mourningwood. You may even find a spouse (or two) amongst the trees.

THE BOWERSTONE RESISTANCE

Bowerstone Industrial is not a place where anyone desires to wind up. It's the end of the road for people whose lives have no future. Children are forced to toil in factories, homeless crowd the streets, and workers are treated like slaves. Walter has been aware of the problems in Industrial for quite some time, and knows of an underground resistance movement. Its leader's name is Page, and she and her men are fueled with an immense hatred for King Logan and have more than enough firepower to back it up. It's time you met her. Whether or not she'll trust you, the King's sibling, is another matter altogether.

BOWERSTONE INDUSTRIAL

FOLLOW SIR WALTER

Walter's knowledge of the Albion sewer network is quite extensive for someone with so little regard for dark, confining spaces. Follow Walter out of the tunnel and onto the paths that line the canals throughout Bowerstone Industrial. Walter waits for you should you desire to have a look around or interact with some of the child laborers or homeless people in the area. You can't draw your weapon right now, so don't spend much time searching for gnomes, as you won't be able to shoot them.

Eagle-eyed players can undoubtedly spot several wooden chests that are currently inaccessible. Follow Walter through town and come back for those treasures later.

AN ADDRESS FROM LOGAN

Follow Walter across the first bridge then take a quick detour down the alley to the right. There is a public address of sorts from Logan to the people of Bowerstone Industrial. This letter shines some light on how Bowerstone Industrial's working poor are treated.

Walter leads you to a demonstration outside of a factory on the far side of Bowerstone Industrial. Here you can see firsthand what happens when a worker tries to fight for his rights. As far as Walter is concerned, handing over control of Bowerstone Industrial to Reaver was among your brother Logan's biggest crimes.

FIND THE BOWERSTONE RESISTANCE HEADQUARTERS

CHOICE	GOLD	GUILD SEALS	MORALITY
GOOD: Meet Page, the leader of the Bowerstone Resistance.	-	50	-
EVIL: N/A	-	-	-

It's time to meet the Bowerstone Resistance. Cross the bridge to the side of the canal near the pub and descend the stairs on the left towards the water. Descend the second set of stairs and open the wooden door to enter the Sewers. The Bowerstone Resistance's headquarters are inside.

The Bowerstone Resistance is headquartered behind this brown wooden door, near the pub. A convenient location!

Follow Walter into the Sewers. There is only one way to go and it isn't far. Members of the Bowerstone Resistance make themselves known. Fortunately for you, their leader Page recognizes Walter and welcomes you both inside. Follow Page deeper into the Sewers to the map room inside their headquarters. Page is fully aware of who you are, but she's not about to hand over the survival of the resistance to you—at least not without vetting you first. You gain 50 Guild Seals for meeting Page, but you have much to do in order to win her trust.

Page trusts Walter. You, on the other hand, must earn her confidence.

ROAD TO RULE

Page is the true leader of the people of Bowerstone Industrial. You may never have met Page before, but Walter knows her well. And he knows you must have her on your side if the revolution is to have any chance of success! Winning the trust of the most oppressed people in Bowerstone is going to take a considerable amount of work. These are people who have been made to feel enslaved. They have had royalty ignore them for too long; winning their hearts and minds will not be easy.

Upgrade Strategy: Your purchases during this visit to the Road to Rule depend entirely on your style of play. The Force Push spell can be quite useful, especially as a complement to melee attacks, but it's hard to recommend it over upgrades to your melee and ranged fighting abilities if you hadn't purchased them already. Return to previous segments along the Road to Rule and see to it that your preferred combat style has been upgraded to its fullest possible extent before purchasing Force Push. Additionally, Level 5 job skills don't come cheap. Purchase the much more affordable Blacksmith Level 4 upgrade first if you haven't already. You'll unlock a new segment along the Road to Rule before long—one that has some costly chests—so consider saving some of your Guild Seals for your next visit.

CHESTS NOW AVAILABLE

CHEST	TYPE	GUILD SEALS	DESCRIPTION
Force Push Spell	Magical Gauntlet	40	Force Push magically propels enemies away from you. Knock them into walls or off ledges for extra damage.
Good Parenting Pack	Expressions	5	Become the world's greatest parent by learning the Tickle Child, Pick Up and Hug Child, and Cuddle Baby expressions.
Hooligan Expression Pack	Expressions	5	Can't wait to be a loud, obnoxious lout? Then learn the Rodeo, Fart on Villager, and Vulgar Thrust expressions.
Blacksmith Level 5	Job Skill Upgrade	60	Become the best blacksmith in Albion.
Pie Maker Level 5	Job Skill Upgrade	60	Become the greatest cook in Albion.
Lute Level 5	Job Skill Upgrade	60	Become the most skilled lute player in Albion.

GATHER 100 MORE GUILD SEALS TO GAIN THE FOLLOWING OF THE PEOPLE OF BOWERSTONE

Page's instructions to earn the following of the people of Bowerstone Industrial are not unlike Samuel's requests in Brightwall Village. Return to the Sanctuary and press the Y button while studying the map table to view the lengthy list of available quests. Many of these quests unlock subsequent quests, often in the same area. The following section details every side quest that is possible to undertake at this time. You needn't do them all now for many are still available later on. There are also a couple quests that you may wish to ignore altogether out of concern for your character's morality rating (note that these same quests of ill-repute are not likely to be available once you become Ruler of Albion). Nevertheless, the more of these quests you complete, the more Guild Seals you'll have to spend later on and the more Silver Keys, gnomes, and other collectibles you're likely to find.

Press the Y button to see a list of all the available quests.

PLANNING FOR FUTURE RICHES

This is a great time to really start focusing on growing your personal wealth and the best way to do that is by purchasing the larger shops. In particular, the pubs, weapons shops, and furniture stores are financial powerhouses. Save enough money to purchase the pub in Bowerstone Industrial along with a few stalls, then watch the money pour in. Thoroughly searching for treasure chests and dig spots further adds to your riches (don't forget to sell gems at the pawnbroker) and it won't be long before you can afford the best shops in Bowerstone Market. Owning a few high-end shops along with some stalls and houses can generate you over 10,000 gold every five minutes you spend playing the game. We're not going to tell you why now, but this is a good time to start shooting for 6,000,000 gold in personal wealth.

SIDE-QUEST | BOWERSTONE INDUSTRIAL

KIDNAPPED

There's been another kidnapping in Bowerstone Industrial. Locate Nigel Ferret's gang, rescue their captive, and shut them down for good.

AVAILABILITY: This quest becomes available after meeting Page in the Sewers.

UNLOCKS: N/A

REWARD: 30 Guild Seals

MORALITY: Tell captive to stay with Laszlo/Linda to earn +100 Morality. Keep captive for yourself to earn -100 Morality. Offering "No Comment" does not affect your Morality.

Make your way over to the boarded-up homeless shelter in Bowerstone Industrial to speak with Laszlo (or Linda if your Hero is female). His fiancée has been kidnapped and he might have to sell the shelter to pay the ransom. That is, unless you can rescue her for him! Follow Laszlo across the street to the gang's hideout and head inside when the door opens. Make your way past the guard and through the cellar door to The Cesspools.

Laszlo informs Ferret that he's not getting his ransom money and that, instead, you're going to kill everyone in his gang. This naturally leads to a battle with the mercenaries in the room. Many are armed with massive cleavers, so keep your distance. Pepper them with pistol or rifle fire and use magic attacks to finish them off. Proceed into the next room to speak with Ferret and learn that the captured fiancée is

stranded at the bottom of the cave below the gang's hideout. Dive off the ledge to continue the search.

DO I KNOW YOU?

The fiancée you're rescuing may look familiar to you depending on your actions earlier in the game. Laszlo's kidnapped beloved is none other than Elise, provided you opted to kill the protestors during the **Life in the Castle** scene before escaping with Walter and Jasper. If you chose to have Elise (or Elliot) killed, the quest giver's fiancé is a villager named Geraldine (Gerald, if your Hero is female).

Lead the fiancée by the hand up the path around the corner to the right and down the hill into the next section of Sewers. Unleash multiple area-of-effect spells to beat back the ravenous bats and locate the chest around the corner to the left. It might contain a Rare Topaz which can be sold for over 9,000 gold during a gem shortage! Proceed through the tunnel to the right-hand turn and note the meat hanging from the ceiling. This is your cue that hobbes are in the area! Inch up the hill with your gun drawn and immediately begin firing on the hobbes as soon as you spot them. Charge a Level 2 magic spell and unleash it as soon as they get close. The hobbes in the red military suits are agile and easily spin away from your melee strikes so rely more on magic and ranged attacks when confronting them.

Lead the fiancée up the hill past the next wave of hobbes to the narrow rock bridge up ahead and continue into the maintenance tunnels beneath the area's factories. The fiancée stops you near the exit to ask for your advice. Should she stick with Laszlo or dump him for you?

Either way, she will return to Laszlo and reunite with him. If you made a play for her, she'll be waiting for you outside the shelter in a few days. At that time you can marry her if you have a Wedding Ring and you've unlocked the Family Pack on the Road to Rule.

THE PEN IS MIGHTIER. . .

Samuel, the librarian in Brightwall, needs your help recovering rare books which have been scattered across Albion and beyond. Return to Samuel to give him any books you find.

AVAILABILITY: This quest becomes available after meeting Page in the Sewers.

UNLOCKS: N/A

REWARD: 50 Guild Seals

MORALITY: N/A

Much like the **Gnomes are Evil!** quest, this is an ongoing quest that takes a considerable amount of time and exploration to complete. To be clear, it's impossible to complete this quest at this moment as many of the areas you must visit are not yet available. Nevertheless, accept the quest now so that you can work on it gradually throughout your travels.

Return to Brightwall Academy and enter the newly opened room to the right of the front desk. Samuel is aware of 30 rare books scattered across Albion (and beyond) that he needs your help in locating and collecting. He has erected a plinth for 25 of the books in this main display room. There is also a special viewing area set aside for the five most valuable books. Accept the quest and follow the glowing trail to each of the pedestals to place any books you may have already found in their proper spaces. The "Albion Atlas" portion of this book details the exact location for each and every rare book. The following table lists the number of discoverable books for each area for those wanting a bit more of a challenge.

25 DISCOVERABLE BOOKS

LOCATION	NO. BOOKS	LOCATION	NO. BOOKS
The Reliquary	2	Bowerstone Castle	1
Mistpeak Valley	1	Millfields	1
Mistpeak Cave	1	Reaver's Mansion	1
The Catacombs	2	Silverpines	1
Dweller Camp	1	Driftwood	1
Mourningwood	1	Bowerstone Old Quarter	1
The Ossuary	1	The Cesspools	1
Sunset House	1	The Hole	1
Bowerstone Industrial	1	Sandfall Palace	1
Bowerstone Market	2	City of Aurora	2

For every five books you return to the Brightwall Academy, Samuel sends you on a specific quest to find one of the special books. The glowing trail guides you to the special book selected by Samuel for collection. You receive 10 Guild Seals for each of the five special books you return to Samuel. Find all 25 discoverable books and each of the five special books to complete the quest and unlock the **Brightwall Book Club** Achievement.

5 SPECIAL BOOKS

BOOK	BOOKS REQUIRED	LOCATION	DESCRIPTION
Book of Mysteries	5	Mistpeak Cave	Defeat the mercenaries beyond the large gate to find the book on a table.
Invocation of the Watchers	10	Bowerstone Old Quarter	Access the basement via a trap door that is only accessible after accepting this quest. Chase down the flit switch to reveal the location of the book.
The Pangs of Sunset	15	Mourningwood	Locate the dig spot within the graveyard to find the book. Defeat the hollow men to make it out alive.
Reaver on Reaver	20	Shifting Sands	Follow your dog to a dig spot in the desert to find the book. Defeat the enemies that attack to keep it.
Book of Doom	25	The Reliquary	Fight past throngs of hollow men to the furthest corner of the Reliquary. Defeat two boss hollow men to claim the book.

A MARRIAGE OF INCONVENIENCE

A married couple in Brightwall has been together for years, and now they've had enough. Perhaps you can help them… separate.

AVAILABILITY: This quest becomes available after meeting Page in the Sewers. You also need the necessary packs for marriage unlocked on the Road to Rule.

UNLOCKS: N/A

REWARD: 20 Guild Seals

MORALITY: Leaving the couple alone to go through with the divorce earns you +50 Morality. Killing either of them earns you -50 Morality.

Accept the quest and cross the bridge over the main road in Brightwall Village to the house where the couple is arguing. Speak with William outside the house to learn about his plan for divorcing Veronica. (If your Hero is female, the couple's names are Wilma and Vincent.) William needs her to file the divorce papers so she doesn't get half of his money! Agree to aid in the divorce by seducing Veronica and enter the house to get started.

Approach Veronica and press the A button to begin interacting with her. Perform a successful series of positive expressions to seduce her. After three expressions she'll begin to talk about how much she adores jewelry. Give her any jewelry you have in your possession (if you have none, you can buy some at the shop near the Academy) to move your relationship from neutral to friends. Perform several more positive expressions with Veronica to seduce her into something beyond mere friendship—love. You'll know when you've succeeded by the heart that appears over her head.

It's time to take Veronica on a date. Grab her by the hand and lead her out of the village and onto the bridge to the south. Kiss her once you get there to really win her over, then propose marriage to seal the deal. She'll hurry home to tell William she wants a divorce. Chase after her to watch her encounter with William inside the house. William is all too happy to accept her divorce papers and lets her know it was all a ruse designed to trick her into leaving him. Veronica won't go down without a fight. She knows the divorce won't be final until William files the papers with the village clerk. That leaves you plenty of time to kill William and marry Veronica, house included. The choice is yours, but the decision you make has a significant effect on your Morality.

AN EVIL PRESENCE

A hellish presence has taken over the Academy. Saul needs a truly heroic exterminator to help clean the place up.

AVAILABILITY: This quest becomes available after meeting Page in the Sewers. You must also have completed **An Ancient Key**.

UNLOCKS: N/A

REWARD: 5 Guild Seals and 250 Gold

MORALITY: N/A

Proceed to the armor display in the Brightwall Academy to chat with Saul about the monsters he's been encountering in the Reliquary. He needs you to clear all the monsters out so that he can continue his research. Accept the quest to receive **The Key of Even More Forbidden Knowledge**.

Equip the Bonesmasher pistol if you haven't already and descend the stairs into the Reliquary. The first wave of hollow men attacks in the initial corridor—don't advance without first killing each and every one. Weave the Vortex spell with another to get the hollow men up into the air, then shoot them one by one as they fly around you in circles. The glowing trail leads you farther into the Reliquary once every hollow man in the previous wave has been destroyed.

Fight your way down the stairs, across the bridge, and back up to the room where you earlier left Saul to his studies. Round the corner in the U-shaped room to the locked door and use the key Saul gave you to continue on to an even older, more isolated part of the Reliquary. Fight your way down the stairs in the rectangular hall until the last of the hollow men have been destroyed. Open the chest at the end of the hall then return to Saul to complete the quest.

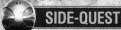

SIDE-QUEST — MOURNINGWOOD

PEACE, LOVE, AND HOMICIDE

Prove how evil you are by murdering someone in Mourningwood.

AVAILABILITY: This quest becomes available after meeting Page in the Sewers.

UNLOCKS: Murder Rhys to unlock the **Excavation** quest in the Dark Sanctum.

REWARD: 15 Guild Seals and 500 Gold

MORALITY: -15

HAMMER AND FORT

Fast travel to Mourningwood using the map table and inspect the cliff beyond the bridge for a Silver Key Chest. Unlock the chest with 10 Silver Keys to claim a new **Legendary Weapon** on your way to Mourningwood Fort. This is also a good time to purchase the fort (~45,000 Gold). Once purchased, you can compete for a high score with the mortar. Score over 2000 points to win another **Legendary Weapon**. The "Albion Atlas" section contains additional info about unlocking each of these weapons, as does the "Weapons of Yore" chapter.

Battle past the hobbes and hollow men to Mourningwood Fort and exit onto the hillside beyond the gate beneath the mortar. Follow the left-hand path to the large wall with the fiery magical barrier. Speak with Lesley, the man in the cloak standing near the flames to hear his complaint about the tree-hugging hippies living in Mourningwood. He'd like nothing more than to see their leader, Rhys, murdered. Would you be so kind as to do this small task for him? Best of all, doing so gains you access to the area beyond the flames.

Follow the glowing trail through the cemetery to the swamp on the west side of Mourningwood. Battle your way past the throngs of hollow men to the hippie camp in the northwest corner of Mourningwood. You'll find Rhys dancing to an imaginary beat near the campfire. Move in behind him, draw your sword, and press Down on the D-Pad to turn the safety off. Yes, Rhys is an innocent man. Strike him down (or shoot him if that is more to your liking), then return to Lesley. There aren't any guards in the woods of Mourningwood so you needn't worry about being arrested or having to pay a fine.

BORED TO DEATH

Max and Sam are dead. And bored. They want you to acquire an ancient tome possessing phenomenal supernatural power.

AVAILABILITY: This quest becomes available after meeting Page in the Sewers.

UNLOCKS: Complete this quest to unlock the **Gone But Not Forgotten** quest.

REWARD: 10 Guild Seals

MORALITY: N/A

Meet up with Max and Sam at the rear of the cemetery in Mourningwood to learn about their desire to read from the Normanomicon, otherwise known as "The Book of the Extremely Dead." They need you to travel to Millfields to dig up the book, which is buried with their mother. The most direct route to Millfields is back through Bowerstone Industrial. Cross the Mourningwood swamp to the Sewer tunnel near the hippie encampment and continue to Bowerstone Industrial. From there, continue south past the pub to Bowerstone Market. Locate the Silver Key Chest near the factory to gain 50,000 gold if you have 10 Silver Keys.

Once in Bowerstone Market, continue running southward to the main bridge and turn left to access Millfields.

Once in Millfields, continue past the Millfields Monorail Station and mining operations to the top of the ridge. Pause for a moment to absorb the views of Bower Lake—*Fable II* fans no doubt recognize this area—before following the glowing trail to the three graves located near the tree on the left. Dig in front of the middle grave to unearth **The Normanomicon**.

Disturbing the book triggers an assault from dozens of hollow men, so ready yourself! Use the Bonesmasher pistol along with the combined Vortex and Fireball spells to blast away the lesser hollow men that attack first. Conserve any Summon Creatures or Slow Time potions you may have until the hollow-man leader escapes from the crypt. This tougher foe is heavily armored and summons additional hollow men into battle. Use a fully charged magic attack to shatter the lesser enemies, then set to attacking the leader with melee strikes. It unleashes an electrifying spell of its own that can inflict some heavy damage if you don't dodge it. Watch for the spell to emanate from within the creature's face to indicate when it's preparing to be unleashed. Dash around the tree to stay away from the creature's heavy attacks and sneak behind it for two quick strikes. This fight is similar to the one against Lieutenant Simmons, only this hollow man doesn't teleport multiple times. Defeat this monstrous foe to earn the rights to keep the book. Return it to Sam and Max in Mourningwood to complete the quest.

EXCAVATION

A man obsessed with evil wants funds for the excavation of the Dark Sanctum.

AVAILABILITY: This quest is unlocked after completion of the **Peace, Love, and Homicide** quest.

UNLOCKS: Provide the funds needed to excavate the Dark Sanctum to unlock the **Awakening** quest.

REWARD: 5 Guild Seals

MORALITY: N/A

Fast travel to Mourningwood and cross through the fort, then travel up the left-hand path to where the fiery magical barrier was. With the barrier removed, you can now access the Dark Sanctum. Continue up the path to where Lesley is standing, just beyond the campfire. Lesley needs 5,000 gold to pay a team of workers to excavate the Dark Sanctum from a rockslide. Give him the money to begin the work.

Check the quest list periodically and return later—Lesley isn't through with you just yet!

GONE BUT NOT FORGOTTEN

Sam's brother Max is getting into trouble. Find him and stop him before something terrible happens.

AVAILABILITY: This quest becomes available after completing the **Bored to Death** quest.

UNLOCKS: N/A

REWARD: 30 Guild Seals & Normanomicon

MORALITY: N/A

Locate Sam in the Mourningwood Cemetery to learn all about what happened after you gave him and his brother the Normanomicon. It turns out things got out of hand. Max had his first taste of alcohol and became a bit belligerent. Now Sam needs your help in tracking

down his wayward brother. Follow him into the crypt to enter an area known as the Ossuary.

Max is just beyond the entrance to the Ossuary. Run up to him, grab him by the hand, and drag him back towards the passage leading to Mourningwood's cemetery. This seems to work just fine, right until Max turns into a wisp and flies to the top of the tomb. Battle the hollow men on the stairs and chase after Max as he flees across the bridge and deeper into the Ossuary.

Leap from the ledge across the bridge and descend the stairs towards the tree where Max moves to next. Max summons a number of deceased partygoers to "entertain" you. Fortunately, these ghostly assailants are not fit for fighting and can be sent back to their graves with one or two shots from the Bonecrusher or a similar weapon. Descend the large staircase beyond the tree to the large clearing. Max again summons the ghosts that were at his party, but this time he calls upon dozens of them! Move to the center of the area and charge up a Level 3 spell. Wait for as many of the enemies to step within the circle as you can safely permit before unleashing the attack. Repeat this to eliminate the ghostly crowd.

Continue your pursuit of Max up the stairs of the large tomb and down the narrow hall to chamber beyond. Max has sprung a trap, but he failed to account for Sam coming to your rescue. Exit the trap room and bypass the holes in the courtyard ahead to reach the two wooden chests. Use the tactics outlined earlier to beat back marauding hollow men to unlock the final door leading to the Organ Room. Of course, you could also minimize your exposure to the hollow men by avoiding the searchlights that move about the area.

Max (and later Sam) uses the organ to summon dozens of ghostly partygoers to the room, followed by several waves of hollow men. Use the spacious area to distance yourself from your enemies and to prevent yourself from being surrounded. Then unleash spell after spell to decimate them and lay them to rest. Use any potions found earlier in the Ossuary to aid you in the battle if necessary, otherwise save them for more difficult fights to come. Watch for the last of the

wisps guarding the book to leave their station, then run to the pedestal and take back the Normanomicon.

GHOST BROTHERS | 10 Points

Complete both the **Bored to Death** and **Gone But Not Forgotten** quests to send Sam and Max back to their graves, alongside their mother, and to unlock this Achievement. Completing these quests involves plenty of combat against hollow men, so have the Bonesmasher equipped and carry plenty of Health Potions and a Summon Creatures potion in case you get into trouble.

MILLFIELDS

RESTORATION

The head of the Albion Historical Restoration Society (AHRS) requires funds to restore the old Dweller Camp bridge.

AVAILABILITY: This quest becomes available after meeting Page in the Sewers.

UNLOCKS: Providing the gold to build the bridge grants access to Driftwood.

REWARD: 5 Guild Seals

MORALITY: N/A

Fast-travel to Millfields and battle through the mercenaries near the mining operation to the ridge overlooking Bower Lake. Follow the signs pointing towards Silverpines beyond the bridge above the river canyon and head up the hill. Fans of *Fable II* should recognize this area as being the place where the young Hero was raised by gypsies. The bridge where that earlier Hero—your father—first talked with Theresa has been destroyed. That is the bridge your donation will help restore.

Speak to Griffith Smith atop the hill, near the sighting scope and trunk, and agree to give him the requisite 750 gold. Return at a later time to cross the bridge, explore the old gypsy camp where your father was raised (though time has not been kind to this area), and continue beyond the area to Driftwood.

THE FINAL INSULT

Arthur urgently needs a letter delivered to Brightwall.

AVAILABILITY: This quest becomes available after meeting Page in the Sewers.

UNLOCKS: N/A

REWARD: 5 Guild Seals

MORALITY: N/A

Meet the rather dapper-looking Arthur on the far side of Bower Lake, near Clixby-Stanners Manor, and agree to deliver his letter to Zachary in Brightwall Village. Make your way back to Brightwall Village on foot or by fast travel and start up the hill in the center of town. Zachary is near the well above the rocks overlooking the shops in the town square. Give him the letter to complete the quest.

SIDE-QUEST DARK SANCTUM

AWAKENING

Lesley's excavation is on hold until someone takes care of a dangerous infestation in the Dark Sanctum.

AVAILABILITY: This quest becomes available after completing the **Excavation** quest.

UNLOCKS: Eliminate the hollow men within the Dark Sanctum to unlock the **Leverage** quest.

REWARD: 5 Guild Seals and 500 Gold

MORALITY: N/A

Fast travel to Mourningwood and ascend the path beyond the fort to enter the Dark Sanctum. Lesley is on the stairs, not far from where you last saw him. Speak with him to learn about the monsters terrorizing his workers and agree to exterminate them.

Enter the central area within the Dark Sanctum and immediately set about slaughtering the dozens of hollow men that rise to attack in front of the giant statue. There's not a ton of room to maneuver, so you may want to rely more on flourish attacks than normal; a charged-up flourish, especially with a hammer weapon, can crush multiple enemies with a single strike. Prepare magic attacks (particularly Vortex) between waves,

unleash them to weaken the enemy ranks, then resume the melee combat. Return to Lesley once the last of the hollow men have been defeated.

LEVERAGE

Lesley needs some assistance bringing the Dark Sanctum to life once more.

AVAILABILITY: This quest becomes available after completing the **Awakening** quest.

UNLOCKS: N/A

REWARD: 10 Guild Seals

MORALITY: Sacrificing the villager (optional) earns you -50 Morality.

Travel to the Dark Sanctum and follow the glowing trail back to the room to the right of the massive statue. Talk with Lesley and agree to search the Dark Sanctum for the missing lever. Take the **Dark Sanctum Key** and ascend the stairs to the locked door behind the statue in the previous room. Run the length of the corridor until you reach the floating platform with the three arrows, similar to those seen in the Reliquary.

There is only one path across the large pit in this room using the floating panels. You must snake your way back and forth across the pit using the two sections of solid ground on the left and right. Proceed along one platform, then cross directly to the left to reach the landing there. Finally, cross the pit to the right. From there you can reach the exit on the other side. You can easily negotiate the pit without triggering any mid-platform hollow men attacks by stepping on the light corresponding to the direction you must go. Stepping on a wrong light doesn't raise a platform into position, but it triggers the appearance of a number of

hollow men. Don't be afraid to step on each of the lights to welcome the battle and earn more Guild Seals.

A DARK SANCTUM PUZZLE

Wondering how you can reach that flit switch in the corner of the room? Well, you're going to have to wait until Lesley's workers get back here and finish cleaning out the debris. Give it some time, then make another trip back here to chase the flit switch back towards the statue for a final puzzle that leads to one of the rare legendary weapons—The Tenderizer! Read how to solve it in the "Albion Atlas" portion of this guide.

Head up the stairs to the rear room within the Dark Sanctum and claim the **Ancient Lever** from the sarcophagus. Slay the hollow men that attack and fight your way back to Lesley. Give him the lever and watch as he prepares a peasant for roasting on the Sacrificial BBQ Pit. Doing the honors is completely optional, but it costs you 50 Morality points. You can now drag someone to the Dark Sanctum for barbecuing

whenever you want—this is a great way to quickly turn 100% evil!

 THE DARK SANCTUM | 10 Points

Unlock this Achievement by completing the entire string of quests in the Dark Sanctum line. This includes the four quests starting with **Peace, Love, and Homicide** and ending with **Leverage**. Your work in the Dark Sanctum isn't over, though. To truly get the most out of this place, see the Dark Sanctum section of the "Albion Atlas."

SIDE-QUEST BOWERSTONE MARKET

THE GAME

Three wizards have a quest for a true Hero: rescue the princess from the evil baron!

AVAILABILITY: This quest becomes available after meeting Page in the Sewers.

UNLOCKS: N/A

REWARD: 40 Guild Seals & Orb of Magicka trophy.

MORALITY: N/A

A LETTER TO THE GAMER GEEKS

Head upstairs before or after taking part in the quest to read the letter to Mark, Jim, and Ben sitting on the table. It's from Arthur, the same Arthur who has been sending insulting letters to everyone in Albion.

Mark, Jim, and Ben are three role-playing gamers who have constructed an elaborate table-top adventure for a Hero of your caliber to participate in. They even wrote a story to go along with it—a story filled with tales of romance, exploration, and even murder!

Take hold of the Orb of Interplanar Transference and watch as the mystical device shrinks you down to the size of a miniature Hero ready to be placed on the board. You find yourself in the village of Lightwater. Go through the gate and up the hill on the right to talk to the villagers. You can overhear the gamers speaking throughout the adventure, and you'll also no doubt notice that speaking to the villagers

is optional. At the least speak with the blacksmith and the poet, as the dialogue is quite entertaining.

Speak with Arturo the gate keeper to learn of the Princess's disappearance. Continue through the gate and up the hill to the castle where the evil Baron lives. Use your gun to kill the wolves that attack on the steps of the castle. Enter the Baron's Tower to discover that the foreboding castle on the hill is harboring little more than a teddy bear factory. Nevertheless, you require the weapon in the chest on the

left—you can't possibly defeat the Baron without the Scimitar of Baron Slaying +3!

SCIMITAR OF BARON SLAYING +3

This weapon comes from the *Artefacts and Armaments Codex* for the popular game *Hollows and Hobbes* (3rd Edition, revision 1.5.2.2.1.7.3.0.0.0.8b) and contains the following bonuses: +30% Sense of Self-Importance, +90% Damage to Space Elves, and -50% Self Awareness. You'll have to unlock that last bonus before taking on the Baron, naturally.

Pursue the Baron into the castle and pull the lever in the room with the checkerboard floor. Stay near the lever as the lights go out and prepare a fully charged magic attack for the hollow men that appear. Finish off the stragglers with your newly found Scimitar of Baron Slaying. Cross the bridge over the ravine to continue the chase up the fiery path to where the Baron flees. Pause momentarily to collect the Legendary Condom of the Gods +5 from the pedestal—even role-playing gamers get lucky every once in a while—and continue to the den of the demonic chickens. These shadowy chickens spit hot fire, so don't

stand too long in one spot. Use the pistol to shoot them from a safe distance to give yourself time to roll away, even though the fireballs inflict minimal damage. No need to take any unnecessary risks, eh?

RETURN TO THE BOWERSTONE RESISTANCE

Exit the cave near the rear of the board, err, Lightwater Village and fight the hobbes preventing you from reaching the princess. Hobbes attack in waves of three and four, giving you plenty of opportunities to defeat them without being surrounded. The hobbes that appear below the ledge are accompanied by a summoner hobbe. Use a magic attack to tie up the hobbes with the military suits so you can focus on the summoner hobbe before he summons a number of skeleton hobbes.

The Princess is just up ahead, guarded by the Baron. Defeating the Baron with the Scimitar of Baron Slaying +3 is as easy as tapping the X button. In fact, that's all you have to do. Show that paper game piece who's boss and rescue the fair Princess! Smoochy-smooch!

Fast travel to Bowerstone Industrial once you've earned at least 100 new Guild Seals to meet Page's demand (you can earn well over 200 by completing all of the quests detailed on the previous pages). You'll find Page in the Sewers, at Bowerstone Resistance headquarters, along with Major Swift, Walter, and Ben Finn.

Some of Page's men broke into Reaver's Manor but they haven't returned, requiring you and her to break them out! Reaver is hosting his weekly masquerade party tonight and it just so happens that Page has secured a couple of Masquerade Suits for the two of you to wear.

Take the Masquerade Suit back to the Sanctuary and put on the entire costume in the dressing room.

 SAVE THE PRINCESS! | 10 Points

Complete "The Game" by surviving the trials and tribulations of Mark, Jim, and Ben's tabletop role-playing game. Battle the wolves and demonic chickens to reach the Princess of Lightwater Village. Defeat the Baron with the Scimitar of Baron Slaying +3 and win a kiss from the Princess and 10 Gamer Points.

REAVER'S MANOR

MEET PAGE AT REAVER'S MANOR

B.Y.O.P.

Things may get ugly at Reaver's party, and his guests have already consumed all the refreshments. Better bring a few potions with you just in case you get thirsty. Take along at least three Health Potions and a couple Summon Creatures potions.

Return to the Sanctuary to put on the entire costume, then fast travel to Millfields; Page is waiting for you outside Reaver's Manor. Fight your way past the mercenaries who prowl the area near the mines in Millfields to the trail leading down to Bower Lake. Reaver's Manor is on the opposite side of the lake. Lead Page into Reaver's Manor and talk to the butler in the foyer. He'll guide you straight to the party and even lets you keep your weapons! Thank goodness for oppressed proletariats!

Head right through the gate to Reaver's Manor to meet up with Page. Don't go inside without first speaking with her.

Follow the butler through the dining room to the main ballroom. You can return to explore the rest of Reaver's mansion during the **Reaver's Unmentionables** quest.

SURVIVE THE MASQUERADE

Reaver not only knew you'd be coming, but he counted on you to provide the evening's entertainment via the Wheel of Misfortune! Reaver is going to spin the wheel, and you'll have to enter the chamber it selects and defeat hordes of enemies that appear. Each chamber has a lone wooden chest near the entrance that contains a potion of some variety—take it! The first few chambers force you to battle more hobbes, hollow men, and mercenaries. You're undoubtedly well acquainted with these enemy types and should have little trouble surviving—especially with Page fighting alongside you! Stand in the center of the chamber and unleash a barrage of area-of-effect magical attacks, preferably weaved with Vortex or Force Push to knock the enemies astray— or right off the ledge. Use targeted spells to inflict even greater damage on the larger creatures that conclude each wave.

Weaving Vortex with Shock both stuns enemies and lifts them up for a ride in the whirlwind. Shoot them as they fly past!

The fourth chamber contains an enemy known as the Sand Fury, a fast-moving enemy with swords that is only human in appearance. Sand furies can be defeated easily—they have no armor and minimal resistance to damage—but they are extremely agile and aggressive. Particularly noteworthy is their ability to leap out of range when you're charging a melee flourish or an area-of-effect spell. Switch to ranged weaponry if you find it hard to land melee strikes. Watch for them to sprint towards you to attack with their swords, flip away, and suddenly fire on you with a hidden crossbow! You can distract them by using a Summon Creatures potion, but that probably isn't necessary. Use magical attacks to occupy them with Vortex while you shoot them from across the chamber. Their crossbow attacks have a limited range and accuracy. The good news is that there aren't any boss-level sand furies to worry about. Slay the roughly two dozen sand furies that spawn then return to the main area.

Sand furies are difficult to hit with melee attacks. Rely on your guns and magic to fend them off.

The final battle takes place in the central ballroom and it's against a pack of balverines, one of Albion's most terrifying creatures! Do not hesitate to fully charge a Level 3 magic attack, then get close to Page and open fire with your gun. If you have a Slow Time or Summon Creatures potion left, this is the time to use it! Keep a close eye on the balverines and immediately begin rolling across the room if you notice one or more leap to the ceiling; they'll drop down somewhere else and dash towards you while performing a vicious melee attack. Balverines only attack in groups of three and usually one keeps to the periphery, leaving you two to focus on. They can sidestep direct melee attacks, so try to sneak up and strike those battling with Page.

Balverine claws are extremely sharp! Keep your distance and take aim on enemies trying to attack Page.

Survive the fight against the balverines to rescue the Bowerstone Resistance member in the cage. Reaver lives to see another day, but you succeeded in letting him know he's up against a true Hero. Your efforts have earned Page's complete support (and the **Balverine Head** trophy), but you must promise her to be different than Logan, to look after the poor and to stop the exploitation of the lower class and homeless. Making this promise not only gains Page's support, but it earns you 50 Guild Seals and the **Resistance** Achievement.

> "I hereby promise to end the exploitation of the people of Bowerstone."

Gaining Page's support brings with it the whole of the Bowerstone Resistance, but there is still more to do. Walter's plan for a revolution is coming together nicely. Major Swift is checking on King Logan's troop movements at this moment, and people all over Albion are on standby, just waiting for your signal. Yet more supporters are needed. And Walter knows where to find them...

Upgrade Strategy: This trip to the Road to Rule should be your most substantial. Depending on how active you were before joining Page for the masquerade party, you should have anywhere between 160 and 300 Guild Seals to spend, even more perhaps! Do not hesitate to purchase the Magic Level 4 upgrade. This is the most important purchase you can make right now. Return to previous segments of the Road to Rule and upgrade your melee and ranged abilities as you see fit, along with any job skills that you would like to have. Level 5 attack abilities will be available before long and you may want to save your Guild Seals to buy them. Those aiming for the **Chest Grandmaster** Achievement need to purchase every chest anyway, so you might as well continue to spend your Guild Seals now.

CHESTS NOW AVAILABLE

CHEST	TYPE	GUILD SEALS	DESCRIPTION
Melee Level 4	Skill Upgrade	80	Do more damage with any melee weapon you use.
Ranged Level 4	Skill Upgrade	80	Do more damage with any gun you use.
Magic Level 4	Skill Upgrade	80	Do more damage with any spell you cast.
Scary Expression Pack	Expressions	5	Learn the Growl, Scary Laugh, and Bloodlust Roar to become the terror of Albion.

TRAITORS

King Logan is calling for the people of Albion to gather at Bowerstone Castle for an important announcement. Demonstrations like these rarely bring good news to the people of Albion. Quite the opposite, actually. Whatever happens at the castle, it's becoming clear that the revolution is coming. Perhaps sooner than expected.

BOWERSTONE CASTLE

MEET BEN FINN AT THE CASTLE

Announcements have gone out all around Bowerstone and the surrounding areas that King Logan is set to deliver an important speech at Bowerstone Castle. Ben Finn knows whatever Logan has to say can't be good, and he wants you to meet him there. Fast travel to Bowerstone Castle to join Ben amongst the crowd that has gathered. Logan's demonstration delivers a blow to your band of revolutionaries, but serves as a grim reminder of just how vital your success is.

The two of you are powerless to save Major Swift, but bide your time—soon Logan will face justice at your hands.

THE RESISTANCE CAN WAIT!

Ben wants to hurry to Bowerstone Industrial to go over what just happened with Page and Walter. That's not a bad idea, but it can wait. This is an excellent opportunity to perform a number of side-quests that are now available. Use this time to search for your first Gold Keys and complete one or two Demon Door challenges.

Meeting with the Bowerstone Resistance is going to set things in motion that aren't easily reversed. You can purchase plenty of potions before you go, but you need to start planning now. Amassing a stockpile of gold can serve you well after the revolution. The best way to do that is to use this time to purchase as many high-end shops, pubs, and mansions as possible. The profits and monthly rent will add up to a sizable fortune by the time you return.

DON'T LET MORALITY GET IN THE WAY OF A GOOD MURDER

Several of the quests that are currently available require you to murder someone. We understand that this presents a bit of a dilemma for those of you who want to complete every quest in the game, but also want to maximize your goody-goody moral image. There are going to be plenty of opportunities to repair (and/or harm) your moral standing later on, so feel free to complete each of these quests now; you'll be able to reverse any damage to your reputation later on. Psst…you are building a sizable nest egg, right?

SIDE-QUEST **MILLFIELDS**

ANIMAL LIBERATION

Break into the pie factory and release the caged animals.

AVAILABILITY: This quest becomes available after leaving the masquerade party with Page.

UNLOCKS: N/A

REWARD: 5 Guild Seals and 500 Gold

MORALITY: N/A

Talk to the woman named Katie near the Demon Door in Millfields to learn of the chickens' plight in Bowerstone Industrial. She wants you to break into the factory and release the birds before they get stuffed into meat pies. Accept the quest to receive the **Factory Gate Key**. This key is used to unlock the gate near the entrance to the Bowerstone Resistance. Travel to Bowerstone Industrial and go past the entrance to the Sewers nearest the pub. Continue up the stairs on the other side of the canal to find a metal gate in an alley.

The area behind the factory is crawling with mercenaries, including two of the taller blokes who throw fireballs. Stay on the move and use the hay bales in the center of the area as cover while you charge up magical attacks and fire your weapon at the lesser thugs. Use a Slow Time potion to halt the attacks of the larger enemies until at least one of them is dead. Stay a few steps away from the larger enemies with the fiery hands to avoid the shockwave from the flaming ground-pound. Finish off the rest of the enemies in the area and climb the stairs on the fire escape. Pull the lever to open the factory door and head inside.

Leap off the balcony and eliminate the mercenaries inside the factory just as you did moments ago outside. The perimeter of the room is stocked with animal cages. Pull the lever in the center of the room to open all of the cages simultaneously. The door in the corner of the factory also opens. Swipe the three Meat Pies from the chest opposite the door and return to Katie in Millfields to complete the quest.

THE DEBT

Cedric isn't exactly taking his loss well.

AVAILABILITY: This quest becomes available after leaving the masquerade party with Page.

UNLOCKS: N/A

REWARD: 5 Guild Seals and 500 Gold

MORALITY: -15 for murder

Meet Cedric along the river walk on the west side of Bowerstone Market and agree to put your weapons to use against the man he lost his money to. Alan, the mark, is at the pub in Bowerstone Industrial and Cedric wants you to kill him as payback for winning all of Cedric's gambling money.

Alan is standing near the bar, rubbing his hands together in a mischievous manner. Approach him slowly, draw your weapon, and turn the safety off by pressing down on the D-Pad. Strike him dead before making your exit from the bar, turning left, and fleeing to Bowerstone Market before anyone else sees you—or worse.

THE MAN WHO KNEW JUST ENOUGH

Bob can't stand the thought of his mate living behind bars.

AVAILABILITY: This quest becomes available after leaving the masquerade party with Page.

UNLOCKS: N/A

REWARD: 5 Guild Seals and 500 Gold

MORALITY: -15 for murder

You can find Bob under the bridge in Bowerstone Market. Talk to him to learn about his business partner who got himself arrested. Ideally, Bob would love for you to kill the sheriff, but that brings too much heat. So, instead, he'd like you to kill his old pal Leonard—after all, dead men tell no secrets!

Cross the bridge to the east side of the river where the jail is and head behind the building on the left. Locate the lever that controls the cell's gate and wait for any nearby guards to leave the area. Once the coast is clear, pull the lever to open the gate, then go inside and kill Leonard. You should try to do this without being detected, but you can kill him right in front of the guards and still come out on top. They'll fine you 250 gold for murder and another 20 for trespassing, but you're going to get 500 gold from Bob anyway.

REAVER'S UNMENTIONABLES

Get a pair of Reaver's underpants for his obsessive fan, Benjamina.

AVAILABILITY: This quest becomes available after leaving the masquerade party with Page.

UNLOCKS: N/A

REWARD: 5 Guild Seals

MORALITY: N/A

Benjamina lives just beyond the city wall, along the road to Millfields. Meet Reaver's adoring fan on her doorstep and agree to find her a pair of Reaver's old underpants. Continue down the road to enter Millfields and make your way around the lake to Reaver's Manor and go inside. Have a look around the downstairs for items (you can find a book in the room on the left and another insulting letter in the kitchen) then ascend the stairs to the second floor.

Head up the short second flight of stairs to the right of the dining room and continue down the hall to the master bedroom. Search the furniture for pajama costume pieces, then investigate the bookshelf in the far right-hand corner to reveal a secret hallway leading to another bedroom containing both a treasure chest and a Silver Key. More important to the mission at hand are **Reaver's Underpants**, located on the nightstand to the right of the bed. Steal the rest of pajama costume from Reaver's furniture, then return to Benjamina to give her the undies.

![SIDE-QUEST] ## BOWERSTONE OLD QUARTER

FRAMED FOR MURDER

Russell believes art is worth dying for.

AVAILABILITY: This quest becomes available after leaving the masquerade party with Page.

UNLOCKS: N/A

REWARD: 5 Guild Seals and 500 Gold

MORALITY: -15 for murder

The art merchant, Russell, operates a stall on the main shopping street in Bowerstone Old Quarter. He's been snatching up Thomas Kaidkin paintings for years and now he wants their value to increase so he can sell them for a profit. He believes the best way to make that happen is to have you kill the artist—it's really a matter of supply and demand.

The artist lives in Brightwall Village. Fast travel to Brightwall to find him outside the pawnbroker's shop, near the main statue. Waiting until guards leave the area and committing the act without detection is great, but the fine is only 250 gold. Move in behind Kaidkin, draw your weapon, turn the safety off, and attack! Pay the fine if you must, then return to Russell in Bowerstone Old Quarter to finish the quest and collect your reward.

ONE RING TO FIND

A clumsy husband-to-be has lost his engagement ring.

AVAILABILITY: This quest becomes available after leaving the masquerade party with Page.

UNLOCKS: N/A

REWARD: 5 Guild Seals

MORALITY: N/A

ALTERNATIVE SEWER ENTRANCE

This quest takes you to a part of the Sewers separate from the Bowerstone Resistance headquarters. If you were wondering how to get the Silver Key beyond the metal bars (visible on the way to meet with Page), then this is the quest for you.

Meet James in Bowerstone Industrial across the bridge from the pub and agree to head into the Sewers and search for his lost engagement ring. Enter the Sewers through the door beneath the large crane near Reaver's large factory. Collect the Silver Key on the right, then turn and make your way deeper into the Sewers on the left.

The small cave beyond the entrance is crawling with hobbes when you pass the first time (it will be patrolled by mercenaries on the return trip). Take a few steps through the crack in the wall and unleash your magical assault on the hobbes to thin them out so they don't follow you deeper into the Sewers. Continue ahead to the next crack in the wall where the mercenaries are located and explore the areas to either side for items. Fight the mercenaries to continue through the room beyond the cracked wall. This leads to another section of the Sewers, where you'll find the ring. Battle the hobbes in this final tunnel to reach the dig spot containing **James's Engagement Ring**. Return the ring to James to complete the quest.

SIDE-QUEST   MOURNINGWOOD

IN MOURNING

A widow wishes to visit the grave of her dead husband.

AVAILABILITY: This quest becomes available after leaving the masquerade party with Page.

UNLOCKS: N/A

REWARD: 5 Guild Seals

MORALITY: N/A

Equip the Bonesmasher along with the Fireball and Shock gauntlets and return to the swampy lands of Mourningwood. Battle past the throngs of hobbes and hollow men to the hippie commune in the northwest corner of Mourningwood. Locate Sarah, who wishes to see her deceased husband's grave, and agree to be her escort. Lead her by the hand back into the swamp where the hollow men are. Follow the glowing trail in the direction of the cemetery in the southeast corner of Mourningwood, but do not hesitate a moment to release Sarah's hand the instant you see the telltale wisps of approaching hollow men. Charge up your weaved spell to stun and weaken the hollow men, then open fire with the Bonesmasher! Three waves of hollow men attack en route. Beat them back and continue guiding Sarah past the statue in the center of the cemetery to the grave just past it, on the right.

SIDE-QUEST   DRIFTWOOD

PEST CONTROL

An offshore infestation of hobbes needs to be dealt with.

AVAILABILITY: This quest becomes available after leaving the masquerade party with Page. You also must first complete the **Restoration** quest and access Driftwood on foot from Millfields.

UNLOCKS: Eliminate the hobbes to unlock the **Gift Wood for Driftwood** and **An Island Getaway** quests.

REWARD: 5 Guild Seals and 500 Gold

MORALITY: N/A

THE OFFSHORE FLIT SWITCH

The flit switch you see on the small outcrop to the right of this island is accessible after the completion of this quest (once you leave the area and return), but you'll need to complete two more quests in Driftwood after that to follow the flit switch to its conclusion. See the Driftwood section of the "Albion Atlas" for full details about that flit switch and the Gold Key to which it leads.

Travel from Millfields to Driftwood and speak to Robin on the beach. The inhabitants of Driftwood wish to expand to the outer islands, but they need someone of your abilities to first eliminate the hobbes who have set up camp there. Locate the chest at the edge of the beach to the right, then swim past the two tiny islands to the larger one straight offshore. The first batch of hobbes is camped amongst the trees near the beach.

The rest of the hobbes are scattered across the two larger islands to the left. The glowing trail leads in that direction, but it's worth taking a moment to swim around the central island in a counter-clockwise direction, opposite the glowing trail, to find some extra collectibles on the outermost island. From there, swim directly to the beach on the backside of the largest island to battle your next group of hobbes. Head counter-clockwise around the island to the channel between this island and the farthest inhabited island offshore of the three. (You'll be able to see Theresa's Tattered Spire in the distance.)

Swim through the channel and follow the glowing trail up onto the beach on the outermost island. The trail on this island leads upwards to a hobbe camp near a collapsed bridge. Dive off the top of the island and resume following the glowing trail clockwise around the middle island. This larger, central island has a trail that spirals upwards to a false summit. The pinnacle of the island is only accessible via a rebuilt bridge. The final batch of hobbes is on a ledge directly above a wooden chest that your dog sniffs out for you. Return to Robin to let him know the islands are hobbe-free!

AN ISLAND GETAWAY

A gambler has lost his fortune and wants you to escort him to the safety of Driftwood before the debt collectors find him.

AVAILABILITY: This quest becomes available after completion of the **Pest Control** quest.

UNLOCKS: N/A

REWARD: 5 Guild Seals and 500 Gold

MORALITY: N/A

Meet the gambler, Rusty, on the second floor of the pub in Bowerstone Market and agree to take him to the newly expanded village of Driftwood. Lead him by the hand across the bridge in Bowerstone Market to Millfields and, from there, across the rebuilt bridge and through the old gypsy camp to Driftwood. This escort quest is similar to others in that you have to release Rusty's hand in order to defend yourself from mercenaries that attack. The mercenaries will likely attack twice near the Millfields mining area and once again near the bridge to the gypsy camp. The thugs you encounter from this point on incorporate grenades into their repertoire of attacks, so stay on the move and be extra careful!

The villagers have expanded onto the islands off the coast and even erected bridges that now link each of the islands. Guide Rusty across the lengthy footbridge to the encampment on the third island to complete the quest. Leave him near the lute player.

GIFT WOOD FOR DRIFTWOOD

The inhabitants of Driftwood need a letter delivered.

AVAILABILITY: This quest becomes available after attending Logan's speech at the castle. You must also first complete the **Pest Control** quest.

UNLOCKS: N/A

REWARD: 10 Guild Seals

MORALITY: N/A

Cross the newly built bridges over the water to the third island in Driftwood and speak with the villager. The residents want to expand to the other islands, but they need a more experienced carpenter to do the work. They need you to deliver the **Letter to a Carpenter** to a man with sufficient carpentry skill, who just so happens to live in Silverpines—one of the most dangerous areas in Albion. It's a patch of dense forest and crumbling mausoleums patrolled by bands of ravenous balverines. It's best to take plenty of Health Potions along for this journey and also wise to equip a weapon that provides benefits against large enemies or balverines or similarly powerful weapon.

Follow the dirt path as it winds its way through the woods, past the collapsed columns of an earlier time, and over a creek to a small settlement to the south. The carpenter doesn't live in this village, but the nearby mine contains a Silver Key worth collecting. Continue out the far side of the settlement along the road

leading eventually to a locked metal gate set in the hillside on the right. The carpenter lives up the hill directly left of this heavy door. Follow the glowing trail to his doorstep and give him the letter to complete the quest.

 ISLAND PARADISE | 10 Points

Complete both the **Pest Control** and **Gift Wood for Driftwood** quests to help the eco-minded folks of Driftwood expand their village throughout the islands in the area. You must first complete the **Restoration** quest in Millfields and visit Driftwood on foot at least once before you can fast travel or accept quests here.

BOWERSTONE INDUSTRIAL

RETURN TO THE RESISTANCE HEADQUARTERS

Major Swift managed to relay an important message to the Bowerstone Resistance before his fateful end.

Travel back to Bowerstone Industrial and make your way into the Sewers to meet with Page and the others. The mood is somber. The group knows Logan is hunting them down at this very moment, but they must continue to build their base of allies. Major Swift was able to send word that the revolution can find allies on the distant shores of Aurora. Walter and Page will see to it that Logan's fleet doesn't follow them across the sea, so it's up to you and Ben Finn to make your way through the back alleys and secure a ship. Ben unlocks the door at the rear of the headquarters room. Follow after him once you're ready.

PREPARE FOR THE LONG TRIP

The journey ahead isn't easy and it's going to be a while before you can return to Bowerstone. Access to your Sanctuary will be limited as well. Purchase several Health Potions before leaving.

FIGHT YOUR WAY TO THE DOCKS

Follow the glowing trail through the back of the Sewers to where the tunnel lets out near the dockside factories in Bowerstone Industrial. The gate leading to the factory you need to cut through is guarded by Logan's men—prepare for a fight!

Move inside the gate as soon as it opens and take aim at the explosive barrels throughout the yard. This considerably reduces the number of soldiers you must face. Logan's men are primarily armed with broadswords so keep your distance as you unleash your magic and blast away with your firearms. Many more troops will emerge from the factory to reinforce their fallen comrades. Hold your ground and maintain the assault! Watch for the soldiers to become distracted by Ben Finn, then run up behind them and pummel them with a hammer attack.

The combination of Shock and Vortex spells is sure to give Logan's men a jolt of excitement!

Shoot the barrels within the factory and ascend the stairs to the wooden chest on the far side. Watch as Ben Finn leaps off this platform to the floor below (behind the crates blocking the path) and follow his lead. This is the only way to the door on the side of the factory as the path is blocked on the ground floor and outside in the alley. Exit the factory via the door on the side and run around to the front in time to see the Bowerstone fleet erupt in a series of fiery explosions.

DEFEAT LOGAN'S SOLDIERS

Circle around to the docks to find one final squad of soldiers standing between you and the ship to Aurora. Quickly target the barrels across the area then finish the rest with magic attacks. Some of these soldiers are carrying rifles, so move swiftly and catch them in crossfire with Ben Finn. Walter joins you near the dock as soon as the fight is over. Board the ship and set sail!

Page is going to stay behind and continue to prepare her men. You'll be shoving off with Walter and Ben Finn.

THE DOCKSIDE CHEST

The explosion on the docks and subsequent crane collapse makes it possible to access the chest on the other dock. You may have seen this chest on your initial visit to Bowerstone Industrial from Mourningwood.

DARKNESS INCARNATE

Setting sail for Aurora was a risky decision and things did not go as smoothly as the crew had hoped. Not only is the group shipwrecked on an unknown shore, but Ben Finn is nowhere to be found. You and Walter are completely lost with no idea where you are in relation to Aurora. You have no choice but to enter the nearby cave in search of civilization, all the while hoping the stories of Aurora's desolate emptiness will prove false.

UNKNOWN SHORE

You and Walter wash ashore on an unknown beach, somewhere far across the sea from Albion. Ben Finn is nowhere to be found. Find the chest on the beach to the left, then join Walter and head into the massive cave. The bats fly by harmlessly and won't attack, so don't worry about them. Just keep close to Walter and proceed through the cave to the large tomb in the distance.

Make your way around the balcony overlooking the mystical pink barrier to the stairs. Locate the chest at the end of the sandy clearing before the stairs, then join Walter and descend the steps. Search the bodies for clues. Walter finds a journal and reads a magical incantation from it that removes the barrier covering the spiral stairs. There's nowhere to go but down!

Walter has a phobia of caves, particularly dark ones. Stay close to his side to explore the cave together.

BRING THE LIGHT!

The enemies you are going to encounter take heavy damage from light, particularly lightning. Equip the Shock Gauntlet if you haven't already. Weaving Shock with Vortex serves you well from this point forward. Also, if you're trying to fully upgrade the Scythe's Hammer weapon (or another weapon that requires Shock magic), this is a great time to have it equipped as you are likely to get dozens of Shock kills in Shadelight.

Descend the stairs to the magical swirling vortex below and search the bodies. Walter stumbles across a way to lift the barrier.

SHADELIGHT

FIND A WAY OUT

Shadelight is pitch black, but your dog finds a torch for Walter to carry. Stick by your mentor's side and make your way down the corridor to the large room with the retracted bridge. Another pink barrier can be seen across the room, but you must first find a way to extend the bridge for Walter. Leap off the ledge on the right and climb the stairs on the other side of the void. Pull the lever to extend the bridge so Walter can cross safely.

Walter manages to dispel the barrier atop the stairs beyond the bridge. A large number of shadowy creatures attacks your party in the corridor to the left. Charge your magic attack and unleash a Level 3 or 4 Shock attack to annihilate them. Repeat as necessary, then continue deeper into the tomb. There's got to be a way out if you keep moving!

NO LOOT TO FIND

Don't worry about searching the corners of Shadelight. Shadelight contains no chests, gnomes, Silver Keys, or any other collectible item you might be looking for. You are far from the beaten path of Albion and if you're lucky you might just be one of the first humans to make it out alive.

Walter's torch shines a path along the right-hand side of the cavern. Leap off the ledge and hug the perimeter of the room to reach the lever.

Battle past the shadow creatures and continue moving. There's only one way to go inside Shadelight, so don't worry about getting lost.

Continue the slow walk into darkness alongside Walter, who soon feels a breeze and runs up the stairs—only to come face-to-ugly-maw with the ruler of Shadelight. Continue searching for an exit until the next batch of shadow children attack. Unleash a Shock attack and immediately begin charging another. In a fit of fear and frustration, Walter tosses the torch at the Nightcrawler to kill it and sinks you further into darkness. Follow the glowing trail up the stairs and through the next corridor, then turn left along a sandy path to a more brightly lit area. Leap down to the sand below the ledge.

Hold your ground and let the shadow children come to you. A charged Shock attack can decimate these transparent entities.

FIND WALTER

Walter's hesitation costs him dearly and now you have to find him. There's no going back the way you came; the ledge is too high to climb back up. You have no choice but to fight your way forward. Shadows emerge from the inky pools of blackness that appear throughout Shadelight, so keep clear of the pools until the creatures stop appearing. Shadow children aren't dangerous as long as you don't get surrounded.

The shadow children emerge from the ink-like pools that appear. Use magic attacks to eliminate any at close range and target more distant ones with your gun.

Follow the glowing trail along the sandy floor of the cave to a series of ledges overlooking a temple of sorts. Leap down to enter the room. Walter is atop the stairs, paralyzed within a blanket of black ink. Don't think about trying to free him just yet. You have to defeat the darkness first!

Move to the middle of the temple floor, away from any pools of shadowy ink, and prepare for battle. Hordes of shadow children attack, but it should only take you three magical area-of-effect attacks to wipe them out. Avoid standing in any of the pools of ink, else a flock of shadow crows rise up and hit you repeatedly.

A high-level Shock attack can rain lightning down on innumerable enemies.

The battle becomes much tougher once the spirits rise and revive the metal-plated statues that line the temple. These bird-like warriors, called "Minions", are equipped with razor-sharp blades and can spin like tops. They are of little threat at a distance but downright deadly at close range. Do not let them get close enough to strike or else you'll certainly get slashed repeatedly and struggle to break free. Use quick strikes with your melee weapon, roll out of the way, and then open fire with your gun or quick-cast repeat magic attacks. Be mindful of the direction in which you roll and try to keep all of the enemies in front of you. This makes it possible to strike multiple enemies with each swing of your sword or hammer.

Roll out of the way of the minion's spinning slash attack, then open fire with your gun.

DEFEAT THE SENTINEL

Defeating the shadow children and minions causes the darkness to drain away from Walter and give life to the Sentinel. The Sentinel is one of the toughest foes you'll ever encounter thanks to its darkness-spreading staff and its ability to summon other enemies. It can be bested while taking minimal damage with the right approach.

The Sentinel does most of its attacking by summoning large pools of darkness to appear on the floor beneath you. Quickly roll or run beyond their diameter to avoid the flocks of birds that emerge from within. The Sentinel's other attack is to stab its staff into the ground and cause the ground to fracture in a line towards your position. Shadow children periodically appear from the pools of darkness but they can be defeated with a quick Level 1 area-of-effect spell.

Keep rolling to avoid the Sentinel's attacks. Get up, attack quickly, then roll again.

The key to defeating the Sentinel is to continuously alternate rolls and targeted magic attacks. Attack quickly, roll to the side, get up and fire your weapon or cast another spell, then roll again. Continue moving in the same direction to encircle the Sentinel and avoid all of its attacks. Don't get close for a melee attack; you are much better off relying purely on magic and ranged attacks.

Look for opportunities to direct a charged (Level 1 or 2 only) spell directly at the Sentinel for maximum effect. Roll away as soon as the spell is cast.

LEAD WALTER INTO THE LIGHT

Help Walter to his feet and take his hand. The darkness has taken his vision and he needs you to escort him out of Shadelight. Descend the stairs and turn left. The lengthy, and somewhat dusty, hallway leads to the Shifting Sands area. Most importantly, it leads outside to fresh air and bright blue skies.

Walter is extremely weak and can no longer see where he's going. Take him by the hand and guide him outside.

SHIFTING SANDS

CROSS THE DESERT

The scorching and windswept dunes provide a stark contrast to the lightless caverns of Shadelight, but the change of scenery has not improved Walter's condition. Guide him up the stairs of the temple to see if there's any sign of nearby civilization.

CONTINUE HELPING WALTER?

CHOICE	GOLD	GUILD SEALS	MORALITY
GOOD: Help Walter	-	-	+50
EVIL: Abandon Walter	-	-	-50

Walter wants you to abandon him. He knows he doesn't have the strength for a long trek across the desert and he's worried that trying to save him may cost you your life. This decision affects only your Morality rating and some dialogue that occurs later on in the game. Make the choice as you see fit. Even if you choose to help him, you can let go of his hand to leave him if you wish.

Do you abandon your friend or do you dig deep within yourself and insist on guiding him across the desert?

Regardless of your choice concerning Walter, there soon comes a point where you have to go on without him and try to get help. Leap off the edge of the temple to the sand and head towards the massive stone arch to the north. Hug the rocky left-hand edge of the desert to avoid getting twisted around amongst the dunes. There are no hidden items to find at this time, so focus on the task at hand: finding help for Walter!

The desert can be a disorienting place. Keep the rocks close by on your left to avoid losing your bearings.

The powers that lord over Shadelight and the darkness that dwells there will toy with your mind as you reach the stone arch. That is not Walter you see, but only an apparition. Follow the glowing path as if nothing is out of the ordinary. Ignore the shade that has blanketed the area, as well as the pleas for help, and run right past the shadow creatures you see. None of this is real! Continue to the stairs leading out of the sand to the city of Aurora and know that help is on the way.

Don't fall for the darkness's tricks. Follow the glowing path and ignore the fakery.

AURORA

SPEAK TO BEN AND KALIN

Despite collapsing on the stairs to Aurora, you are safe now. Ben and the leader of Aurora, Kalin, brought you within the walls of the city and nursed you back to health, and Walter too. You awaken in the temple at the south end of Aurora, atop a hill overlooking the city. Have a look around and follow Ben and Kalin outside as you learn of your rescue and this place Ben calls the "City of Nightmares."

■ Ben explains how he came to be in Aurora and got Kalin and her people to help search for you and Walter.

EXPLORE AURORA

Kalin believes the best way for you to understand the plight of her people is to explore Aurora on your own and read the letters posted throughout the city. These are memories written by surviving family members about their deceased loved ones. Your dog can help sniff them out.

TREASURE HUNTING IN AURORA

You encounter several chests and dig spots during your stroll around Aurora, but you cannot draw your weapons at this time nor are you able to shoot any gnomes you encounter. You'll have to return for them later. One thing that should not wait is the nearby **Legendary Weapon**. Locate the Silver Key Chest to the left of the temple entrance to claim another new and powerful weapon.

The first memory letter is on the base of the stairs. Descend the left-hand flight of steps to the bottom to find it. There are five others attached to the sides of houses, shrines, and memorials throughout the city. Much of the city is blocked off at the moment by rubble so the area you have to explore is rather limited. Follow the perimeter of the town and duck into each little alleyway to find all of the letters. Read the memories while you search for chests. You only encounter a single Auroran during your exploration, Selan the Auroran. Speak to him after reading the letter he posted.

Speak to Selan the Auroran to learn the significance of the letters. Don't overlook the letter near the statue beside him.

RETURN TO KALIN

Head up the stairs to the first platform and speak with Kalin and Ben once you're done looking around Aurora. Listen to Kalin's story as you follow her back up the stairs to the temple entrance. Ben told her about your quest and she's willing to lend you the support of her ships in exchange for a promise to rebuild and protect Aurora. Agree to the promise to earn 50 Guild Seals and unlock the **Distant Friends** Achievement and complete your recruitment of allies.

"I hereby promise to rebuild Aurora and protect its people."

ROAD TO RULE

Your promise to Kalin has earned you the final ally needed to launch the revolution against your brother. He too had promised Kalin his support, but went back on his word and left Aurora to suffer its terrible fate. Though they are a town ravaged by the darkness, their ships could aid you greatly in the coming assault. Can you ever repay them?

Upgrade Strategy: There is only one new chest available to purchase and it's an important one—Blades! Weaving Blades with either Shock or Fireball provides you with a devastating combination that can decimate foes of every variety. There is one more segment along the Road to Rule after this and its three chests cost 100 Guild Seals each to purchase. Spend your excess Guild Seals wisely, as you'll need every Guild Seal you can get your hands on once that next section is unlocked.

CHESTS NOW AVAILABLE

CHEST	TYPE	GUILD SEALS	DESCRIPTION
Blades Spell	Magical Gauntlet	40	Blades conjures magical swords which seek out and impale enemies.

BOARD THE SHIP

The Auroran priestess is successful in coaxing the darkness out of Walter, whose expressions upon waking up differ based on whether or not you abandoned him. With Walter back on his feet, the time has come to leave. The time to revolt against King Logan is upon you. Board the ship to set sail for Albion.

Board the ship to sail back to Albion and gather your generals. Page and Sabine no doubt want their say in planning the assault!

THE BATTLE FOR ALBION

The preparations have been made; hearts have been won, and allegiances sworn. It is time to embrace the role of traitor and wage war against your brother's rule. It won't be easy, war never is, and both property and life will be lost. But this battle is both noble and necessary and the legacy of your rebellion will survive long after the bodies have been buried and the rubble has been swept away.

BOWERSTONE OLD QUARTER

DESTROY THE MORTAR

With the revolution under way you find yourself on the coast of Bowerstone Old Quarter alongside Walter, Ben Finn, and a small group of soldiers who have sworn their allegiance to you. The path before you winds its way up to the city gate and is guarded by dozens of Logan's men. Worse still, there is a mortar positioned at the top of the hill that is taking out your men and keeping the Auroran ships at bay. You must get to the top of the hill and take out that mortar!

RED IS FRIENDLY, PURPLE IS NOT

It can be hard to tell some of your soldiers apart from the enemies you're trying to defeat; after all, they do look quite similar. One way to tell them apart is the color of their uniform. It's a relatively subtle difference but the soldiers fighting in support of the revolution are dressed in red jackets. The soldiers who maintain their allegiance to King Logan wear purple.

Use the trees for cover and harry the enemy's flank while they engage Walter at close range.

Follow Walter's lead up the path, but keep your distance. It's much safer to use a rifle and pick off the enemy soldiers from afar while Walter draws their attention. Move into a flanking position by leaping over the wall and climbing up the grassy slopes on either side. This allows you to slip unnoticed into a prime sniping position. Avoid staying in one spot for more than a few seconds or else the mortar will fire on you!

Use the newly-acquired Blades spell together with either Shock or Fireball to attack a number of enemies at once with deadly accuracy. Even area-of-effect attacks spread out and impale individual enemies. This alone makes Blades an excellent spell to use when battling small groups. Blades is also a good spell to use in quick bursts when targeting enemies directly ahead of you, particularly if weaved with Shock.

Cast Blades repeatedly while aiming at the enemies on the path. You won't have to worry about shooting the wrong person—the Blades know who to hit!

Defeat the final batch of enemies beyond the final switchback, then shoot the explosive barrel near the mortar to silence the cannon.

FIND LOGAN

Kalin and her fleet move into position and blast through the city gate, giving you access to the Old Quarter. Fight your way into position beside the statue in the town center. From here you can open fire on the enemy troops farther up the road without straying into harm's way. Target any barrels you see and resist advancing past this statue until you've defeated all enemies.

Wait for multiple enemies to take cover behind the sandbags near the explosive barrel. Use this battle to inch closer to unlocking the **Barrel of Laughs** Achievement.

Let Walter engage the enemy at close range while you lend support from a safe distance.

You'll know when Sabine is on the scene, as a giant explosion rocks the town and a building topples to the ground. Lead your team through the rubble to the road that curves around to the left, and onto the bridge you went under before the explosion. Lend some support to any Dwellers you see engaged in combat and continue up the road to where it wraps around the small park. Cast your Blades spell against the enemies around the bend, then roll away and allow Walter and the others to take them on at close range. After all, Walter and Ben Finn don't need to worry about using Health Potions like you do!

Logan's men have assembled a significant defense atop the bridge. Use your rifle to detonate the barrels near each of the rows of sandbags to reduce their numbers. Hang back and wait for Walter to move in and distract the remaining troops, then take them out as soon as you get a clean shot!

Don't take unnecessary risks. Some of Logan's men are armed with pistols. Use the superior range of your rifle to take them down while staying safely out of their range.

Though it looks as if the route is blocked, you can leap from the wreckage on the right down into the building Sabine blew up earlier. Snake your way through the burning building to the solid ground beyond. You're almost to the castle! Join the Dwellers in the street and fight your way up the slope to the next roadblock. Cut through the house on the right in time to see Page and her men racing towards you from the other direction.

Round the bend in the road slowly and use your rifle to target the barrel in the distance. Fire before the soldiers start moving and you just might take out a half-dozen enemies with a single shot! Climb the stairs on the right to find a chest atop the wall, then return to the street. The gate to Bowerstone Castle—and King Logan—are steps away.

Don't let the heavy wooden gate stop you! Leap into the burning building and make your way around the gate.

Stick close to the wall on the left to avoid being spotted early, and shoot the barrel to eliminate half of the remaining royal guard.

CORONATION

Your brother offers no resistance, and Walter and the rest of your generals usher you in as the new ruler of Albion, to much fanfare. Ruling a land as vast as Albion poses unique challenges, heretofore unknown to you. Walter introduces you to your new personal assistant, Hobson. Jasper remains in the Sanctuary to provide support for your journeys afield, while Hobson helps manage your daily tasks and budgetary matters. Your rule begins immediately.

WEIGHT OF THE WORLD

Life in such a time is difficult, not only for the people of Albion, but for the ruling class as well. You will soon learn the motive behind many of Logan's actions and be faced with the same challenging decisions that cast him in such unfavorable light. Will you fare better? Balancing your desire to do what is popular and good with what is in the kingdom's best, long-term interests is no easy task. It is the endless challenge that faces all leaders, as you are about to experience...

BOWERSTONE CASTLE

King's Schedule

Days Left Until Attack: 365

- Judge Logan, former King of Albion.

- Set tax policy.

- Talk to Reaver in Bowerstone Industrial.

- Consider proposal to rebuild the Bowerstone Old Quarter.

GO TO THE THRONE ROOM

YOUR ROYAL DAY PLANNER

Hobson has set out a schedule of tasks for you to accomplish on your first day as King of Albion. These tasks must be tackled in order. Hobson guides you through the choices you must make, seeing to it that you fully understand the options—and consequences—you have to choose from. Many tasks are purely decision making in nature, but don't hang up your sword and pistol just yet! There are still are plenty of opportunities to go adventuring, even as King!

Exit the planning room and head down the hall to the throne room where your people anxiously await your arrival. Walter presents the issue at hand—the fate of your brother—and each of your allies speak on the matter. Public hearings often take this format, though Reaver often speaks in defense of the less charitable option.

Being King isn't easy. You'll have many voices in your ear, each of them trying to sway your opinion.

DECIDE YOUR BROTHER'S FATE

CHOICE	GOLD	GUILD SEALS	MORALITY
GOOD: Pardon Logan.	-	-	+100
EVIL: Execute Logan.	-	-	-100

Some believe Logan should be executed while others feel that killing Logan would only mean a continuation of the type of rule you fought to overthrow. Listen carefully to Logan's explanation for his actions and, more importantly, his warning. If what he says is true, you may well indeed need his soldiers. This decision reveals a great deal about your character and has one of the largest affects on your morality rating. Logan's life rests in your hands.

You swore you'd never forgive Logan for what he did before you ran away with Walter. Are you still angry enough to kill him?

ROAD TO RULE

You've made your first ruling as King of Albion, but many decisions are still to come, some of which have a far greater impact on the kingdom's future. Logan's warning was true; Theresa confirms as much. You have exactly one year to prepare Albion for the inevitable attack. Albion needed a Hero and you heeded the call, but are you able to make the hard choices necessary to ensure its longevity?

Upgrade Strategy: This is the final segment of the Road to Rule and each of the three chests costs 100 Guild Seals each. You need to purchase the Melee Level 5 (or Ranged Level 5 if fully upgrading a gun) upgrade in order to open the Demon Door in Mourningwood. You may well not have enough Guild Seals to purchase any of these upgrades right now, but you can return to the Road to Rule whenever you want. Visit the Sanctuary and step into the light to return here. You can also tap Up on the D-Pad when the Guild Seal icon is present.

CHESTS NOW AVAILABLE

CHEST	TYPE	GUILD SEALS	DESCRIPTION
Magic Level 5	Skill Upgrade	100	Become a master of magic.
Ranged Level 5	Skill Upgrade	100	Become a master of guns.
Melee Level 5	Skill Upgrade	100	Become a master of melee weapons.

FOLLOW HOBSON

It is time to learn about the Kingdom's finances. Follow Hobson through the door to the treasury. The treasury contains all of the Kingdom's gold. Despite your brother's iron-fisted rule, the treasury contains a meager 400,000 gold. You're going to have to bring in a lot more gold if Albion is to have any chance of surviving the invasion.

A LIFE WORTH SAVING

You have exactly one year to build the treasury's total to 6,500,000 gold if you are to save the maximum number of people from the impending attack (and unlock the **Tough Love** Achievement). There are 6.5 million residents in Albion and there is a 1:1 ratio of gold to lives saved. You have the opportunity to make numerous decisions that impact the treasury's total. Making what are generally considered popular and benevolent choices significantly reduces the treasury's total. Making the hard, unpopular choices increases the amount of gold in the treasury, but makes the people hate you.

Making only the most popular and morally good choices as ruler leaves you with a treasury deficit of **-2,000,000** gold, exactly **8,500,000** short of your target!

Choosing the hard, unpopular options while avoiding the temptation to embezzle money (you have the opportunity to donate the value of found items to the treasury or your own personal savings) nets you a total of **5,650,000** gold. An impressive sum and only a mere **850,000** gold short of your target. However, that translates into nearly a million people you didn't save.

So how do you possibly save everyone? The only way is to donate the necessary funds from your personal savings. Use the ledger in the treasury room to transfer gold between your personal savings and the treasury. This can be done in both directions though your morality is affected accordingly.

SET ANNUAL TAX LEVEL

CHOICE	TREASURY GOLD	GUILD SEALS	MORALITY
GOOD: Lower taxes.	-400,000	-	+25
EVIL: Raise taxes.	+200,000	-	-25
STATUS QUO	-	-	-

This is a one-time decision that affects how your people view you for quite some time. Raising the taxes increases the treasury, but this no doubt leads to increased homelessness, crime, and starvation. The people will surely hate you for it. Lowering the taxes brings great joy to the people of Albion, but wipes out what little gold there is in the treasury. Maintaining Logan's current tax rate is also an option.

No choice comes without a consequence. Is the extra 200,000 gold worth the effect it will have on the populace?

MEET REAVER IN BOWERSTONE INDUSTRIAL

Hobson has arranged a public meeting for you with Reaver in Bowerstone Industrial. You can be assured that the public turns out in droves to shower you with praise. You automatically travel to Bowerstone Industrial. Follow the glowing trail past the crowds of onlookers to the area outside Reaver's factory. Reaver is an excellent fundraiser—perhaps too good—and he is proposing that child labor be reinstated as a way of bringing in more money to the treasury. Page is there to remind you of your promise to her and ask that the factory be turned into a school.

Deciding the fate of the factory has no effect regarding future quests or exploration. It does, however, have a significant effect on your relationship with Page. Reaver is guaranteeing a deposit of 500,000 gold to the treasury. You can't opt for the status quo this time; you must make a decision. The money or your word?

DECIDE THE FACTORY'S FATE

CHOICE	TREASURY GOLD	GUILD SEALS	MORALITY
GOOD: Turn factory into a school.	-200,000	-	+25
EVIL: Reinstate child labor.	+500,000	-	-25
STATUS QUO	N/A	N/A	N/A

Saving the lives of Albion's residents is important, but what about the quality of those lives?

GO TO THE THRONE ROOM

Take this opportunity to explore the castle, both inside and out. There are several collectibles to be found in the gardens, as well as in the kitchen and royal bedroom. Make your way to the throne room as soon as you're ready to tackle the last item on the day's agenda. Reaver and Page await you in the throne room to discuss the fate of the Old Quarter.

The revolution to overthrow King Logan took a heavy toll on the Old Quarter. Buildings were toppled, shops set aflame, and walls torn down. People have lost their jobs and homes and have been forced into the streets. Nevertheless, the battle against the darkness is just a year away. Is there any guarantee the Old Quarter won't get decimated again? What good is a rebuilt city if half a million residents may lose their lives to pay for it? Rebuilding the city costs the treasury a substantial amount of money, but any shops and homes you own will once again generate revenue for your personal savings. Perhaps you can buy enough shops to refund the treasury?

DECIDE THE FATE OF THE OLD QUARTER

CHOICE	TREASURY GOLD	GUILD SEALS	MORALITY
GOOD: Rebuild the Old Quarter.	-550,000	-	+25
EVIL: Leave the Old Quarter in ruins.	0	-	-25
STATUS QUO	N/A	N/A	N/A

It was your revolution that left the Old Quarter in ruins, but is this the right time to restore it?

BOWERSTONE CASTLE

King's Schedule

Days Left Until Attack: 339

- Set guard budget.

- Decide on castle's decoration.

- Rule on the status of Aurora.

- Embark on a journey of adventure and exploration.

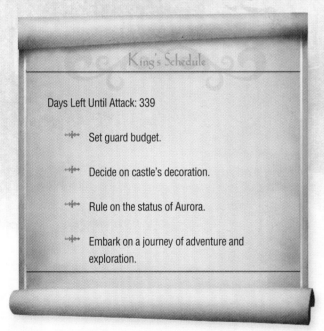

JOIN HOBSON IN THE TREASURY

And just like that, you're 26 days closer to the impending attack. Hobson is in the treasury room, as anxious as ever to discuss budgetary matters with you, namely, the guard budget. It's time to decide the coming year's allotment of funds for the Bowerstone law enforcement.

SET THE GUARD BUDGET

CHOICE	TREASURY GOLD	GUILD SEALS	MORALITY
GOOD: Raise the guard budget.	-200,000	-	+25
EVIL: Lower the guard budget.	+200,000	-	-25
STATUS QUO	0	-	-

The people of Albion are asking for an increase in the guard budget in hopes of reducing the crime that plagues Bowerstone's streets. Increasing the guard budget was something your brother was never comfortable doing due to other more pressing needs. You can leave the budget as it is, raise it and lower the crime rate, or sink extra funds into the treasury by reducing the amount spent on guards. The citizenry react accordingly.

Cutting the guard budget increases crime and may have a negative effect on the rent and profits your real estate investments generate.

GO TO THE THRONE ROOM

A pair of interior designers is awaiting your arrival in the throne room. They are here to present their ideas regarding the new decorating scheme for the castle. Matters like this may seem trivial to a ruler with far more important matters to tend to, but don't disregard the effect these seemingly innocuous decisions have on the servants' attitudes. You remain in the throne room to decide the fate of Aurora immediately after deciding on the interior design. So is the life of a ruler: one minute you're picking out curtains and the next you're condemning an entire city to a life of darkness.

CHOOSE AN INTERIOR DESIGN

CHOICE	TREASURY GOLD	GUILD SEALS	MORALITY
GOOD: Select the bright, celestial design.	-	-	-
EVIL: Select the dark, intimidating design.	-	-	-
STATUS QUO	N/A	N/A	N/A

Choose the design that suits your mood and reflects the style of leader you wish to be.

Finally a choice that doesn't affect the budget! Your opinion on this matter is purely cosmetic and does not impact the treasury or your morality. Do you wish for the castle's wallpaper and decorations to be bright and enlightening or do you want them to make visitors cower in fear?

DECIDE THE FATE OF AURORA

CHOICE	TREASURY GOLD	GUILD SEALS	MORALITY
GOOD: Keep your promise and rebuild Aurora.	-700,000	-	+25
EVIL: Break your promise and mine Aurora.	+500,000	-	-25
STATUS QUO	N/A	N/A	N/A

Kalin is here to remind you of the promise you made to her when you were in need of Aurora's help and now she wants you to keep your word. Doing so costs a significant amount of gold, but Aurora will be a brighter and safer place to live. In contrast, Reaver's mining proposal actually nets the kingdom 500,000 gold in revenue. It also opens up a new area in Aurora for you to explore, as well as an optional side-quest. The choice is yours to make.

Going back on a promise is never easy, but can you really afford to turn down Reaver's mining operation?

GO TO THE AURORAN CAVE

The "journey of adventure and exploration" that Hobson put on your schedule could prove quite lucrative if you manage to succeed. Explorers have found a diamond in the Auroran desert believed to be worth a fortune. It's located in an ancient temple within the Shifting Sands area known as Sandfall Palace. Dangerous creatures are said to guard the palace, but it's nothing a Hero can't handle. Right?

Fast travel to the City of Aurora and have a look around town to see the changes that have occurred as a result of your recent ruling. Scour the city for collectibles and pay a visit to each of the shops; you may just find a new dog training book or article of clothing you haven't seen before. You couldn't draw a weapon in Aurora during your initial visit so use this time to shoot any gnomes you noticed before.

Improving your dog's ability to sniff out treasure and collectibles like Auroran Flowers is worth every penny!

FLOWER GATHERING

Your dog is likely to draw your attention to a number of Auroran Flowers. These flowers are exceptionally rare and come in six different colors. Pick up any that you come across. You can't do anything with them just yet, but they become useful soon enough. There are five of each color: Green, Orange, Blue, Purple, Red, and Yellow.

Exit the city via the gate at the top of the hill across the city from the temple. This leads out into the desert of Shifting Sands. You exit onto the steps where you collapsed so many days ago. The area's most dominant feature, its arch, lies directly ahead of you. To the left is a canyon leading to an area known as the Veiled Path. The cave you seek is at the end of the short canyon to the right. Pass under the red banners strung across the canyon and fight past the Sand Furies to enter the area known as Sandfall Palace.

Exit Aurora and follow the glowing trail through the canyon with the red banners.

SANDFALL PALACE

FIND THE AURORAN DIAMOND

The cave doesn't look much like a palace at first glance, but it will shortly. Follow the ribbon of sand to the stairs looking out over the oasis below and draw the Sand Furies out of hiding. Unleash your woven Blades and Shock spells to destroy them and head down the stairs to the water on the left. The area contains multiple dig spots, dive spots, and Auroran Flowers. Cross the stairs beyond the doorway.

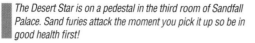
Sand furies aren't nearly as tough as they act. Hit them with the Blades spell to cut right through them!

The upper area contains an expansive pool of shallow water that wraps around a larger central platform. Explore the watery area to the left of the statues and large stone wheels then follow the glowing trail up the stairs to the wraparound walkway. Fight past the sand furies around the corner and continue through the door to the room containing the diamond. Get the Silver Key in the corner then collect **The Desert Star**.

The Desert Star is on a pedestal in the third room of Sandfall Palace. Sand furies attack the moment you pick it up so be in good health first!

ESCAPE THE CAVE

Unleash a charged magic attack as soon as you collect the diamond, then roll to the larger center area of the room. Additional sand furies come streaming in through the side door that opens once the first batch is killed. Take them out then head through the door they entered through—this is an alternate path to the exit.

Shock the sand furies to temporarily immobilize them then open fire with your gun.

Battle along this corridor to the walkway above the water and collect the items from the chests en route. Dive off the ledge where there's a gap in the railing and swim ashore. One final wave of sand furies meets you on the stairs—wipe them out and exit the cave. Return to Hobson at Bowerstone Castle via the Sanctuary's map table.

THE FLIT SWITCH DOOR

Climb the stairs to the sandy path leading to the exit and inspect the area above the door on the right. Stand back and shoot the flit switch above the door three times (it moves after each hit) to open the door. Enter the small side area to find a chest and another Silver Key.

DECIDE HOW TO SPEND THE DIAMOND MONEY

CHOICE		TREASURY GOLD	GUILD SEALS	MORALITY
	GOOD: Donate the diamond's value to the treasury.	+700,000	50	+25
	EVIL: Keep the diamond's value for yourself.	0	50	-25
STATUS QUO		N/A	N/A	N/A

You risked your life (somewhat) to locate the Desert Star and now that you're back safe and sound in Bowerstone Castle, it's time to decide what to do with it. The diamond is worth 700,000 gold. You can donate the value of the diamond to the treasury and help fund the coming war or you can keep the gold for yourself and deposit all 700,000 into your personal savings.

Even if you are planning to later donate all the gold you have to the treasury to fund Albion's defense, embezzling money along the way results in a net-negative concerning your morality. Unless you are truly playing to be as evil as possible, the only reason to keep the gold is if you are really close to reaching the Gold Key in the Sanctuary and need this to put you over the top. Otherwise, it's a good idea to donate the funds.

The Desert Star is almost too big for Hobson to lift!

King's Schedule

Days Left Until Attack: 294

- Determine fate of Child Benefits.

- Consider proposal to renovate Bowerstone Shelter & Orphanage.

- Consider proposal on how to deal with excess sewage in Bowerstone Industrial.

- Meet with Page.

MEET HOBSON IN THE TREASURY

Hobson is not about to let much time pass before presenting you with your next agenda. Stay in the treasury after deciding the fate of the Desert Star diamond to get started on the next agenda (allow for 45 days to pass during the saving and loading period).

DETERMINE THE FATE OF CHILD BENEFITS

CHOICE	TREASURY GOLD	GUILD SEALS	MORALITY
GOOD: Restore child benefits.	-200,000	-	+25
EVIL: Introduce child fines.	+200,000	-	-25
STATUS QUO	0	-	-

The people of Albion had grown accustomed to a sizable tax benefit for their children, a policy that Logan had abolished some time ago. The people want the child benefit reinstated at a cost of 200,000 gold. Maintaining Logan's policy has no effect on the treasury, but Hobson has another option. Rather than provide the citizenry with a benefit for having children, why not fine them for each kid they have! This devilishly clever policy would actually bring in money to the treasury, but at what cost to your popularity?

Do you dare fine the populace for having children? Not even Logan went that far.

SIDE-QUEST AURORA

TEMPLE'S TREASURE

Priestess Mara needs help restoring the lost treasure of her temple.

AVAILABILITY: This quest becomes available after retrieving the Desert Star diamond.

UNLOCKS: N/A

REWARD: 60 Guild Seals (10 per color)

MORALITY: N/A

This is a fine time to ignore the guests waiting in the throne room and return to Aurora. Climb the steps of the temple and enter the room to the right of the altar to speak with Priestess Mara about her missing treasure. The Aurorans used to collect the rare Auroran Flowers and make valuable, and highly ritualistic, dyes out of them. Priestess Mara is willing to share these dyes with you (for changing the color of your tattoos) if you can find the flowers.

There are 30 flowers in total, five each of six different colors. The flowers are spread across the Auroran continent and can be found in City of Aurora, Shifting Sands, Sandfall Palace, the Veiled Path, and the Enigma. Thorough exploration of these areas, along with the flower-sniffing ability of your dog, leads you to them. Consult the table below for the breakdown of flowers in each area. The maps in the "Albion Atlas" show the locations of all 30 flowers. Find all 30 flowers to unlock the **Flower Power** Achievement. Return to Priestess Mara whenever you find all five of a given color to receive 10 Guild Seals. Approach the vessel of dye on any one of the pedestals to change the color of your tattoos.

AURORAN FLOWER BLOOM DISTRIBUTION

AREA	GREEN	RED	BLUE	PURPLE	ORANGE	YELLOW
City of Aurora	1	0	1	1	1	1
Shifting Sands	0	0	1	2	2	2
Sandfall Palace	2	2	1	0	0	0
The Veiled Path	1	2	2	2	2	2
The Enigma	1	1	0	0	0	0

PERFORM RULINGS IN THE THRONE ROOM

DETERMINE THE FATE OF BOWERSTONE SHELTER AND ORPHANAGE

CHOICE		TREASURY GOLD	GUILD SEALS	MORALITY
	GOOD: Renovate the shelter and orphanage.	-50,000	-	+25
	EVIL: Convert shelter into a brothel.	+1,250,000	-	-25
	STATUS QUO	N/A	N/A	N/A

Page has come to request funds for the restoration of the Bowerstone shelter and orphanage in Bowerstone Industrial and Reaver is there to propose turning it into a brothel instead. As with the school you decided on earlier, denying Page's request amounts to going back on your promise to her. She won't take it easily. That said, the vast amount of profits the treasury stands to receive from Reaver's proposed bordello does indeed test one's best intentions. The decision you make is not purely financial: restoring the shelter provides a much-needed orphanage to the city of Bowerstone and everyone, including unwed monarchs like yourself perhaps, can adopt the child of their liking. Or ten, for that matter. On the other hand, opening a brothel grants you access to the Whorezone quest.

*An orphanage makes it possible to adopt children. A brothel unlocks the **Whorezone** quest. Tough call.*

Everyone must make this decision based on their own style of play, but there are certain tactical considerations. If you are low on personal funds and wanting to save as many civilians as possible, then the brothel makes a lot of sense. If you've already satisfied the Auroran Demon Door's request to see a purely Evil or Good Hero then you needn't worry about trying to achieve a perfectly good morality and can select the brothel.

ADOPT A DEMON DOOR OPENING

If you've been too focused on questing and treasure-hunting to stop and raise a family, then now is the time to open the Demon Door in Brightwall Village. Visit the orphanage and adopt a child. Pick out a house in Brightwall Village for the child to live in (you must own the house) and agree to hire a nanny to care for him/her. Visit the location later and lead the child to the Demon Door to get it to open.

DECIDE ON BOWERSTONE'S SEWAGE SOLUTION

CHOICE	TREASURY GOLD	GUILD SEALS	MORALITY
GOOD: Build a sewage plant in Bowerstone.	-150,000	-	+25
EVIL: Flood Mourningwood with raw sewage.	+0	-	-25
STATUS QUO	N/A	N/A	N/A

The next item on the docket deals with Bowerstone's sewage problem. Reaver has come to the castle to propose increasing the volume of sewage disposed of in the Mourningwood marsh. Currently a little of Bowerstone's sewage is piped into the marsh; Reaver would like to see all of it be disposed of there. Of course, one of Mourningwood's resident hippies has come to offer the counterpoint. Dumping the sewage in Mourningwood does not affect your ability to visit the area, nor does it unlock or cancel any possible questing opportunities. Your decision on this matter can be based purely on finances and morality. It is worth pointing out that you never promised the people of Mourningwood anything so you at least don't have to fret over going back on your word.

Nobody wants their neighborhood flooded with sewage, but is it worth spending 150,000 gold to protect the marsh?

MEET PAGE AT THE REBEL HQ

Page wishes to meet with you at the old rebel headquarters in the Sewers beneath Bowerstone Industrial. Return there at once to learn about the rampant crime spree sweeping across Bowerstone. She says it's all linked to one man—Nigel Ferret. Ferret's gang is planning to rob the tavern in Bowerstone Market: it's a perfect opportunity for you to stop them in the

act and learn about their secret hideout.

Page isn't used to royalty meeting her in the Sewers, but she's happy to have your help.

STOP THE ROBBERY IN THE BOWERSTONE MARKET PUB

Exit the Sewers and follow the glowing trail to Bowerstone Market. It is night when you arrive and the pub is closed for business. Approach the door and hold the A button to slip inside and interrupt the robbery. Ferret isn't on hand, but one of his lieutenants is and he gives the order for the other gang members to attack you. Immediately open fire with your gun before they can turn their rifles on you. The thugs that come running towards you can be downed with just one or two shots each, assuming you've been leveling up your ranged ability. The gang members who stand in place are a bit harder to kill. Alternate shooting them with targeted magic attacks. Defeat all of them to obtain **Nigel Ferret's Instructions**. The note contains directions on how to enter the gang's hideout.

Page isn't used to royalty meeting her in the Sewers, but she's happy to have your help.

Head out of the pub and across the bridge to the stairs on the right. Descend the stairs to a steel door leading to the Hideout area. This area can only be accessed during this quest.

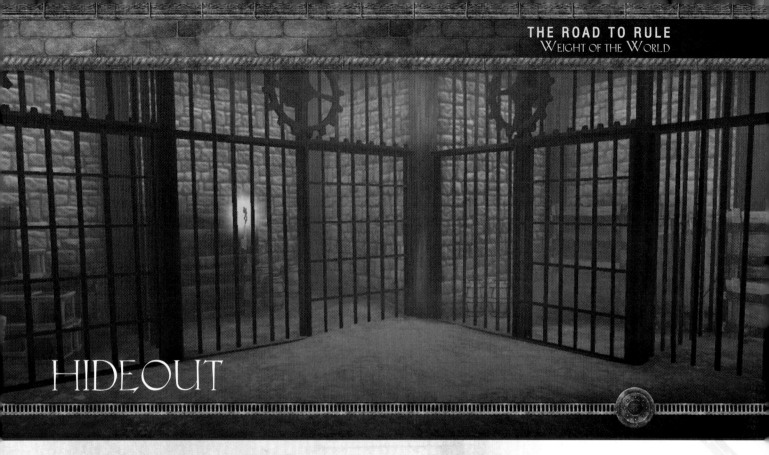

HIDEOUT

CAPTURE NIGEL FERRET

Open the door to the interior of the hideout to meet up with Nigel Ferret and his gang of thugs. Ferret quickly locks the door to the room he's in and tells his men to attack. Use the time it takes them to get up from their seats to begin charging a powerful magic attack. Continue charging it until the area of effect envelops the entire room then unleash it. Finish off any surviving gangsters with your gun or melee strikes.

A Level 4 or 5 Fireball spell won't leave many standing. Use your gun to finish off those who survive the initial attack.

The Hideout is actually three stories in height and though the door to Nigel Ferret's inner sanctum is locked, you can access it via the back passages on the middle level. Descend the stairs in the corner of the room to the lower level storage and prisoner area. The path ahead loops in a clockwise direction past numerous cells and other small rooms to a staircase on the other side of the Hideout. You can stop and open the cells to let the prisoner out, but don't overlook the door on the right leading down to the lower level where you can find a Silver Key.

Follow the path to the door near the stairs leading back to the upper level. Ferret seals himself behind the bars in a cell he believes has a secret escape—he's wrong—and leaves you to fight two of his henchmen. These much larger thugs are capable of tossing molotov cocktails as well as Fireballs. You can't afford to spend too much time charging a spell, as they won't hesitate to attack. Instead, quickly hit them with a Level 2 spell then roll towards one of the enemies and begin slashing away at him. Focus your attacks on a single thug to halve the number of attacks you have to face. Roll around the area to avoid their fiery projectiles then get up, open fire with your gun if you are across the room or strike twice quickly with your sword or hammer.

You may not survive the time it takes to charge a high-powered magic attack while both thugs are standing. Soften them with a lesser spell instead.

OPEN THE CHEST

Don't overlook the chest in the corner of the room, to the left of Ferret's cell. You won't get a chance to open it after winning the fight and the contents may well come in handy during the battle.

Don't let these two bruisers corner you! Stay on the move and focus your attacks on a single enemy until there's only one left.

Ferret pleads with you to release him. He even bribes you with 100,000 gold to take mercy on him. Ferret has been running a crime operation in Bowerstone for as long as anyone can remember and he certainly deserves to be left in the cell to rot. That said, there is another option. It's possible to accept the bribe then shoot and kill Ferret as he escapes the Hideout. This still counts against your morality rating, but not as significantly and you get the gold. The choice is yours.

DECIDE FERRET'S FATE

CHOICE		TREASURY GOLD	GUILD SEALS	MORALITY
	GOOD: Reject Ferret's bribe and let him stay locked up.	0	50	+25
	EVIL: Accept the bribe and release Ferret.	+100,000	50	-25

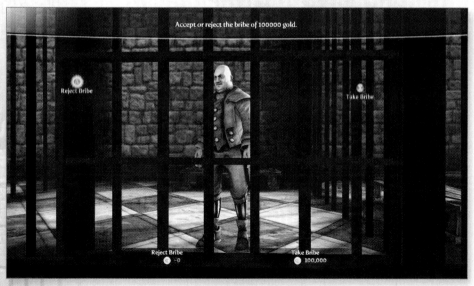

Ferret deserves to spend the rest of his life in the cell, but will you accept the bribe?

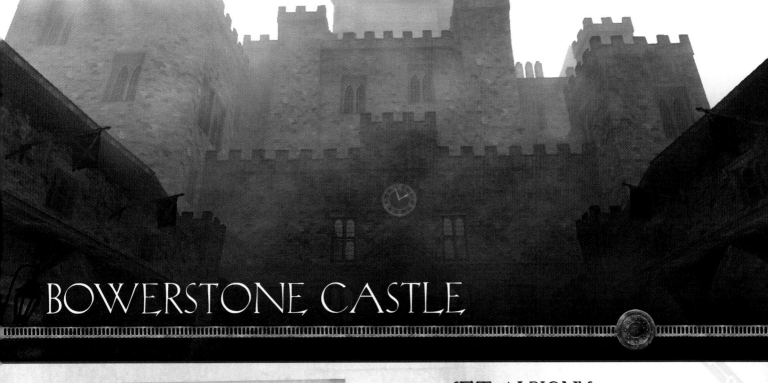

BOWERSTONE CASTLE

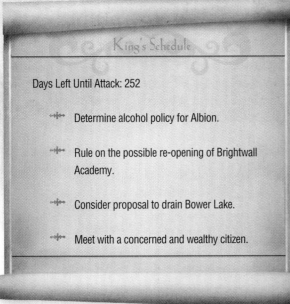

King's Schedule

Days Left Until Attack: 252

- Determine alcohol policy for Albion.

- Rule on the possible re-opening of Brightwall Academy.

- Consider proposal to drain Bower Lake.

- Meet with a concerned and wealthy citizen.

SET ALBION'S ALCOHOL POLICY

The time has come to focus once again on the laws of Albion and less on adventuring and treasure hunting. Hobson greets you in the treasury room and eagerly gives you an update concerning the fate of the kingdom's defenses. The next item on the agenda concerns Albion's drinking policies.

SET ALBION'S ALCOHOL POLICY

CHOICE		TREASURY GOLD	GUILD SEALS	MORALITY
	GOOD: Remove the drinking limit.	-100,000	-	+25
	EVIL: Outlaw alcohol consumption.	+100,000	-	-25
	STATUS QUO	0	-	-

Since the alcohol policy only affects the commoners, the noblemen and noblewomen of Albion are willing to contribute 100,000 to the treasury in exchange for a complete ban on alcohol consumption. The current policy merely limits consumption and is unpopular among both classes. The nobles don't think it goes far enough and the commoners feel it is an infringement on their rights. The commoners are only pleased by a complete lifting of all drinking limits. Doing so is seen as a morally just thing to do—live and let live as the saying goes—but it costs the kingdom additional funds due to the increase in public drunkenness. Those puddles of vomit aren't going to clean themselves, you know!

Removing the drinking limit will further increase your popularity, along with the occurrences of housewives throwing up in the streets.

RULE ON BRIGHTWALL ACADEMY

CHOICE		TREASURY GOLD	GUILD SEALS	MORALITY
	GOOD: Reopen the Brightwall Academy to all.	-150,000	-	+25
	EVIL: Charge tuition for Brightwall Academy.	+300,000	-	-25
STATUS QUO		N/A	N/A	N/A

Your father helped create the Brightwall Academy as a place where anyone, regardless of income, could study and learn. The institution was closed during King Logan's rule and now Samuel wants it reopened. He's here to remind you of the promise you made when you were looking for the people of Brightwall Village to assist the Dwellers. Reaver too wants to open the Academy, but he believes in giving nothing away for free. He proposes that you charge a significant tuition for use of the Brightwall Academy, ultimately guaranteeing that only the rich could ever learn. It's only fitting that the owner of so many sweatshops would aim to keep the population ignorant.

Do you break your promise or do you ignore the pending attack and open the Academy free of charge for all who wish to learn?

DECIDE THE FATE OF BOWER LAKE

CHOICE		TREASURY GOLD	GUILD SEALS	MORALITY
	GOOD: Reject the proposal to mine the lake.	-50,000	-	+25
	EVIL: Drain Bower Lake so mining can begin.	+400,000	-	-25
STATUS QUO		N/A	N/A	N/A

Reaver has reason to believe that vast mineral deposits are located beneath Bower Lake and he wishes to have the lake drained and a quarry constructed. Mining Bower Lake would bring a wealth of gold to the treasury, but rob the people of Albion of their one natural park. Page pleads with you not to take away the one place the people of Bowerstone can go to escape the city and enjoy nature.

Think what you want about draining Bower Lake, Reaver certainly knows how to frame a convincing argument.

Agreeing to drain Bower Lake and open the quarry loses you some favor and sets your morality back a bit, but it doesn't violate any promises you've made. Furthermore, draining Bower Lake actually unlocks two different optional side-quests along with an entire mining area you'd otherwise never get to explore. You won't miss any critical items by not draining the lake, but it is something worth considering.

MEET THE WEALTHY PATRON IN MILLFIELDS

Lady Muriel can't be expected to track down a thief and recover the statue herself (and the guards certainly won't do it). This is a job for a Hero!

Hobson has learned of a wealthy citizen who wishes to make a sizable donation to the treasury in order to help protect the kingdom. Travel to Millfields at once and follow the glowing trail to the house near the entrance to Silver Pines and speak with Lady Muriel. Lady Muriel was going to donate a valuable statue, but it has been stolen. The thief ran into Silverpines and she needs you to recover it at once!

SILVERPINES

FIND THE THIEF

Your dog picks up the scent of the thief within moments of entering the forest—it belongs to a white balverine! Sprint down the path in the direction of the balverine to give chase. The balverine leaps high into the air and retreats deeper and deeper into the woods as you proceed. Just keep pursuing it until you reach the settlement in the center of the forest.

You won't get a friendly welcome to the settlement, but that's because the inhabitants are a little jumpy due to the increased balverine activity. They keep silver nitrate lamps burning to ward off the balverines—there's one hanging near the entrance. Have a look around the settlement and nearby cemetery then return to the main path and continue after the white balverine.

Listen to the man's story about the silver nitrate torch and what recently happened when a man named Connor let one go out.

Follow the main path past the crumbling ruins in the corner of Silverpines to a circular clearing where the man named Connor sits, guarded by several balverines. Connor has no further need for the stolen statue and hands it over, but not without first presenting an ultimatum: aid Connor in exacting revenge on the village or be attacked by Connor's pet balverines.

The stolen statue has given Connor the power to transform into a white balverine. Proceed with caution.

CONNOR'S OFFER OF VENGEANCE

CHOICE	GOLD	GUILD SEALS	MORALITY
GOOD: Defend the village from the balverines.	-	-	+25
EVIL: Extinguish the lanterns to aid the balverine attack.	-	-	-25

You stand to retrieve the stolen statue regardless of your choice here, so make your decision based on the morality of the situation and whether or not you wish to do much battling against balverines. By choosing to defend the village you are thrust into battle against a pair of balverines sent to distract you while Connor and the other balverines attack the village. Immediately cast a woven Fireball + Blades attack to destroy them then head down the path to the settlement. Use magic and ranged attacks to fight past the balverines that attack en route and keep moving towards the village. Kill the four balverines seen rampaging through the village to lure Connor out of hiding.

Connor transforms into a balverine sire right before your eyes and immediately summons additional balverines to the fight. Counter his call for reinforcements by using a Summon Creatures potion. Your shadowy allies distract Connor's lesser balverines leaving you to focus on the main enemy. Roll out of the bedlam to get a clean line of sight on Connor and charge up a Blades + Fireball attack to hit him with. Follow this with ranged and/or melee strikes depending on positioning. Ideally, you should be able to maintain separation from him and use your guns, but this may not be possible given his speed. Don't hesitate to use a Health potion the moment you start to take significant damage, especially if Connor has you within striking range.

Use ranged attacks to get past the balverines quickly. Depending on weapon and level, it may only take 3 shots to kill a balverine.

AIDING THE ATTACK

So you want to help Connor attack the village? Follow the glowing trail back to the village and use your melee weapon to destroy each of the three silver nitrate torches that keep the balverines at bay. The man you met earlier continues to threaten you through the process, and ultimately attacks once the last torch has been extinguished. Defend yourself as necessary, while Connor and his balverines begin their attack on the village. Connor hands over the stolen statue as soon as he feels justice has been served.

Connor's bite is every bit as bad as his bark. Don't take him lightly!

Defeat Connor (or conclude the attack on the village) to retrieve the **White One** statue that was stolen. Return to Lady Muriel's house in Millfields to let her know you found it.

ACCEPTING THE STATUE DONATION

CHOICE		TREASURY GOLD	GUILD SEALS	MORALITY
	GOOD: Donate the value of the statue to the treasury.	+500,000	50	+25
	EVIL: Keep the gold for yourself.	0	50	-25

Hand over the statue to Hobson and consider the choice before you. The White One statue is worth 500,000 gold and you can either donate it to the treasury or keep the gold for yourself. Regardless of your choice, you can always transfer the gold back and forth between your personal savings and the Treasury (unless the Treasury is negative) so base this decision on morality and your desire to pay off any debts in the Treasury.

Try to distance yourself from the summoned creatures and the other balverines and focus ranged and magic attacks on Connor.

The 500,000 gold donation can help pay for those feel-good causes you've likely been subsidizing.

BOWERSTONE CASTLE

King's Schedule

Days Left Until Attack: 121

- Address collapse of Albion economy.
- Consider proposal to build a military outpost.
- Rule on the future of Mistpeak.

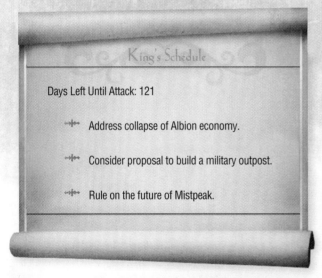

You recently received a 500,000 gold donation from Lady Muriel. Do you use it to bail out the economy?

ADDRESS COLLAPSE OF ALBION'S ECONOMY

Much time has passed since the last schedule was set and the attack is just 121 days away. Panic has gripped Albion and the already tenuous financial situation has grown far worse. The financial institutions are on the brink of ruin and the economy is in tatters. This is an urgent matter that demands a bold course of action.

DETERMINE THE FUTURE OF ALBION'S ECONOMY

CHOICE	TREASURY GOLD	GUILD SEALS	MORALITY
GOOD: Bail out the economy.	-500,000	-	+25
EVIL: Let the economy collapse.	+0	-	-25
STATUS QUO	N/A	N/A	N/A

The people of Albion are counting on you to guarantee that their savings are protected, but what good is a functioning economy if no one survives the coming attack? This can be a tough decision to make, especially if your personal wealth is not substantial enough to fund the necessary defenses. You can offset the hit in morality by loaning money to the Treasury later, but your popularity certainly takes a hit if you allow the economy to collapse.

GO TO THE THRONE ROOM

Though the calendar says there are still 121 days left before the attack, we must warn you that this is your last opportunity to stash away enough money to save the citizens of Albion. Delay your trip to the throne room for as long as necessary if you want to save everyone and let the money pour in from your investments. Transfer enough gold to the Treasury to exceed 3,250,000 gold so that at least half of all citizens are spared. You still have some more rulings to make, and they'll impact your final numbers as well, so read ahead and gear up. Concluding this final session in the throne room sets in motion events that cannot be stopped. The darkness is coming. This is your final chance to prepare.

BOW TO YOUR CHICKEN!

This is your last chance to unlock the **Coronation Chicken** Achievement by putting on the Chicken Suit before going to the throne room. Conduct the final rulings wearing this comical suit and leave your royal subjects clucking for days.

DECIDE ON PROTECTION FOR AURORA

CHOICE		TREASURY GOLD	GUILD SEALS	MORALITY
	GOOD: Build a desert outpost for protection.	-300,000	-	+25
	EVIL: Reject proposal to build outpost.	+0	-	-25
STATUS QUO		N/A	N/A	N/A

Kalin has returned to Bowerstone Castle to ask for additional protection in Aurora. She wants the kingdom to provide her people with a desert outpost near the large stone arch in Shifting Sands. This outpost would help to defend Aurora from the darkness and also provide a settlement in an otherwise barren landscape. Reaver, naturally, is on hand to argue for rejecting the proposal. Building the outpost changes the landscape of Shifting Sands and does give you a new location to explore in the days following the battle, but it does not come cheap.

How much protection can you afford to give the people of Aurora knowing your own city and castle are about to be attacked?

DETERMINE THE FATE OF MISTPEAK

CHOICE	TREASURY GOLD	GUILD SEALS	MORALITY
GOOD: Keep your promise to Sabine.	-50,000	-	+25
EVIL: Break promise and log Mistpeak for resources.	+400,000	-	-25
STATUS QUO	N/A	N/A	N/A

Sabine has finally made it to Bowerstone Castle in order to remind you of the promise you made—reverse Logan's

History will not judge you kindly if the Treasury doesn't have at least enough gold to save half the citizenry. Consider this before deciding Mistpeak's fate.

policies and return control of the mountains and forests of Mistpeak to the Dwellers. This ensures the area's health and natural splendor for generations to come, but does come at the expense of lost assets. Reaver proposes expanding Logan's policies by logging Mistpeak.

Building a logging camp not only changes the landscape and adds a significant amount of gold to the Treasury, but it also unlocks an optional side-quest. But is that worth going back on a promise after Sabine and his men risked their lives to put you in the throne you now occupy?

ROAD TO RULE

It is the one-year anniversary of your coronation and the time has come for you to show your true form—your Hero form—and guide the people of Albion in battle against the darkness. Theresa judges your performance over the past year and comments on your intentions in relation to the number of people you managed to save. Were you a kind, benevolent ruler who succeeded in making the "right" decision? Did your inability to make hard decisions cost your kingdom their lives? Or were you a tyrant who maximized personal gain over the common good? Regardless, what's done is done and it's now up to you to save what remains of the kingdom. You must lead Walter and Ben Finn into battle. You must fight for Albion!

Upgrade Strategy: This is your final chance to visit the Road to Rule before the climactic battle to save Albion. In demonstrating your true form, your Hero Level has been maximized but it still does not hurt to have Level 5 ranged, magic, and melee abilities. Run back along the Road to Rule and buy any all upgrades you can afford starting with the final attack skill upgrades. This is also a good time to purchase and equip Force Push if you haven't already.

DO THE ENDS JUSTIFY THE MEANS?

The day all of Albion has feared is finally here. Theresa's warning has proven true, as has Logan's, and the darkness has spread across the sea to Albion. Defense of your lands is the only option and you must now fight to save them. The fate of Albion's people has been cast by the decisions you made over the past year and the money you allocated for their survival. You will undoubtedly survive the battle, but will your subjects? What about your friends? You alone are responsible for the outcome of the invasion. Will the ends justify the means?

BOWERSTONE MARKET

SAVE THE PEOPLE OF BOWERSTONE

The battle has begun and your army of allies is once again by your side, particularly Walter and Ben Finn. You enter Bowerstone Market from the road leading to the castle and the battle is already well underway. Dozens of shadow creatures have invaded the area near the clock tower and additional reinforcements are flooding in. Open fire with your gun as you descend the stairs towards the pools of ink then hack and slash through the throngs of attackers to clear the area. Most of the shadow creatures fall from a single strike, but do not let down your guard! Their strength is in their numbers.

Stay clear of the large pools of ink and look for opportunities to slay multiple shadow creatures with a single blow.

Follow the glowing trail through the alley near the weapons shop and around the corner to an apparition of Page before doubling back towards the bridge. The approaching darkness has brought large swaths of sand with it from Aurora and much of Bowerstone Market is being blanketed in it. The darkness is also eating away at the barrels and other detritus strewn across the city. You must end their assault before there's nothing left to save.

Defeat the shadow creatures and their armored comrades near the bridge. Use magic attacks to thin their numbers then attack with flourishes and quick strikes. The armored enemies can harm you with their spinning slice attacks; do your best to avoid them. Make your way down the street alongside the river, near the clothing store, to the turn in the road. Multiple enemies unleash their assault here, but you can defeat them in an instant by detonating the barrel on the left. Cast a low-level Blades spell to ensure there aren't any survivors.

Detonate the barrel alongside the armored minions to blast them to pieces before they can start their spinning attack.

Proceed to the end of the road and turn right to cross the bridge on the outskirts of town. A sentinel appears in the center of the bridge so allow your health to recover before getting too close. It attacks with Blades magic of its own so you've got to work fast—Blades are deadly! Open fire on the sentinel from afar while he uses his staff to extend the darkness in your direction. Roll out of the way then get up and open fire again. Gradually close on the sentinel and finish it with melee strikes.

Pepper the sentinel with ranged and magic attacks while you gradually close the distance for a melee strike.

Continue across the bridge to the junction with the road on the other side of the river. Many enemies attack here, but the most deadly are the armored foes taking cover behind the sandbags to the right. Use your gun to take them out before they begin throwing their bladed discs at you. Target the barrels in the area to expedite their demise. Defeat the final sentinel up the road leading to the jail and continue to the clearing near the main bridge.

Stand back from the ranged enemies behind the sandbags to allow Ben Finn and Walter to draw their flying discs while you shoot them.

Maintain a steady barrage of Blades attacks from a safe distance to weaken Walter and keep him on the defensive.

DEFEAT THE POSSESSED

Walter has been possessed by the Nightcrawler and there's nothing you can do to break the spell other than defeat him in combat. This is not the Walter who you knew and trusted—it's a creature of the darkness now. The crawler is using Walter's body to try and kill you so don't hesitate to fight back with all you have!

Possessed Walter carries a sword and a pistol but he has no magical abilities. Keep your distance from him and repeatedly cast low-level magic attacks one after the other to keep him on the defensive and to gradually soften him up. The combination of Blades + Fireball or Shock works well given the ease at which the Blades spell hits its mark.

Walter jabs his sword into the ground to create ink attacks much like the sentinel, but you can avoid these by staying on the move. Use a Summon Creatures potion in the center of the area to have reinforcements ready to distract Walter if he gets too close.

Evade to the side whenever Walter jabs his sword into the ground then quickly stand up and open fire.

The pace of the battle picks up significantly the weaker Walter gets. Not only does he attack with greater fervor, but he also begins teleporting into position alongside you for a quick strike. Stay on the move and continue to use flourish attacks whenever he gets close. You can typically beat Walter to the draw with your gun so watch for him to raise his pistol, then quickly open fire.

The darkness within Walter is no match for your charged flourish attacks. Spread your wings and end this fight!

The best way to finish the fight once you've softened him up is to move in close and charge up a flourish attack. Charging a flourish attack not only spreads the wings of your true form but you are untouchable while the wings are spread. Unleash the flourish to deal devastating amounts of damage to Walter. Continue this process to vanquish the darkness from Bowerstone and put your dear friend out of his misery.

ALBION IS SAVED

Ben Finn and each of the allies to whom you kept your word will be there in the castle garden to bid their farewells and memorialize Walter. The scene you see and the comments you hear—especially from Walter in his final moments and from Theresa—are based upon the actions you took as Ruler of Albion. How you accomplished the task of saving Albion matters not in the eyes of Theresa, only that you succeeded in saving more than half of all the citizens. The others, however, will not even be on hand to congratulate you if you went back on your promises to them. Did the ends justify the means? What would your allies have done in your shoes?

BUT THERE IS STILL MORE TO DO

Life in Bowerstone and throughout Albion continues, but not without changes. The population, particularly in the cities, directly reflects upon your success or failure in preparing for the darkness. Several quests are now available, along with potentially new areas to explore based on the rulings you made. This is also an excellent time to continue your search for gnomes, books, and other collectibles. Visit other lands with a friend over Xbox LIVE or perhaps raise a family. The choices are endless. The story ends with the defeat of the darkness, but the game is far from over. Sure, Hobson and Reaver are saying their farewells, but you still have Jasper and your dog too! Turn the page to continue the adventure with our endgame coverage of the remaining quests.

THE ENDGAME

You've vanquished the darkness from Albion and lived to tell the tale. The main story of your rise from Prince to Heroic Ruler is over, but there is still much to do. There are a handful of quests that only become available after the darkness has been defeated. There are also several quests that are dependent on your rulings. This is the perfect time to complete some of these additional quests and finish your search for the silver keys, books, and gnomes. This chapter helps show you the way. Still, there may be more to explore even when the quests outlined below have been exhausted. Turn to the "Albion Atlas" after reading this section for additional guidance in uncovering the many secrets of Albion.

BOWERSTONE MARKET

AFTER THE WAR

SIDE-QUEST · **AURORA**

THE NEW WORLD

An Auroran explorer needs funding for an ambitious new expedition.

AVAILABILITY: This quest becomes available after you defeat the darkness.

UNLOCKS: N/A

REWARD: 5 Guild Seals

MORALITY: N/A

Journey to the City of Aurora and speak to the lady on the beach near the docks. She's seeking 8,000 gold to finance an expedition across the great ocean in search of a distant continent. She's convinced that, if funded, she can return with a ship full of exotic treasures and spices and other valuables. Give her the gold to complete the quest.

This investment is not merely for Guild Seals (which you may no longer need). Allow for a half day to pass in-game then travel to Driftwood. Swim out to the smaller islands off the coast in search of a shipwreck. The ship belongs to the explorer you funded and four treasure chests loaded with roughly 5000 gold each can be found scattered around the island as a result of the wreck. Help yourself to their contents as payment for funding the trip. You can also find and read pages from the ship's log, which reveal the explorer's fate.

THE PROPHETIC HERMIT

A follower of an Auroran prophet wants you to deliver a package into the desert.

AVAILABILITY: This quest becomes available after you defeat the darkness.

UNLOCKS: N/A

REWARD: 5 Guild Seals

MORALITY: N/A

Speak to the quest-giver near the shops in the center of the city to learn about the prophetic hermit who lives in the desert. The hermit can predict the future and communicate with the dead. Accept the **Brain** and head out into the desert of Shifting Sands. Follow the glowing trail into the canyon to the left to enter the area known as The Veiled Path.

The Veiled Path is crawling with Sand Furies and armored minions; you may have banished them from Albion, but a few still roam the lands of Aurora! Weaving the Blades and Force Push spells makes for a potent attack and leaves you with some room to maneuver. Battle past the hordes of enemies all the way to the far end of the area. Ascend the stairs past the entrance to The Enigma to the sentinel standing between you and the prophet. Use a Slow Time or Summon Creatures potion to aid you in this last, difficult battle and use a Level 5 Blades + Force Push spell to decimate the opposition. Deliver the Brain to the hermit to complete the quest.

A RELIC OF AGES PAST

Help the temple recover an important item.

AVAILABILITY: This quest becomes available after you defeat the darkness.

UNLOCKS: N/A

REWARD: 5 Guild Seals

MORALITY: N/A

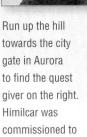

Run up the hill towards the city gate in Aurora to find the quest giver on the right. Himilcar was commissioned to find the lost statue of Tannar the Great for the temple in Aurora, and though he knows the statue's whereabouts, he's far too weak to battle the inhabitants of the Shifting Sands. Accept the quest and venture out into the desert.

Battle past the stone arch and take a bearing straight through the heart of the desert towards the ruins near the exit from Shadelight. Your dog detects a dig spot near the ruins where you can unearth **Tannar's Statue**. There are a lot of enemies in this area so take a Health Potion with you and be ready for battle.

Return to Himilcar the way you came and hand over the statue. You can return to Aurora at a later time and see the statue on display in the temple.

THE KEY TO A GREATER KEY

An Auroran businessman has an interesting proposition for you.

AVAILABILITY: This quest becomes available after you defeat the darkness.

UNLOCKS: N/A

REWARD: 5 Guild Seals

MORALITY: N/A

Speak to the businessman near the tattooist in Aurora to hear his deal. He wishes to sell you a special key for 4,000 gold. This key is said to unlock an area containing an even greater key which, in turn, can unlock a door to greater treasure. Purchase the **Ancient Key** from the man to complete the quest, as far as the businessman is concerned.

The Ancient Key unlocks a door in the far northwestern corner of Shifting Sands. Journey across the desert, beyond the arch, and angle to the left of Shadelight. There are many ruins in this area and hidden among them is a narrow staircase leading to a locked door. Use the Ancient Key you purchased to unlock a small area known as the Crossroads of Passing.

Step on the blue-lit switches to make your way over to the alcove on the left-hand side of the room. Numerous enemies attack as you step on the switches in the area, unless you only step on the correct switch (see the map in "Albion Atlas"). Go ahead and step on all of the switches swiftly to draw all of the enemies in the area into battle and unleash a charged magic attack, preferably woven with Force Push, to knock them right off the platform! Step onto the floor plates in the left and right alcoves to light the nearby cauldrons and make the final panels and stairs rise into place. Go through the door to find a **Gold Key**.

HOBNOBBING WITH HOBBES

Take Dans Mourir to a hobbe cave so he can study the creatures.

AVAILABILITY: This quest becomes available after you defeat the darkness.

UNLOCKS: N/A

REWARD: 5 Guild Seals

MORALITY: N/A

Journey to Millfields and speak to the author, Dans Mourir, where he stands near the Bower Lake bridge. Dans wants you to escort him into the nearby hobbe cave, Dankwater Cavern, where he plans to live amongst the hobbes to conduct much-needed research for his next book. Take Dans by the hand and lead him around the edge of the lake and up the hill leading towards the mining area in Millfields. Leave the trail as you reach the fence on the right and explore the area to the left, above the pond. Defend Dans against any attackers you meet along the way and enter the cave.

Battle past the few hobbes you encounter as you escort Dans Mourir to the far end of the cave. Dankwater Cavern is essentially split in two halves: an upper dry, rocky portion and a lower water-filled center. You cannot access the watery portion of the cave just yet—that comes after Dans does his research. Lead Dans to the far end of the cave where he can stay and observe the hobbes. There's nothing else you can do in this area now. Accept the Guild Seals (and promise of being mentioned in the foreword of Dans's next book) and leave the area. Allow for some time to pass and return to this spot in Dankwater Cavern to gain access to the lower half of the cave. We'll let you discover the author's fate on your own. Consult the "Albion Atlas" portion of this book for details on what you can find later on.

SIDE-QUEST   BOWERSTONE INDUSTRIAL

WHOREZONE

Deirdre is in the world's oldest profession. She's looking to hire someone in the world's second-oldest profession.

AVAILABILITY: This quest becomes available after you defeat the darkness, but only if you ruled in favor of converting the Bowerstone Shelter & Orphanage into a brothel.

UNLOCKS: N/A

REWARD: 5 Guild Seals and 750 Gold

MORALITY: -15 if you kill Lucy

Travel to Bowerstone Industrial and speak with Deirdre. She's standing on the corner across from the hedges that wrap around the newly converted brothel. Deirdre has encountered some competition that she would like eliminated. She's willing to pay you to travel to Bowerstone Market and kill the prostitute named Lucy. You don't have to, of course, but there's a good chance that if you were truly worried about your morality rating, you probably wouldn't have converted the orphanage into a brothel in the first place.

SIDE-QUEST BOWERSTONE INDUSTRIAL (CONT)

Accept the quest and follow the glowing trail to Bowerstone Market. Lucy is located in an alley behind the pawnbroker near the clocktower. Draw your weapon, turn off the safety, and let dying be the last trick she ever turns. Return to Deirdre to collect your reward—and to spend some of it if you're into that sort of thing.

 **SIDE-QUEST** MILLFIELDS

RESCUE THE MINER'S BROTHER

Get the miner's brother out of a nasty predicament.

AVAILABILITY: This quest becomes available after you defeat the darkness, but only if you decided to drain Bower Lake and open the Millfields Mine area.

UNLOCKS: N/A

REWARD: 5 Guild Seals

MORALITY: N/A

Visit the Millfields area and descend into the massive quarry pit where the lake used to be. Locate the house beneath the old cupola in the center and talk to the distressed man about his brother. The missing brother works in the mine and has been cornered by violent hobbes. He needs you to fight your way past the hobbes and escort his brother to safety.

Enter Millfields Mine via the entrance next to the quest-giver (as opposed to the entrance near the tracks) and descend the rocky path to the first wave of hobbes. Focus your early attacks on the Summoner Hobbe to minimize the number of hobbes you'll encounter, then battle the others. Use a Fireball + Vortex or Blades to devastate the lesser hobbes then finish those still standing with powerful flourish attacks. Another wave of hobbes is in position at the base of the stairs leading onto the wooden platform. Expedite the battle by knocking them off the ledge into the abyss!

The final wave of hobbes contains two Summoner Hobbes so be extra careful; defeat them quickly to avoid being overrun. The missing brother is up the stairs and around the corner on the wooden platform. With the hobbes eliminated you are free to grab him by the hand and lead him on an uninterrupted journey back to the surface, where his brother awaits.

ALBION ATLAS

Our Hero's rise from adolescent to Ruler of Albion takes place in a sprawling expanse of land that includes a diverse array of towns, mountainous terrain, and underground caverns. The struggle to build an army capable of carrying out a successful revolution will lead you from the mountains to the sea, through long-forgotten tombs, and to faraway island beaches. Since even the best explorer would be lost without a good set of maps, we have compiled a definitive cartographical collection for every area in Albion. These maps include the whereabouts of every piece of treasure, collectible item, and Demon Door in the kingdom.

ABOUT THIS SECTION

The contents of dig spots, dive spots, and unlocked chests are random based on your Hero's level and the exploration rating required of your dog to detect them. The contents of silver key chests are random, however, they may hold Legendary Weapons.

The item tallies shown when selecting a settlement on the map table in the Sanctuary also includes those items found within the given settlement's sub-areas. Consult the list of sub-areas of each major area to see which locations you must also search in order to account for any discrepancies between the map table and the listings in this section.

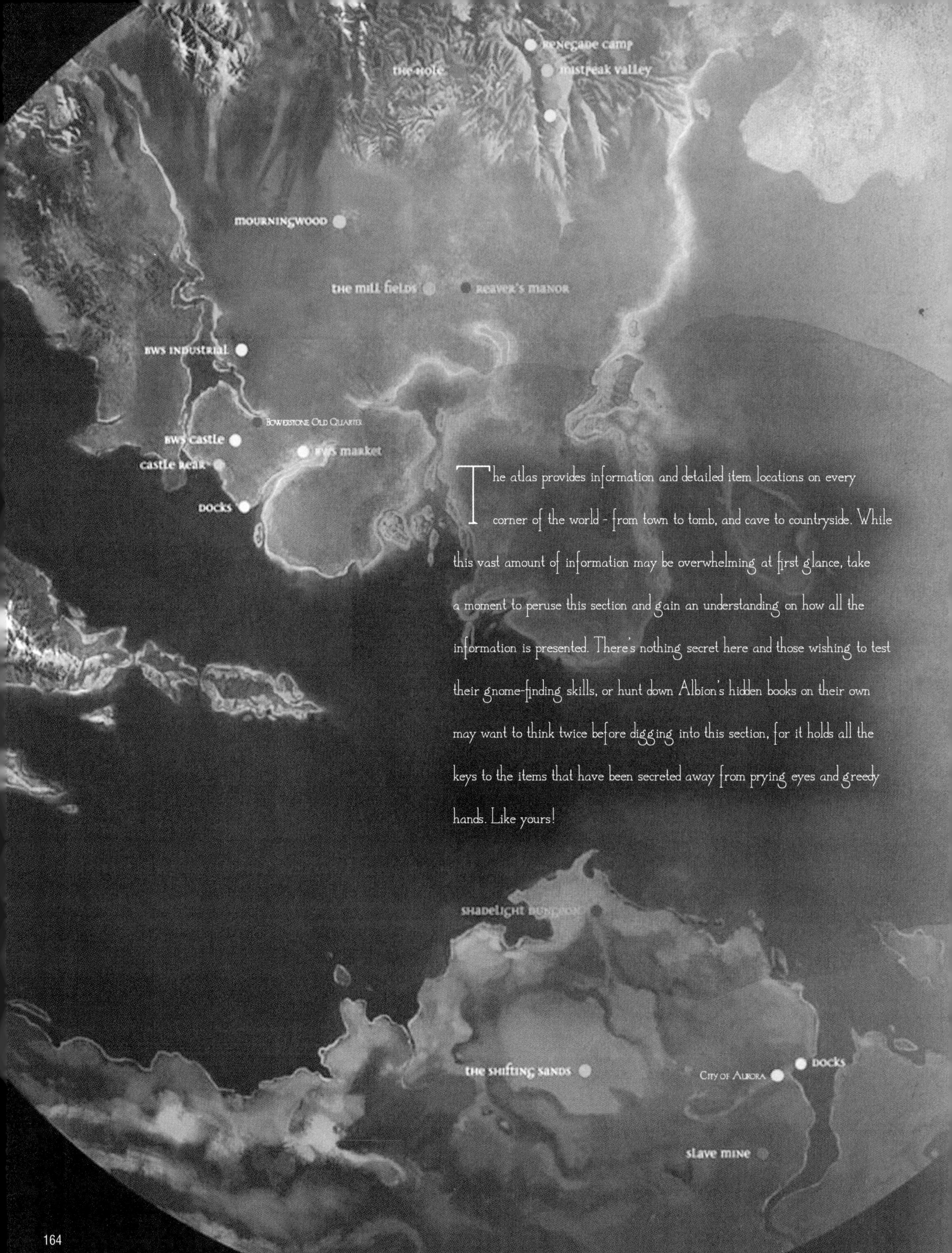

RENEGADE CAMP

THE HOLE

MISTPEAK VALLEY

MOURNINGWOOD

THE MILL FIELDS   REAVER'S MANOR

BWS INDUSTRIAL

BOWERSTONE OLD QUARTER

BWS CASTLE

CASTLE KEEP   BWS MARKET

DOCKS

The atlas provides information and detailed item locations on every corner of the world - from town to tomb, and cave to countryside. While this vast amount of information may be overwhelming at first glance, take a moment to peruse this section and gain an understanding on how all the information is presented. There's nothing secret here and those wishing to test their gnome-finding skills, or hunt down Albion's hidden books on their own may want to think twice before digging into this section, for it holds all the keys to the items that have been secreted away from prying eyes and greedy hands. Like yours!

SHADELIGHT DUNGEON

THE SHIFTING SANDS   CITY OF AURORA   DOCKS

SLAVE MINE

HOW TO USE THIS ATLAS

1	AREA NAME	Along with the Area Name, the Area Info breaks down the Area Type, lists the Neighboring Regions, and indicates whether there are Sub-Areas within the area.
2	AREA INFORMATION	
3	REGION SYNOPSIS	A bit of history and area data provide a glimpse into the area and a proper introduction before you decide to rush in. Take a second to read this to see if you're ready for it.
4	TREASURE TABLE	Here's a quick glimpse at what treasures are available in the region: Chests, Silver Key Chests, Dig Spots, and Dive Spots.
	Chests & Silver Key Chests	A listing of each chest in the region provides detailed information on how many keys are required to open them, what may be inside, and directions to the goods. What more could you want?
	Dig Spots	Your dog sniffs out treasure as you roam the lands. The golden trail is great, but a bit of off-trail exploration is required to give your dog the chance to find some of the more out-of-the-way spots.
	Dive Spots	Feel like taking a dip? There's always something worthwhile at the bottom of these little pools of goodness.
5	COLLECTIBLES TABLE	Those goodies are calling you! This table provides a summary of how many Silver & Gold Keys, Gnomes, Books, and Flowers are in the area.
	Auroran Flowers	Take a second to stop and pick the flowers after finding out exactly where they can be found.
6	JOBS & SHOPS	Feel like working? Shopping? These quick lists indicate what jobs and shops are available.
7	MAP	These beautiful maps provide callouts for *everything*! Chests, Demon Doors, Dig Spots, Dive Spots, Gnomes, Silver & Gold Keys, and Flowers. A peek at this will help you find that missing item for which you've been hunting.
8	TREASURES OF THE LAND	The devil is in the details and this section provides detailed explanations on how to get each of the treasures in the region and, if available, what rewards can be gained by finding them.
9	SILVER KEYS	Vigilance and persistence are required to find each of the silver keys. However, the reward for doing so is great!
10	GNOMES	If following the slew of insults and vulgarities aren't enough, explanations on how to find each of these miniature hecklers should do the trick.
11	BOOKS	Bibliophiles! Raise your hands and give thanks. The locations for each of the world's books are provided, along with the rarest among them!
12	DEMON DOORS	Yes, the devious and demanding doors have been unearthed once again. Along with detailing what the doors require, these entries provide some tips on how best to open each. You'll have to do some pretty odd things to open them all, but you knew that.
13	ITEMS OF INTEREST	Repeatable Quests, Puzzle Solutions, Secret Areas, and Golden Riches (Gold Keys & Chests) are all detailed here. These are those elements that draw you back for more, make you scream in anger, and lead you on to riches. Take a moment to read through these sections to find the treasures, solve the puzzles, and find the secrets.

CITY OF
AURORA

AREA TYPE: RESIDENTIAL
NEIGHBORING REGIONS: SHIFTING SANDS
SUB-AREAS: AURORAN MINE

REGION SYNOPSIS

The City of Aurora is located across the sea from Bowerstone and is inhabited by an autonomous civilization of people known as Aurorans. The city is built on the outskirts of the Shifting Sands, a massive and monster-inhabited desert. The Aurorans have suffered tremendously in recent time at the hands of a powerful force known as the Darkness. The city has experienced mass casualties and a vast amount of destruction. It's a desolate and somber place in need of heavy restoration. With the right support, the City of Aurora can be made over into a bright and prosperous settlement with bustling streets and thriving shops. Your first visit to Aurora is restricted to visiting certain parts of the city and the temple atop the hill. Return after becoming Ruler to experience the full breadth of what this faraway city has to offer.

TREASURE

🎁 CHESTS	🎁 SILVER KEY CHESTS	👆 DIG SPOTS	💧 DIVE SPOTS
6	1	10	0

COLLECTIBLES

🗝 SILVER KEYS	🗝 GOLD KEYS	🗿 GNOMES	📖 BOOKS	❀ AURORAN FLOWERS
2	0	2	2	5

JOBS: Blacksmith, Lute Hero

SHOPS: Pawnbroker, General Goods, Food, Tattooist, Stylist, Weapons, Gifts, Trade Goods, Potions

TREASURE OF THE LAND

SILVER KEY CHESTS

CHEST	SILVER KEYS	CONTENTS	LOCATION
1	20	Legendary Weapon	Behind the rocks to the left of the temple entrance.

SILVER KEYS

Make your way up the path leading to the city's gates and continue past the Demon Door. The silver key is in a small hollow on the right-hand side.

Follow the looping path beneath the city gate to the small rocky path near the large shrine. Follow this path out onto the stone arch with the hanging laundry and leap onto the lower roof. Continue vaulting onto lower rooftops to reach the lower arch where the silver key is located.

GNOMES

This gnome calls to you near the docks. With your back to the water, head left around the first house and look up to spot it. You cannot draw a weapon in Aurora until returning after the revolution.

This gnome is on the side of a house, directly above a shrine near one of the arches. Follow the looping path away from the temple and listen for it.

BOOKS

Climb the stairs to the temple in Aurora and approach the altar. *The Amazing Exploits of Baron Barnaby Beadle* is near the candles on the right.

The *Very Unsafe Book for Boys, Vol. I: Hang Gliders* is sitting on the edge of the shrine near an arch, on the looping path leading away from temple, just uphill from gnome #2.

DEMON DOOR

REWARD: Legendary Weapon

The Demon Door in Aurora isn't accessible during your first visit and only after you return to Aurora following the revolution can the rubble blocking the path to it be cleared. The Demon Door is clearly visible on the left side of the path leading to the city gate. You'll climb this path whenever you want to exit to Shifting Sands.

This is one of the more difficult Demon Doors to unlock as it requires an unwavering devotion to your chosen moral path.

You must achieve absolute goodness or evil in order for it to open. However, opening the door reveals one major surprise: the region beyond the Demon Door reflects which moral direction you've chosen. Refer to the player stats screen in the Sanctuary to see how you're doing. You will find that it's not terribly hard to become absolutely good as long as you avoid killing innocents, stealing, and breaking promises. Similarly, doing all of these things certainly tilts you towards pure evil. You can push yourself to the limit by transferring gold from your personal savings to the Treasury (good) or embezzling money from the Treasury (evil).

Satisfy the Demon Door's requirement to gain access to the tiny area known as The Moral View. This region consists of no more than a short path leading to a chest with a random **Legendary Weapon** inside it.

RECURRING QUESTS

MINERS REQUIRED

- 1000 to 6000 Gold

- -10 Morality

This quest only appears if you decide to exploit the City of Aurora and force the people to pay for their protection in the reopened mine. If so, return to Aurora and locate the entrance to the Auroran Mine atop the hill where the large shrine used to be. The factory supervisor is just outside the entrance to the mine and he needs an additional "volunteer" to work the mine. Descend the path into the city and grab the first person you encounter, so long as they're not listed as a factory worker or miner. Drag that person back to the supervisor to enslave them in the mine. It's not an especially nice thing to do, but if you were worried about nice you probably wouldn't have opened the mine in the first place. There is one thing to keep in mind if you're interested in lining your pockets as much as possible. More gold is given for bringing people of higher social standing. Beggars working in the mine are worth less than having a nobleman.

AURORAN MINE

The Auroran Mine is a sub-area of City of Aurora.

REGION SYNOPSIS

The City of Aurora had long ago closed the mine within their city and erected a shrine where the mine entrance once was. As Ruler of Albion, you are given the opportunity to reopen the Auroran Mine and force the citizens to work in the mine as a way of repaying Albion for their protection. The Auroran Mine is located at the top of the hill on the looping road in the city. Open the closed metal gate to access it. The Auroran Mine contains no enemies, but does have several chests including one that contains a Legendary Weapon.

TREASURE

📦 CHESTS	📦 SILVER KEY CHESTS	⛏ DIG SPOTS	💧 DIVE SPOTS
5	0	1	0

COLLECTIBLES

🗝 SILVER KEYS	🗝 GOLD KEYS	🧙 GNOMES	📖 BOOKS	❀ AURORAN FLOWERS
0	0	0	0	0

JOBS: None

SHOPS: None

GODDESS PUZZLE

REWARD: Legendary Weapon

The Auroran Mine, at first glance, seems to contain little more than a network of walkways and scaffolding that leads to a handful of unlocked chests. Then you notice the massive goddess statue and unlit braziers at the rear of the cave and realize there is more to this area than meets the eye. In fact, there are eight flit switches hidden throughout the cave that you must shoot/strike to send to the central platform. Once on the central platform, the flit switches turn red. Move to the central dais and perform a Level 3 magic attack to simultaneously activate all eight of them. This makes the statue's hands spread wide, revealing a chest containing a **Legendary Weapon**.

That may sound straightforward, but the challenge lies in finding each of the eight flit switches. Make your way around the perimeter of the cave, on both the high and low paths, and seek out the eight flit switches detailed on the next page. Once found, use a Fireball spell to light the braziers on the left-hand side to extend a bridge leading to the central platform. Charge an area-of-effect spell wide enough to hit all eight flit switches a second time then retrieve the treasure.

The first flit switch is on the left, as soon as you climb the first set of stairs. This is the one that lets you know there is a puzzle in the area.

Continue in a clockwise direction along the platforms on the left-hand side to the stairs in the far corner. The flit switch is on the left, beside the stairs.

Descend the ramp in the far left-hand corner and turn to face the central platform. This flit switch is on the platform support.

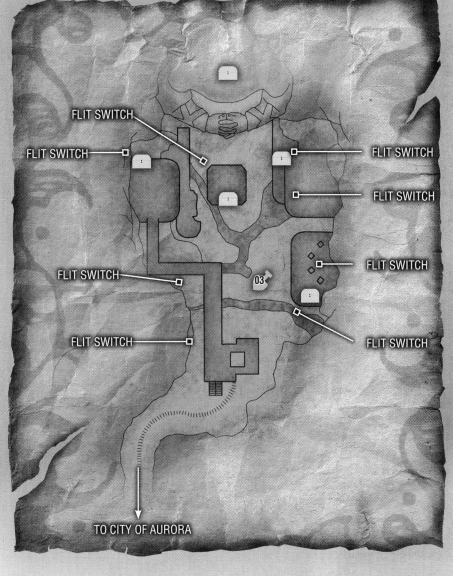

FLIT SWITCH

FLIT SWITCH

FLIT SWITCH

FLIT SWITCH

FLIT SWITCH

FLIT SWITCH

FLIT SWITCH

FLIT SWITCH

03

TO CITY OF AURORA

This flit switch is beneath the wooden walkways in the near right-hand corner of the cave. Descend to the rocky ledge and walk counter-clockwise until you see it.

Walk along the upper path in a counter-clockwise direction to the pillars on the right side of the cave. This flit switch is across from the right-side of the central platform.

The final flit switch may be the most difficult to find of all. It's on the underside of the ceiling, near the four columns in the near right-hand corner.

Shoot this flit switch on the far right-hand corner, on a pillar facing away from the statue. It's nearly as far as you can travel on the upper right-hand path.

This flit switch is on the rocky wall of the cave below the wooden walkway in the near left-hand corner. A good place to shoot it from is on the bridge that extends when you light the braziers leading to the central platform.

BOWERSTONE CASTLE

AREA TYPE: RESIDENTIAL
NEIGHBORING REGIONS: BOWERSTONE MARKET
SUB-AREAS: THE CATACOMBS

REGION SYNOPSIS

Bowerstone Castle is your home as King Logan's younger sibling and, later, as the Ruler of Albion. The two-story castle contains numerous rooms including a dining room, kitchen, library, and bedrooms, among others. The castle is alive with servants and nobles in the castle, many of whom can be found strolling the gardens overlooking Bowerstone. Bowerstone Castle is off-limits to you for much of the game, but you'll have ample opportunity to explore it thoroughly later on. The silver key chests in the garden requires 50 silver keys to open, but is more than worth the effort, especially if the Albion treasury is running low.

TREASURE

🎁 CHESTS	🎁 SILVER KEY CHESTS	👆 DIG SPOTS	💧 DIVE SPOTS
0	1	2	0

COLLECTIBLES

🔑 SILVER KEYS	🔑 GOLD KEYS	🧙 GNOMES	📖 BOOKS	❀ AURORAN FLOWERS
1	0	2	1	0

JOBS: N/A

SHOPS: N/A

TREASURE OF THE LAND

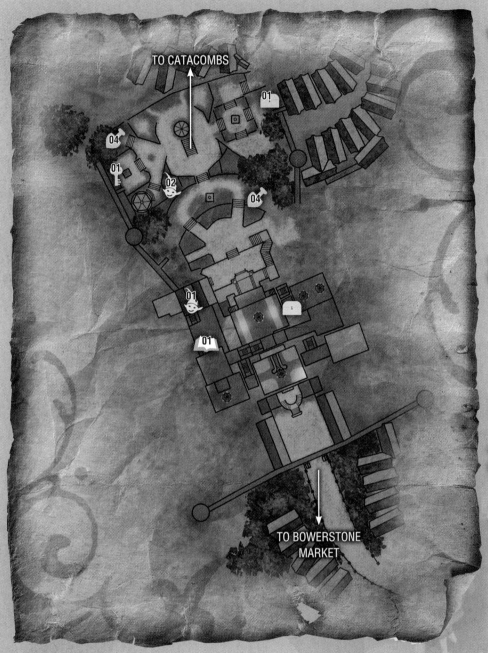

TO CATACOMBS

TO BOWERSTONE MARKET

SILVER KEYS

Make your way to the back of the gardens behind the castle and turn left at the steps leading to the Catacombs. The silver key is behind the statue.

GNOMES

Enter the kitchen on the ground floor of the castle to find this gnome. He's sitting atop the giant cask in the corner.

This gnome is on the birdbath in the corner of the garden. Exit the castle via the kitchen and head down the steps. Look to the left to find this heckler.

BOOKS

Head up the stairs inside the castle and turn left to reach the royal bedroom. The *Alchemy and Immortality* book is on one of the beds in the small room to the right.

SILVER KEY CHESTS

🗝 CHEST	⚷ SILVER KEYS	CONTENTS	LOCATION
1	50	Legendary Weapon & 2,000,000 Gold	In the far right-hand corner of the gardens behind the castle.

THE LIBRARY'S SECRET

Explore the lower floor of the castle to find the library (the room with the four tables in it). You can reach this area by descending the stairs in the hallway between the foyer and the dining room. The locked door in the library can be opened by reading a story written on the four statues in the correct order. Inspect each of the statues to see their messages then go to the statues and read them in the order listed here to complete the story. Unlock this door to gain access to a small room containing a chest.

- There were once three great Heroes… (left of locked door)

- The second was the Hero of Strength… (right of locked door)

- The third was perhaps the most powerful of all… (right of door leading outside)

- But before they died… (left of door leading outside)

GOLDEN RICHES IN THE SANCTUARY

The Sanctuary isn't *literally* in the castle, but you are highly unlikely to be able to access the gold key in the Sanctuary until you are Ruler of Albion, so we include this information here. Remember, though, this refers to the treasure room in the Sanctuary, *not* the Treasury area within Bowerstone Castle. Use the gold key found in the Sanctuary to unlock the special chest buried beneath the gold in the Sanctuary.

SPECIAL GOLD KEY

There is an important gold key in the recess high above the floor of the treasure room that you've likely seen since the beginning of the game. The only way to reach this key is to accumulate enough wealth—at least 5,000,000 gold—to be able to run up the pile of gold coins and grab it. The best way to build the necessary wealth is to use all of your early earnings to purchase as many high-priced shops as possible. Purchase pubs, furniture shops, pawnbrokers, and weapon shops throughout Albion to generate substantial shop income every five minutes spent playing the game. Additionally, visit the Demon Door in Sunset House once you've become Ruler to gain access to a chest containing 1,000,000 gold. Spending time in another Hero's game (Xbox Live co-op play) and working as blacksmith, pie maker, or lute player are also great ways to earn the requisite amount of gold.

GOLD CHEST

REWARD: Legendary Weapon

You may or may not be aware that there is a chest on the floor of the treasure room inside the Sanctuary. This chest is typically buried beneath your gold, but if you've ever gone broke, you may have seen it. Regardless, the only way to unlock this chest is with the special gold key you collected by climbing the mountain of gold coins! You can access the chest by transferring all of your gold to the Albion Treasury. Transfers can only be done up to 1,000,000 gold at a time so this may require several transfers to accomplish.

Leave the treasure room once you've transferred all of the gold in your personal savings then return to access the chest. Unlock the chest with a gold key to obtain another **Legendary Weapon**.

BOWERSTONE INDUSTRIAL

AREA TYPE: INDUSTRIAL
NEIGHBORING REGIONS: BOWERSTONE MARKET, MOURNINGWOOD
SUB-AREAS: CESSPOOLS, SEWERS

REGION SYNOPSIS

Bowerstone Industrial is Albion's seedy underbelly. True, it's the machinery that keeps the great city humming along, but it's nowhere anyone wants to be. This is the home of the downtrodden, the abused, and the overlooked. Crime, homelessness, and miserable working conditions plague the region-not unintentionally. Bowerstone Industrial is run by the greedy businessman Reaver, a nobleman who has yet to find a person, piece of land, or idea that he can't exploit for his own gain. He masks his dealings as being good for the kingdom, but ultimately come at the expense of its subjects. Bowerstone Industrial is crossed with canals leading to the factories positioned alongside the docks. It is a lawless place that is ripe for organized crime-and organized resistance!

TREASURE

🧰 CHESTS	🗝 SILVER KEY CHESTS	🖐 DIG SPOTS	💧 DIVE SPOTS
7	2	10	3

COLLECTIBLES

🔑 SILVER KEYS	🔑 GOLD KEYS	🧙 GNOMES	📖 BOOKS	✿ AURORAN FLOWERS
2	0	3	1	0

JOBS: None

SHOPS: Drinks, Trade Stock, Food

TREASURE OF THE LAND

SILVER KEY CHESTS

🔒 CHEST	🗝 SILVER KEYS	CONTENTS	LOCATION
1	10	50,000 Gold	In a small triangular clearing just south of the factory with the children workers.
2	5	5x Slow Time Potion	On the upper walkway inside Reaver's factory near the crane. This is the factory where you see the demonstrator get shot.

SILVER KEYS

01 There is a silver key inside the factory where the children are working (near the tunnel from Mourningwood), but you have to manipulate the levers in a particular order to turn off the steam vents in order to reach it. Climb the stairs to the first valve and pull the lever. Cross to the far right-hand corner and throw the lever there. Cross to the back left-hand corner and throw that lever next. Now pull the lever nearest the stairs you climbed to reach the balcony. This turns the valves off to allow you access to the silver key from the far right-hand side. The fourth lever, the one on the near right-hand side of the room, isn't used.

02 Return to the military warehouse nearest the docks after you become Ruler of Albion and climb the stairs to the upper level. There is a small elevator car at the top that is now open. It has a silver key inside it.

GNOMES

BOOKS

The gnome is in an alcove under the bridge beyond where the worker demonstration was. This is the bridge closest to the path leading to Bowerstone Market.

Accept the **Animal Liberation** quest and unlock the entrance to the pie factory. The gnome is inside an animal cage beneath the upper entrance to the factory.

This gnome is high on the wall of the building on the west side of the bridge closest to the docks. Enter the alley to get a clear shot at it.

The *Famous Killers: Terrence Posture* has been left on the table nearest the piano inside the pub. Pick it up the next time you drop by for a pint.

RECURRING QUESTS

FACTORY "VOLUNTEERS"

- 1000 to 6000 Gold

- -10 Morality

The factory supervisor in the factory nearest the tunnels leading to Mourningwood occasionally looks for additional workers. Of course, nobody actually wants to work for him so he needs your help to "recruit" some volunteers by dragging them into the factory. Bowerstone Industrial is crawling with people, many of them homeless, so finding someone who isn't already a factory worker shouldn't be hard. It doesn't hurt to drag a factory worker to him either, as there's a good chance they're actually employed at a different factory anyway. You'll receive more gold for dragging someone of higher social standing to do the hard labor.

BOUNTY HUNTING

- 1000 to 6000 Gold

- +10 Morality

Bowerstone Industrial has a problem with jailbreaks and you may come across a guard who needs your help catching one of the escaped prisoners. Accept the quest and follow the glowing trail to the target. He'll likely take off running at the first sight of you so chase after him. The farther he runs, the more pleasure you'll feel when you finally do get him to surrender. Hold the A button to sprint after the criminal so he doesn't get away. He'll eventually throw his arms in the air and surrender—drag him back to the guard when he does.

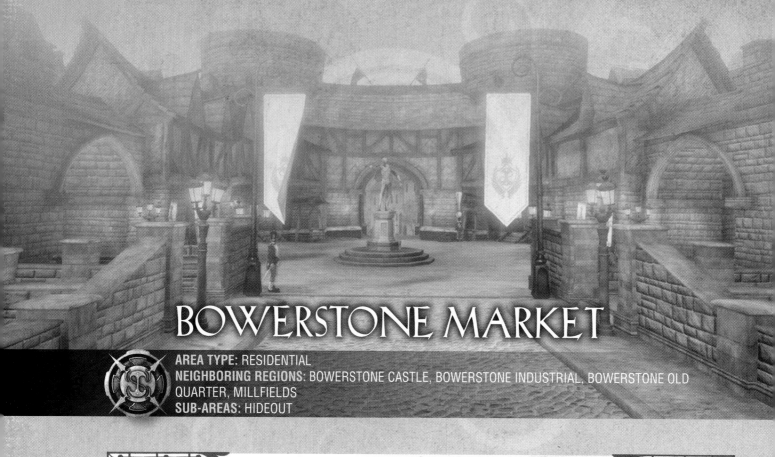

BOWERSTONE MARKET

AREA TYPE: RESIDENTIAL
NEIGHBORING REGIONS: BOWERSTONE CASTLE, BOWERSTONE INDUSTRIAL, BOWERSTONE OLD QUARTER, MILLFIELDS
SUB-AREAS: HIDEOUT

REGION SYNOPSIS

Bowerstone Market is the crown jewel of Albion civilization. It is an area of the city kept free of crime and neglect that plagues the other areas. Bowertone Market sits at a crossroads between Millfields, Bowerstone Castle, and the other sections of the city. This is where the city's entrepreneurs come to live and work, in the shadow of a timeless clock tower that has stood watch over so many important events in Albion's history. Bowerstone Market has every shop you can desire and is home to many of the finer homes in Albion, though none quite as luxurious as those in nearby Millfields. Bowerstone Market even has its own jail, though it is occasionally prone to breakouts.

TREASURE

🗝 CHESTS	🗝 SILVER KEY CHESTS	👆 DIG SPOTS	💧 DIVE SPOTS
4	1	9	2

COLLECTIBLES

🔑 SILVER KEYS	🔑 GOLD KEYS	🔥 GNOMES	📖 BOOKS	✿ AURORAN FLOWERS
2	0	3	2	0

JOBS: Lute Hero, Blacksmith, Pie Maker

SHOPS: Pawnbroker, Stylist, Drinks, Food, Gifts, Potions, Furniture, Tattoos, Clothes, Weapons, General Goods

TREASURE OF THE LAND

TO BOWERSTONE
OLD QUARTER

TO MILLFIELDS

TO BOWERSTONE
CASTLE

TO BOWERSTONE
INDUSTRIAL

SILVER KEY CHESTS

🗃 CHEST	🔑 SILVER KEYS	CONTENTS	LOCATION
1	15	20 Guild Seals	Behind the clothing shop near the clock tower.

SILVER KEYS

Cross the bridge to the side of the river nearest Millfields and descend the stairs to the river walk. The silver key is beyond the food stall, near the sailboats at the end of the walkway.

Approach the path leading to the Bowerstone Castle exit and enter the last house on the left before the wall. The house is called Hauteville Heights and has a silver key in its backyard. Cross through the interior of the house to reach it.

GNOMES

This first gnome is in the alley near the stairs leading up onto the city wall, nearest the entrance from Bowerstone Industrial. It's in the corner just past the stairs.

Ascend the stairs nearest the entrance from Bowerstone Industrial onto the city wall and proceed south towards the jail. This gnome is in the circular lookout on the wall.

Walk through the house to the left of the pub and straight out the backdoor into the yard behind the house. The gnome is on the back of the house, to the right of the door.

BOOKS

Enter the Cock in the Crown pub in the center of the market and climb the stairs to the second floor. Follow the balcony around to the table and chairs near the window to find the *Tyranny of Tyrants*.

Cross the bridge and continue beyond the city wall as if heading towards Millfields. Purchase the third house on the right, Dollhouse, and enter the second floor via the outside door. *The Grasping Avarice of Kings and their Lackeys* is on the bed in the corner.

RECURRING QUESTS

ESCAPED CONVICT

- 1000 to 3000 Gold

- +10 Morality

Talk to the guard near the jails within the main city wall near the road leading to Millfields to accept an **Escaped Convict** quest. These repeatable quests require you to track down an escaped prisoner somewhere in the area. Follow the glowing trail to the convict and interact with him. Some run, others try to put up a fight, and others go quietly. Usually firing an errant shot with your weapon is enough to scare the escapee into surrendering. Take him by the hand and drag the criminal back to the guard to complete the quest.

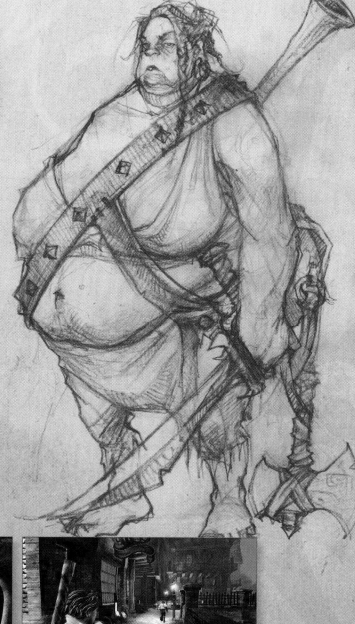

BOWERSTONE OLD QUARTER

AREA TYPE: RESIDENTIAL
NEIGHBORING REGIONS: BOWERSTONE MARKET
SUB-AREAS: NONE

REGION SYNOPSIS

Few places in Albion contain as much history as Bowerstone Old Quarter. This quaint residential section of Bowerstone has undergone substantial gentrification over the decades since the former Ruler groveled on its cobblestone streets as a child. A bustling main street is now home to attractive shops and stalls and the neighborhood has been virtually swept free of crime. Bowerstone Old Quarter sits atop a hill that leads to the shores of Albion and is all that stands between Bowerstone Castle and an invading force.

TREASURE

CHESTS	SILVER KEY CHESTS	DIG SPOTS	DIVE SPOTS
5	0	9	1

COLLECTIBLES

SILVER KEYS	GOLD KEYS	GNOMES	BOOKS	AURORAN FLOWERS
2	0	2	2	0

JOBS: None

SHOPS: Potions, Gifts, General Goods, Trade Stock, Dog Books, Food

TREASURE OF THE LAND

TO BOWERSTONE MARKET

SILVER KEYS

Make your way past the rows of shops in the center of town and turn left at the end of the path. Climb the steps to where the path turns and purchase the Nightshade House on the right. The silver key is on the second floor.

Kill a few birds with one stone and locate this key during the "Battle for Albion" portion of the story. It's far to the left of the path leading up from the water, in the corner of the area beneath the city wall.

GNOMES

This gnome is on the right-hand side of the House of Stains, near the main entrance to Bowerstone Old Quarter from the zigzagging path leading down to the water.

Make your way uphill past the main shopping area in Old Quarter and turn left at the end of the road. The gnome is on the side of the house to the right of the small steps in the path.

BOOKS

Dangerous Things: Industrial Machinery is located on the base of the statue in the circular park where the road curves tightly up the hill.

RARE BOOK: THE INVOCATION OF THE WATCHERS

Return a total of 10 books to the Academy and accept Samuel's quest to find *The Invocation of the Watchers*. Samuel gives you the **Trapdoor Key** needed to access the basement of a house in Bowerstone Old Quarter where the book is being held. The man of the house was a bit of a collector of Albion history and was unwilling to donate the book to the library. Now he's dead and, as Samuel puts it, he's not going to miss it if you take it.

Visit Bowerstone Old Quarter and follow the glowing trail around to the rear of Throckbibble Mansion and use the key to unlock the trapdoor to the basement. Locate the flit switch in the far right-hand corner of the area and shoot it. The three hobbe statues in the center come to life after you shoot it a second time. Defeat the hobbes and continue to hit the flit switch first with magic, then with a melee attack, then with a final magic attack. This moves the bookshelves and reveals the book Samuel requested.

FABLE AND FABLE II ARTIFACTS

This basement contains a museum collection of various artifacts from previous *Fable* games. Fans of the series will no doubt identify many of the pieces on display. Read the signposts near each exhibit for details.

BRIGHTWALL VILLAGE

AREA TYPE: RESIDENTIAL
NEIGHBORING REGIONS: MISTPEAK VALLEY
SUB-AREAS: THE RELIQUARY

REGION SYNOPSIS

Brightwall Village is among Albion's most peaceful settlements, and certainly one of its most scenic. The village is set across the chasm beyond Mistpeak Valley and has all the comforts of a larger city with the natural splendor of a slower pace that comes with living in the country. Brightwall Village certainly has its share of socially awkward people-gnome lovers and chicken racers to name a few. It is also home to the famed Brightwall Academy, Albion's most prestigious place of higher learning. The academy is currently closed by order of King Logan, but perhaps you'll find a way to reopen it...

TREASURE

🧰 CHESTS	🧰 SILVER KEY CHESTS	⛏️ DIG SPOTS	💧 DIVE SPOTS
5	1	7	0

COLLECTIBLES

🔑 SILVER KEYS	🔑 GOLD KEYS	🧙 GNOMES	📖 BOOKS	❀ AURORAN FLOWERS
3	0	3	3	0

JOBS: Lute Hero, Pie Maker

SHOPS: Dog Books, Potions, Drinks, Weapons, Furniture, Pawnbroker, Gifts, Stylist, Food

SILVER KEY CHESTS

🧰 CHEST	🔑 SILVER KEYS	CONTENTS	LOCATION
1	10	50,000 Gold	On a hill overlooking the plaza in front of Brightwall Academy.

TREASURE OF THE LAND

BRIGHTWALL
ACADEMY

DEMON
DOOR

TO MISTPEAK VALLEY

SILVER KEYS

The map table in the Sanctuary lists five silver keys for Brightwall Village. Two of these are located within the Reliquary.

01 Beneath the small stone archway near the house outside the village. This house is located across the main bridge from Brightwall.

02 This is to the left of the entrance to Brightwall Academy. It's behind the rocks between the Academy and the nearby house.

03 This silver key is behind Bernard and Patsy's house, near the chicken coop. Circle their house in a clockwise direction to find it.

GNOMES

The first gnome is inside Brian's house (the quest giver). It's high on the wall opposite the entrance.

This gnome is on the side of the chimney of the large house east of the little stone bridge.

Gnome #3 is on the rocks behind the Bumbler's Gruff house near the bridge that goes over the main path through town.

BOOKS

Famous Kings of History: Markus Ivy is on the second floor of the pub in Brightwall Village. Climb the stairs on the outside of the pub to enter the second floor. The book is on the bedside table.

Approach the furniture shop on the hill near the large frog statues and loop around the left-hand side of the building to the back corner. *Attack of the Killer Puffins* is on the windowsill at the rear of the house.

Use the stairs on the side of the house nearest the Brightwall Academy to enter the second floor. You'll find *The Very Unsafe Book for Boys, Vol. 2: Ovens* on the railing inside the house.

DEMON DOOR

REWARD: 25 Guild Seals and 3x Summon Creature potions

The Demon Door is located up the path behind the pub, in the cliffs that ring the village to the east. The Demon Door greatly desires to bear witness to a soul of utter purity that hasn't been corrupted with greed or evil thoughts. In short, the Demon Door needs to see a child. Since you cannot hold a strange child's hand and lead them anywhere, you're going to have to bring a child of your own to it. There are two ways to go about doing this: 1) you can buy a house, get married, and raise a family of your own (preferably right in Brightwall Village), or 2) you can adopt a child from the Bowerstone

Orphanage. You can accomplish this after the Bowerstone Resistance portion of the story or you can wait until you're Ruler of Albion and restore the orphanage. Assign her to a house you own in Brightwall Village (a nanny cares for her if necessary), then go and visit her. Take her by the hand to the Demon Door to show it the purity which it seeks.

The area beyond this Demon Door is known as Last Orders. It's a small area containing no more than a two-story pub filled with jovial skeletons. You can't interact with the skeletons, but you can watch them drink and dance for as long as you wish. You're likely to be more interested in the chest on the second floor. Ascend the stairs on the side of the building and enter the bedroom to the right. Here you'll find the chest containing **25 Guild Seals** and **three Summon Creature potions**.

REPEATABLE QUEST

ESCAPED PRISONER

- 1000 to 3000 Gold

- +10 Morality

Talk to the guard near the stairs leading up to the second floor of the pub to accept an **Escaped Prisoner** quest. These repeatable quests require you to track down an escaped convict somewhere in the area. Follow the glowing trail to the escapee and interact with him. Some run, others try to put up a fight, and others go quietly. Take him by the hand and drag the criminal back to the guard to complete the quest.

CATACOMBS

Catacombs is a sub-area of Bowerstone Castle.

REGION SYNOPSIS

Catacombs is a large cavern underneath the Bowerstone Castle gardens, accessed via the family crypt during the "Leaving the Castle" portion of the story. Aside from being home to a number of bats, the Catacombs primarily serves as a means to reach the Cullis Gate leading to the Dweller Camp. Your time in Catacombs is limited early on, but return after becoming Ruler of Albion to investigate the area beyond the golden door.

TREASURE

CHESTS	SILVER KEY CHESTS	DIG SPOTS	DIVE SPOTS
2	0	7	0

COLLECTIBLES

SILVER KEYS	GOLD KEYS	GNOMES	BOOKS	AURORAN FLOWERS
1	0	1	0	0

JOBS: None

SHOPS: None

TREASURE OF THE LAND

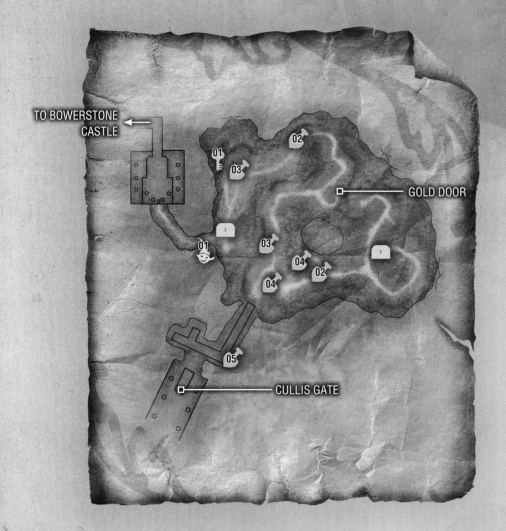

TO BOWERSTONE CASTLE

GOLD DOOR

CULLIS GATE

SILVER KEYS

Descend the steps from where you first enter the Catacombs from the Castle and found the Guild Seal. Continue down the path to the overlook and turn left near the ruins.

GNOMES

Return to the Castle after the revolution and enter the Catacombs. Traverse the initial tunnel leading away from the crypt and turn immediately to the right to spot this gnome.

GOLDEN RICHES

GOLDEN DOOR

REWARD: 40 Guild Seals

Descend into the Catacombs from the garden tomb in Bowerstone Gardens. Follow the rocky ledge just as you did when escaping the castle then turn left at the fork to descend the stairs to the golden door. Unlock the door with a gold key found elsewhere and continue along the path to the enemies across the shallow pool of water. Slay the balverines at the base of the stairs then ascend the circling path to a chest high above the water. Open it to gain **40 Guild Seals**.

Return the way you came and make a left at the bottom of the stairs (where you fought the balverines). The path forks ahead. The right fork leads to a dig spot while the left branch takes you to a ledge overlooking the entrance to the tunnel leading to Mistpeak Valley.

CESSPOOLS

Cesspools is a sub-area of Bowerstone Industrial.

REGION SYNOPSIS

The Cesspools is a small dungeon-like area beneath Bowerstone Industrial that can only be accessed through a basement door inside the house across from the orphanage. Dive off the edge in the basement to enter the caves that run below the factories in the area (not to be confused with the Sewers area). Be thorough on your initial visit to the area and you won't have to worry about returning. Grabbing all of the collectibles during the **Kidnapped** quest is a great idea as they're all available at that time. However, you can also enter the orphanage and use the trapdoor after you've become ruler.

TREASURE

🗝 CHESTS	🗝 SILVER KEY CHESTS	✊ DIG SPOTS	💧 DIVE SPOTS
3	0	5	0

COLLECTIBLES

🗝 SILVER KEYS	🗝 GOLD KEYS	🍶 GNOMES	📖 BOOKS	✿ AURORAN FLOWERS
1	0	1	1	0

JOBS: None

SHOPS: None

TREASURE OF THE LAND

TO BOWERSTONE INDUSTRIAL

SILVER KEYS

Dive off the ledge and head up the path and around the corner to the right. Smash the wooden boards on the left-hand side of the tunnel to find this silver key.

GNOMES

Proceed through the tunnel at the base of the hill past the turn to the right, to the dead end up ahead. The gnome is on the far wall just beyond the light shining down from above ground.

BOOKS

Dangerous Things: Gunpowder is located on a table just inside the entrance.

191

CHILLBREATH CAVERNS

Chillbreath Caverns is a sub-area of Mistpeak Valley.

REGION SYNOPSIS

Chillbreath Caverns is the largest of the underground caverns and contains no fewer than four unique entrances from Mistpeak Valley. These entrances lead to two separate portions of the cave system. You'll explore a dead-end section of the cave during the **Missing Child** quest. One of the three remaining entrances to the cave leads to a well-hidden gold key in Mistpeak Valley that is only accessible by finding this secluded exit from Chillbreath Caverns. The icy, multi-level cave system contains a number of valuable collectibles, including a rare quest-specific book. It's also home to numerous hobbes, wolves, and other monsters. Proceed with caution and search every available path to exhaust this sprawling location of items.

TREASURE

🧰 CHESTS	🧰 SILVER KEY CHESTS	✌ DIG SPOTS	💧 DIVE SPOTS
8	1	8	0

COLLECTIBLES

🗝 SILVER KEYS	🗝 GOLD KEYS	🔮 GNOMES	📖 BOOKS	✿ AURORAN FLOWERS
1	0	2	2	0

JOBS: None

SHOPS: None

TREASURE OF THE LAND

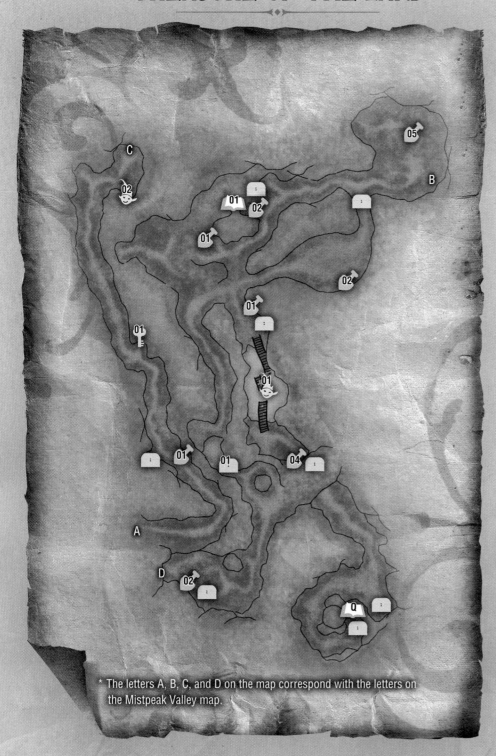

* The letters A, B, C, and D on the map correspond with the letters on the Mistpeak Valley map.

SILVER KEYS

You'll likely spot this silver key during the **Missing Child** quest but not see a way to get it. To reach it, enter Chillbreath Caverns via the entrance near the bridge strung above the path leading to the Mistpeak Valley Demon Door. Once inside the cave, follow the path across the rocky bridge to the silver key.

GNOMES

Enter the cave via the entrance uphill from the monorail station. Follow the path to the frozen lake and head out onto the ice. The gnome is standing atop the taller stalagmite.

Enter Chillbreath Caverns via the entrance closest to the bridge near Mistpeak Valley Demon Door. The gnome is high atop the stalactites just inside the entrance.

SILVER KEY CHESTS

CHEST	SILVER KEYS	CONTENTS	LOCATION
1	15	75,000 Gold	Use the cave entrance nearest the monorail station and follow the upper path above the frozen lake.

BOOKS

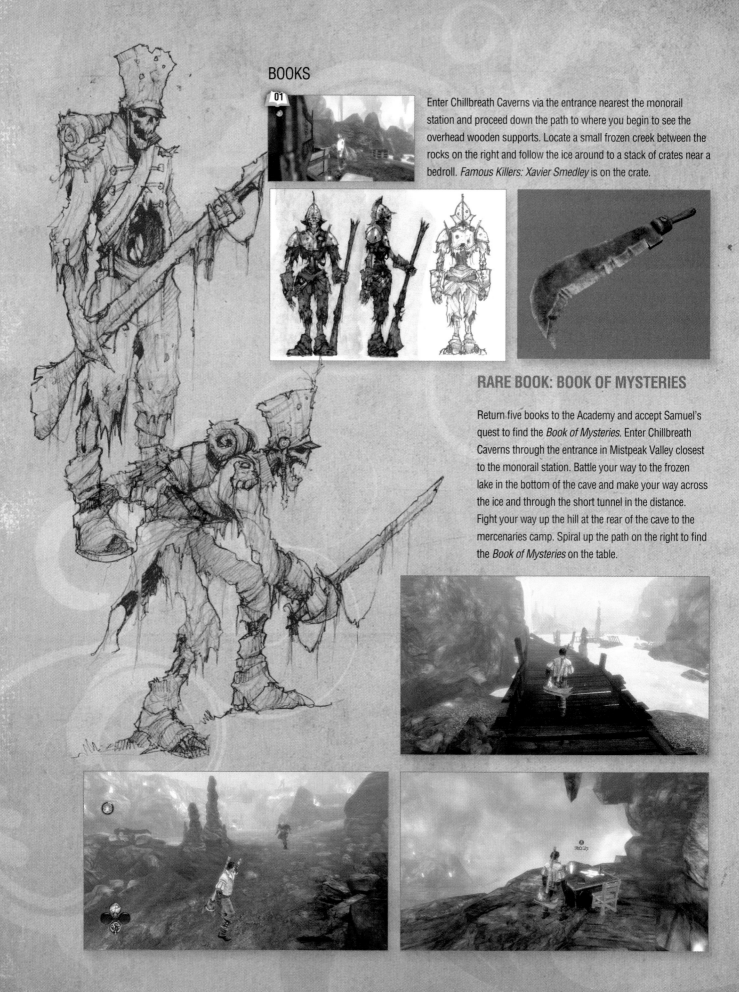

01 Enter Chillbreath Caverns via the entrance nearest the monorail station and proceed down the path to where you begin to see the overhead wooden supports. Locate a small frozen creek between the rocks on the right and follow the ice around to a stack of crates near a bedroll. *Famous Killers: Xavier Smedley* is on the crate.

RARE BOOK: BOOK OF MYSTERIES

Return five books to the Academy and accept Samuel's quest to find the *Book of Mysteries*. Enter Chillbreath Caverns through the entrance in Mistpeak Valley closest to the monorail station. Battle your way to the frozen lake in the bottom of the cave and make your way across the ice and through the short tunnel in the distance. Fight your way up the hill at the rear of the cave to the mercenaries camp. Spiral up the path on the right to find the *Book of Mysteries* on the table.

DANKWATER CAVERN

Dankwater Cavern is a sub-area of Millfields.

REGION SYNOPSIS

Dankwater Cavern is a spacious, two-level cave located beneath Millfields. It is home to a sophisticated clan of hobbes and contains several valuable items and its dive spots tend to yield valuable gems. There is little reason to explore this area until accepting the **Hobnobbing with Hobbes** quest during the endgame portion of the story as much of the cavern is off-limits until that quest has been completed. Leave the area after completing the quest then return some time later to gain access to the lower, watery portion of the cave. That's where the valuables are!

TREASURE

CHESTS	SILVER KEY CHESTS	DIG SPOTS	DIVE SPOTS
2	0	5	3

COLLECTIBLES

SILVER KEYS	GOLD KEYS	GNOMES	BOOKS	AURORAN FLOWERS
2	0	2	1	0

JOBS: None

SHOPS: None

TREASURE OF THE LAND

SILVER KEYS

Return to Dankwater Cavern after completing the **Hobnobbing with Hobbes** quest and enter the water via the slope where you left Dans Mourir. Swim far to the left to the bank with the branching path leading up out of the water. Take the right-hand path and follow it up to the silver key you may have seen upon entering the cavern.

Return to Dankwater Cavern after completing the **Hobnobbing with Hobbes** quest and enter the water near the hobbe camp. Swim a counter-clockwise spiral through the rocks immediately to the right to work your way to the sloping path in the far right-hand corner and the silver key.

TO MILLFIELDS

GNOMES

Enter Dankwater Cavern and follow the narrow path above the water towards the waterfalls. The gnome is on the rocks beside the waterfalls.

Proceed down the narrow path to where the route circles around a pile of rocks and stalactites in the southwest corner. The gnome is behind the rocks on a short offshoot path on the outer edge of the circle.

BOOKS

You must complete the **Hobnobbing with Hobbes** quest in order to access this book. Return to where you left Dans Mourir and enter the water. Swim all the way to the far left end of the cave. *Liver of Darkness* is on a table below the cliff where you first enter the cavern.

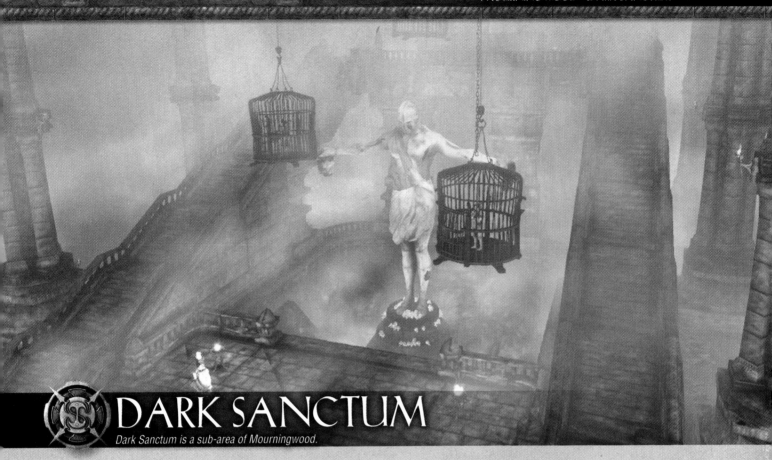

DARK SANCTUM

Dark Sanctum is a sub-area of Mourningwood.

REGION SYNOPSIS

The area known as the Dark Sanctum is hidden behind a fiery magical barrier in Mourningwood and can only be accessed after completing a series of quests beginning with **Peace, Love, and Homicide**. Suffice to say, only those who don't mind dabbling in the murder of innocents will gain entry to this space. Though there are no collectibles within the Dark Sanctum, and it does require an extensive commitment to unlock in its entirety, there are a pair of puzzles within the area that lead to Legendary Weapons. Members can also use the Sacrificial Barbecue Pit whenever they are hungry-and don't mind the taste of grilled villager.

TREASURE

🗃 CHESTS	🗃 SILVER KEY CHESTS	🖐 DIG SPOTS	💧 DIVE SPOTS
3	0	0	0

COLLECTIBLES

🗝 SILVER KEYS	🗝 GOLD KEYS	🧙 GNOMES	📖 BOOKS	❀ AURORAN FLOWERS
0	0	0	0	0

JOBS: None

SHOPS: None

TREASURE OF THE LAND

TO MOURNINGWOOD

FLIT SWITCH PUZZLES

THE STATUE FLIT SWITCH

The Dark Sanctum contains two flit switches that, if hit, can be used to access to previously inaccessible areas. In order to access these two flit switches, you must first complete the entire Dark Sanctum quest line, starting with **Peace, Love, and Homicide** and ending with the opening of the Sacrificial BBQ Pit in the **Leverage** quest.

The first flit switch is at the base of the large statue in the center of the main hall. Approach the edge between the two stairs and use your gun to shoot the flit switch. Follow the flit switch past the Sacrificial BBQ Pit to the door behind it. There is a chest containing a Summon Creatures potion within this room.

UNLOCKING THE TENDERISER

The second flit switch is located in the deepest, darkest corner of the Dark Sanctum, right where you found the lever needed to complete the **Leverage** quest. Equip the Bonesmasher (preferably after you've gained the Cleric upgrade's 80% damage bonus against hollow men) and bring a healthy supply of Health potions to the rear of the Dark Sanctum. Slowly and methodically fight your way through the hordes of hollow men that line the serpentine path winding its way to the rear of the area. Dozens of hollow men attack at once in this section so be extra careful. Use high-level magic attacks—Fireball weaved with Shock, Blades, or Vortex works well—to buy yourself some time, then unload with the Bonesmasher. Roll backwards away from the hollow men whenever you need to reload.

Strike the flit switch in the corner of the room where the lever was and chase it back the way you came. Shoot it when it stops and chase it to the area where the hollow men were. It descends into a slot in the floor and four pedestals with extinguished cauldrons will rise. Target each cauldron with the Fireball spell to ignite them. Light the four to make two additional flit switches appear near the exit. Hit the right-hand one with magic then quickly shoot the one on the left.

Follow the two flit switches through the hallway, but stop at each archway to hit the third and fourth flit switches that appear. One drops from the ceiling as the first two pass through the arch. Chase all four flit switches to the landing atop the stairs and quickly hit all four at once with a Level 2 magic attack. Once all four have been hit with a magical attack, they'll move to the door down the stairs on the right and open access to a new area.

This final area within Dark Sanctum is a puzzle of sorts. You must gradually make your way back and forth across the area to light the four extinguished cauldrons. New sections of walkway and stairs move into position with each lit cauldron. Each cauldron is guarded by the wisps of hollow men, so be on guard! Head left first to the cauldron even with the entrance then climb the stairs that appear when that cauldron is lit. Use your gun to shoot the sniping hollow men positioned throughout the area and continue to the far left-hand corner to light the next cauldron.

Circle back past the entrance and extend the walkway in a counter-clockwise direction. Leap off the walkway onto the lower ledge and climb the stairs to the third cauldron. Leap off the corner of the platform where the cauldron is to land on the path leading to the fourth, directly below the chest. Light the final cauldron and climb the stairs that appear to reach the chest containing a **Legendary Weapon**.

DRIFTWOOD

AREA TYPE: COUNTRYSIDE
NEIGHBORING REGIONS: MILLFIELDS
SUB-AREAS: NONE

REGION SYNOPSIS

The coastal settlement of Driftwood can only be accessed after completing the **Restoration** quest in Millfields. This area lies beyond the gypsy camp where the former Ruler of Albion had been raised, hence the need to rebuild the bridge located there. Driftwood is a community in progress, and one that needs your help. Complete a series of quests in Driftwood to help the villagers expand their settlement across the water to the three large islands off the coast. Only then are you able to fully explore this scenic area. The bridges, walkways, and mines that are created after completing the **Giftwood for Driftwood** quest expand your ability to collect its most valuable treasures.

TREASURE

🗃 CHESTS	🗃 SILVER KEY CHESTS	⚒ DIG SPOTS	💧 DIVE SPOTS
6	0	12	4

COLLECTIBLES

🗝 SILVER KEYS	🗝 GOLD KEYS	🧪 GNOMES	📖 BOOKS	❀ AURORAN FLOWERS
2	1	2	1	0

JOBS: None

SHOPS: General Goods, Food, Gifts

TREASURE OF THE LAND

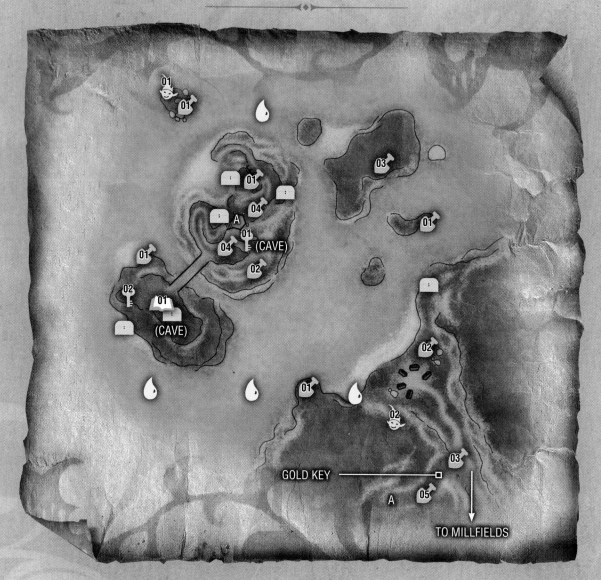

GOLD KEY

A

TO MILLFIELDS

SILVER KEYS

01 Swim offshore to the large island in the center of the three inhabited islands and locate the small cave on the side of the island facing the main coast. Enter this tiny cave to find the silver key.

02 Climb the outermost of the three large islands to the hobbe camp beyond the ledge where the chest is located. Leap off the plateau with the camp onto a ledge on the outer edge of the island to find this silver key.

GNOMES

01 This gnome sits on a small island far off the coast of Driftwood, beyond the larger islands where the hobbes (and later the villagers) are located.

02 Stand on the beach facing Robin's coastal commune and locate the faint trail leading between the rocks to the right of the caravans. Follow this path to a small group of trees—the gnome is on a tiny caravan in the center.

BOOKS

Make your way out to the right-most large island and enter the mine on the side facing the shore (after completing the **Giftwood for Driftwood** quest). *Dangerous Things: Stargazing in Remote Areas* is on one of the crates to the left as you enter.

GOLDEN RICHES

GOLD KEY

Complete the **An Island Getaway**, **Pest Control**, and **Gift Wood for Driftwood** quests and leave the Driftwood area. Return after a short visit to another area (once the **Island Paradise** Achievement is unlocked) and cross over to the island camp. Use the newly-built bridge to reach the flit switch on the tiny island to the right and strike it. Chase after the flit switch and continue shooting and striking it. You can reach each position that it moves to thanks to the carpenter's work.

Swim across the channel to the other island to continue your pursuit of the flit switch and chase it all the way up the mountain to where the collapsed bridge was. A new wooden bridge has been erected in its place, so long as you gave the carpenter enough time before returning. Continue chasing the flit switch up the spiraling mountain of the center island to the Cullis Gate. Use this gate to warp to a secluded path near the entrance to Driftwood containing the gold key.

DWELLER CAMP

AREA TYPE: RESIDENTIAL
BORDERING REGIONS: MISTPEAK VALLEY
SUB-AREAS: NONE

REGION SYNOPSIS

Dweller Camp is a small settlement located high in the snow-covered mountains of Mistpeak. The residents-Dwellers as they like to be called-are lead by a village elder named Sabine who, together with his bodyguard Boulder, seek to protect what remains of the Dweller culture. The Dweller Camp can be accessed directly via the World Map Table or on foot from Mistpeak Valley. Dweller Camp contains few collectibles, shops, or desirable real-estate investments. The Dwellers have been oppressed under King Logan's rule and find their struggle against the government's policies even more challenging than the battle they wage against the elements. Return to the Dweller Camp to gain access to Sabine's inner compound.

TREASURE

🗃 CHESTS	🗃 SILVER KEY CHESTS	🪏 DIG SPOTS	💧 DIVE SPOTS
3	1	9	1

COLLECTIBLES

🗝 SILVER KEYS	🗝 GOLD KEYS	🧙 GNOMES	📖 BOOKS	✿ AURORAN FLOWERS
1	0	1	1	0

JOBS: Lute Hero

SHOPS: Clothing, General Goods, Tattoos

TREASURE OF THE LAND

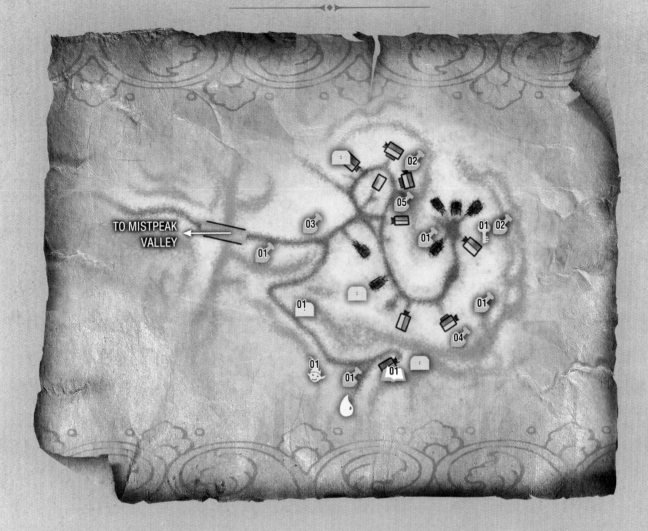

SILVER KEY CHESTS

CHEST	SILVER KEYS	CONTENTS	LOCATION
1	5	10 Guild Seals and a Health Potion	On a ledge overlooking the wagons, near the pond.

SILVER KEYS

Return to the Dweller Camp to find the gate to Sabine's inner camp open. Enter this private area and look behind the wagon on the right to find the silver key.

GNOMES

This gnome is on the rocks beyond the silver key chest. Head up the path southeast of the wagons to the chest and shoot the gnome from there.

BOOKS

Famous Kings of History: King Cedric is on the table inside the lone wagon near the top of the switchbacking trail that leads up to the pond. It is inside the "Wimpet's Sniffle" wagon.

HIDEOUT

Hideout is a sub-area of Bowerstone Market.

REGION SYNOPSIS

Hideout is a small area beneath Bowerstone Market, accessed only after meeting with Page about the recent crime spree during the "Weight of the World" portion of the story. Use the key obtained during the quest to unlock the door to the Hideout along the river path in Bowerstone Market. The Hideout consists of multiple levels and contains multiple rooms and cells where prisoners are kept hostage. Explore the lowermost level for the silver key before heading back up the stairs to where the quest culminates.

TREASURE

CHESTS	SILVER KEY CHESTS	DIG SPOTS	DIVE SPOTS
1	0	0	0

COLLECTIBLES

SILVER KEYS	GOLD KEYS	GNOMES	BOOKS	AURORAN FLOWERS
1	0	0	0	0

JOBS: None

SHOPS: None

TREASURE OF THE LAND

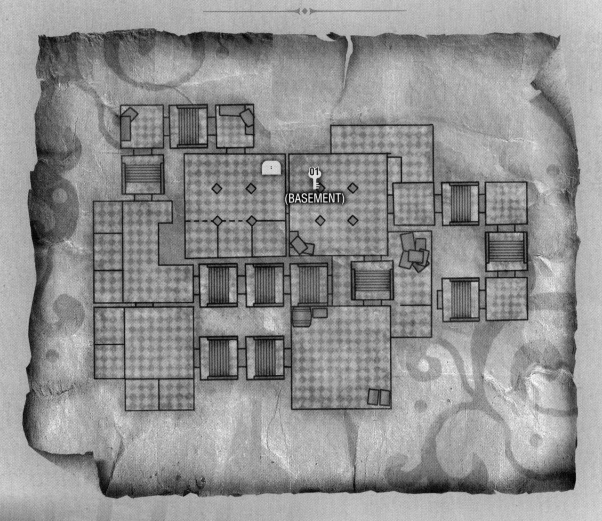

(BASEMENT)

SILVER KEYS

Open the door across from the jail cells on the middle floor of the Hideout and descend the stairs to the lowermost level. Open the cell around the corner to get the silver key.

THE HOLE

The Hole is a sub-area of Mistpeak Valley, but a small portion of it can also be accessed via Millfields.

REGION SYNOPSIS

The Hole is the name given to the hobbe-infested cave that lies between the Mistpeak and Millfields Monorail Stations. There are essentially three portions to the cave that you must explore in hopes of finding all of the silver keys in Albion. You'll visit the main portion of the cave as you travel from Mistpeak to Mourningwood during the "Mistpeak Monorail" portion of the story. Find the Technicians Key before exiting so you can return and explore the area beyond the gate near the crash site. It's also possible to enter The Hole via the Millfields Monorail Station entrance, though this area only consists of a small transit station. The cave itself can be dangerous to navigate given the population of hobbes. Carry a long-range rifle and target the exploding barrels whenever possible.

TREASURE

🗝 CHESTS	🗝 SILVER KEY CHESTS	🗝 DIG SPOTS	🗝 DIVE SPOTS
5	0	10	1

COLLECTIBLES

🗝 SILVER KEYS	🗝 GOLD KEYS	🗝 GNOMES	📖 BOOKS	✿ AURORAN FLOWERS
3	0	2	0	0

JOBS: None

SHOPS: None

TREASURE OF THE LAND

SILVER KEYS

Follow the cart tracks down the hill from the monorail wreckage to the storage area. The silver key is behind the rack of barrels along the far wall.

Enter the Millfields Monorail Station to access the southeast corner of The Hole. Climb the stairs to the monorail platform and locate the key around the far side of it.

Use the Technician's Key to unlock the gate beyond the monorail wreckage and follow the upper path to the ledge above the arena. Battle the army of hobbes and claim the key.

GNOMES

This nasty fellow is hanging onto the lamppost near the wrecked monorail. Shoot him before crossing the wooden bridge.

Defeat the hobbes in the arena then face the entrance to the arena, look up and to the left to spot this gnome on the column near where you came in.

TO MISTPEAK VALLEY

TO MILLFIELDS

TECHNICIAN'S GATE

ARENA

TO MOURNINGWOOD

BEYOND THE TECHNICIAN'S GATE

Collect the Technician's Key from the chest at the end of the path beyond the bridge leading out of the Hobbe Arena (near the exit into Mourningwood) and return to the Mistpeak Monorail Station where you first enter The Hole. Descend in the elevator once again and continue past the monorail wreckage to the locked gate left of the rack of barrels. Climb the stairs and explore the upper section of the cave as it wraps around a previously unexplored area towards the arena. Listen to your dog's barking and locate the dig spots, chest, and silver key in this area. But be careful! The hobbes that live in this upper area are a bit tougher than the ones you may have faced earlier.

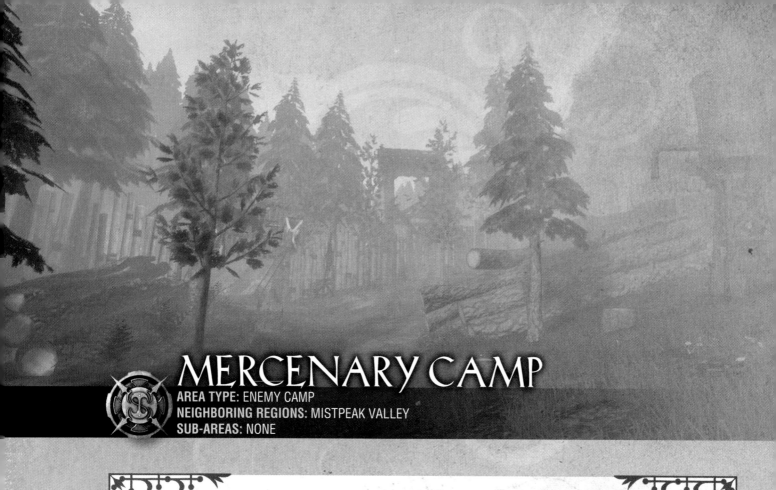

MERCENARY CAMP

AREA TYPE: ENEMY CAMP
NEIGHBORING REGIONS: MISTPEAK VALLEY
SUB-AREAS: NONE

REGION SYNOPSIS

The Mercenary Camp is a heavily fortified stronghold where the renegades that plague Mistpeak Valley live. It's located on the far shore of the lake, opposite the entrance to the Mistpeak Monorail Station. The renegades may be brutish thugs, but they knew what they were doing when they built their camp. There is only one route through the camp and it's lined with watchtowers, checkpoints, and multiple fortifications. Only a Hero could possibly make it through to the arena-like inner sanctum atop the hill! The one good thing about the mercenaries is that they are true to their word. Spare their leader's life and you'll be welcomed back to the camp anytime you wish, free of hassle.

TREASURE

CHESTS	SILVER KEY CHESTS	DIG SPOTS	DIVE SPOTS
6	0	9	0

COLLECTIBLES

SILVER KEYS	GOLD KEYS	GNOMES	BOOKS	AURORAN FLOWERS
1	0	1	0	0

JOBS: None

SHOPS: None

TREASURE OF THE LAND

JEWELRY

MISTPEAK VALLEY

SILVER KEYS

Under the watchtower at the top of the hill, near the wolf cages. This is the last watchtower you can ascend before reaching Saker's inner sanctum.

GNOMES

Return to the Mercenary Camp after initiating the **Gnomes are Evil!** quest and make your way to the inner fortified area. The gnome is atop the water tower where the path switchbacks to the left.

MILLFIELDS

AREA TYPE: COUNTRYSIDE
NEIGHBORING REGIONS: BOWERSTONE MARKET, DRIFTWOOD, SILVERPINES
SUB-AREAS: DANKWATER CAVERN, MILLFIELDS MINES, PEPPERPOT CAVE, REAVER'S MANOR

REGION SYNOPSIS

Millfields is the name given to the region known as Bower Lake decades ago. Though the hills are alive with history, time has erased much of the features that would have been recognizable to the former ruler. The lake is still present but the gypsies have been pushed out of the area to make room for picturesque country cottages and even an ornate mansion on the lake's northern shore. The hills to the south are home to a mining operation and farm fields. Despite the changes, Millfields is every bit the major crossroads that Bower Lake once was. Those traveling between Bowerstone Market, Driftwood, and Silverpines have no choice but to traverse this sprawling region. Millfields also has access points to a number of caves, including the Millfields Mines which can be created once you are in position to determine the fate of Bower Lake—would you dare drain the lake your parent swam in as a child?

TREASURE

🎁 CHESTS	🎁 SILVER KEY CHESTS	🦴 DIG SPOTS	💧 DIVE SPOTS
5	1	26*	4

* To maximize the usability of this map, extraneous callouts for level 1 and 2 dig spots have been removed. Only those dig spots requiring a Level 3 and above dog exploration rating are shown.

COLLECTIBLES

🗝 SILVER KEYS	🗝 GOLD KEYS	🧙 GNOMES	📖 BOOKS	❀ AURORAN FLOWERS
3	0	3	1	0

JOBS: None

SHOPS: None

TREASURE OF THE LAND

TO SILVERPINES

REAVER'S MANOR

TO DRIFTWOOD

DEMON DOOR

TO DANKWATER CAVERN

TO THE HOLE (MONO STATION)

TO PEPPERPOT CAVE

TO BOWERSTONE MARKET

SILVER KEY CHESTS

🗝 CHEST	⚷ SILVER KEYS	CONTENTS	LOCATION
1	20	Tee Killer Shooter	Beside the statue near the Demon Door.

SILVER KEYS

01

Ascend the path beyond the fence opposite Pepperpot Cave to reach the large factory atop the hill. The silver key is inside a small shack on the far side of the building.

02

Make your way past the mining factories and over the ridge towards the Bower Lake side of Millfields. Take the first path on the left and immediately turn left again to spot this silver key sitting out in the open.

03

Ascend the hill from the lake towards the mining area and venture cross-country to the left towards the entrance to Dankwater Cavern. Descend to the pond directly below the cave entrance and swim over to the silver key on the left. The key is directly below the statue with the telescope.

BOOKS

01

Accept the quest **Bored to Death** in Mourningwood and dig up the Normanomicon in Millfields. Defeat the hollow men that attack, then enter the crypt where the leader of the hollow men was to find *AdventureQuest: A Select Your Own Endeavour* book.

GNOMES

01

Enter Millfields from Bowerstone Market and continue past the mining operations and monorail station. Follow the path to the right beyond the entrance to Pepperpot Cave and venture off the path near the rocks on the right to find the gnome.

02

This gnome is high on the ruins near the bridge leading out to the island on Bower Lake. It's directly below the hill where the suspension bridge waits to be restored.

03

Swim across Bower Lake towards Reaver's Manor and climb out onto the dock. This third gnome is in the left-hand corner of the terraced garden, near the tree with the white bark.

DEMON DOOR

REWARD: 40 Guild Seals

The Demon Door in Millfields is what some may call a contrarian, particularly as it relates to what passes for style and beauty. The Demon Door has grown tired of seeing the stylish and fit parade past on their way to the lake. The people of Millfields strive far too hard to dress attractively and keep their bodies thin. The Demon Door craves to see someone with absolutely no care as to how they look. It wants to see someone put effort into looking as ugly and unfit as possible.

The Demon Door's request is actually comprised of two parts: dressing ugly and letting yourself gain a lot of weight. The first part is easy: simply swap out your outfit for pyjamas. The pyjamas are sure to fit the bill and are among the easiest to find. You can exacerbate your ugliness by coloring each piece of your outfit a different color. This is sure to earn the Demon Door's approval. The second part of the request can be a little trickier. The easiest way to pack on the pounds is to consume a number of fattening pies and pieces of meat. Depending on how long you wait to open the Demon Door, there is a chance that the majority of your cities' vendors don't survive during the Weight of the World portion of the story. Fortunately, you can always visit the pubs! Beer, wine, and spirits are all high in calories and help you pack on the pounds. Keep eating and drinking until your weight meter (visible on the Hero Status screen at the Sanctuary) reaches the far right-hand side of the meter. Return to the Demon Door to impress him with your ugliness and girth. Enter the Twitcher's Curtains area and open the chest within it to gain an extra 40 Guild Seals.

RECURRING QUESTS

CONVICT ON THE RUN

⊶ 1000 to 5000 Gold

⊶ +10 Morality

Talk to the guard near Reaver's Mansion to accept an **Escaped Convict** quest. These repeatable quests require you to track down a criminal on the loose somewhere in the area. Follow the glowing trail to the escapee and interact with him. Some run, others try to put up a fight, and others go quietly. Take him by the hand and drag the criminal back to the guard to complete the quest.

MINERS REQUIRED

⊶ 1000 to 6000 Gold

⊶ -10 Morality

This quest only appears if you decide to drain Bower Lake and open a quarry during the rulings phase. If so, return

to Millfields after battling the darkness and talk to the supervisor about the need for additional laborers. He's willing to pay you for your trouble if you locate someone who isn't already employed at the mine and drag him/her to the foreman for forced labor. The key to completing this quest is to pick out a person who isn't already working at the mine—ignore those with the title of crate carrier, miner, or factory worker. Your best bet is to find a nobleman and drag him to the supervisor. You'll know you got a good candidate if he resists being dragged; they're probably already working at the mine if they go willingly.

MILLFIELDS MINES

Millfields Mines is a sub-area of Millfields.

REGION SYNOPSIS

Millfields Mines is created through a ruling during the Weight of the World portion of the story. Those who decide to drain Bower Lake in order to create a quarry gain access to the underground mine. This area mainly consists of several wooden platforms and a section of solid ground. Creating the mine opens up the **Rescue the Miner's Brother** quest and gains you access to several chests and dig spots. The mine has two entrances, both of which can be accessed from the bottom of the quarry, where Bower Lake used to be. This is a completely optional area and those who decide to preserve Bower Lake will not miss out on any valuables items or rare collectibles.

JOBS: None

SHOPS: None

TREASURE

🗃 CHESTS	🗝 SILVER KEY CHESTS	⛏ DIG SPOTS	💧 DIVE SPOTS
2	0	3	0

COLLECTIBLES

🗝 SILVER KEYS	🗝 GOLD KEYS	🍄 GNOMES	📖 BOOKS	🌸 AURORAN FLOWERS
0	0	0	0	0

MISTPEAK VALLEY

AREA TYPE: WILDERNESS
BORDERING REGIONS: BRIGHTWALL VILLAGE, DWELLER CAMP, MERCENARY CAMP
SUB-AREAS: CHILLBREATH CAVERNS, THE HOLE, HUNTER'S LODGE

REGION SYNOPSIS

Mistpeak Valley is one of the largest regions in Albion, comprising both the highland mountains near the Dweller Camp and a lush, lowland valley containing endless trees and a large lake. The snow-covered mountains of Mistpeak are laced with wooden bridges leading from one peak to the next. There are numerous ruins–and monsters–in the mountains and mercenaries and hobbes in the valley. Though it can be tricky to navigate the mountains at first, thorough exploration brings considerable rewards in the form of rare collectibles and three different entrances to Chillbreath Caverns. Don't overlook the forested hillside above the monorail station!

TREASURE

🗝 CHESTS	🗝 SILVER KEY CHESTS	⛏ DIG SPOTS	💧 DIVE SPOTS
5	1	42*	2

*To maximize the usability of this map, extraneous callouts for Level 1 and 2 dig spots have been removed. Only those dig spots requiring a Level 3 and above dog exploration rating are shown.

COLLECTIBLES

🔑 SILVER KEYS	🔑 GOLD KEYS	🧙 GNOMES	📖 BOOKS	❀ AURORAN FLOWERS
2	1	3	1	0

JOBS: None

SHOPS: None

TREASURE OF THE LAND

* The letters A, B, C, and D on the map correspond with the letters on the Chillbreath Caverns map.

SILVER KEY CHESTS

CHEST	SILVER KEYS	CONTENTS	LOCATION
1	5	55 Guild Seals and Summon Creatures potion	Atop the mountain near Dweller Camp. Ascend the walkway and spiral up the snowy path.

SILVER KEYS

There is a silver key behind the piles of logs near the clear-cut swath of forest on the banks of the lake. This area is downhill from the Demon Door, not far from the Mercenary Camp.

Face the Mistpeak Monorail Station entrance and head up the hill directly to the right. There is a faint trail here that soon fades away. Continue ascending between the rocks and trees to the ridge.

BOOKS

Enter the ticket booth outside the Mistpeak Monorail Station to find *How to be a Crack Shot* on the counter near the cash register.

GNOMES

This gnome is atop the frozen waterfall near the Demon Door. This small frozen valley is the farthest to the right when leaving the lake and heading up into the mountains.

This particular gnome is directly to the right of silver key #2. Climb the hill to the right of the Mistpeak Monorail Station entrance all the way to the top to find it.

Head to the section of ruins in the lower mountains where the table, crates, and shovels are and look over the edge of the cliff. The gnome is on the rocks to the right.

GOLDEN RICHES

GOLD KEY

Mistpeak Valley contains a gold key on a ledge not far from the Demon Door, but it cannot be accessed without first making a lengthy trek through Chillbreath Caverns. Enter Chillbreath Caverns (B) via the entrance uphill from the Mistpeak Monorail Station and proceed to the frozen lake inside the cave. Head up the slope to the right of the lake and continue in a straight path, bypassing the rocky land bridge on the left. Fight your way past the mercenaries and hobbes that dwell within the cave to the exit far in the distance. You'll exit the cave near some ruins high on the hillside of Mistpeak Valley, steps away from the gold key.

DEMON DOOR

REWARD: Legendary Weapon

The Demon Door in Mistpeak Valley is located in an icy clearing just uphill from the stacks of felled trees. This particular Demon Door longs to see the physical expression of affection between friends. Invite a friend to join your game, either via Xbox Live, or as a local co-op partner and take a minute to make sure he/she has the Lovers Expression Pack from the Road to Rule. The chest only costs 5 Guild Seals and can be acquired quickly by a new henchman if necessary. Once both members have the necessary expression pack, head to the Demon Door and listen to its request. The Demon Door wants to see you perform the Kiss, Hug, and Tickle expressions. The order doesn't matter, but you must perform them successfully which means holding the A button until the meter fills to the 12 o'clock position and the controller vibrates. Perform each of the expressions to unlock the door to Demon Door Retirement Home.

Demon Door Retirement Home is exactly what it sounds like; a place where Demon Doors go to live out their days in tranquility. Though the Demon Doors in this area are quite funny to listen to, the main allure of the place is the chest containing a **Legendary Weapon**.

RECURRING QUESTS

LUMBERJACKS WANTED!

✦ 1000 to 6000 Gold ✦ -10 Morality

This quest only appears if you decide to exploit Mistpeak Valley and log the forests for use in the war against the darkness. If so, return to the shores of the lake in Mistpeak Valley after battling the darkness and talk to the supervisor about the need for additional laborers. He's willing to pay you for your trouble if you locate someone who isn't already employed as a lumberjack and drag him/her to the foreman for forced labor. There aren't a lot of people in Mistpeak Valley, and many of them are already working at the lumber camp (sometimes listed as 'factory worker'), so you may need to search far and wide to find someone. The key to completing this quest is to pick out a person who isn't already working as a lumberjack. Follow the path around the lake towards the Mercenary Camp for your best chance of finding someone. There aren't many, but you may find a housewife who has gone out for a walk—drag her to the factory supervisor to put her to work!

LCE BONUS: HUNTER'S LODGE

Those who purchased the Limited Collector's Edition of the game receive a code that can be entered to unlock this special area located in the far northern corner of Mistpeak Valley. This small property contains two dig spots and a chest outside and a chest inside the house that contains the men's and women's Auroran outfits along with a Boxer Dog potion. Give the dog the potion while in the Sanctuary to change his breed to a boxer.

MOURNINGWOOD

AREA TYPE: WILDERNESS
NEIGHBORING REGIONS: BOWERSTONE INDUSTRIAL, SUNSET HOUSE
SUB-AREAS: DARK SANCTUM, THE OSSUARY

REGION SYNOPSIS

Mourningwood is a sprawling marshland that exists as much to house the dead as it does to serve as a receptacle for Bowerstone's waste. Your first introduction to Mourningwood comes after making a lengthy trek through The Hole. Mourningwood isn't without human inhabitants of the living variety though. Mourningwood Fort is home to a small garrison of Albion soldiers and the distant reaches of the swamp are home to a small band of eco warriors. The rest of Mourningwood is the domain of the hollow men, particularly the maze-like network of trenches dug into the hillside east of the cemetery. Mourningwood is a place where bad deeds often go rewarded—only those who don't mind killing the occasional innocent gain access to the Dark Sanctum.

TREASURE

🧰 CHESTS	🧰 SILVER KEY CHESTS	👆 DIG SPOTS	💧 DIVE SPOTS
8	1	12	0

COLLECTIBLES

🗝 SILVER KEYS	🗝 GOLD KEYS	🔖 GNOMES	📖 BOOKS	❀ AURORAN FLOWERS
2	0	2	2	0

JOBS: Blacksmith

SHOPS: Tattooist, Food and Potions,

TREASURE OF THE LAND

MOURNINGWOOD FORT

TO DARK SANCTUM

TO THE HOLE

DEMON DOOR

TO OSSUARY

TO SUNSET HOUSE

TO BOWERSTONE INDUSTRIAL

SILVER KEY CHESTS

🗝 CHEST	🔑 SILVER KEYS	CONTENTS	LOCATION
1	10	Legendary Weapon	On a ledge above the path spiraling down under the bridge on the way to Mourningwood Fort.

SILVER KEYS

The World Map Table lists four silver keys for Mourningwood. Two are located in Mourningwood proper, and the other two are located in The Ossuary.

GNOMES

The map table lists three gnomes for Mourningwood, but one of them is located at The Ossuary.

Detonate the barrels near the wooden barricade sealing off the key inside this bunker. Either shoot the barrels with your gun or fire a mortar close enough to rupture the barrels from splash damage.

Follow the western edge of Mourningwood northward past the chest near the tree to the ruined wall. The silver key is within one of the arches on this wall.

Follow the main path away from Mourningwood Fort to where the paths come together to the south. The gnome is on the back of a semi-circular ruin atop a small hill between the paths. If you reach the cemetery you went too far.

This gnome is located on the rocks between the two large sewer tunnels in the northwest corner of Mourningwood. Approach the left-hand tunnel then look to the rocks on the right to spot it.

BOOKS

Fight your way to the hippie camp and approach the house nearest the storage platform set outside the ring of homes. *The Mibbs-Spagno Theory of Gluttony* is atop a crate next to the house nearest that platform.

RARE BOOK: THE PANGS OF SUNSET

Samuel requests that you find *The Pangs of Sunset* after you return 15 of the discoverable books scattered across the landscape. This book is located in a grave in Mourningwood and is among the most straightforward to recover. Equip the Bonesmasher in preparation for the hordes of hollow men that patrol the cemetery and return to the area. Fight your way past the Mourningwood Fort and up the hill straight ahead to the large cemetery. Slay the hollow men that appear by focusing on the larger one with the two swords—he'll continue to summon lesser hollow men for as long as he's standing.

Follow the glowing trail to the statue in the center of the cemetery then look to the left. Your dog leads you to the grave site you seek. It's just to the right of the large tree. Return the book to Samuel.

DEMON DOOR

REWARD: Military Costume and Summon Creatures potion

The Demon Door in Mourningwood is located slightly southeast of the eco warrior village. This particular Demon Door craves to see a fully upgraded weapon, and not one of those Hero weapons your father left you, but a **Legendary Weapon**. Consult the "Weapons of Yore" chapter for a breakdown of each weapon's upgrade requirements and see which of them most closely matches your style of play then set to meeting all three requirements to fully upgrade it. Doing so unlocks the **My Weapon's Better Than Yours** Achievement.

Once you have that done, make your way to the end of the Road to Rule and purchase the Melee or Ranged Level 5 upgrade. This upgrade costs 100 Guild Seals (assuming you've already purchased Level 4) so save up for it. Now you are ready to show off your weapon! Return to the Demon Door and draw the weapon to impress him.

The Demon Door opens to an area named Planet One. Step through the portal to emerge on a distant lunar landscape. Follow the path up the hill to the chest containing the Military Costume and Summon Creatures potion. The chest is not the only thing on this otherwise barren landscape; there is also a mysterious apparatus. Pull the lever in front of it to change the color of the planet you stand upon. We're quite fond of the green, but perhaps you prefer red? Either way, this is purely cosmetic and cannot be seen back in Albion. Enjoy.

MORTAR AND MOURNING

Purchase the Mourningwood Fort for approximately 45,000 gold. This is a special property that can't be rented out or sold, so only do this if you've already purchased a good number of shops and are flush with cash. Once the Mourningwood Fort is in your possession, head up onto the rampart and inspect the mortar to trigger the **Mortar and Mourning** mini-game.

Jammy has come back from the dead to help you bombard the hollow men once again! You have 200 seconds to rack up as many points as you can with the mortar. Each hollow man is worth 10 points and you need to score 2000 points to win the top prize—a **Legendary Weapon!** Focus your attention on large groups of hollow men, preferably while they are still spawning to ensure a direct hit before they split up. That being said, you can't score points when you're not firing and it only takes three seconds to ready another shot. Pan the area back and forth in sweeping semi-circular motions and keep firing! It's better to fire on a single hollow man than to pass over it and fire no shot at all. This plays exactly like the scene during "The Hollow Legion" part of the story. You are free to play the mini-game as many times as you'd like. After all, it's your fort!

MORTAR AND MOURNING PRIZE INFO

SCORE	TITLE	PRIZE
500	Private	Goblet (random item)
1000	Sergeant	Box of Fish (random item)
1500	Lieutenant	Amethyst (random item)
2000	General	Souldrinker

THE OSSUARY

The Ossuary is a sub-area of Mourningwood.

REGION SYNOPSIS

The Ossuary is accessed through a crypt in Mourningwood, during the **Gone But Not Forgotten** quest. You can return to this dreadful place at anytime once that quest has been completed. The Ossuary isn't a large location, but it is crawling with hollow men and can be terrifying to those who arrive unprepared for battle. This underground extension of the Mourningwood cemetery contains several collectibles, along with one of the extremely rare golden doors. Don't miss out visiting this area.

TREASURE

CHESTS	SILVER KEY CHESTS	DIG SPOTS	DIVE SPOTS
4	0	2	0

COLLECTIBLES

SILVER KEYS	GOLD KEYS	GNOMES	BOOKS	AURORAN FLOWERS
2	0	1	1	0

JOBS: None

SHOPS: None

TREASURE OF THE LAND

GOLD DOOR

TO MOURNINGWOOD

SILVER KEYS

In the open crypt near the entrance to the area from Mourningwood. It's the fourth crypt from the right.

Climb the stairs of the tomb nearest the entrance from Mourningwood and turn left at the first landing (before the golden door). Leap off the ledge here to land on an otherwise unreachable level containing a silver key.

GNOMES

Circle around the perimeter to the left of the large central tree to reach the row of five crypts near the wooden chest. The gnome is behind the short wall between the third and fourth crypts.

BOOKS

Famous Kings of History: Old King Oswald is resting atop the stone railing on the balcony, just beyond the golden door.

GOLDEN RICHES

GOLDEN DOOR
REWARD: Legendary Weapon

Beyond the golden door in the Ossuary lies a small room strewn with wooden coffins and little else. Ascend the steps on the right to the lone sarcophagus in the room and push back the lid to discover another **Legendary Weapon**.

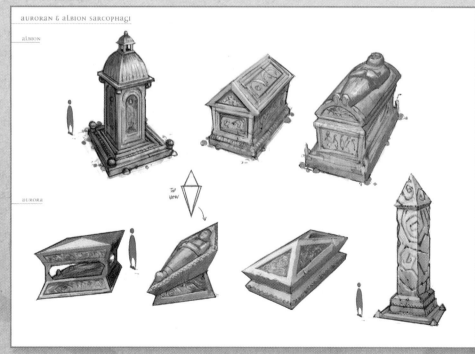

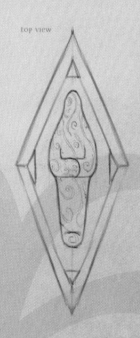

PEPPERPOT CAVE

Pepperpot Cave is a sub-area of Millfields.

REGION SYNOPSIS

Millfields is loaded with small sub-areas and Pepperpot Cave is one of the first, and most easily accessible, ones you can visit. This narrow, serpentine cave near the mining and farming portion of Millfields is home to a small group of hobbes and contains a silver key. You don't need to complete any quests to access it or ever return to it later, except to perhaps locate a higher level dig spot. Pepperpot Cave is just a small cave that offers a change of scenery—and enemy—from the greater Millfields area.

TREASURE

CHESTS	SILVER KEY CHESTS	DIG SPOTS	DIVE SPOTS
1	0	2	0

COLLECTIBLES

SILVER KEYS	GOLD KEYS	GNOMES	BOOKS	AURORAN FLOWERS
1	0	0	0	0

JOBS: None

SHOPS: None

TREASURE OF THE LAND

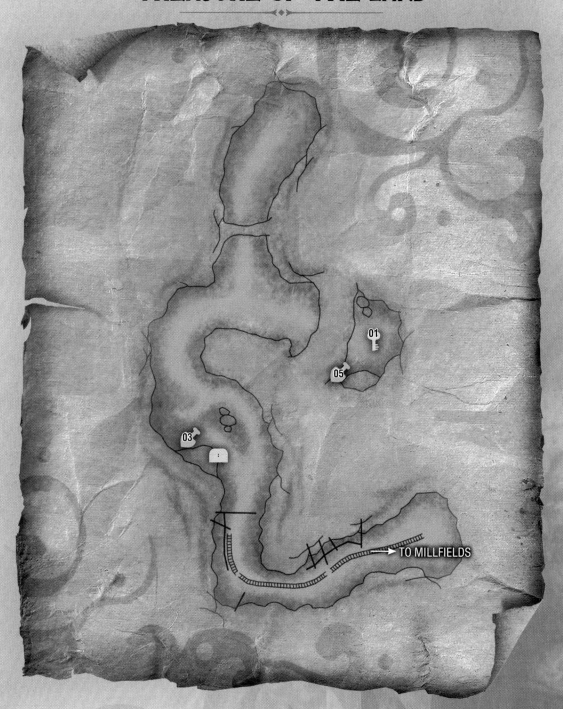

TO MILLFIELDS

SILVER KEYS

Fight past the hobbes to the far end of the cave and swim across the small pool of water to find the silver key.

REAVER'S MANOR

Reaver's Manor is a sub-area of Millfields.

REGION SYNOPSIS

The hated leader of Bowerstone Industrial lives in a stylish mansion on the shore of Bower Lake in Millfields. You first enter this house during the Bowerstone Resistance portion of the story, but are restricted to certain areas. Return later to explore the mansion more fully. Reaver's bedroom is on the second floor—don't miss the secret corridor beyond the bookcase to find a second, top-secret bedroom.

TREASURE

🎁 CHESTS	🎁 SILVER KEY CHESTS	⛏ DIG SPOTS	💧 DIVE SPOTS
7	0	0	0

COLLECTIBLES

🔑 SILVER KEYS	🔑 GOLD KEYS	🧙 GNOMES	📖 BOOKS	🌸 AURORAN FLOWERS
1	0	0	1	0

JOBS: None

SHOPS: None

TREASURE OF THE LAND

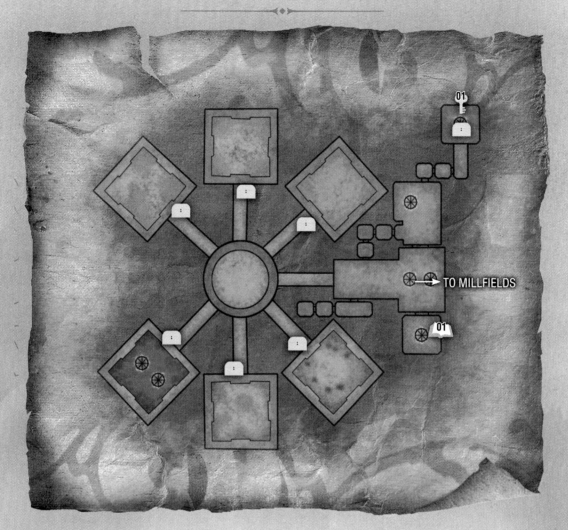

SILVER KEYS

Enter the bedroom to the right of the second floor dining room and inspect the bookshelf to reveal the secret hallway. Follow this to Reaver's private bedroom. The silver key is behind his bed.

BOOKS

Enter Reaver's Manor during the **Reaver's Unmentionables** quest (or by purchasing it) and enter the room to the left of the stairs. *Dangerous Things: Lightning* is on the table near the windows.

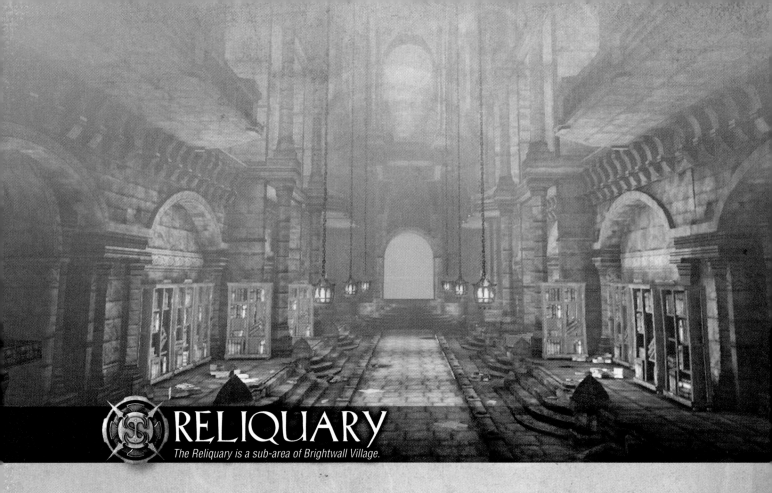

RELIQUARY

The Reliquary is a sub-area of Brightwall Village.

REGION SYNOPSIS

The Reliquary is a haunted and crumbling depository of ancient tomes located deep underground beneath Brightwall Academy. You access the Reliquary during your first Hero Test and are free to return whenever you desire after that point. The Reliquary is filled with hollow men and represents one of the best places to go when looking to earn Guild Seals through combat. The area is much larger than it first seems thanks to a large multi-level section of library in the southwest corner that can only be explored upon accepting several unique quests. Keep your eyes peeled for flit switches and seemingly out-of-place levers, as there are a number of secrets within these hallowed halls.

TREASURE

🧰 CHESTS	🗝 SILVER KEY CHESTS	✋ DIG SPOTS	💧 DIVE SPOTS
10	1	7	1

COLLECTIBLES

🗝 SILVER KEYS	🗝 GOLD KEYS	🧙 GNOMES	📖 BOOKS	❀ AURORAN FLOWERS
2	0	2	3	0

JOBS: None

SHOPS: None

TREASURE OF THE LAND

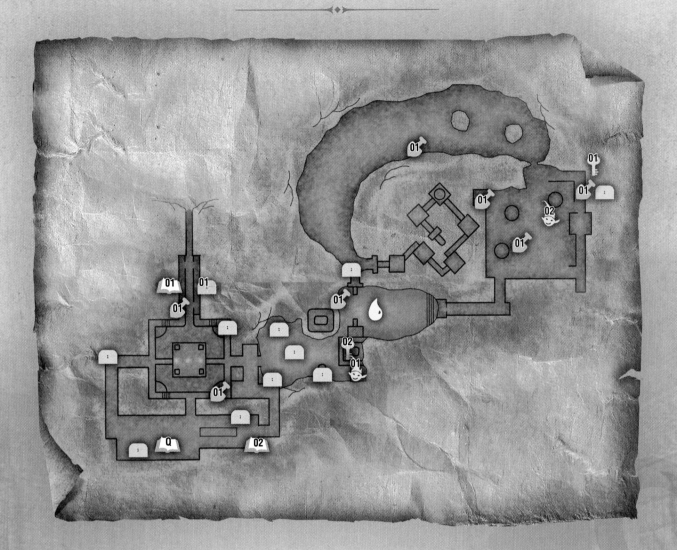

SILVER KEY CHESTS

🔒 CHEST	🔑 SILVER KEYS	CONTENTS	LOCATION
1	1	Dog Training Combat 2 book	In the hallway to the left of the main entrance from the Academy.

SILVER KEYS

These two silver keys are included within the map table's tally for Brightwall Village.

Use the Fireball spell to light the six cauldrons near the locked door to find this silver key. This is in the area beyond the circular vault-like door you must open with a magic spell.

Return to the room with the grid of floating platforms and chests and throw the lever in the nearby temple (you need to make a lengthy loop through the cavern to reach it). This makes a staircase rise into position near the rocky ledge with the chest on it. Ascend the stairs to a small tomb containing this silver key and a sarcophagus.

GNOMES

Cross the grid of floating platforms to the stairs leading down to the temple on the far side of the area. The gnome is behind a column on the right-hand side.

Dive off the ledge into the water and follow the path up to the room with the large cylindrical columns. The gnome is on a wall to the right of the vault near the six braziers.

BOOKS

Descend the steps from within Brightwall Academy to enter the Reliquary and immediately turn to the right. *How to be a Master Swordsman* is on a stand on the right.

Complete the **An Ancient Key** quest to reach a locked library within the Reliquary. *Famous Killers: Carl Tendency* is on a stand in the corner of the room.

RARE BOOK: BOOK OF DOOM

This is the final book in the **Pen is Mightier Than The...** quest. You must find and return all 29 other books before Samuel gives you the key needed to access the part of the Reliquary containing this book, which means also having completed **The Ancient Key** quest. Accept the quest—and key—and descend into the Reliquary. Use the key to unlock the first locked door on the right, just down the stairs wrapping around the cave. Of course, you must fight through throngs of hollow men to reach it!

Slash your way through the hollow men in the corridor beyond the locked door and follow the hallway to the lowermost floor in the collapsed portion of the Reliquary. Ascend the stairs past the rubble to the first landing. The book you seek is on the pedestal to the right.

GOLDEN RICHES

GOLDEN DOOR

REWARD: Male and Female Highwayman Costumes

The Reliquary contains a golden door that can be quite hard to spot and impossible to reach if you haven't been completing each of the available side-quests. Accept **The Ancient Key** quest (you must first complete the **Special Delivery** quest) and use the Key of Forbidden Knowledge to lead Saul to the locked library within the Reliquary. Once there, shoot the flit switch on the wall three times to unlock the door in the center of the room.

Ascend the stairs to a balcony high above the room with the floating platforms and open the door on the left to find a second flit switch. This one requires melee strikes to move it. Strike the flit switch then vault down to the lower level and strike it again. Defeat the large squad of hollow men that appears in order to trigger the arrival of the first in a lengthy series of stairs and floating platforms. Descend the spiraling series of platforms to the golden door at the base of the central tower. Use a gold key to access the Cullis Gate inside and transfer to an area known as The Prism.

THE PRISM

The Prism contains four short platforms flanking a lengthy central one. Each landing has a chest containing a different piece of the male and female Highway Man costume—the only way to collect the full outfit and exit The Prism is to visit all five areas. Each platform contains one or two Cullis Gates that you must use to warp around the area, from platform to platform. Hollow men attack in each area, so be ready with the Bonesmasher or magic attacks as soon as you appear.

Consult the lettered callouts on the accompanying map to master the route through The Prism. You begin on the northeast corner. Take the lone Cullis Gate on platform A to reach platform B. Platform B has two Cullis Gates. Face the edge of the balcony and take the left Cullis Gate to reach platform C. Take the left-hand Cullis Gate on platform C to return to B. Now take the right-hand Cullis Gate on B to visit platform D. Collect the item from the chest then use the left-hand Cullis Gate to make your way to platform E. The Cullis Gate on platform E takes you back to Gate A and the exit.

SANDFALL PALACE

Sandfall Palace is a sub-area of Shifting Sands.

REGION SYNOPSIS

Sandfall Palace is an ancient temple located at the end of a narrow canyon in the corner of Shifting Sands nearest the City of Aurora. This tranquil palace is an oasis in the desert, complete with watery lagoons, palm trees, and marauding packs of sand furies! Sandfall Palace is the rumored home of a legendary diamond that you'll need to hunt during the "Weight of the World" portion of the story, but it's got much more. Many of the collectibles you seek can be found here as well. Explore the palace, take a swim, and keep your eyes peeled for the beautiful Auroran Flowers, so highly prized by the Auroran people.

TREASURE

🗝 CHESTS	🗝 SILVER KEY CHESTS	⛏ DIG SPOTS	🜄 DIVE SPOTS
4	0	5	2

COLLECTIBLES

🗝 SILVER KEYS	🗝 GOLD KEYS	🧙 GNOMES	📖 BOOKS	❀ AURORAN FLOWERS
2	0	1	1	5

JOBS: None

SHOPS: None

TREASURE OF THE LAND

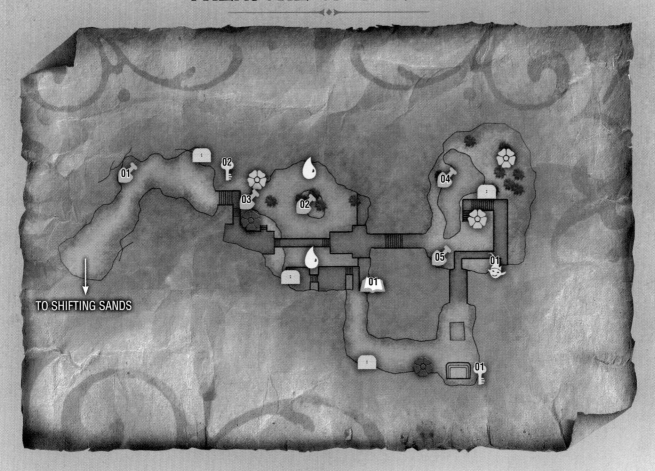

TO SHIFTING SANDS

SILVER KEYS

The silver key is in the far corner of the room containing the diamond. It's directly left of the diamond.

Locate the locked door on the left, before reaching the first oasis. Shoot the flit switch above the door three times to open the door. The silver key is on a ledge just beyond this door.

GNOMES

The gnome is high on the wall in the far right-hand corner of the second large oasis room. You can shoot it from underneath the walkway.

BOOKS

Cross the bridge over the first section of water to the door on the far side of the room and descend the stairs on the right. *Dangerous Things: Ladders* is on the railing near the trees.

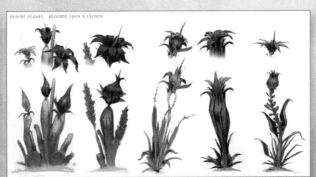

SEWERS

The Sewers are a sub-area of Bowerstone Industrial.

REGION SYNOPSIS

The Sewers beneath Bowerstone Industrial are not to be confused with the tunnels that connect Mourningwood and the docks. The Sewers are far more habitable than that! The Bowerstone Resistance makes their home in the Sewers, accessed via a door down the stairs outside the pub. Page and her crew have built quite a home within this section of the Sewers and have even eliminate all signs of monsters or other nasty creatures. The other half of the Sewers is not quite as sanitized. Accept the **One Ring to Find** quest to gain access to another section where hobbes and mercenaries roam free. This part of the Sewers is much more dangerous, but it also contains some of the collectibles you'll likely be hunting.

TREASURE

CHESTS	SILVER KEY CHESTS	DIG SPOTS	DIVE SPOTS
2	0	4	0

COLLECTIBLES

SILVER KEYS	GOLD KEYS	GNOMES	BOOKS	AURORAN FLOWERS
1	0	1	0	0

JOBS: None

SHOPS: None

TREASURE OF THE LAND

TO BOWERSTONE INDUSTRIAL

RESISTANCE HEADQUARTERS

TO BOWERSTONE INDUSTRIAL

TO BOWERSTONE INDUSTRIAL

SILVER KEYS

Enter the Sewers through the door beneath the crane in the far corner of Bowerstone Industrial (used during the **One Ring to Find** quest) and turn right at the first junction. The silver key is around the corner, near the metal bars. This is the key you could see but not reach when heading to Bowerstone Resistance headquarters.

GNOMES

Enter the Sewers via the door under the crane (used during the **One Ring to Find** quest) and turn left at the first junction. Continue straight ahead through the distant crack in the wall to a room with light shining down through a ceiling grate. The gnome is stuck in the grate.

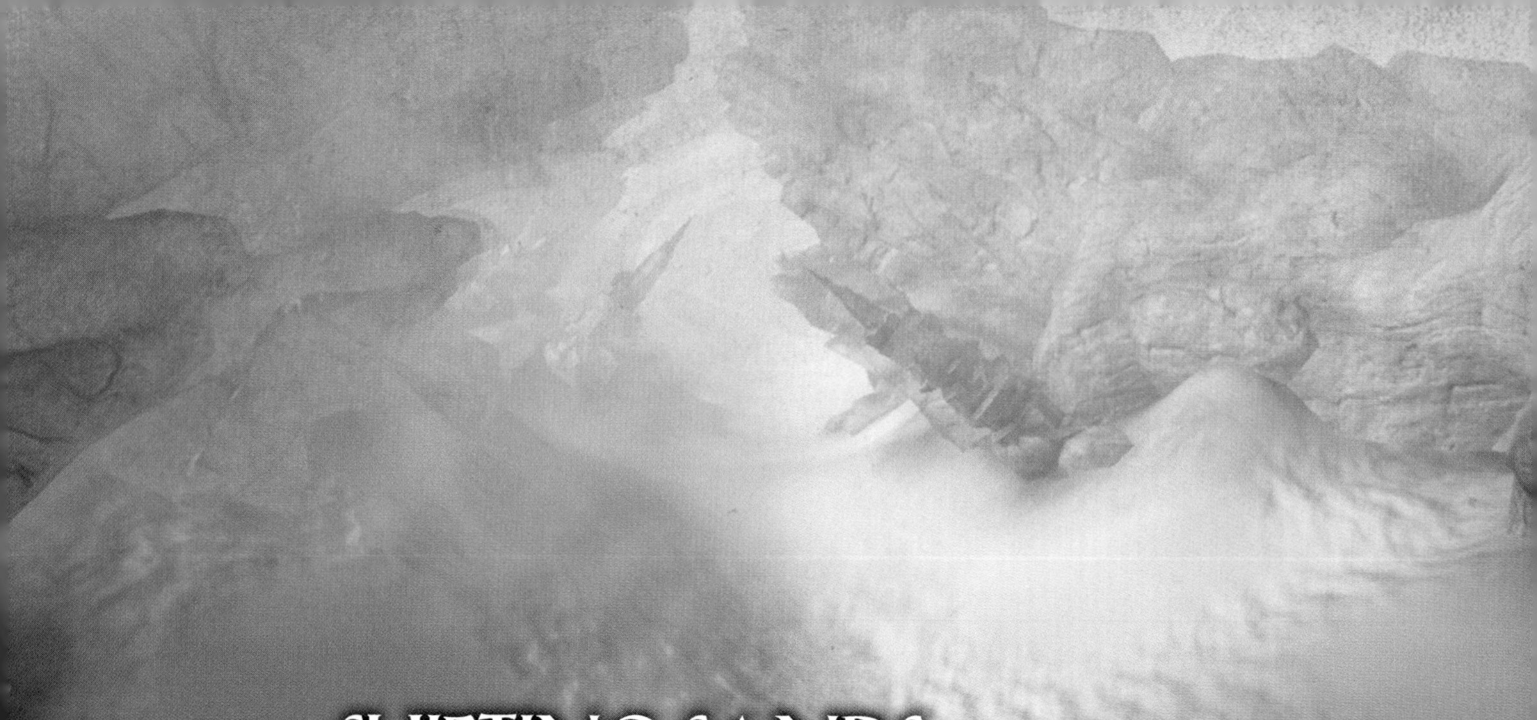

SHIFTING SANDS

AREA TYPE: WILDERNESS
NEIGHBORING REGIONS: CITY OF AURORA, VEILED PATH
SUB-AREAS: CROSSROADS OF PASSING, SANDFALL PALACE

REGION SYNOPSIS

Shifting Sands is an expansive desert, home to violent sand furies and creatures of the darkness. It stretches from Shadelight in the north all the way to the City of Aurora in the south. Navigating the giant sand dunes isn't as disorienting as it could be thanks to a solitary stone arch located roughly in the center of the area. Aim for this arch when heading south towards the City of Aurora; the arch serves as gateway to the canyons where The Veiled Path, Sandfall Palace, and the City of Aurora are located. Scouring the desert for items can be difficult given the terrain. Try crossing back and forth along an imaginary grid so you don't miss anything.

TREASURE

📦 CHESTS	📦 SILVER KEY CHESTS	⛏ DIG SPOTS	💧 DIVE SPOTS
1	1	8	0

COLLECTIBLES

🗝 SILVER KEYS	🗝 GOLD KEYS	🧙 GNOMES	📖 BOOKS	🌸 AURORAN FLOWERS
3	1	3	1	7

JOBS: None

SHOPS: None

TREASURE OF THE LAND

TO CROSSROADS OF PASSING

FROM SHADELIGHT

03

03

Q

01

04

02

01   01

TO VEILED PATH

03

04

01

05

01

01   01

02

TO CITY OF AURORA

TO SANDFALL PALACE

BUILD A SETTLEMENT

Visit Shifting Sands if you elect to construct the security outpost as Ruler of Albion. A settlement has been constructed near the large stone arch in the center of Shifting Sands. You won't find any rare collectibles, but the fort does contain multiple chests that may yield some valuable items to bring to a pawnbroker.

SILVER KEY CHESTS

🗝 CHEST	⚷ SILVER KEYS	CONTENTS	LOCATION
1	10	50,000 Gold	On the lookout beneath the large stone arch.

SILVER KEYS

Approach the large stone arch from the Aurora end of Shifting Sands and look for a path leading up the dunes to the right. The silver key is up this path, before the arch.

Head under the large stone arch in the direction of Shadelight and immediately turn to the left. Follow the rocks over the dunes to the key.

This silver key is under the large slab of rock sticking out of the sand in front of the exit from Shadelight. Cross the center of the dunes to reach it.

GNOMES

Exit the City of Aurora out onto the stairs in Shifting Sands and look to the column down the stairs, on the left. The gnome is on the column, near the top.

Enter the narrow canyon leading to Sandfall Palace and keep your eyes on the left-hand wall. The gnome is on the rocks on that side, just before the entrance to the cave.

Leave Aurora and head through the narrow passage leading to the large stone arch. The gnome is high on an overhanging rock to the left.

BOOKS

RARE BOOK: REAVER ON REAVER

Accept Samuel's request to find this special book after returning 20 or more discoverable books. Use the World Map Table in the Sanctuary to travel directly to Shifting Sands. This places you on the steps leading down into the desert outside the walls of Aurora. Head north through the canyon leading to the large stone arch and continue into the expansive desert beyond. Battle past the sand furies and other creatures to a depression in the dunes near the edge of the desert on the right. Your dog guides you to a spot in the sand where you can dig up the valuable book. You should notice a shovel and crate in the area. Return the book to Samuel to collect another 10 Guild Seals.

GOLDEN RICHES

GOLD KEY

Return to the City of Aurora after defeating the darkness on your anniversary as Ruler of Albion. Locate the man near the tattooist and purchase the **Ancient Key** for 4,000 gold. This key unlocks a door in the far northwest corner of the Shifting Sands area. Cross the desert towards Shadelight and veer to the left to discover a narrow staircase behind the ruins in the corner of the desert. Unlock the door with the purchased key to enter the area.

CROSSROADS OF PASSING

The Crossroads of Passing consists of a large room with a series of floating panels that rise up from the abyss when the correct triangular switch is stepped on. Stepping on the incorrect switch triggers the arrival of numerous enemies, and sometimes both a platform and enemies! Use Force Push to knock the enemies off the platforms and make your way to the alcove on the left. Stand on the floor plate to light the two cauldrons and make a set of stairs rise into position.

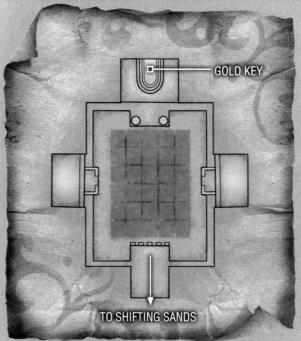

GOLD KEY

TO SHIFTING SANDS

Double-back the way you came and battle your way to the alcove on the right side of the room. Step on the floor plate there to light the second set of cauldrons and gain access to the door on the far side of the room. The door opens as you get close. Enter the small vault beyond it to collect what is likely to be the final gold key you need.

SILVERPINES

AREA TYPE: COUNTRYSIDE
NEIGHBORING REGIONS: MILLFIELDS
SUB-AREAS: NONE

REGION SYNOPSIS

Silverpines is arguably the most dangerous place in Albion, due to the packs of balverines that patrol these haunted woods. The only way into the area is via a trail from Millfields. Silverpines isn't without human residents; you'll find a small settlement to the south and a lone carpenter living in the northwest corner. However, the remainder of the region is crawling with monsters and can be quite dangerous if you're not prepared. The Silverpines area is also home to an elaborate quest exclusive to those who purchase the Limited Collector's Edition of the game.

TREASURE

🗝 CHESTS	🗝 SILVER KEY CHESTS	⛏ DIG SPOTS	💧 DIVE SPOTS
3	0	9	0

COLLECTIBLES

🗝 SILVER KEYS	🗝 GOLD KEYS	🧙 GNOMES	📖 BOOKS	✿ AURORAN FLOWERS
2	0	2	1	0

JOBS: None

SHOPS: General Goods

TREASURE OF THE LAND

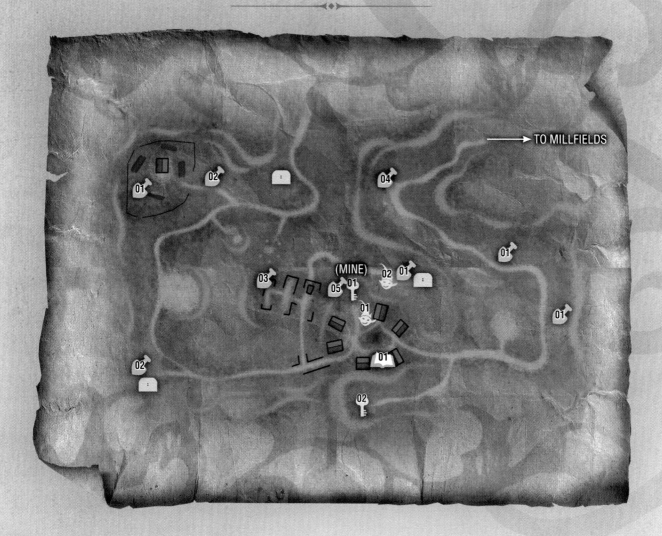

→ TO MILLFIELDS

SILVER KEYS

Follow the path southward to the small settlement and enter the Silverpines Mine, a small cave considered part of the general Silverpines area. The key is at the rear of the cave.

Proceed down the main path towards the settlement in the center of the forest. Turn left just before the settlement and follow this side-trail up the hill to the silver key.

GNOMES

The gnome is atop the wooden supports outside the Silverpines Mine, in the small settlement at the south edge of Silverpines.

Climb the hill to the cemetery above the settlement and locate the trail behind the crypt. This path wraps around to the right, to a wooden tower above the mine. There is a gnome on this structure.

BOOKS

Follow the path to the settlement in the center of the forest and walk around the first cabin on the left. *The Very Unsafe Book for Boys, Vol. 3: Boxing* is on the crates beside the house.

WOLF'S BANE LCE QUEST

REWARD: Legendary Weapon

The goal of this quest is to assemble a wolf skeleton to gain access to the large tomb near the carpenter's house. Use the key you receive with the code included in the exclusive Limited Collector's Edition of the game to unlock the door of the crypt uphill from the settlement. Open the sarcophagus to retrieve the first piece of the wolf skeleton. Head up the stairs in the cemetery and locate the altar to the right. Place the first piece of the skeleton—the skull—on the altar. Now you need to find the other three pieces. Head to the ruins near the lake and enter the cave (only accessible during twilight). Open the chest to find the wolf torso, return it to the altar, then proceed to the third location: the lake. Swim out towards the ghost that appears at the dive spot. Dive down to retrieve the third piece of the wolf skeleton. Place the third piece of the skeleton on the altar and quickly sprint to the dig spot at the nearby ruins. The dig spot has the final piece of the skeleton.

Follow the ghost wolf that appears once the skeleton is complete. It will lead you to the locked door to the tomb near the carpenter's house. Enter the tomb and collect the **Legendary Weapon** from the sarcophagus. Watch out! Ghost soldiers, along with their leader, ambush you as soon as you open the lid to the sarcophagus. Spring your own ambush on them and turn the tables before grabbing your reward.

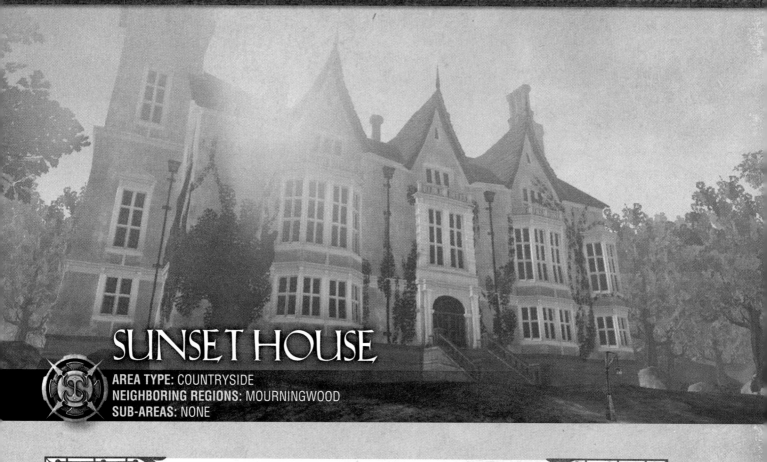

SUNSET HOUSE

AREA TYPE: COUNTRYSIDE
NEIGHBORING REGIONS: MOURNINGWOOD
SUB-AREAS: NONE

REGION SYNOPSIS

Sunset House is arguably one of the most confounding areas in all of Albion. At first glance, it is little more than a dilapidated mansion set on a large parcel of land under the control of monsters. It seems to contain a Demon Door and a golden door, but little else. In fact, Sunset House is home to several secrets. Secrets that test your fighting ability as well as your ability to solve puzzles. Of course, you'll have to visit at night if you're to have any hope of gaining access to the area's namesake house. Read all about the curse of Sunset House on the following pages.

TREASURE

🧰 CHESTS	🗝 SILVER KEY CHESTS	⛏ DIG SPOTS	💧 DIVE SPOTS
5	0	0	0

COLLECTIBLES

🗝 SILVER KEYS	🗝 GOLD KEYS	🧙 GNOMES	📖 BOOKS	❀ AURORAN FLOWERS
2	0	1	1	0

JOBS: None

SHOPS: None

TREASURE OF THE LAND

X4 (IN HOUSE)

01

01

GOLD DOOR

01

DEMON DOOR

02

TO MOURNINGWOOD

SILVER KEYS

Head up the path to the large clearing in Sunset House and follow the perimeter in a counter-clockwise direction halfway up the hill to the mansion. The silver key is amongst the rocks and trees on the right.

This silver key is amongst the rocks to the left of the Demon Door. Look for the glow of the key emanating from the boulders.

GNOMES

This gnome sits atop the rocks to the right of the Sunset House mansion. It appears during both day and night.

BOOKS

Approach the cupola with the statues and look to the park bench near the hedges behind it. *The Extraordinary Homunculus of Baron Von Orfen* is sitting on this bench.

GOLDEN RICHES

GOLDEN DOOR

REWARD: Legendary Weapon

Enter Sunset House from Mourningwood and proceed down the path to the large clearing. Turn immediately to the right and hug the perimeter while approaching the rocks and trees. Proceed along the path between the rocks to a golden door. Unlock the golden door with a single gold key to locate a chest containing a new **Legendary Weapon**.

DEMON DOOR

REWARD: 1,000,000 Gold

The Demon Door in Sunset House is located to the left of the path leading up to the clearing. It is hidden behind trees and rocks and requires a small bit of roaming to find. This particular Demon Door is only impressed by supreme royalty and will not open for anyone other than the King or Queen of Albion. Return to Sunset House after the coronation—perhaps on your way to Aurora during the search for the Desert Star diamond—and approach the Demon Door as King or Queen to have it open.

The area beyond the Demon Door is known as the Pools of Sorrow. Descend the steps to the chest at the end of the walkway and help yourself to **1,000,000 Gold**! There's also a note on the railing for you to read, but it's there purely for your entertainment.

INVESTIGATE THE CURSE

Visit the Sunset House area during the night. If it's not night when you arrive, simply exit to Mourningwood then turn around and come back. It will be night when you return. Make your way over to the ghostly cupola with the four statues and approach one of them. Press the A button to interact with any single statue four times to make it cycle through its various stances and match the stances that the statues exhibit during the day. Now do this for each of the other statues in a counter-clockwise direction until you have cycled through all four animations for each of the four statues in order. Do this correctly and the ghostly statues turn solid, as does the mansion atop the hill.

Read the letter on the table inside the mansion then continue through the open door. Climb the stairs to the flaming bedroom and, despite the pleas telling you otherwise, lay down in the bed and go to sleep. It doesn't matter for how long.

CHESTY'S CHESS

You'll awake in a dreamscape outside on a giant chessboard. Open the chest in the center of the chessboard to read a message from everyone's favorite sadistic chest, Chesty! Chesty wants to play chess with you and it doesn't matter if you don't know how to play because Chesty, as he's known to do, is going to cheat anyway. Move the selector around the board and select a white chess piece with the A button. Move the piece to any of the valid places on the board (acceptable moves light up to help guide you). Press the B button to deselect a piece if you so wish. Take turns playing what appears to be a normal game of chess until, that is, Chesty just calls the game off.

Return to the center of the board and read another message from Chesty. Chesty has decided to change the rules and create a new game. One that involves attempted murder—prepare for battle! Chesty is going to animate his chess pieces and send them to attack you in waves. Ready a magic spell to annihilate his pawns (hobbes). Speak to Chesty after each wave to initiate the next fight. He'll send his bishops and knights after you next (sand furies and hollow men). Rooks (giant hobbes) attack in the third wave followed by his king and queen (mercenary and hollow men leaders). Unleash a Level 3 or 4 magic attack then finish off any surviving foes with a couple of gun shots. Complete this quest to earn 20 Guild Seals.

KNIGHT JUMPS CHESTY   10 Points

Investigate the curse of Sunset House and defeat Chesty in chess. The battles are not difficult, provided you have leveled up your magic and either your ranged or melee attacks to Level 3 or higher.

CO-OP CHESS BATTLES

You can return to Sunset House and play chess with a friend during co-op play. Approach the two chessboards on the grass alongside the life-sized board to play.

SHATTER THE MIRROR

Head down the hallway to the right to the dusty, abandoned dining room and approach the barrier on the far side of the room. This magical barrier is actually a mirror reflecting the image of a happier, brighter time in Sunset House's past. Pay attention to the position of the furniture and paintings on the wall to see that you are indeed looking at a fresher mirror image of the decrepit room you are actually in. Notice the three black slots on the wall (two on the left and one on the far right). You must move to the corresponding position in the room and guide the ghostly head within the mirror to the flit docks. It may help to swing your sword at the wall to ensure you get close enough for the head to dock within the flit switch. The flit switch appears in the mirror image and lights the corresponding receptacle. Light all three to earn the ability to leap through the mirror. The flit switch locations essentially correspond to where the suits of armor are positioned—it helps to knock down the armor to hit the switches.

The first is on the right-hand side of the room you're in, near the couch to the right of the bust.

The second one is next to the couch in the near left-hand corner as you enter the dining room.

The third flit switch location is in the center of the room on the left, to the left of the globe.

Strike all three flit switches then approach the mirror and leap through it to go back in time before Sunset House was cursed. Return to the foyer and shoot the green orb (now in the opposite corner of the room) to unlock the door on the other side. This leads to a chest containing a **Legendary Weapon**. Locate the chest in the bedroom upstairs then leap back through the mirror. Shoot the green orb in the present day to open that same door—this time the chest contains 175 Guild Seals and a Slow Time potion!

THE VEILED PATH

AREA TYPE: WILDERNESS
NEIGHBORING REGIONS: SHIFTING SANDS
SUB-AREAS: THE ENIGMA

REGION SYNOPSIS

The Veiled Path is a lengthy, narrow canyon that gradually climbs away from Shifting Sands up the steps of an ancient temple. Sentinels, sand furies, and other soldiers of the darkness fight to protect it with fierce determination. The Veiled Path is quite possibly the single most dangerous area you will visit, so travel with caution. This area is home to numerous Auroran Flowers and also a special puzzle-laden area known simply as The Enigma. Crack its code to earn a gold key for your efforts.

TREASURE

📦 CHESTS	🗄 SILVER KEY CHESTS	⛏ DIG SPOTS	💧 DIVE SPOTS
2	0	7	0

COLLECTIBLES

🗝 SILVER KEYS	🗝 GOLD KEYS	🧙 GNOMES	📖 BOOKS	✿ AURORAN FLOWERS
2	1	4	0	13

* The totals listed in the above tables also include items found within The Enigma.

JOBS: None

SHOPS: None

TREASURE OF THE LAND

TO ENIGMA

TO SHIFTING SANDS

SILVER KEYS

Fight your way to the far end of The Veiled Path. This silver key is in the right-hand corner, at the top of the stairs.

Enter the area known as The Enigma and shoot the flit switch to enter the second room. Light the second brazier with an unwoven Fireball spell to open the nearby door. Go through the opening on the right to find the silver key atop a small circular platform.

GNOMES

This first gnome is almost directly to the right of the entrance to this area. Take a few steps forward and look along the rocks to your right.

This gnome is on the rocks beneath the lengthy approach to the rear of The Veiled Path. It's just below the entrance to The Enigma.

Ascend the lengthy staircase at the far end of the area to where the next batch of enemies attack. Kill the enemies and look to the top of the rock spire near the stairs. The gnome is standing on top of it.

Enter The Enigma and shoot the flit switch to enter the second room. Light the second brazier on the left with a pure Fireball spell to open the nearby door. Cross this next room to find the gnome in a small alcove across from the entrance.

GOLDEN RICHES

GOLD KEY

Fight your way to the lengthy staircase at the rear of The Veiled Path and enter the small area on the right known as The Enigma. The door is just above the stairs leading up out of the sand (see map table).

THE ENIGMA

The Enigma looks quite small at first glance—just a room with a chest in it—but there is a series of interconnected rooms beyond this initial entryway. The hexagonal shaped rooms will go unexplored, however, unless you notice the flit switch above the door at the end of the first room.

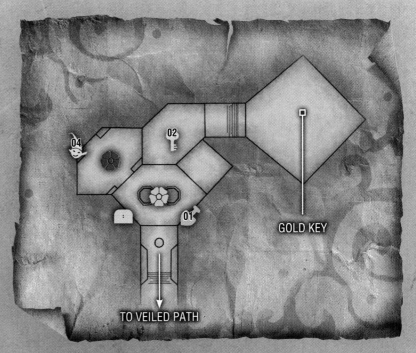

GOLD KEY

TO VEILED PATH

Defeat the enemies that attack and collect the Green Auroran Flower in the center of this room. Note the three unlit braziers around the periphery of the room. Each one is near a currently closed door. Return to the Sanctuary and equip only the Fireball gauntlet then return and target the braziers with fire to open a nearby door. Light the brazier to your immediate left to find a chest and the one to your immediate right to find a dig spot. Far more valuable treasures lie behind the door linked to the middle unlit brazier.

Light the brazier and enter this next major room to find a Red Auroran Flower and numerous enemies. Locate the gnome across the room then venture to the third room, located to the right. This room contains a silver key, but more importantly a series of colored platforms: red, blue, and yellow. Stand in the middle of the room and look to the two groups of colored flames on the altars flanking another large door. You must step on each of the colored platforms in the order that matches the colored flames (from left to right). Be careful not to step on the wrong color, else you'll have to start over. Each platform chimes and emits a bright glow when approached in the correct order. The order is as follows: yellow, blue, yellow, red, blue, red, blue, red. Go through the door between the flames to find the gold key.

REAL ESTATE MAGNATE

For you, the road to rule in Albion isn't optional...that's the point of the game! The road to riches is definitely an optional path, however. Whether you invest time in jobs, real estate, and/or treasure hunting is up to you, but eschew being wealthy at your own risk, for money certainly comes in handy in Albion. Through purchasing homes and businesses, you are able to provide shelter for your family (or families), decorate properties with new furniture and sell them for a profit, and receive continuous income every five minutes of gameplay from incoming rent and store profits.

After acquiring the appropriate ability upgrades along the Road to Rule, you can transact on properties from the World Map Table.

You can also buy properties while hoofing it through town. Properties you already own have a symbol indicating ownership above the real estate sign.

BARRIERS TO ENTRY

It's not quite the same in Albion as it is in our world; a Hero's first worry in this era isn't likely to be a land deed. For a fair time your concern simply is survival, and the mobilizing of a revolutionary army. You can't start building your real estate empire until a little ways into the events of the game. New real estate-related abilities are acquired along the Road to Rule, by spending Guild Seals to open special treasure chests. Soon enough, you can buy just about every property on the map.

ABILITY PACK	AVAILABILITY	GUILD SEAL COST	DESCRIPTION
Landlord Pack	Road to Rule 2: After Music Box	2	Become Albion's greatest land baron by learning how to buy, rent, and decorate houses.
Family Pack	Road to Rule 3: After Saker	5	Want to start a family? Unlock Marriage, House Buying, Having Children, and Adoption. (Also unlocks the Lover Expression Pack.)
Entrepreneur Pack	Road to Rule 5: After The Hole	5	Learn how to haggle and own shops and you soon can be running your own business empire.
Theft Pack	Road to Rule 6: Swift Promise	5	Become a master thief by learning how to steal. Just be careful you don't get caught.

Included on this list of real estate-relevant treasure chest unlocks is the Theft Pack. While theft isn't expressly an aspect of land ownership, the ability to finagle items from furniture figures in heavily once you start setting foot in a lot of different houses. If you own a home and live there, theft doesn't enter into it; take whatever you want, it's your house after all. If you are renting out a home, though, or if you don't have a stake in a property whatsoever, then any attempt to remove valuables constitutes theft. This includes the attendant -5 morality ding per thieving incident, as well as the pressures of the law over your head should you be caught stealing. If you really want to search a home you own without worrying about a drop in morality, simply swap it from a rental to a personal home before rifling through the drawers. Once done, switch the property back to a rental. Those of us who are renters are glad it does not work this way outside of Albion!

HOUSES

Most buildings are homes, used by families of Albion. After you unlock either the Landlord or Family Pack, you are able to buy houses. Immediately after purchasing a house you can either choose it as your domicile, or rent it out. You need a home for each spouse you marry in your travels. Apart from that you don't have to have a personal home at all; you could simply assign all available properties to accrue rent. Rent for your rental units is tabulated and added to your reserves roughly every five minutes. You can certainly also maintain personal homes if you choose, and you may find value in decorating with furniture and seeing what kind of purchase offers you generate.

Available properties are called out by this sign at the map table.

Owned Property

Family Home

Rented Property

The status of your property, whether shop, rental, or family home, is called out with a flag.

Properties naturally max out at a condition of 100%. Over time, properties degrade in condition due to normal wear and tear. Active vandalism of properties diminishes their condition. For a price, you can repair any property that you own. Properties with a condition over 50% have a clean, blue display flag. Properties that have degraded to under 50% condition have a brown display flag.

Houses can be surveyed and purchased either on foot, or while looking over the map table.

Once purchased, the door to your new abode swings open invitingly.

UPKEEP

All housing degrades over time, whether through weather, age, misuse, vandalism, or proximity to major incidents of inflammatory political upheaval. Properties won't show their full sale value if upkeep is not maintained. If wear and tear goes unchecked long enough to reduce a property's condition to 0%, the occupying tenant will stop paying rent altogether! Additionally, a spouse in a family home will be completely unsatisfied at that point. There is no rental penalty for a condition of at least 1%, however. Rent is not affected unless condition falls to 0%. You will be alerted that properties approach dire physical straits via the contextual D-Pad menu. However, the contextual D-Pad menu keeps track of so many things, and the game itself is so fast-paced, that it is easy to miss this small visual cue.

So, if you're assembling a portfolio of properties, make it a habit to check on building status whenever you happen to be looking at the map table. Blue property flags over your buildings? No problem! Brown flags, however? You might want to do some quick repairs! The costs of upkeep are a small price to pay to keep your buildings in tip-top shape.

DECORATIONS

A house you own can be redecorated, whether you reside there or rent it out. Be careful entering a rental property to redecorate at night, though—your tenants may get upset, considering this trespassing! Once inside a house, the contextual D-Pad menu gives you some prompts to follow. By pressing Up on D-Pad, you can signal for Jasper to redecorate the entire property as best he can, from your reserve of unused furniture. If you'd rather do it yourself, or if you're unhappy with the job Jasper does, you can enter Manual Redecoration mode by pressing Down on D-Pad. From here, go up to individual furniture objects and press Ⓐ to swap them out for other furniture in your inventory. You can also press Down on the D-Pad again from within Manual Redecoration mode to alter the wallpaper, as well.

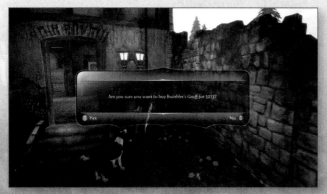

You cannot redecorate a property until you've purchased it, of course.

Swap furniture out for other pieces in your inventory by accessing Manual Redecoration mode with Down on D-Pad. Change wallpaper by pressing Down again.

Or, press Up on D-Pad to have Jasper redecorate the whole place as best he can. He uses the most expensive pieces of furniture you have.

Replacing furniture alters the value of the home, usually for the better.

NOTHING GOING ON BUT THE RENT

In addition to choosing whether to rent out a property, you also choose how much to rent it out for. How your prices for a given region trend in general, whether unreasonably high or generously low overall, is one of the most important factors for determining what people in that area think of you. Set all properties to have normal rent and you won't see any change in the public's opinion whatsoever; they're content paying an honest price for shelter. Set the rent too low, or even eliminate it altogether, and everyone thinks a little bit better of you each time the rent comes due, as their portion is either nil or marginal. The same holds true for heartless rent skewed in the other direction; buy up all the rentals and jack up the rates, and watch a town slowly start to hate you after just a few rent cycles. Of course, the highest prices are extremely high indeed, and there's no penalty to spreading your overpriced monopoly on homes apart from the public scorn. So, if you value money more than you worry about derision, this path is open to you.

SHOPS

■ *Shops are a serious cash cow, but require a steeper payment up front.*

Shops are less customizable and numerous than houses, but shops offer a more direct revenue stream. The purchase cost tends to be much higher, but shops also tend to generate more money. Shops also don't have upkeep; just buy the shop, set your desired price range, and that's all there is to it. Shops can be sold, though it is always at a loss against what you paid for it. As a substantial bonus, you receive a discount buying wares from any shop you own! As with rental homes, skewing the price away from normal greatly influences what citizens think of you. Charge more for goods than normal, and the citizenry won't be pleased. Charge less than normal, or even nothing at all, and they'll be naturally overjoyed.

ALBION REAL ESTATE LISTINGS

Listed here are the properties, broken down by area. While base prices and income values are included, remember the fluid nature of politics and the fickle whims of the people; property values can change for any number of reasons, often before you even think about approaching to purchase a prospective plot. Let these numbers serve most usefully as guidelines. With them, you can tell which properties in each region are most valuable, relative to one another. Whether or not you get what's listed here - you probably won't - is less important than knowing whether you're getting a good bang for your buck.

PROPERTY VALUES

A few factors can influence the costs of just about anything in a given area. What the public thinks of you is a good place to start: have you done anything to make a city's populace furious, or ecstatic? Are you perhaps such a terror that they fear more than abhor you, or are you the apple of every eye? Finally, what do you *already* own? As you purchase more and more properties in a given town, the remaining properties grow ever-so-slightly in cost, reflecting a shrinking market. If you've a fat enough wallet to go for a lot of real estate in the first place, though, the difference won't be a big deal.

These are things that can alter a property's value before you ever even see it. After your purchase, you can further alter the value of your homes by repairing them and sprucing them up with swank new furniture.

DWELLER CAMP

The first settlement you see after escaping the castle is a jarring experience indeed…living sheltered behind the walls of Bowerstone Castle blinds one to the reality of life for the downtrodden in Albion. Property values and returns are predictably low, but that just makes it easier to buy everything. Those little returns add up.

The amenities of the Dweller Camp could be charitably described as sparse. You buy your first new outfit here, but that's about it.

Owning a lot of properties can be useful even if the money earned per each isn't much. All the little amounts add up, and each additional property that is offset from normal prices is one more property affecting your influence every time costs are accrued.

DWELLER CAMP SHOPS

PROPERTY	BASE PURCHASE PRICE	BASE SELL PRICE	INCOME: SHOP SALES			
			LOW	NORMAL	HIGH	HIGHEST
The Raggle Taggle (Clothing)	2700	2430	40	81	121	162
Summit Supplies (General Goods)	2700	2430	40	81	121	162
Albion Ink (Tattooist)	2760	2484	41	82	123	165

DWELLER CAMP HOMES

PROPERTY	BASE PURCHASE PRICE (100%)	BASE SELL PRICE	INCOME: RENT			
			LOW	NORMAL	HIGH	HIGHEST
Obscure Reference House	990	810	18	36	54	72
The Rat House	990	810	18	36	54	72
Mrs Tibbins's Caravan	990	810	18	36	54	72
The House of Riddles	990	810	18	36	54	72
The Crooked Caravan	990	810	18	36	54	72
Old Reliable	990	810	18	36	54	72
Caravan of Poom	1023	837	18	37	55	74
The Slaughter House	1023	837	18	37	55	74
The Caravan of Love	1023	837	18	37	55	74
Wimpet's Sniffle	1105	904	20	40	60	80
Winter Wagon	1204	985	21	43	64	86

BRIGHTWALL VILLAGE

Brightwall Village is quite a step up from the Dweller Camp in every way except being covered in snow. There's more diversity of people and property, for a much wider spectrum of investment opportunities. Here you begin to see that the real money in real estate comes from high-dollar shops. The initial outlay can be daunting, but the money comes back double-time.

The Dweller Camp doesn't have much in the way of shopping. In contrast, Brightwall has it all. Keep an eye out for sales in stores, and offers for extra money for certain goods at the pawnbroker.

The gem of the bunch here is the pawnbroker. The price might not be right, though. To earn fast, short-term money to use towards housing investments, figure out which job is the easiest for you, then level that job up to 5 on the Road to Rule. With a maxed multiplier of 10x on a Level 5 job, you can make more than 3000 for each brief round. Keep that going for a while and you won't be fretting so much at the steep costs of some buildings.

BRIGHTWALL SHOPS

PROPERTY	BASE PURCHASE PRICE	BASE SELL PRICE	INCOME: SHOP SALES			
			LOW	NORMAL	HIGH	HIGHEST
Brightwall Banquets (Food)	950	855	14	28	42	57
Brightwall Booze (Drinks)	950	855	14	28	42	57
Brightwall Bling (Gifts)	2850	2565	42	85	128	171
Brightwall Medicinal Potations (Potions)	2850	2850	42	85	128	171
Buy 'n Sell 'n Buy (Trade Items)	3800	3420	57	114	171	228
Good Boy (Dog Books)	3865	3420	57	114	171	228
Mustache Mansions (Stylist)	15,410	13,869	231	462	693	924
Frou Frou Frocks (Clothing)	40,050	36,045	600	1201	1802	2403
Fabulous Furnishings (Furniture)	48,100	43,290	721	1443	2164	2886
Brightwall Blades (Weapons)	60,950	54,855	914	1828	2742	3657
Ye Quill & Quandry (Pub)	76,990	69,291	1154	2309	3463	4618
Brightwall Brokerage	142,650	128,385	2139	4279	6419	8559

BRIGHTWALL HOMES

PROPERTY	BASE PURCHASE PRICE (100%)	BASE SELL PRICE	INCOME: RENT			
			LOW	NORMAL	HIGH	HIGHEST
Misgnomer House	-	-	-	-	-	-
House of Cluck	-	-	-	-	-	-
Fluff Cottage	-	-	-	-	-	-
The Old Smokehouse	2302	1883	41	83	124	166
Mourir's Mansion	2302	1883	41	83	124	166
House of Slats	3502	2865	63	127	190	254
Two-Knock House	4039	3304	73	146	219	292
Bumbler's Gruff	4533	3708	82	164	246	328

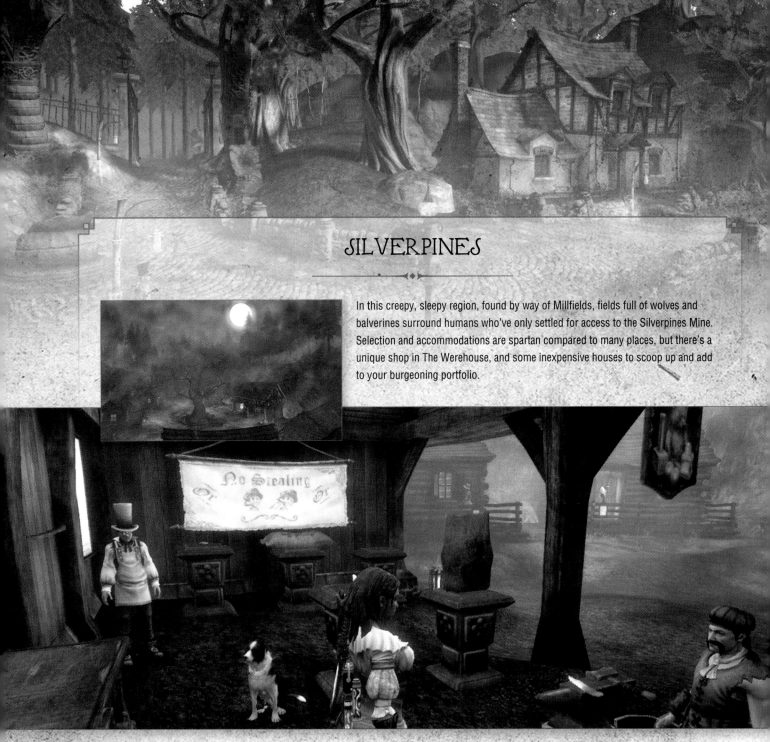

SILVERPINES

In this creepy, sleepy region, found by way of Millfields, fields full of wolves and balverines surround humans who've only settled for access to the Silverpines Mine. Selection and accommodations are spartan compared to many places, but there's a unique shop in The Werehouse, and some inexpensive houses to scoop up and add to your burgeoning portfolio.

The Werehouse offers a strange menagerie of trade goods and rare items.

SILVERPINES SHOPS

PROPERTY	BASE PURCHASE PRICE	BASE SELL PRICE	INCOME: SHOP SALES			
			LOW	NORMAL	HIGH	HIGHEST
The Werehouse	25,000	22,500	375	750	1125	1500

SILVERPINES HOMES

PROPERTY	BASE PURCHASE PRICE (100%)	BASE SELL PRICE	INCOME: RENT			
			LOW	NORMAL	HIGH	HIGHEST
Finkelhouse Farm	2405	2164	48	96	144	192
Lupine Lodge	2670	2185	48	97	145	194
House of Hulshoff	2670	2185	48	97	145	194
The Skidz	2776	2271	50	100	150	200
Moonshine Cabin	2776	2271	50	100	150	200
Carpenter's Lodge	2745	2470	66	133	199	266

MILLFIELDS

There's not much in Millfields save for members of the aristocracy huddled in their mansions around Bower Lake, fearful of roving mercenaries in the surrounding lands. Bower Lake is one of a shrinking number of nature's treasures that hasn't yet been plundered for the sake of the industrial revolution. Of course, the cost for these spacious waterfront properties is outrageous, but in return you garner the best rental fees.

And who said Bower Lake would escape the wrath of onrushing progress forever? You may have a say in the destiny of the lake at some point…

MILLFIELDS HOMES

PROPERTY	BASE PURCHASE PRICE	BASE SELL PRICE	INCOME: RENT			
			LOW	NORMAL	HIGH	HIGHEST
Chavington Hall	-	-	-	-	-	-
Timmins Towers	189,794	155,286	3450	6901	10351	13802
Clixby-Stanners Manor	215,900	176,645	3925	7850	11775	15700
Fakeney Hall	240,928	197,123	4380	8761	13141	17522

DRIFTWOOD

Driftwood is an area socked away along the southern coast of Albion. In the distance, views can be had of both Bowerstone Castle and the tattered, looming Spire. A city can be slowly built up along the islands of Driftwood by completing a series of quests, starting with **Pest Control**.

*More of the town is opened up by completing **An Island Getaway**.*

*Complete the **Giftwood for Driftwood** quest to completely round out this sleepy aquatic getaway.*

DRIFTWOOD SHOPS

PROPERTY	BASE PURCHASE PRICE	BASE SELL PRICE	INCOME: SHOP SALES			
			LOW	NORMAL	HIGH	HIGHEST
Tradewinds (Trade Goods)	4000	3600	60	120	180	240
Drifter's Miscellany (General Goods)	2700	2430	40	81	121	162
Drifter's Fishery (Food)	2000	1800	30	60	90	120
Giftwood (Gifts)	2700	2430	40	81	121	162

DRIFTWOOD HOMES

PROPERTY	BASE PURCHASE PRICE (100%)	BASE SELL PRICE (100%)	INCOME: RENT			
			LOW	NORMAL	HIGH	HIGHEST
Driftwood Cabin	2302	1883	41	83	124	166
Cart of the Solution	990	810	18	36	54	72
Sparrow's Caravan	990	810	18	36	54	72
The Caravan of Damien Brundish	990	810	18	36	54	72
The Sticky Caravan	990	810	18	36	54	72
Old Creaky	990	810	18	36	54	72
Old Reliable	990	810	18	36	54	72
Caravan of Mogo	990	810	18	36	54	72
The Fat Wagon	990	810	18	36	54	72
The Wobbly Wagon	990	810	18	36	54	72

MOURNINGWOOD

The area of Mourningwood is that patrolled by Captain Swift and his men, ever-vigilant against the encroaching hoards of squat hobbes and skeletal hollow men. Also present here is Mourningwood Village, a hippie commune. Situated as it is among the trees, it's a totally groovy place for the enlightened free-thinkers of Albion to gather in unison with nature, to exchange their organic, fair-trade eats, to explore their sexuality, and to—ah, what were we saying, man? Nearby, Mourningwood Fort itself can be purchased, which unlocks the **Mortar and Mourning** mini-game that repeats the defense event in the main quest. Go after Captain Swift's record to snag a **Legendary Weapon** as your prize!

Mourningwood is no Brightwall or Bowerstone for bustle, but the eco warriors here have a charm all their own. Perhaps that comes from not showering.

The fort itself is semi-expensive and offers no recurring rental compensation in return, but on the bright side you can play the **Mortar and Mourning** mini-game as often as you want for item rewards.

MOURNINGWOOD SHOPS

PROPERTY	BASE PURCHASE PRICE	BASE SELL PRICE	INCOME: SHOP SALES			
			LOW	NORMAL	HIGH	HIGHEST
Organic Ink (Tattooist)	4500	4050	67	135	202	270
The Mellow Emporium (General Goods)	6300	5670	94	189	283	378
Peas and Love (Food and Potions)	7200	6480	108	216	324	432

MOURNINGWOOD HOMES

PROPERTY	BASE PURCHASE PRICE (100%)	BASE SELL PRICE	INCOME: RENT			
			LOW	NORMAL	HIGH	HIGHEST
Mourningwood Fort	45,000	-	-	-	-	
Drop-out House	3036	2484	55	110	165	220
Raven's Nest	3168	2592	57	115	172	230
Happy Hippies' Hut	3329	2724	60	121	181	242

BOWERSTONE INDUSTRIAL

The choking smokestacks of progress can be seen (and smelled) from far away. The consequent property values of establishments and residences situated here are some of the lowest in Albion, an air of smog and forced child labor being discouraging to land appreciation.

The heart of the industrial revolution is here, carried on the backs of the poorest people in the land.

The Riveter's Rest, a place of drunken respite for the workers of the area, is the only property here that offers solid individual value on its own.

BOWERSTONE INDUSTRIAL SHOPS

PROPERTY	BASE PURCHASE PRICE	BASE SELL PRICE	INCOME: SHOP SALES			
			LOW	NORMAL	HIGH	HIGHEST
Hot, Yummy, and Circular (Food)	840	756	12	24	37	49
The Fair Trader (Trade Items)	3360	3024	50	100	150	201
The Riveter's Rest (Pub)	27,240	24,516	408	816	1225	1633

BOWERSTONE INDUSTRIAL HOMES

PROPERTY	BASE PURCHASE PRICE (100%)	BASE SELL PRICE	INCOME: RENT			
			LOW	NORMAL	HIGH	HIGHEST
Woodle-Fuddlebuck-Glimborg Mansion	-	-	-	-	-	-
Bumfrey House	3014	2466	54	109	163	218
Captain's Lodge	3151	2578	57	114	171	228
The Smoggles	3323	2754	61	122	183	244
Sailor's Retreat	3455	2862	63	127	190	254
Rotter's Flump	3156	2876	63	127	190	254
Flannigan's Chump	3537	2930	65	130	195	260
House of Bilge	3603	2984	66	132	198	264
Crunge House	3620	2997	66	133	199	266
The Cruddocks	3966	3281	72	145	217	290
House of Filth	4109	3362	74	149	223	298
Futtock's End	4251	3478	77	154	231	308
Guiltford	4444	3636	80	161	241	322
Plum House	4643	3834	85	170	255	340

BOWERSTONE MARKET

Finally, a metropolis to make Brightwall Village seem quaint. This market, located near the seat of power for Albion, is the most expansive in the land. Like Brightwall Village, there are options for every budget. Many store kiosks and houses can be acquired on the cheap, yet there are still options for a larger lay-down of currency should you desire.

Bowerstone Storage isn't exactly a house nor a shop, but owning it gives you solid payouts, and a treasure chest is contained within.

Bowerstone Market has a few noteworthy shops for a potential owner to consider. Like most pawnbrokers, the one here offers huge payouts, but only with an equally huge up-front purchase. Several shops here represent investments that are almost as good, but not quite as committing.

BOWERSTONE MARKET SHOPS

PROPERTY	BASE PURCHASE PRICE	BASE SELL PRICE	INCOME: SHOP SALES			
			LOW	NORMAL	HIGH	HIGHEST
The Old Trout (Food)	1060	954	15	31	47	63
Bowerstone Beverages (Drinks)	1060	954	15	31	47	63
Flower Bower (Food)	1060	954	15	31	47	63
Num Num Pies (Food)	1060	954	15	31	47	63
Jewell Be Sorry (Gifts)	4240	3816	63	126	190	253
Tat's the Way to Do It! (Tattooist)	6359	5723	95	190	285	381
I'll Cut You (Stylist)	16,960	15,264	254	508	762	1017
The Magic Bottle (Potions)	32,159	28,943	482	964	1446	1929
Gifts & Gumf (General Goods)	42,474	38,226	636	1273	1910	2547
We've Got Wood (Furniture)	53,149	47,834	796	1593	2390	3187
Bower Threads (Clothing)	61,479	55,331	922	1844	2766	3688
The Iron Hoof (Weapons)	67,840	61,056	1017	2034	3052	4069
The Cock in the Crown (Pub)	82,649	74,384	1239	2478	3718	4957
Bowerstone Broker (Pawnbroker)	265,000	238,500	3975	7950	11925	15900

BOWERSTONE MARKET HOMES

PROPERTY	BASE PURCHASE PRICE (100%)	BASE SELL PRICE	INCOME: RENT			
			LOW	NORMAL	HIGH	HIGHEST
Bowerstone Storage	107,428	96,685	-	3222	-	-
The Gate House	4834	3955	87	175	262	350
Treacle's Slump	4914	4021	89	178	267	356
Lollipop Lodge	5034	4119	91	183	274	366
House of a Thousand Roofing Nails	5057	4138	91	183	274	366
The Shrine	5239	4286	95	190	285	380
The Last House on the Left (My Left)	5640	4615	102	205	307	410
The Dollhouse	6029	4932	109	219	328	438
Shackleton Rickets	6103	4994	110	221	331	442
The Bricks	6103	4994	110	221	331	442
Infestation Cottage	6103	4994	110	221	331	442
Hole in the Head House	6261	5122	113	227	340	454
The Antique Roadhouse	6261	5122	113	227	340	454
The Old Townhouse	6470	5293	117	235	352	470
Black Stack Shack	8159	6676	148	296	444	592
Riverside Studios	9123	7464	165	331	496	662
Watery Grove	9639	7886	175	350	525	700
The Saltbox	10,212	8355	185	371	556	742
House of Cards	16,901	13,828	307	614	921	1228
The Fat Count	16,188	14,569	323	647	970	1294
Hauteville Heights	24,863	20,342	452	904	1656	1808
The Doghouse	25,732	21,053	467	935	1402	1870

BOWERSTONE OLD QUARTER

This poor, weathered district of the city has taken more punishment over the years than just about any borough could stand. At some point later in the story you have the opportunity to help revitalize this area, re-instilling commerce and family to the district. The houses and shops are modest both in form and value, but there is worth in having more shops to check and citizens to influence.

Don't worry, it's not hard to pinpoint when the Bowerstone Old Quarter decision is made.

Properties here are humble, but the shops may have inventory you can't find elsewhere, and the people couldn't be more full of gratitude.

BOWERSTONE OLD QUARTER SHOPS

PROPERTY	BASE PURCHASE PRICE	BASE SELL PRICE	INCOME: SHOP SALES			
			LOW	NORMAL	HIGH	HIGHEST
Ms Elaine Neous's Goods (General Goods)	1500	1350	22	45	67	90
Potion Emotion (Potions)	2000	1800	30	60	90	120
Eat It! (Food)	2000	1800	30	60	90	120
Merchant's Mile (Trade Goods)	4000	3600	60	120	180	240
Cultured Mutts (Dog Books)	4000	3600	60	120	180	240
Gimme, Gimme, Gimme! (Gifts)	4000	3600	60	120	180	240

BOWERSTONE OLD QUARTER HOMES

PROPERTY	BASE PURCHASE PRICE (100%)	BASE SELL PRICE	INCOME: RENT			
			LOW	NORMAL	HIGH	HIGHEST
The Baubles	4709	3852	85	171	256	342
Harried House	5247	4293	95	190	285	380
The Krannocks	6171	5049	112	224	336	448
Simmons House	6171	5049	112	224	336	448
Nightshade House	6171	5049	112	224	336	448
Cheese Cottage	6171	5049	112	224	336	448
Duckworth House	6171	5049	112	224	336	448
Sod House	6224	5093	113	226	339	452
Shingles' End	6278	5137	114	228	342	456
Tumbledown Arms	6315	5166	114	229	343	458
The Shambles	6315	5166	114	229	343	458
Throckbibble Mansion	6536	5347	118	237	355	474
House of Stains	6602	5401	120	240	360	480
Crumble's Topping	6655	5445	121	242	363	484
Fattie's Retreat	6866	5617	124	249	373	498
Curmudgeons' Cottage	6966	5699	126	253	379	506
Poggle's Knocker	6966	5699	126	253	379	506
I Know We Can Make This Work Manor	7115	5822	129	258	387	516

AURORA

Like the Bowerstone Old Quarter, Aurora is also an area whose condition—and potential for profit—depends largely on your actions. A rebuilt Aurora offers copious residences and shops for the frequenting, on top of an aesthetic that's radically different from the conventions used across the sea, in Albion.

The ancient majesty in Aurora is matched in few other places. Pictured here, our Hero wears the Auroran Suit, only available with the Limited Collector's Edition of Fable III.

Your best bests here are the weapons store, or the pawnbroker. So, pretty much the same as everywhere else.

AURORA SHOPS

PROPERTY	BASE PURCHASE PRICE	BASE SELL PRICE	INCOME: SHOP SALES			
			LOW	NORMAL	HIGH	HIGHEST
Delectable Delights (Food)	1920	1728	28	57	85	114
Vegetables of Aurora (Food)	1920	1728	28	57	85	114
The Curiosity Shop (Gifts)	3840	3456	57	114	172	229
Sketchy Tattoos (Tattooist)	4800	4320	72	144	216	288
Misca Tonics (Potions)	4800	4320	72	144	216	288
Styles of Aurora (Stylist)	17,280	15,552	259	518	777	1036
Honest Omar's (General Goods)	23,040	20,736	345	690	1036	1381
Robes Are Us (Clothing)	30,720	27,648	460	921	1381	1842
The Armoury (Weapons)	49,920	44,928	748	1497	2245	2994
Flotsam's Jetsam (Pawnbroker)	144,000	129,600	2160	4320	6480	8640

AURORA HOMES

PROPERTY	BASE PURCHASE PRICE (100%)	BASE SELL PRICE	INCOME: RENT			
			LOW	NORMAL	HIGH	HIGHEST
The House of Tannar the Great	4275	3498	77	155	232	310
House of Platitudes	4275	3498	77	155	232	310
The Dunes	4275	3498	77	155	232	310
House of Quiet	4275	3498	77	155	232	310
Desert View	4275	3498	77	155	232	310
Wanderer's Retreat	4275	3498	77	155	232	310
Curious Cottage	4275	3498	77	155	232	310
Sandsky House	4275	3498	77	155	232	310
Warrior's Rest	4275	3498	77	155	232	310
Hermione's Hermetic Hermitage	4275	3498	77	155	232	310
Shackleram House	4275	3498	77	155	232	310
House of Himilcar	4275	3498	77	155	232	310
Ka-Lev's Cottage	4275	3498	77	155	232	310
Cold Star Manor	4275	3498	77	155	232	310

ALBION LOVE CONNECTION

A kingdom like Albion, stretching as it does from sea to sea and encompassing dozens of settlements, towns, and cities, is bustling with people. People going to and fro, attending to their daily business, chatting each other up, falling in and out of love, and raising children. These are the people you seek to protect from your brother Logan, among other threats. This is who you fight for! But your relationship with the people of Albion at large isn't just about your struggle against the King, or your valiance in battle, for you can also engage each person on an individual level.

Are you kind to the people, considerate of their wants and needs? Or are you no different from your brother? It's up to you.

Many Legendary weapon bonuses and Achievement unlocks are contingent upon fraternizing directly with the citizenry.

THE PUBLIC TRUST

Your contact with each person can have an effect on both that individual's opinion of you, as well as the opinion of the townspeople at large. If your contact comes in the form of whacking villagers into oblivion with a hammer, or grossly overcharging for rent or goods on your properties, then these activities are noticed by those citizens not directly victimized. On the other hand, kindness and charity to the populace are likewise likely to be lauded by the group. Of course, while these overarching behaviors alter what people think about you, they are not direct means to familiarity. For that, you must roll your sleeves up and address the populace directly. This is accomplished through **Expressions**. Aside from during a few moments in the main story, you don't *have* to cultivate relationships, but great rewards are found in doing so.

YOU CAN LEAD A HORSE TO WATER...

Face a villager, stand still for a second, then pull the left trigger to hold their hand. Once your hands are clasped together, you can lead the villager wherever you'd like. You can still hold the A button while moving to sprint, as though you were running alone. You cannot fight or engage with other objects or villagers, however. You must first release your grasp by pulling the left trigger once again. Trying to force them to run through too tight a squeeze (or through other people or objects) can also cause the bond to be broken, though your partner tries to catch up if possible. Note that villagers only go willingly if they feel neutral or better about you. If they're hateful or fearful, "Hold Hands" becomes "Drag!" You can still haul them wherever you'd like, but it takes longer to do so. From going on dates, to leading scared citizens back from the wilderness, to dragging escaped criminals back to jail, or bringing "volunteers" to a new place of employment, there are many uses for handholding throughout the game.

Citizens with nothing to fear from you come quickly and willingly when led by the hand.

Those whose opinion of our Hero is less than sterling must be dragged. Whatever gets the job done, yes?

272

AN EXPRESSIVE PERSONALITY

Expressions are your most direct means of influencing your relationships in Albion. Expressions are performed by interacting with a person, then pressing and holding either the A, X, or Y button. You can release the button at any time to get credit for the expression, and therefore any available Guild Seal reward for interacting with that person during whichever state they're in at the time, but the effect of the expression on the relationship is much more potent if you wait until the gauge charges to the sweet spot to release the button. Once the expression plays out, you return to the interaction screen with that same person, ready to perform more expressions.

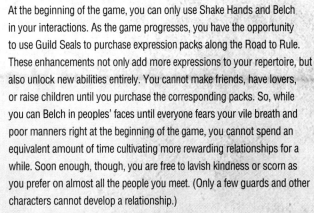

The effect of expressions is far more pronounced if you hold the button and release during the sweet spot.

Expressions do not have a pass or fail chance, as they did in Fable II. *Expressions simply work.*

At the beginning of the game, you can only use Shake Hands and Belch in your interactions. As the game progresses, you have the opportunity to use Guild Seals to purchase expression packs along the Road to Rule. These enhancements not only add more expressions to your repertoire, but also unlock new abilities entirely. You cannot make friends, have lovers, or raise children until you purchase the corresponding packs. So, while you can Belch in peoples' faces until everyone fears your vile breath and poor manners right at the beginning of the game, you cannot spend an equivalent amount of time cultivating more rewarding relationships for a while. Soon enough, though, you are free to lavish kindness or scorn as you prefer on almost all the people you meet. (Only a few guards and other characters cannot develop a relationship.)

EXPRESSION PACK	AVAILABILITY	GUILD SEAL COST	DESCRIPTION
Friend Expression Pack	After Music Box	2	Learn Whistle, Hero Pose and Chat expressions in order to become friends with the people of Albion.
Lover Expression Pack	Road to Rule 3: After Saker	5	Take your relationship to the next level by learning Dance, Hug, and Kiss in order to become best friends or even lovers with the people of Albion.
Joker Expression Pack	Road to Rule 4: Sabine Promise	5	Become a comedian by learning the Tickle, Pat-A-Cake, and Chicken Dance expressions.
Bully Expression Pack	Road to Rule 6: Swift Promise	5	Learn how to coerce people and bend them to your will with the Insult, Point and Laugh, and Threaten expressions.
Good Parenting Pack	Road to Rule 7: Page Meeting	5	Become the world's greatest parent by learning the Tickle Child, Pick Up and Hug Child, and Cuddle Baby expressions.
Hooligan Expression Pack	Road to Rule 7: Page Meeting	5	Can't wait to be a loud, obnoxious lout? Then learn the Rodeo, Fart on Villager, and Vulgar Thrust Expressions.
Scary Expression Pack	Road to Rule 8: Reaver's Manor	5	Learn the Growl, Scary Laugh, and Bloodlust Roar to become the terror of Albion.

WEAPONS TO EQUIP WHILE EARNING GUILD SEALS USING EVIL EXPRESSIONS

WEAPON NAME		LEGENDARY BONUS	OBJECTIVE	REWARD
SWORD	Souldrinker	Thug	Earn Guild Seals from evil expressions.	+15 Extra Damage
	The Inquisitor	Extort	Earn Guild Seals from evil expressions.	Gain Money per Hit
	Really Sharp Pair of Scissors	Despot	Earn Guild Seals from evil expressions.	Earn Guild Seals Faster in Combat.
HAMMER	Trollblight	Regeneration	Earn Guild Seals from evil expressions.	Gain Health with Each Hit
	Sorrow's Fist	Menace	Earn Guild Seals from evil expressions.	+14 Extra Damage
	The Tenderiser	Fiend	Earn Guild Seals from evil expressions.	Earn Guild Seals Faster in Combat
PISTOL	The Ice Maiden	Sledger	Earn Guild Seals from evil expressions.	+ Shotgun Spray
	Gnomewrecker	Insulter	Earn Guild Seals from evil expressions.	+10 Extra Damage
RIFLE	The Sandgoose	Aggressive	Earn Guild Seals from evil expressions.	+1 Gold per Hit

GOOD EXPRESSIONS
- Shake Hands
- Whistle
- Hero Pose
- Chat
- Dance
- Hug
- Kiss
- Tickle
- Pat-A-Cake

GOOD EXPRESSIONS FOR CHILDREN
- Tickle Child
- Pick Up and Hug Child
- Cuddle Baby

SILLY EXPRESSION
- Chicken Dance

EVIL EXPRESSIONS
- Belch
- Insult
- Point and Laugh
- Threaten
- Rodeo
- Fart on Villager
- Vulgar Thrust
- Growl
- Scary Laugh
- Bloodlust Roar

AN ALBION STATE OF MIND PUBLIC TRUST

Each person's appraisal of their relationship with you is readily available. For information at a glance, hold down the right trigger. Any villagers in sight who can be influenced have a symbol above their heads to give you a general idea where you stand with them. For more detail, approach a given person to prompt new display elements to appear to help you gauge their opinion. The relationship gauge at the bottom of the screen shows their state of mind toward you. To begin direct interactions with a particular person, press the A button while this meter is present. From here, you can hold the right trigger to gain more insight into their personality and preferences.

Villagers come in all shapes and sizes, with all sorts of different preferences. Straight, gay, joyous, humorless, silly, serious, and so on. In the end, though, the choice is really still just between using either good expressions to build trust, or evil expressions to torpedo it.

FRIEND

Positive Expressions + Relationship Quest (Sexually Incompatible)

BEST FRIEND

Positive Expressions + Relationship Quest

NEUTRAL

Positive Expressions + Date (Sexually Compatible)

LOVER

Negative Expressions

HATE

Negative Expressions

FEAR

Propose

SPOUSE

Unprotected Sex

CHILD

NEUTRAL

Neutral

The first time you interact with a person their state is almost always neutral, indicating they have no solid opinion, neither good nor ill. (Their opinion may be influenced in advance of your personal meeting, however, if you've committed global negative acts against their area, such as needless murder or overcharging.) By interacting with the person and performing either good or evil expressions, you can tilt their opinion towards friendship or hatred. If you bottom-out the neutral gauge, their lack of opinion readily gives way to hate, even at the start of the game. On the other hand, provided you have the friend expression pack, max out the neutral gauge and the citizen offers a **Relationship** quest. Complete this quest and they become your friend.

HATE

If you heckle, ridicule, and otherwise annoy a citizen continually, their opinion of you slowly slides from neutral to hate. Unlike ascending in the other direction, towards friendship and love, no expression packs are required to steer someone towards hate. This state is pretty self-explanatory; they won't like you much. You must weather their derision whenever you wander nearby, and their prices toward you (assuming they own a shop of some sort) are negatively influenced. The relationship is always salvageable, though, if you start acting nicely toward them. If you manage to max out hate, you must do a **Relationship** quest to progress back to neutral. Perpetuate evil behavior, though, and hatred can give way to fear.

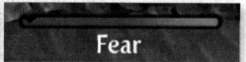

FEAR

Continue down the path of annoying or threatening someone who already hates you, and they eventually teeter from hatred to outright fear. In this state, they shudder and cower in your presence. You see an opposite effect on benefits in this state. If they own a shop, their prices are likely to be favorable toward you, out of fear for their well-being. It's possible to create a fear state in lots of villagers without ever talking to them at all if you run roughshod through their village killing people. In this case, people who fear you without ever talking to you directly cough up Guild Seals as a reward when you simply bump into them going about your normal business. You can still retrieve relationships from fear, but of course the going is longer than if they simply abhor you. You must complete a **Relationship** quest to go back from fear to hate, and then another to go from hate to neutral.

There are a few Legendary weapons with bonuses that you can only unlock if you walk the path of a murderous despot. If you're going to make people fear and hate you anyway, you might as well kill some of them with these weapons too.

Having everyone hate you isn't necessarily useful, but it is more or less guaranteed if you play the game a certain way. Raise prices, grind your morality and corruption into the dirt, pass judgments that lower quality of life, and kill the innocent, then hate, and eventually fear, is inevitable.

RELATIONSHIP BENEFITS/DISADVANTAGES

RELATIONSHIP STAGE	GIFTS*	SHOP/STALL PRICES**
Love/Best Friends	100%	-20% Discount
Friends	75%	-10% Discount
Neutral	—	—
Hate	5%***	+10% Overcharge
Fear	10%	-10% Discount

*This is the chance that one of the people with whom you have a relationship (good or bad) will have a gift for you when you enter the region.

**Pawnbrokers don't offer the same discounts or overcharges.

***This isn't a gift so much as it is a bribe to make you leave.

WEAPONS FOR KILLING VILLAGERS AND SOLDIERS

WEAPON NAME		LEGENDARY BONUS	OBJECTIVE	REWARD
SWORD	The Inquisitor	Bloodsucker	Kill 300 villagers or soldiers.	Gain Health per Hit
HAMMER	Jack's Hammer	Murderer	Kill 100 villagers or soldiers.	+20 Extra Damage
PISTOL	Bloodcraver	Blood Drainer	Kill 300 villagers or soldiers.	Gain Health with Each Hit

FRIEND

If, from a neutral state, you shower a citizen with good expressions, their neutral gauge eventually fills up. Then, if you have the friend expression pack, they offer you a **Relationship** quest. Complete the quest and this person is promoted from the neutral state to become your friend. Once you're friends with a citizen, you can continue to regale them with positive expressions to max out their friend gauge. At that point, the next step depends on whether you are sexually compatible with that person. (Straight villagers are only compatible with opposite sex Heroes, while gay villagers are compatible with same-sex Heroes.) If not sexually compatible, then a **Relationship** quest is triggered that, upon completion, transforms a friend into a best friend. If compatible, then you can take the friend on a date. Complete the date successfully and the friend becomes a lover!

Friends

Fetch: Citizens sometimes request that you retrieve a misplaced item for them. This item is always found in a dig spot, which you can find with the help of your dog, and the glowing trail.

Gift: The villager may just want a present. If you don't have an appropriate trinket stowed away in your inventory, check out Brightwall Bling in Brightwall Village, Jewell Be Sorry or Gifts & Gumf in Bowerstone Market, Gimme, Gimme, Gimme! in Bowerstone Old Quarter, or The Curiosity Shop in Aurora.

Courier: You have to deliver a package or letter for your prospective friend. After a successful delivery, return to confirm the delivery, complete the quest, and progress the relationship.

WEAPONS TO EQUIP WHILE MAKING FRIENDS

WEAPON NAME		LEGENDARY BONUS	OBJECTIVE	REWARD
SWORD	The Casanova	Charmer	Become friends with 30 villagers.	Earn Guild Seals Faster in Combat.
HAMMER	Mallett's Mallet	Big Hitter	Become friends with 30 villagers.	+10% Chance of Knockback vs All Enemies
	The Absolver	Party Animal	Become friends with 30 villagers.	Earn Guild Seals Faster in Combat
	The TYPO	Chum	Become friends with 30 villagers.	Gain Money with Each Hit
PISTOL	The Barnumificator	Popular	Become friends with 30 villagers.	+12 Extra Damage
RIFLE	Arkwright's Flintlock	Socialite	Become friends with 30 villagers.	Earn Guild Seals Faster in Combat
	The Sandgoose	Popularity	Become friends with 30 villagers.	Gain Money with Each Hit

Best Friends

SEXUALLY INCOMPATIBLE: BEST FRIEND

From friends to best friends. If you aren't sexually compatible with a citizen, this is the course the relationship takes at the end. Once their friend gauge is full, they send you on another **Relationship** quest, as with any positive transition from one relationship state to another, such as neutral to friend. This can be a fetch, courier, or gift-giving quest. As before, if you don't have an appropriate gift on hand, head to a gift shop in Brightwall, Bowerstone Market, Bowerstone Old Quarter, or Aurora to make a purchase.

Love

SEXUALLY COMPATIBLE: LOVER

If you ARE sexually compatible with a friend, pushing the relationship to the next step leads to gaining a lover. A compatible friend with a maxed-out friend gauge can be taken on a date. On a date, you have to hold hands with your new love interest and lead them to the rendezvous, as indicated by the glowing trail. Here, you kiss them to affirm the new commitment.

■ *Love is the first step toward first marriage, then sex and possibly children.*

WEAPONS TO EQUIP WHILE GAINING LOVERS

WEAPON NAME		LEGENDARY BONUS	OBJECTIVE	REWARD
SWORD	The Love Sword	Phwoar	Make 5 villagers love you.	+25% Attractiveness, Immunity to Scarring
	Casanova	Beloved	Make 5 villagers love you.	+25% Attractiveness, Immunity to Scarring
	Avo's Lamentation	Blessed	Make 5 villagers love you.	Earn Guild Seals Faster in Combat.
HAMMER	Aurora's Shield	Faith	Make 5 villagers love you.	Earn Guild Seals Faster in Combat
	Faerie Hammer of the Moon King	Loved	Make 5 villagers love you.	Earn Guild Seals Faster in Combat
	Champion	Heartbreaker	Make 5 villagers love you.	Earn Guild Seals Faster in Combat
	The TYPO	Popular	Make 5 villagers love you.	Earn Guild Seals Faster in Combat
PISTOL	Mirian's Mutilator	Beloved	Make 10 villagers love you.	Lose Weight with Each Hit
RIFLE	The Shrieking Pilgrim	Saintly	Make 5 villagers love you.	Earn Guild Seals Faster in Combat

WEAPONS FOR KILLING LOVERS

WEAPON NAME		LEGENDARY BONUS	OBJECTIVE	REWARD
HAMMER	Sorrow's Fist	Lovestruck	Kill 5 villagers who love you.	Extra Knockdown vs Human Enemies
PISTOL	Mirian's Mutilator	Vanity	Kill 5 people who love you.	+8 Extra Damage
	Bloodcraver	Blood Drinker	Kill 20 villagers who love you.	Earn Guild Seals Faster in Combat

WEAPONS THAT CAN BOOST ATTRACTIVENESS

WEAPON NAME		LEGENDARY BONUS	OBJECTIVE	REWARD
SWORD	The Love Sword	Phwoar	Make 5 villagers love you.	+25% Attractiveness, Immunity to Scarring
	The Casanova	Beloved	Make 5 villagers love you.	+25% Attractiveness, Immunity to Scarring
PISTOL	Reaver Industries Perforator	Player	Have an orgy with 4 other people.	+25% Attractiveness, Immunity to Scarring

MARRIAGE

You can propose to a lover at any time by interacting with them, then pressing the right bumper. Assuming you have a wedding ring (available at jewelry and gift shops), and a home (or enough money to buy a home), the proposal is accepted! You immediately have to select both a marital home and a wedding ceremony. Most homes and weddings are expensive, so be aware of the costs of matrimony going in. After your ceremony you can let passion take hold and lead your new spouse to a bed, in order to consummate the union. If you have a condom on hand, you are able to choose between protected or unprotected sex. Unprotected sex can lead to the transmission of STDs, but you may also be blessed with a child!

You can propose marriage to any lover with the right bumper. In order to go through with the marriage, you have to select a marital home. A different home must be selected for each new spouse, naturally, and prudence might dictate not placing different households too close together

On top of selecting a home, you also have to select a ceremony. More expensive ceremonies are more lavish and well-attended, but you have a marriage whether your choice is frugal or opulent.

Ah, the fun part! Use protection if you don't want a little one.

WEDDING CEREMONIES

LOCATION	THEME	COST
Brightwall Village	Street Wedding	0
Mourningwood	Swamp Wedding	1
Bowerstone Market	Vagrant Wedding	25
Dweller Camp	Winter Wedding	75
Millfields	Muddy Wedding	100
Mourningwood	Far Out Wedding	200
Brightwall Village	Bridge Wedding	400
Bowerstone Industrial	Back Alley Wedding	500

LOCATION	THEME	COST
Aurora	Simple Wedding	500
Dweller Camp	Dweller Wedding	775
Millfields	Monument Wedding	1000
Mourningwood	Fort Wedding	1000
Bowerstone Market	Town Square Wedding	2000
Aurora	Festive Wedding	2000
Dweller Camp	Dweller Court Wedding	2500
Bowerstone Industrial	Factory Wedding	3500

LOCATION	THEME	COST
Brightwall Village	Academy Wedding	4000
Millfields	Lake Wedding	5000
Bowerstone Market	Royal Mile Wedding	5000
Bowerstone Industrial	Canal Wedding	6000
Bowerstone Castle	Garden Wedding	6000
Aurora	Lavish Wedding	8000
Bowerstone Castle	State Wedding	12,000
Bowerstone Castle	Royal Wedding	20,000

In the afterglow of post-marital and post-coital bliss, you must take care of some bookkeeping regarding your new next-of-kin, and you have to start thinking about the long-term contentedness of your spouse. You receive a dowry for marrying, along with a small stipend from your spouse each time incoming profits and rent are tabulated. However, familial upkeep also represents an ongoing drag on your pocketbook. You also want to keep your marital home in good condition, and your spouse is likely to ask for a change of furniture and an improvement in the condition and value of the property every once in a while. Ignore the requests of a spouse at your own peril; while you can divorce spouses you've tired of by interacting with them and pressing the right bumper, *they* can divorce *you* just as quickly if you neglect them. The relationship decays over time based on the home and upkeep. The relationship can actually increase gradually over time if the house and upkeep are good. If it's bad, however, your relationship will deteriorate at a rate based on how bad the home and upkeep are. Keep in mind that wealthier villagers want nicer (more valuable) homes and more upkeep. The flipside to that is that they give bigger dowries and some better, potentially even rarer, gifts. There's another bonus to having a happy spouse; they increase the condition of the family home over time by making repairs! It's good to have a happy & handy person in the home. Set upkeep as high as you comfortably can, give them occasional tender loving care, and swap out their furniture for nicer pieces in order to keep them sated. The final resort may be to move. If your spouse is constantly nagging about the quality of the home and amount of upkeep, and new decorations don't seem to do the trick, consider moving. Take your spouse by the hand and lead them to the building sign of a brand new, better house (select the family home option when there). This should appease them. You may also use the map table to do this. Happy spouses lavish you with gifts, as do happy children, and this can be a fantastic source of goodies. These offerings can be quite valuable, allowing you to obtain some of the rarer items in the game: furniture, make-up, hairstyles, tattoos, etc. A spouse/child may have a gift for you every couple of days—provided you keep them in the top relationship stage.

You can choose how much to give each family per day, from 0 all the way to a max of 1000.

WEAPONS FOR KILLING SPOUSES

WEAPON NAME		LEGENDARY BONUS	OBJECTIVE	REWARD
HAMMER	The Tenderiser	Soul Burner	Kill 3 spouses.	Lose Weight and Purity with Each Hit.
RIFLE	Skorm's Justice	Unholy Blast	Kill 3 spouses.	+ Shock Damage

WEAPONS TO WEAR DURING SEX WITH WOMEN

WEAPON NAME		LEGENDARY BONUS	OBJECTIVE	REWARD
SWORD	The Love Sword	Lover	Have sex with women 20 times.	+8 Extra Damage

WEAPONS TO WEAR DURING SEX WITH MEN

WEAPON NAME		LEGENDARY BONUS	OBJECTIVE	REWARD
PISTOL	The Ice Maiden	Seduction	Have sex with men 15 times.	+ Flame Damage

MARRIED WITH CHILDREN

Marriage followed by unprotected lovemaking can lead to the birth of a child. You may be blessed with a new child by adopting one from the Bowerstone Industrial Orphanage. A nanny will automatically be hired if there's no spouse assigned to the family home. The baby initially appears in a crib in the marital home, where they mature for a while before becoming a fully-fledged kid. The apple tends not to fall too far from the tree; as you are generally good, evil, serious, or flirty, so too may your child inherit your master traits. Can babies be evil? In Albion, yes!

Your offspring grows in a crib for a bit, where you can encourage him or her with expressions meant for children. Eventually, your child matures beyond the crib and begins living in earnest, walking amongst the townspeople and vying for your attention just like any other citizen.

WEAPONS TO WEAR WHILE GAINING SPOUSES

WEAPON NAME		LEGENDARY BONUS	OBJECTIVE	REWARD
PISTOL	Miriam's Mutilator	Marriage Addict	Get married 5 times.	+8 Extra Damage
RIFLE	Defender of the Faith	Settled	Get married.	Earn Guild Seals Faster in Combat

WEAPONS TO WEAR WHILE HAVING CHILDREN

WEAPON NAME		LEGENDARY BONUS	OBJECTIVE	REWARD
SWORD	The Love Sword	Breeder	Have 5 children.	+8 Extra Damage
RIFLE	The Hero's Companion	Family	Have 2 children.	Earn Guild Seals Faster in Combat

PITFALLS OF POLYGAMY

It's entirely possible to have multiple lovers, and - ultimately - multiple spouses. This creates interesting logistical problems, though. Naturally, different spouses are none too happy about having to share, and their displeasure increases in direct proportion to the proximity of other husbands or wives. Spouses aware of each other bicker at each other and you constantly, and their happiness plummets. As your main preventative measure, position your primary families in different cities. If you must cultivate marital harems in the same town, try to keep the houses far apart, keep the houses repaired and well-furnished, take a hands-on approach to checking in with your families, and last but definitely not least, set family upkeep for each domicile to 1000 per day. This solution isn't cheap, but who ever said juggling families and spouses is easy? Well, it isn't!

Uh-oh…

> Neglect spouses, or situate them close together and aware of one another, and you might find yourself the dumpee rather than the dumper, divorce-wise. It's possible to maintain multiple marriages where the spouses are aware they aren't alone, but it's difficult.

HOUSES OF ILL REPUTE, SOCIAL DISEASES, AND ORGIES

In accordance with the social mores of Albion, sex takes place within the sanctity of a marriage bond and under the marital roof, for purposes of pair bonding and reproduction. However, rules were made to be broken. Just because you're not married doesn't mean you can't engage in adult dalliances. Should you find them streetwalking, prostitutes can be commissioned to follow you to a bed for some consenting entertainment. You can even enlist multiple prostitutes at once for an orgy; a few Legendary weapons even have this as a requirement for unlocking bonuses! Finally, STDs are an extant nuisance in Albion, though at least the actual effects are innocuous; the only reason you notice you've acquired these embarrassing ailments is from inter-area loading screens!

WEAPONS TO WEAR DURING ORGIES

WEAPON NAME		LEGENDARY BONUS		OBJECTIVE	REWARD
HAMMER	Sorrow's Fist		Loose Morals	Have an orgy with 4 other people.	Earn Guild Seals Faster in Combat
PISTOL	Reaver Industries Perforator		Player	Have an orgy with 4 other people.	+25% Attractiveness, Immunity to Scarring
	Tee Killer Shooter		Hedonist	Have an orgy with 4 other people.	+11 Extra Damage

WEAPONS OF YORE

Uniting a kingdom, toppling its ruler, and then taking his place—these are blood-drenched undertakings. At every step along the way, fierce and loathsome adversaries seek to stop you in your tracks. As luck would have it, though, you trained under the mighty Sir Walter Beck, a formidable warrior who once served your parent, the Hero of the Spire, Albion's previous ruler. Add to that the inheritance of magic (in the form of spell gauntlets) from the previous Hero and we have a formidable warrior indeed. For each weapon type—melee, guns, and magic—there's an Achievement acquired by killing 500 enemies.

WEAPONS SAFETY

If you brandish a weapon or cast a spell near villagers, the safety symbol appears in the bottom-left of the screen, where D-Pad commands are shown. Pressing down on the D-Pad while this symbol is visible toggles whether you can attack villagers. Harming innocents strikes fear into the hearts of those you spare, while skewing your morality naturally towards evil. The morality of the Hero is 0 at the outset. This value can soar as high as 1000, for pure good, or plunge as low as -1000, for pure evil. Morality can be checked at the **Hero Status panel** in the **Hero's Sanctuary**.

Friendly fire off! Swing away near the innocent, you won't hurt them. Windows can be broken to the tune of -5 morality each.

Weapons free! Show the puny townspeople your wrath. You'll garner -5 morality for assault, and -15 for murder. Villagers tend to die in one hit, but soldiers can give you a bit of a fight.

WEAPON FOR KILLING VILLAGERS AND SOLDIERS

WEAPON NAME		LEGENDARY BONUS		OBJECTIVE	REWARD
SWORD	The Inquisitor		Bloodsucker	Kill 300 villagers or soldiers.	Gain Health Per Hit
HAMMER	Jack's Hammer		Murderer	Kill 100 villagers or soldiers.	+20 Extra Damage
PISTOL	Bloodcraver		Blood Drainer	Kill 300 villagers or soldiers.	Gain Health With Each Hit

WAY OF THE WARRIOR

SWORDS, HAMMERS, PISTOLS, AND RIFLES

❌ controls melee attacks and defense. The first time you press ❌ your current sword or hammer is simply drawn and readied. To put the weapon away, press Ⓐ. Direct strikes are accomplished by holding 🕹 in the desired direction while pressing ❌. (Simply pressing ❌ without a specific direction causes your hero to attack straight ahead.) Press ❌ repeatedly to string continuous attacks together. Hold ❌ (without moving 🕹) to block incoming strikes.

Ⓨ controls ranged attacks. The first time you press Ⓨ, your current gun is drawn and cocked. To holster your firearm, press Ⓐ. Direct the gunshots by holding 🕹 in the desired direction while pressing Ⓨ. Firearms can only discharge so many shots before a reload is required. Your Hero reloads automatically when necessary. Magazine size is determined by the current ranged attack unlock level along the **Road to Rule**. The higher the level, the more shots per reload. Don't worry about overall ammo—your reserve is limitless.

Fortune favors the bold. Melee swings allow you to get right into the thick of battle.

RANGED LEVEL (INCREASE ON ROAD TO RULE)	PISTOL SHOTS PER RELOAD	RIFLE SHOTS PER RELOAD
Lv0 (Game start)	3	2
Lv1	4	3
Lv2	4	3
Lv3	5	4
Lv4	5	4
Lv5	6	5

Discretion is the better part of valor. Pepper the enemy with gunfire from afar.

You can't block with a gun. If enemies close in, lay on a charged area-of-effect spell, then roll away from them with 🕹+Ⓐ. Resume the barrage when clear. This works best with spells that get enemies off your case for a few seconds, like Vortex.

FLOURISHES

By focusing his or her martial prowess, a Hero can tense up and unleash a powerful flourish technique. Flourishes take a second to ready, but are much more powerful than normal attacks. Flourishes can be performed with both melee weapons and guns. For swords and hammers, ready a flourish by holding ⓧ while moving 🕹 in the direction of the intended target. Your Hero adopts a different stance than when you simply hold ⓧ (without 🕹) for a blocking posture. Release ⓧ to unleash the flourish. For guns, hold ⓨ to ready a flourish, then release ⓨ to fire (this fires in the direction the Hero is facing. Fire in a different direction with 🕹). You can be interrupted while readying a flourish,

◼ *Hold, then release 🕹+ⓧ for swords and hammers, or ⓨ for guns.*

but not once you've released the button and started the attack. Added damage aside, flourishes are terrific because all but the stoutest foes will be knocked down. Prone, dazed foes are completely susceptible to gunfire, spells, finishing blows with ⓧ, or fatal attacks from your trusty canine companion.

◼ *In battle, screen contrast changes and the controller vibrates to indicate your Hero is focused and ready to let loose the flourish.*

◼ *Stand still over foes that are knocked down, but still alive, then press ⓧ so they don't get up again.*

LEGENDARY WEAPONS TO USE FLOURISHES WITH

WEAPON NAME		LEGENDARY BONUS	OBJECTIVE	REWARD
SWORD	Wolfsbane	Overkill	Kill 50 enemies with flourishes.	Earn Guild Seals Faster in Combat.
	Mr Stabby	Massacre	Kill 60 villagers or soldiers with flourishes.	+15 Extra Damage
	Beadle's Cutlass	Killer	Kill 100 enemies with flourishes.	+15 Extra Damage
	Really Sharp Pair of Scissors	Surgeon	Kill 80 human enemies with flourishes.	+30% Damage vs Human Enemies
	Thunderblade	Show-off	Kill 200 enemies with flourishes.	Earn Guild Seals Faster in Combat.
HAMMER	Faerie Hammer of the Moon King	Assassin	Kill 100 enemies with flourishes.	+1 Gold per Hit
	Trollblight	Giantbane	Kill 10 large enemies with flourishes.	+80% Damage vs Large Enemies
	Dragonbone Hammer	Headsmacker	Kill 100 human enemies with flourishes.	Extra Knockdown vs Human Enemies
	Lunarium Pounder	Thud!	Kill 100 enemies with flourishes.	+10% Chance of Knockback per Hit
	Tannar's Glory	HolyFire	Kill 150 enemies with flourishes.	+ Flame Damage
	The TYPO	Thwack!	Kill 100 enemies with flourishes.	Earn Guild Seals Faster in Combat
	The Tenderiser	Tenderise	Kill 150 villagers or soldiers with flourishes.	+20 Extra Damage
	Jack's Hammer	Blademaster	Kill 50 villagers or soldiers with flourishes.	+30% Damage to Humans
PISTOL	The Bonesmasher	Shotgunner	Hit 500 enemies with a flourish attack.	+ Shotgun Spray
	Gnomewrecker	Smasher	Kill 100 enemies with flourishes.	+10 Extra Damage
	Bloodcraver	Overkill	Kill 100 human enemies with flourishes.	+16 Extra Damage
	Dragonstomper .48	Dragon's Breath	Kill 150 enemies with flourishes.	+ Flame Damage
	Scattershot	Hard Hitter	Hit enemies with 200 flourishes.	+8 Extra Damage
RIFLE	Defender of the Faith	Avenger	Kill 200 enemies with flourishes.	+ Shock Damage
	Scattershot	Scattergun	Kill 10 large enemies with flourishes.	+ Shotgun Spray
	Facemelter	Giant	Kill 10 large enemies with flourishes.	+13 Extra Damage
	The Marksman 500	Flourisher	Kill 50 human enemies with flourishes.	Extra Knockdown vs Human Enemies

FINISHING MOVES

When you attack an enemy who is near death, a finishing move can occur. Finishing moves occur more frequently as you open combat-oriented treasure chests along the Road to Rule, increasing your melee and ranged skill levels. When you score a finishing move, you'll know it—your Hero downs the foe lavishly in a brief cinematic sequence. Each weapon type has its own finishing moves, which are different against each type of enemy! With hammers against balverines, for example, the coup de grace may be a brutal head crush, while against hobbes a tremendous hammer golf swing punts them into the distance. Experiment with various weapons and level them all up to see all the finishing moves.

SPELL GAUNTLETS

Ⓑ controls magic attacks. Press **Ⓑ** for a quick, area-of-effect spell that strikes anything nearby. Alternately, press **Ⓑ**+🕹 in the direction of an enemy to focus a more powerful version of the spell on just one target. This is just with tapping **Ⓑ**, however; you can increase the power of any spell, whether area-of-effect or focused, by pressing and holding **Ⓑ**, then releasing to cast. A spell can be charged up to five levels, and unlike charging flourish attacks with swords, hammers, or guns, the Hero cannot be interrupted while charging an enhanced spell! This makes spells perfect for getting out of overwhelming situations. Gunslingers and sword-swingers can both be overwhelmed by hordes of foes, but spell users rarely will (although be aware that while you can't be interrupted while charging, you do still take damage). Ultimately, weapons and spells go hand-in-hand…spells can serve as a crucial supplement to users of any sword, hammer, or gun.

Spells can be mixed in fluidly with conventional combat.

ROLLING

Rolling is accomplished during combat by pressing **Ⓐ** while moving with 🕹. Rolling is an even better defensive option than guarding. Our Hero is invulnerable while rolling, so with well-timed rolls you can avoid every attack in the game. This indispensable defensive technique is useful in all situations—from escaping crowds of hollow men or hobbes, to leaping out of a blast of explosives thrown by mercenary bosses, to dodging the scattershot barrages of enemy marksmen.

*There are six different spell gauntlets. Eventually, through **spell weaving**, different gauntlets can be paired in numerous ways for tons of different spell effects. There's an Achievement available for using every possible spell effect!*

When in doubt, roll!

THE SCARS OF BATTLE

Healing over time—simply avoid foes until the red blotches on the screen fade away.

Damage in combat is represented by deepening red blotches around the perimeter of the screen, and around the D-Pad display in the lower left-hand corner. Continue to take damage, and the screen continues to redden. Once your heart starts pounding, the end is awfully close. Take too much damage, and you'll be knocked out. Eating a knockout erases your progress to the next Guild Seal, and can lead to scarring. Luckily, there are several ways to heal up during battle to avoid being knocked out.

 Potions restore health instantly. If you're in dire straights, available potions are accessible by pressing right on ⊙.

 Various food items also restore health. The currently equipped food item is available in combat by pressing left on ⊙.

Getting knocked out even **once** means you can't get the **You Can't Bring Me Down** Achievement!

LEGENDARY WEAPONS THAT CAN HELP YOU STAY HEALTHY

WEAPON NAME		LEGENDARY BONUS	OBJECTIVE	REWARD
SWORD	The Inquisitor	Bloodsucker	Kill 300 villagers or soldiers.	Gain Health per Hit
	Really Sharp Pair of Scissors	Artist	Kill 400 human enemies.	Gain Health with Each Hit
HAMMER	Trollblight	Regeneration	Earn Guild Seals from evil expressions.	Gain Health with Each Hit
PISTOL	Holy Vengeance	Paladin	Drag 10 criminals to jail.	Gain Health with Each Hit
	Desert Fury	Man-Eater	Kill 150 men.	Gain Health with Each Hit
	Bloodcraver	Blood Drainer	Kill 300 villagers or soldiers.	Gain Health with Each Hit

TOOLS OF THE TRADE

Very early on in the events of *Fable III* you acquire the weapons of your forebear—a sword, hammer, pistol, and rifle. These are the **Hero weapons**. As you increase your weapon levels along the **Road to Rule**, the damage ratings on weapons also increase. In addition to increasing in power when leveled up, Hero weapons also morph in response to your behavior in Albion. Use one type of magic primarily, for example, and your Hero weapons may adopt the color hue or effect of that spell.

All kinds of things can alter the physical traits of Hero weapons: the spells you use, the enemies you fight most often, whether you're aligned with good or evil, even whether you use potions frequently or spend lots of money.

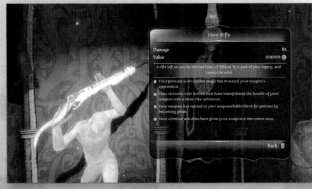

Higher weapon levels from Road to Rule treasure chests mean more unique traits on each Hero weapon.

On top of the four Hero weapons, there are also over fifty **Legendary weapons** to collect. The Hero weapons are completely adequate for the entire game and develop unique traits, but most Legendary weapons hit harder. Most importantly, Legendary weapons are customizable too, in specific ways. Each Legendary weapon has three powerful bonuses that can be unlocked if the right objectives are fulfilled *while that weapon is equipped*. Many bonuses are fabulous, but the work to achieve them is grueling. You'll have to pay attention to which weapons you're wielding as you go about various tasks—from making friends, to spending money, to using certain attacks or killing certain enemies. There are a few things to consider when leveling up Legendary weapons. First, when possible, double up by equipping a melee weapon and a gun with similar unlock objectives! Second, look for bonuses that "overlap" each other—for example, the Bonesmasher pistol rewards killing hollow men, killing enemies during the day, and killing with flourishes. Kill a hollow man with a flourish during the day, and you make progress toward all three rewards! As bonuses are unlocked, different weapons become more effective in specific situations. To aid you as a reference, we've included tables of related weapons in various places throughout this guide.

Some bonus prerequisites are easy to achieve, while most are not. Compare bonuses in the Hero's Sanctuary, or in this very chapter.

Unlocked: Vandal
Result: Extra Knockdown

Weapon store owners restock what they sell, so you can buy extra weapons to have on hand for online bartering.

Some Legendary weapon bonuses grant abilities available nowhere else, like giving spell effects to normal melee swings, or adding shotgun spray to gunfire.

Oh, and another couple things about Legendary weapons—first, you can't get them all by yourself! **On a given Gamertag, only 26 of the Legendary weapons are obtainable solo: 12 from shops and 12 more from treasure chests, and 2 from quest rewards.** Second, the weapons you can receive per playthrough are also, more or less, random. The contents of stores, rewards for some quests, and contents of some treasure chests are simply "random Legendary weapon," so the weapons won't all show up on a given playthrough. Don't fret though, this is the point—it's encouragement to hop on Xbox LIVE to trade for the weapons you need with other players. You can also take part in commerce in their kingdoms, making money far more quickly than is possible offline, so there's plenty of incentive!

From the Xbox LIVE Online room of the Hero's Sanctuary you can interact with Heroes from other worlds.

WEAPON COLLECTION

Any given playthrough of *Fable III* may see a different lineup of Legendary weapons for sale in stores and waiting in treasure chests. While a handful of Legendary weapons are always found in a couple chests or received at the end of a few quests, most of the time what you get is up to chance. For this reason, we only list an acquisition method for those weapons that can always be acquired. If no acquisition method is listed, then that weapon must be received as loot, either as a random treasure chest reward or quest spoils. Weapons neither found in a store nor a chest must be tracked down in trades over Xbox LIVE. As your own trade bait, you have the contents of the weapon shops in Brightwall Village, Bowerstone Market, and potentially Aurora. These blacksmiths always restock the same weapons on a given playthrough, so this pool of weapons represents your bargaining chips with other players online, who will themselves have different stocks of weapons available from the stores in their worlds.

LEGENDARY WEAPON ACQUISITION

LOCATION	RESULT
Treasure Chest in Mourningwood	The Bonesmasher
Mourningwood Silver Key Chest (10)	Random Legendary weapon
Mill Fields Silver Key Chest (20)	Random Legendary weapon
Aurora Silver Key Chest (20)	Random Legendary weapon
Sunset House Gold Key Door	Random Legendary weapon
Treasure Chest in Hero's Sanctuary Trophy Room	Random Legendary weapon
Mistpeak Valley Demon Door	Random Legendary weapon
Aurora Demon Door	Random good or evil Legendary weapon, depending on Hero alignment
Beat high score at Mourningwood Fort mortar	Random Legendary weapon
Complete Limited Collector's Edition Quest in Silverpines	Wolfsbane
Complete Slave Mine Puzzle	Random Legendary weapon
Complete Dark Sanctum Quests	The Tenderiser
Gnomewrecker	Collect and turn in all 50 gnomes
The Ossuary Gold Key Door Reward	Random Legendary weapon – Relic
Bowerstone Castle Silver Key Chest (50)	Random Legendary weapon – Relic

COMBAT POWER

The strength of your swings, shots, and spells increases as the game progresses, based on the damage ratings of the weapons that are equipped, and the combat stats of your character. Damage can also be influenced by unlockable bonuses on Legendary weapons, along with weaknesses particular enemies have to certain attacks.

STATS (INCREASE THROUGH USE)	ATTACK TYPES (POWER UP ON THE ROAD TO RULE)	WEAPONS
Hero Level & Strength	Melee Attacks	Swords
Hero Level & Strength	Melee Attacks	Hammers
Hero Level & Stature	Ranged Attacks	Pistols
Hero Level & Stature	Ranged Attacks	Rifles
Hero Level & Magical Aura	Magic Attacks	Spell Gauntlets

DAMAGE AND ATTACK LEVEL

Each attack type (melee, guns, and spells) starts at level 0. This level can be increased by opening treasure chests along the **Road to Rule**. There are five chests for each attack type, for five upgrades each. You can check the current level for a given type in the **Armory** of the **Hero's Sanctuary**, or at the **Hero Status** panel. As you open level-increasing Road to Rule chests for melee or ranged attacks, you uniformly upgrade the damage rating of every related weapon. Finishing moves appear more often in combat with higher-level weapons, too. Every weapon's appearance also changes, and your Hero weapons morph according to your behavior up to that point. Opening higher-level chests for magic spells increases the power and overall effect of all spells, while also decreasing the time required to charge up high-level spells. However, there is a special case. There are 4 levels of Legendary weapons: Common, Uncommon, Rare, and Relics. The weapon's level determines how much damage each inflicts. The damage gaps between these weapons increases as the Hero levels up that attack skill.

ROAD TO RULE COMBAT SKILL TREASURE CHESTS

UPGRADE LEVEL	AVAILABILITY	GUILD SEAL COST
Lv1	Road to Rule 2: After Music Box	20 for each type
Lv2	Road to Rule 3: After Saker	40 each
Lv3	Road to Rule 6: Swift Promise	60 each
Lv4	Road to Rule 8: Page Promise	80 each
Lv5	Road to Rule 10	100 each

COMBAT STATS—STRENGTH, STATURE, AND MAGICAL AURA

Dealing damage and scoring kills with a given attack type grants experience toward the related stat. The more experience you have, the higher your combat multiplier is for that type of attack. These three stats together give your Hero his power, and the more powerful you are, the more damage you do in combat, and the better the loot you get from chests.

STRENGTH, STATURE, AND MAGICAL AURA PROGRESSION

STAR RATING (AS SHOWN BY THE HERO STATUS PANEL)	ACTUAL EXPERIENCE SPECTRUM	COMBAT MULTIPLIER
—	0~17%	1~1.17x
★	18~33%	1.18x~1.33x
★★	34~50%	1.34x~1.5x
★★★	51~71%	1.51x~1.71x
★★★★	72~83%	1.72x~1.83x
★★★★★	84~100%	1.84x~2x

You won't know exactly where you are in statistic progression, but that's fine. You were going to hit things anyway, weren't you?

Strength, and therefore melee damage, is increased by pounding enemies into submission with swords and hammers. Your Hero grows brawnier the higher their strength grows.

Stature, and therefore gun damage, is increased by gunning down foes. As stature increases, so too does height.

Magical aura, and therefore spell damage, is increased by pulverizing the opposition with spells. A high magical aura stat makes the Hero glow with power while charging flourishes or spells.

HERO LEVEL

Hero level is one of the most important numbers in the game. It determines the numbers and types of enemies you face, and the quality of random loot you receive. Hero level is set at 1 at the beginning of the game, and it can increase to a max of 10. Hero level is an aggregate of three stats—**strength**, **stature**, and **magical aura**.

HERO LEVEL	ACTUAL EXPERIENCE SPECTRUM*
1	0~9%
2	10~19%
3	20~29%
4	30~39%
5	40~49%
6	50~59%
7	60~69%
8	70~79%
9	80~89%
10	90~100%

Derived from strength, stature, magical aura, and Road to Rule weapon skill unlocks

COMBAT STRATEGY —FOR ALBION!

Actual battles in *Fable III* are almost always against large groups of assailants—this revolutionary leader can hardly catch a break, eh? Groups of wolves, corrupt soldiers, mercenaries, hobbes, hollow men, or any of a host of other vile creatures surround you and close in cautiously. At lower Hero levels these groups are fairly weak in strength, and similarly unprepared in tactics.

Against disorganized groups of wildlife or humans, any battle plan you like should see the day won.

Further in the game, as the story progresses and you develop your power, renown, and Hero level, enemy numbers swell and their formations become more robust. Increasingly, enemy ranks are broken down between melee combatants and armed backlines. You'll have to choose between dealing with melee attackers first while being peppered with bullets from afar, or charge past enemy fighters to close in on their pesky, gun-toting support.

Enemy marksmen usually miss you if you keep moving laterally around them, but their gunfire interferes if you stop to attack some of their bludgeon-wielding friends. Rush for the gunmen to take them out. They are predictably weak in close-quarter combat.

Eventually, larger, boss-type enemies begin to appear in enemy formations. These burlier baddies have access to attacks their lesser brethren lack, such as firebombs or magic of their own. Some of these enemy leaders can even summon more foes if you kill members of their contingent. Thus, the strategy here becomes further complicated; you still have to deal with melee fighters and enemy marksmen, choosing which to prioritize, but now you also have their boss to contend with. Focus on the minor foes and their boss may nail you with powerful, explosive attacks from afar, meanwhile any lower-ranking foe you dispatched may just be replaced. Against these groups, you'll want to bring your strongest abilities to bear clearing out minor foes while you focus the majority of your attention on the boss. On the other hand, if you're confident, these large-scale skirmishes also represent an ideal opportunity to "grind" experience toward Hero level or bonuses for Legendary weapons. You can simply keep murdering whatever aides the boss-type enemies throw at you, for as long as you please!

Heftier foes include mercenary bosses, fearsome undead, and elite hobbe magicians. While you can shrug off plenty of stray blows and bullets from normal foes, these stronger enemies can knock you out in just a few hits. Ignore or bat aside lesser enemies while focusing your damage—and your damage avoidance—on the beefiest of the bunch.

MELEE WEAPONS

SWORDS

Swords are the more agile of the two melee weapons; you won't hit as hard with a blade as with a hammer, but you can make up for it in speed.

HERO SWORD

A sword left to you by the last Hero of Albion. It is part of your legacy, and cannot be sold.

ACQUISITION: *Story progress.*

VALUE	LV0 DMG	LV1 DMG	LV2 DMG	LV3 DMG	LV4 DMG	LV5 DMG
4000~104,000	10	15	23	30	54	76

THE SCIMITAR OF BARON SLAYING +3

This weapon comes from the Artefacts and Armaments Codex for the popular game *Hollows and Hobbes* (3rd Edition, revision 1.5.2.2.1.7.3.0.0.0.8b).

ACQUISITION: *Only available during* **The Game** *quest.*

Lv5

VALUE	LV0 DMG	LV1 DMG	LV2 DMG	LV3 DMG	LV4 DMG	LV5 DMG
1,005,000	10	15	23	30	54	76

LEGENDARY BONUS	OBJECTIVE	REWARD
Know-It-All	Learn all the rules, even the really obscure ones.	+30% Sense of Self-Importance
Space Geek	Memorize quotes from fictional science fiction plays.	+90% Damage vs Space Elves
Oh, The Irony	Try desperately hard to make fun of stereotypes.	-50% Self Awareness

THE LOVE SWORD

Created by Lawrence the Licentious (also known as Lusty Larry), who was famous for his many, many conquests, and who left behind a legacy of many, many illegitimate children.

Lv5

VALUE	LV0 DMG	LV1 DMG	LV2 DMG	LV3 DMG	LV4 DMG	LV5 DMG
4200	11	16	24	31	55	77

LEGENDARY BONUS	OBJECTIVE	REWARD
Breeder	Have 5 children.	+8 Extra Damage
Lover	Have sex with women 20 times.	+8 Extra Damage
Phwoar	Make 5 villagers love you.	+25% Attractiveness, Immunity to Scarring

THE MERCHANT'S BODYGUARD

Created by the ancient order of Darkwood Traders, the Merchant's Bodyguard was used to protect the caravan while generating more income.

ACQUISITION: *Shops.*

Lv5

VALUE	LV0 DMG	LV1 DMG	LV2 DMG	LV3 DMG	LV4 DMG	LV5 DMG
2300	12	17	25	32	56	78

LEGENDARY BONUS	OBJECTIVE	REWARD
Big Spender	Spend 8,000 of your personal gold.	+20% Damage in Multiplayer
Profiteer	Kill 400 mercenaries.	+10 Extra Damage
Trader	Give gifts to 20 players over Xbox LIVE.	Gain Money with Each Hit.

THE SPLADE

This ingenious multipurpose killing tool is equally capable at digging treasure from the ground, or the heart out of a man.

ACQUISITION: *Shops.*

Lv5

VALUE	LV0 DMG	LV1 DMG	LV2 DMG	LV3 DMG	LV4 DMG	LV5 DMG
2200	13	18	26	33	57	79

LEGENDARY BONUS		OBJECTIVE	REWARD
	Scrounger	Dig up 30 items.	Earn Guild Seals Faster in Combat.
	Stabber	Kill 300 human enemies.	+10% Chance of Knockback vs Human Enemies
	Purge	Kill 50 nobles.	+10 Extra Damage

THE CASANOVA

This weapon was developed by Reaver Industries to help some of the less outgoing members of the royal guards find love.

ACQUISITION: *Shops.*

Lv5

VALUE	LV0 DMG	LV1 DMG	LV2 DMG	LV3 DMG	LV4 DMG	LV5 DMG
8200	15	23	32	40	65	88

LEGENDARY BONUS		OBJECTIVE	REWARD
	Charmer	Become friends with 30 villagers.	Earn Guild Seals Faster in Combat.
	Perfectionist	Kill 200 ugly enemies.	+12 Extra Damage
	Beloved	Make 5 villagers love you.	+25% Attractiveness, Immunity to Scarring

SLIMQUICK

The Slimquick line of weapons has achieved notoriety for the counterintuitive way it allows users to lose weight by putting it on.

ACQUISITION: *Shops.*

Lv5

VALUE	LV0 DMG	LV1 DMG	LV2 DMG	LV3 DMG	LV4 DMG	LV5 DMG
8100	14	22	31	39	64	87

LEGENDARY BONUS		OBJECTIVE	REWARD
	Scrounger	Dig up 30 items.	Earn Guild Seals Faster in Combat.
	Stabber	Kill 300 human enemies.	+10% Chance of Knockback vs Human Enemies
	Purge	Kill 50 nobles.	+10 Extra Damage

MR STABBY

For a short period, Mr Stabby was the most popular weapon for personal defense in Albion. Its popularity waned with time, as most of its owners were ultimately stabbed.

ACQUISITION: *Shops.*

Lv5

VALUE	LV0 DMG	LV1 DMG	LV2 DMG	LV3 DMG	LV4 DMG	LV5 DMG
8100	15	23	32	40	65	88

LEGENDARY BONUS		OBJECTIVE	REWARD
	Massacre	Kill 60 villagers or soldiers with flourishes.	+15 Extra Damage
	Assassin	Decrease your moral standing.	Gain Money and Evil with Each Hit
	Taskmaster	Drag 8 villagers to work.	Gain Money and Evil with Each Hit

WOLFSBANE

It is said that this sword was forged by wolves during the great Lupine Wars over a thousand years ago.

ACQUISITION: *Complete Limited Collector's Edition quest in Silverpines.*

Lv5

VALUE	LV0 DMG	LV1 DMG	LV2 DMG	LV3 DMG	LV4 DMG	LV5 DMG
8600	15	23	32	40	65	88

LEGENDARY BONUS		OBJECTIVE	REWARD
	Overkill	Kill 50 enemies with flourishes.	Earn Guild Seals Faster in Combat.
	Lupinator	Kill 50 wolves or balverines.	+40% Damage vs Wolves and Balverines
	Moonglow	Kill 50 enemies at night.	+40% Damage at Night

THE CHANNELER

Forged by the legendary spellcaster Garth. His research into the marriage of magic and steel allowed him to imbue this weapon with some of his impressive abilities.

Lv5

VALUE	LV0 DMG	LV1 DMG	LV2 DMG	LV3 DMG	LV4 DMG	LV5 DMG
8200	16	24	33	41	66	89

LEGENDARY BONUS		OBJECTIVE	REWARD
	Quester	Complete 30 quests.	+ Shock Damage
	Researcher	Spend 8,000 of your personal gold.	Earn Guild Seals Faster in Combat.
	Bladestorm	Kill 100 enemies with an unwoven Blades spell.	+15 Extra Damage

SHARDBORNE

Made from a shard washed up in Bloodstone Bay, this weapon emits pure evil. It becomes a powerful tool in the wrong hands.

Lv5

VALUE	LV0 DMG	LV1 DMG	LV2 DMG	LV3 DMG	LV4 DMG	LV5 DMG
8400	16	24	33	41	66	89

LEGENDARY BONUS	OBJECTIVE	REWARD
Unholy	Decrease your moral standing.	+5 Extra Damage, +30% vs Non-Evil Enemies
Darkness	Kill 200 enemies at night.	+15 Extra Damage
Heartless	Drag 8 villagers to work.	Gain Money per Hit

THE INQUISITOR

Reaver used the Inquisitor to spread his influence throughout Bloodstone. Any who stood in his way were ruthlessly dealt with.

Lv5

VALUE	LV0 DMG	LV1 DMG	LV2 DMG	LV3 DMG	LV4 DMG	LV5 DMG
8500	16	24	33	41	66	89

LEGENDARY BONUS	OBJECTIVE	REWARD
Extravagant	Spend 3000 of your personal gold.	+15 Extra Damage
Extort	Earn Guild Seals from evil expressions.	Gain Money per Hit
Bloodsucker	Kill 300 villagers or soldiers.	Gain Health per Hit

BEADLE'S CUTLASS

Called 'the greatest weapon ever made' by its creator, Barnaby Beadle. Weapon experts agree that this is an exaggeration, and that it is in fact the 28th best weapon ever made.

Lv5

VALUE	LV0 DMG	LV1 DMG	LV2 DMG	LV3 DMG	LV4 DMG	LV5 DMG
8500	16	24	33	41	66	89

LEGENDARY BONUS	OBJECTIVE	REWARD
Dayripper	Kill 300 enemies in the daytime.	Earn Guild Seals Faster in Combat.
Killer	Kill 100 enemies with flourishes.	+15 Extra Damage
Braggadocio	Complete 30 quests.	+30% Damage vs Human Enemies

REALLY SHARP PAIR OF SCISSORS

Hoping to cultivate a fearsome legend, blacksmith Harvey Bindle named this dastardly weapon after the scariest thing he could think of.

Lv5

VALUE	LV0 DMG	LV1 DMG	LV2 DMG	LV3 DMG	LV4 DMG	LV5 DMG
12,100	17	28	38	48	74	98

LEGENDARY BONUS	OBJECTIVE	REWARD
Surgeon	Kill 80 human enemies with flourishes.	+30% Damage vs Human Enemies
Despot	Earn Guild Seals from evil expressions.	Earn Guild Seals Faster in Combat.
Artist	Kill 400 human enemies.	Gain Health with Each Hit

SOULDRINKER

No one knows who forged this sword. It is said to have been summoned from a black abyss by a necromancer.

Lv5

VALUE	LV0 DMG	LV1 DMG	LV2 DMG	LV3 DMG	LV4 DMG	LV5 DMG
8300	16	24	33	41	66	89

LEGENDARY BONUS	OBJECTIVE	REWARD
Blackguard	Decrease your moral standing.	Earn Guild Seals Faster in Combat.
Shadow Drain	Kill 100 enemies found near Aurora.	30% Damage vs Human Enemies
Thug	Earn Guild Seals from evil expressions.	+15 Extra Damage

THUNDERBLADE

The great old Hero Thunder is said to have been able to rend the sky with this. The rumour was started by Thunder himself, and was widely discredited by his sister, Whisper.

Lv5

VALUE	LV0 DMG	LV1 DMG	LV2 DMG	LV3 DMG	LV4 DMG	LV5 DMG
12,100	18	29	39	49	75	99

LEGENDARY BONUS	OBJECTIVE	REWARD
Show-off	Kill 200 enemies with flourishes.	Earn Guild Seals Faster in Combat.
Electrocutioner	Kill 200 enemies with an unwoven Shock spell.	+ Chance to Stun Enemy
Hero	Complete 30 quests.	Earn Guild Seals Faster in Combat

AVO'S LAMENTATION

A sister to the legendary Avo's Tear, this weapon was forged at the same time, but was lost for centuries.

Lv5

VALUE	LV0 DMG	LV1 DMG	LV2 DMG	LV3 DMG	LV4 DMG	LV5 DMG
12,700	18	29	39	49	75	99

LEGENDARY BONUS	OBJECTIVE	REWARD
Righteous	Increase your moral standing.	+20% Damage vs Evil Enemies
Blessed	Make 5 villagers love you.	Earn Guild Seals Faster in Combat.
Holy Blast	Kill 200 hollow men.	+ Shock Damage

THE SWINGING SWORD

Often misidentified as 'The Singing Sword', this weapon thrives on a wielder who is, shall we say, generous with their affections.

Lv5

VALUE	LV0 DMG	LV1 DMG	LV2 DMG	LV3 DMG	LV4 DMG	LV5 DMG
16,700	20	35	47	55	83	108

LEGENDARY BONUS	OBJECTIVE	REWARD
Man's Best Friend	Have sex with men 15 times.	Earn Guild Seals Faster in Combat.
Ladykiller	Have sex with women 15 times.	Earn Guild Seals Faster in Combat.
Swinger	Have an orgy with 4 other people.	+25 Extra Damage

HAMMERS

Hammers hit hard, and are more likely to knock enemies about than swords. For these privileges, hammers are a little slower. The weight might have something to do with it, too.

HERO HAMMER

A hammer left to you by the last Hero of Albion. It is part of your legacy, and cannot be sold.

ACQUISITION: *Story progress.*

Lv5

VALUE	LV0 DMG	LV1 DMG	LV2 DMG	LV3 DMG	LV4 DMG	LV5 DMG
4000~104,000	14	20	30	40	71	100

AURORA'S SHIELD

Wielded by the long-dead champion Saler the Righteous and his soldiers, this model of hammer has crushed untold legions of Aurora's enemies.

ACQUISITION: *Shops.*

Lv5

VALUE	LV0 DMG	LV1 DMG	LV2 DMG	LV3 DMG	LV4 DMG	LV5 DMG
2000	15	21	31	41	72	101

LEGENDARY BONUS	OBJECTIVE	REWARD
Protector	Kill 30 enemies found near Aurora.	+40% Damage vs Enemies Found Near Aurora
Policeman	Drag 10 criminals to jail.	+30% Damage vs Evil Human Enemies
Faith	Make 5 villagers love you.	Earn Guild Seals Faster in Combat

FAERIE HAMMER OF THE MOON KING

Many have looked askance at the fragile, unassuming aspect of this hammer, shortly before it bashed their heads into very small pieces.

ACQUISITION: *Shops.*

Lv5

VALUE	LV0 DMG	LV1 DMG	LV2 DMG	LV3 DMG	LV4 DMG	LV5 DMG
2200	16	22	32	42	73	102

LEGENDARY BONUS	OBJECTIVE	REWARD
Assassin	Kill 100 enemies with flourishes.	+1 Gold per Hit
Loved	Make 5 villagers love you.	Earn Guild Seals Faster in Combat
Adventurer	Complete 30 quests.	+10 Extra Damage

TROLLBLIGHT

A set of weapons commissioned by Logan to exterminate every last troll from Albion. As anyone travelling through the kingdom can testify, the campaign was entirely successful.

ACQUISITION: *Shops.*

Lv5

VALUE	LV0 DMG	LV1 DMG	LV2 DMG	LV3 DMG	LV4 DMG	LV5 DMG
2100	17	23	33	43	74	103

LEGENDARY BONUS	OBJECTIVE	REWARD
Giantbane	Kill 10 large enemies with flourishes.	+80% Damage vs Large Enemies
Trollbane	Kill 150 enemies with an unwoven Fireball spell.	+ Flame Damage
Regeneration	Earn Guild Seals from evil expressions.	Gain Health with Each Hit

DRAGONBONE HAMMER

Made from the vertebra of an ancient dragon, this hammer is shrouded in mystery. The principal mystery is: what sort of person goes around making hammers out of dragon bones?

ACQUISITION: *Shops.*

Lv5

VALUE	LV0 DMG	LV1 DMG	LV2 DMG	LV3 DMG	LV4 DMG	LV5 DMG
8200	18	27	39	51	84	115

LEGENDARY BONUS	OBJECTIVE	REWARD
Headsmacker	Kill 100 human enemies with flourishes.	Extra Knockdown vs Human Enemies
Dragonfire	Kill 150 enemies with an unwoven Fireball spell.	+ Flame Damage
Overseer	Drag 8 villagers to work.	+14 Extra Damage

SORROW'S FIST

Found deep in an Auroran cave, Sorrow's Fist is blighted by the shadows that inhabit its dark steel.

Lv5

VALUE	LV0 DMG	LV1 DMG	LV2 DMG	LV3 DMG	LV4 DMG	LV5 DMG
8300	18	27	39	51	84	115

LEGENDARY BONUS	OBJECTIVE	REWARD
Lovestruck	Kill 5 villagers who love you.	Extra Knockdown vs Human Enemies
Menace	Earn Guild Seals from evil expressions.	+14 Extra Damage
Loose Morals	Have an orgy with 4 other people.	Earn Guild Seals Faster in Combat

LUNARIUM POUNDER

The blacksmith Caramax Incunabulus created this line of powerful hammers to work with the rare substance lunarium, until then thought to be completely immalleable.

ACQUISITION: *Shops.*

Lv5

VALUE	LV0 DMG	LV1 DMG	LV2 DMG	LV3 DMG	LV4 DMG	LV5 DMG
7800	18	27	39	51	84	115

LEGENDARY BONUS	OBJECTIVE	REWARD
Night Watchman	Kill 200 enemies at night.	Extra Knockdown vs All Enemies
Thud!	Kill 100 enemies with flourishes.	+10% Chance of Knockback per Hit
Hunter	Kill 100 wolves or balverines.	+40% Damage vs wolves and balverines

MALLETT'S MALLET

Made by master blacksmith Timothy Mallett, this weapon is especially good at inflicting head trauma on smaller humanoids.

ACQUISITION: *Shops.*

Lv5

VALUE	LV0 DMG	LV1 DMG	LV2 DMG	LV3 DMG	LV4 DMG	LV5 DMG
8000	19	28	40	52	85	116

LEGENDARY BONUS	OBJECTIVE	REWARD
Vandal	Smash 40 crates.	Extra Knockdown
Bleurgh!	Kill 200 short enemies.	+15 Extra Damage
Big Hitter	Become friends with 30 villagers.	+10% Chance of Knockback vs All Enemies

THE ABSOLVER

Hammer used this weapon to mete out justice in the name of her father, murdered in the Temple of Light.

Lv5

VALUE	LV0 DMG	LV1 DMG	LV2 DMG	LV3 DMG	LV4 DMG	LV5 DMG
8500	19	28	40	52	85	116

LEGENDARY BONUS	OBJECTIVE	REWARD
Big Hearted	Make yourself fatter.	+15 Extra Damage
Party Animal	Become friends with 30 villagers.	Earn Guild Seals Faster in Combat
Absolution	Kill 200 evil enemies.	+20% Damage vs Evil Enemies

TANNAR'S GLORY

Tannar was an ancient Auroran warrior who dedicated his life to defending his people. He protected the Auroran city from the many threats that beset it from the deserts.

Lv5

VALUE	LV0 DMG	LV1 DMG	LV2 DMG	LV3 DMG	LV4 DMG	LV5 DMG
9000	20	29	41	53	86	117

LEGENDARY BONUS	OBJECTIVE	REWARD
Defender	Kill 30 enemies found near Aurora.	+30% Damage vs Enemies Found Near Aurora
Enforcer	Drag 10 criminals to jail.	+16 Extra Damage
Holy Fire	Kill 150 enemies with flourishes.	+ Flame Damage

HAMMER OF WILMAGEDDON

This rare weapon was forged by famed blacksmith Henry Geddon under the direction of his wife Wilma, who was said to have magical aptitude.

Lv5

VALUE	LV0 DMG	LV1 DMG	LV2 DMG	LV3 DMG	LV4 DMG	LV5 DMG
8350	20	29	41	53	86	117

LEGENDARY BONUS	OBJECTIVE	REWARD
Fire Mage	Kill 100 enemies with an unwoven Fireball spell.	+ Flame Damage
Blast	Kill 200 enemies with an unwoven Shock spell.	+ Shock Damage
Bonebreaker	Kill 150 hollow men.	+15 Extra Damage

THE CHAMPION

Found in the ruins of the old Hero Guild, this weapon has an engraving indicating it was wielded by the Guild's greatest champion.

Lv5

VALUE	LV0 DMG	LV1 DMG	LV2 DMG	LV3 DMG	LV4 DMG	LV5 DMG
8500	20	29	41	53	86	117

LEGENDARY BONUS	OBJECTIVE	REWARD
Heartbreaker	Make 5 villagers love you.	Earn Guild Seals Faster in Combat
Wrath	Increase your moral standing.	+ Flame Damage
Adventurer	Complete 30 quests.	+15 Extra Damage

SCYTHE'S WARHAMMER

It is foretold that one day Scythe will return to Albion. When he does, he might want his hammer back. Just a heads-up.

Lv5

VALUE	LV0 DMG	LV1 DMG	LV2 DMG	LV3 DMG	LV4 DMG	LV5 DMG
11,800	21	33	47	61	96	129

LEGENDARY BONUS	OBJECTIVE	REWARD
Avenger	Kill 300 evil enemies.	+21 Extra Damage
Stormlord	Kill 200 enemies with an unwoven Shock spell.	+ Shock Damage
Legendary	Complete 30 quests.	Earn Guild Seals Faster in Combat

THE TENDERISER

This hammer was used by the Dark Sanctum Brotherhood to prepare their older, tougher sacrifices.

ACQUISITION: *Complete Dark Sanctum quests.*

Lv5

VALUE	LV0 DMG	LV1 DMG	LV2 DMG	LV3 DMG	LV4 DMG	LV5 DMG
12,500	22	34	48	62	97	130

LEGENDARY BONUS	OBJECTIVE	REWARD
Soul Burner	Kill 3 spouses.	Lose Weight and Purity With Each Hit.
Fiend	Earn Guild Seals from evil expressions.	Earn Guild Seals Faster in Combat
Tenderise	Kill 150 villagers or soldiers with flourishes.	+20 Extra Damage

THE TYPO

A weapon designed not only for fighting enemies, but also for winning the hearts and minds of civilians. Its name is an acronym for Tactical Personal Offensive Weapon.

Lv5

VALUE	LV0 DMG	LV1 DMG	LV2 DMG	LV3 DMG	LV4 DMG	LV5 DMG
11,700	21	33	47	61	96	129

LEGENDARY BONUS	OBJECTIVE	REWARD
Popular	Make 5 villagers love you.	Earn Guild Seals Faster in Combat
Chum	Become friends with 30 villagers.	Gain Money with Each Hit
Thwack!	Kill 100 enemies with flourishes.	Earn Guild Seals Faster in Combat

JACK'S HAMMER

Imbued with pure evil, this hammer was used by the infamous Jack of Blades to activate magical focal sites hundreds of years ago.

Lv5

VALUE	LV0 DMG	LV1 DMG	LV2 DMG	LV3 DMG	LV4 DMG	LV5 DMG
16,500	24	39	55	71	108	143

LEGENDARY BONUS	OBJECTIVE	REWARD
Blademaster	Kill 50 villagers or soldiers with flourishes.	+30% Damage to Humans
Shade	Kill 400 shadow creatures.	+30% Damage to Dark Minions and Sentinels
Murderer	Kill 100 villagers or soldiers.	+20 Extra Damage

RANGED WEAPONS

PISTOLS

Pistols are quicker to fire than rifles, and also hold one more round per reload. The shells from a pistol don't pack as hefty a wallop, though.

HERO PISTOL

A pistol left to you by the last Hero of Albion. It is part of your legacy, and cannot be sold.

ACQUISITION: *Story progress.*

Lv5

VALUE	LV0 DMG	LV1 DMG	LV2 DMG	LV3 DMG	LV4 DMG	LV5 DMG
4000~104,000	14	19	26	32	53	73

GUNS THAT CAN HAVE A SHOTGUN SPRAY EFFECT

WEAPON NAME		LEGENDARY BONUS	OBJECTIVE	REWARD
PISTOL	Holy Vengeance	Avenger	Kill 200 evil enemies.	+ Shotgun Spray
	The Bonesmasher	Shotgunner	Hit 500 enemies with a flourish attack.	+ Shotgun Spray
	Briar's Blaster	Blaster	Earn 10,000 gold from jobs.	+ Shotgun Spray
	The Ice Maiden	Sledger	Earn Guild Seals from evil expressions.	+ Shotgun Spray
RIFLE	Scattershot	Scattergun	Kill 10 large enemies with flourishes.	+ Shotgun Spray
	Ol' Malice	Explosive	Kill 100 enemies with an unweaved Fireball spell.	+ Shotgun Spray
	Simmon's Shotgun	Exhumation	Dig up 30 items.	+ Shotgun Spray
	The Equaliser	Woodward	Drag 10 criminals to jail.	+ Shotgun Spray
	The Shrieking Pilgrim	Sanctify	Kill 150 hollow men.	+ Shotgun Spray

MIRIAN'S MUTILATOR

Used by Lady Mirian and all of her followers and admirers, this pistol model was used on anyone who didn't agree she was the fairest in the land.

ACQUISITION: *Shops.*

Lv5

VALUE	LV0 DMG	LV1 DMG	LV2 DMG	LV3 DMG	LV4 DMG	LV5 DMG
2300	15	20	27	33	54	74

LEGENDARY BONUS	OBJECTIVE	REWARD
Vanity	Kill 5 people who love you.	+8 Extra Damage
Beloved	Make 10 villagers love you.	Lose Weight with Each Hit
Marriage Addict	Get married 5 times.	+8 Extra Damage

HOLY VENGEANCE

The noble Marcus the Pure crafted this line of extraordinary pistols in his war against evil. He was forced to use one on himself after having impure thoughts one morning.

ACQUISITION: *Shops.*

Lv5

VALUE	LV0 DMG	LV1 DMG	LV2 DMG	LV3 DMG	LV4 DMG	LV5 DMG
2100	16	21	28	34	55	75

LEGENDARY BONUS	OBJECTIVE	REWARD
Paragon	Increase your moral standing.	Earn Guild Seals Faster in Combat
Paladin	Drag 10 criminals to jail.	Gain Health with Each Hit
Avenger	Kill 200 evil enemies.	+ Shotgun Spray

THE BONESMASHER

The latest technology has gone into creating this pistol, especially designed to shatter hollow men into very small pieces.

ACQUISITION: *Treasure chest in Mourningwood.*

Lv5

VALUE	LV0 DMG	LV1 DMG	LV2 DMG	LV3 DMG	LV4 DMG	LV5 DMG
8200	18	23	30	36	57	77

LEGENDARY BONUS	OBJECTIVE	REWARD
Cleric	Kill 300 hollow men.	+7 Extra Damage, +80% vs hollow men
Solar	Kill 250 enemies in the daytime.	+30% Damage to Enemies in Daytime
Shotgunner	Hit 500 enemies with a flourish attack.	+ Shotgun Spray

THE BARNUMIFICATOR

Barnum, one of Albion's great entrepreneurs, bought the rights to this weapon hoping to make a fortune. Sadly, he died before he could witness its success.

ACQUISITION: *Shops.*

Lv5

VALUE	LV0 DMG	LV1 DMG	LV2 DMG	LV3 DMG	LV4 DMG	LV5 DMG
7800	19	27	36	44	67	89

LEGENDARY BONUS	OBJECTIVE	REWARD
Hard Worker	Earn 10,000 gold from jobs.	+1 Gold per Hit
Popular	Become friends with 30 villagers.	+12 Extra Damage
Philanthropist	Give gifts to 20 players over Xbox LIVE.	Gain Money with Each Hit

DESERT FURY

According to legend, the sand furies used pistols like this to kill every last male of the sand fury tribe. Their procreation habits remain a mystery to this day.

ACQUISITION: *Shops.*

Lv5

VALUE	LV0 DMG	LV1 DMG	LV2 DMG	LV3 DMG	LV4 DMG	LV5 DMG
2200	15	23	32	40	63	85

LEGENDARY BONUS	OBJECTIVE	REWARD
Fury	Kill 30 enemies found near Aurora.	+30% Damage vs Enemies Found Near Aurora
Sunblasted	Kill 400 enemies in the daytime.	+30% Damage to Enemies in Daytime
Man-Eater	Kill 150 men.	Gain Health with Each Hit

TEE KILLER SHOOTER

Tee Killer was actually a very nice man when sober. As soon as he got drunk though, he was a fearsome assassin. Nobody really knows why he'd lick salt with every shot.

Lv5

VALUE	LV0 DMG	LV1 DMG	LV2 DMG	LV3 DMG	LV4 DMG	LV5 DMG
8400	20	28	37	45	68	90

LEGENDARY BONUS	OBJECTIVE	REWARD
Nightowl	Kill 200 enemies at night.	+40% Damage at Night
Accumulator	Spend 10,000 of your personal gold.	Gain Money with Each Hit
Hedonist	Have an orgy with 4 other people.	+11 Extra Damage

REAVER INDUSTRIES PERFORATOR

A pistol manufactured by Reaver Industries, combining reliability, accuracy, and a marked tendency to kill anyone shot with it.

ACQUISITION: *Shops.*

Lv5

VALUE	LV0 DMG	LV1 DMG	LV2 DMG	LV3 DMG	LV4 DMG	LV5 DMG
8100	18	26	35	43	66	88

LEGENDARY BONUS	OBJECTIVE	REWARD
Fiend	Decrease your moral standing.	+7 Extra Damage, +30% vs Non-Evil Enemies
Retail Therapy	Spend 10,000 of your personal gold.	Earn Guild Seals Faster in Combat
Player	Have an orgy with 4 other people.	+25% Attractiveness, Immunity to Scarring

BRIAR'S BLASTER

Briar Rose was a greatly misunderstood Hero. The fact that she was rather annoying didn't help her reputation. One thing is indisputable though, she was a great shot.

Lv5

VALUE	LV0 DMG	LV1 DMG	LV2 DMG	LV3 DMG	LV4 DMG	LV5 DMG
8500	20	28	37	45	68	90

LEGENDARY BONUS	OBJECTIVE	REWARD
Blaster	Earn 10,000 gold from jobs.	+ Shotgun Spray
Girl Power	Kill 150 men.	+12 Extra Damage
Heroine	Complete 30 quests.	Earn Guild Seals Faster in Combat

THE ICE MAIDEN

The infamous assassin Scarlet Frost used the Ice Maiden to liquidate any men who stood in her way, and a few who were not in her way but had made inappropriate remarks.

Lv5

VALUE	LV0 DMG	LV1 DMG	LV2 DMG	LV3 DMG	LV4 DMG	LV5 DMG
11,900	21	31	41	50	74	97

LEGENDARY BONUS	OBJECTIVE	REWARD
Man-Hater	Kill 200 men.	+15 Extra Damage
Sledger	Earn Guild Seals from evil expressions.	+ Shotgun Spray
Seduction	Have sex with men 15 times.	+ Flame Damage

GNOMEWRECKER

The ancient Gnomemaker made this weapon to keep his minions in check. After hearing their insults day after day, he found the easiest solution was to use it on himself.

ACQUISITION: *Complete Gnome quest.*

Lv5

VALUE	LV0 DMG	LV1 DMG	LV2 DMG	LV3 DMG	LV4 DMG	LV5 DMG
12,300	21	31	41	50	74	97

LEGENDARY BONUS	OBJECTIVE	REWARD
Shortist	Kill 200 short enemies.	+30% Damage vs Short Enemies
Insulter	Earn Guild Seals from evil expressions.	+10 Extra Damage
Smasher	Kill 100 enemies with flourishes.	+10 Extra Damage

BLOODCRAVER

The Bloodcraver craves blood. It used to be called The Fury of the Poppy Seed Bun, but was renamed after the weapon manufacturer's marketing division got wind of it.

Lv5

VALUE	LV0 DMG	LV1 DMG	LV2 DMG	LV3 DMG	LV4 DMG	LV5 DMG
12,300	22	32	42	51	75	98

LEGENDARY BONUS	OBJECTIVE	REWARD
Blood Drinker	Kill 20 villagers who love you.	Earn Guild Seals Faster in Combat
Overkill	Kill 100 human enemies with flourishes.	+16 Extra Damage
Blood Drainer	Kill 300 villagers or soldiers.	Gain Health with Each Hit

CHICKENBANE

The scourge of chickens across Albion. This weapon could easily have been called Chickenscourge, but that name didn't test well.

Lv5

VALUE	LV0 DMG	LV1 DMG	LV2 DMG	LV3 DMG	LV4 DMG	LV5 DMG
16,200	23	36	48	59	95	110

LEGENDARY BONUS	OBJECTIVE	REWARD
Kicker	Kick 100 chickens.	+10% Chance of Knockback per Hit
Scratcher	Dig up 30 items.	+12 Extra Damage
Swashbuckler	Complete 30 quests.	+12 Extra Damage

DRAGONSTOMPER .48

Only six of these fine weapons were ever made. Reaver has collected five of them. You now possess the sixth.

Lv5

VALUE	LV0 DMG	LV1 DMG	LV2 DMG	LV3 DMG	LV4 DMG	LV5 DMG
16,700	24	37	49	60	96	111

LEGENDARY BONUS	OBJECTIVE	REWARD
Revolutionist	Kill 50 nobles.	Earn Guild Seals Faster in Combat
Dragon's Breath	Kill 150 enemies with flourishes.	+ Flame Damage
Workaholic	Earn 10,000 gold from jobs.	+18 Extra Damage

RIFLES

Mirroring the relationship of hammers to swords, rifles are more powerful than pistols, but at some cost to speed. Rifles also discharge one less round per reload.

HERO RIFLE

A rifle left to you by the last Hero of Albion. It is part of your legacy, and cannot be sold.

ACQUISITION: *Story progress.*

Lv5

VALUE	LV0 DMG	LV1 DMG	LV2 DMG	LV3 DMG	LV4 DMG	LV5 DMG
4000~104,000	19	22	29	37	60	81

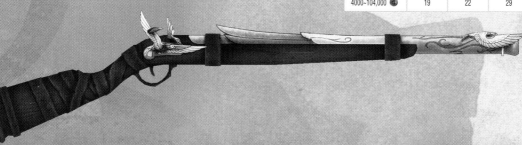

DEFENDER OF THE FAITH

Rifles like this were once carried by Karl the Misguided and his followers, Temple of Light monks who were not entirely clear on the meaning of the word 'pacifist'.

ACQUISITION: *Shops.*

Lv5

VALUE	LV0 DMG	LV1 DMG	LV2 DMG	LV3 DMG	LV4 DMG	LV5 DMG
2200	20	23	30	38	61	82

LEGENDARY BONUS	OBJECTIVE	REWARD
Settled	Get married.	Earn Guild Seals Faster in Combat
Sunblessed	Kill 400 enemies in the daytime.	+30% Damage to Enemies in Daytime
Avenger	Kill 200 enemies with flourishes.	+ Shock Damage

THE HERO'S COMPANION

This weapon is aptly named as it performs better for those Heroes who have a number of companions of their own.

ACQUISITION: *Shops.*

Lv5

VALUE	LV0 DMG	LV1 DMG	LV2 DMG	LV3 DMG	LV4 DMG	LV5 DMG
8100	22	28	37	47	72	95

LEGENDARY BONUS	OBJECTIVE	REWARD
Family	Have 2 children.	Earn Guild Seals Faster in Combat
Benefactor	Give gifts to 20 players over Xbox LIVE.	+12 Extra Damage
Saviour	Complete 30 quests.	+20% Damage in Multiplayer

SCATTERSHOT

Created to spray bullets in all directions, the Scattershot, if properly used and maintained, can be adapted into an impressive blunderbuss.

ACQUISITION: *Shops.*

Lv5

VALUE	LV0 DMG	LV1 DMG	LV2 DMG	LV3 DMG	LV4 DMG	LV5 DMG
2100	20	23	30	38	61	82

LEGENDARY BONUS	OBJECTIVE	REWARD
Hard Hitter	Hit enemies with 200 flourishes.	+8 Extra Damage
Scattergun	Kill 10 large enemies with flourishes.	+ Shotgun Spray
Donor	Give gifts to 20 players over Xbox LIVE.	+20% Damage in Multiplayer

FACEMELTER

This weapon's name is a bit misleading, as it can actually melt more or less any part of an opponent's body.

ACQUISITION: *Shops.*

Lv5

VALUE	LV0 DMG	LV1 DMG	LV2 DMG	LV3 DMG	LV4 DMG	LV5 DMG
8100	23	29	38	48	73	96

LEGENDARY BONUS	OBJECTIVE	REWARD
Giant	Kill 10 large enemies with flourishes.	+13 Extra Damage
Melter	Kill 150 enemies with an unwoven Fireball spell.	+ Flame Damage
Unholy	Decrease your moral standing.	Earn Guild Seals Faster in Combat

OL' MALICE

Some say this weapon emanates evil. Others prefer the term 'exudes'.

ACQUISITION: *Shops.*

Lv5

VALUE	LV0 DMG	LV1 DMG	LV2 DMG	LV3 DMG	LV4 DMG	LV5 DMG
2200	21	24	31	39	62	83

LEGENDARY BONUS	OBJECTIVE	REWARD
Hooligan	Smash 50 crates.	Earn Guild Seals Faster in Combat
Featherbrained	Kick 100 chickens.	Earn Guild Seals Faster in Combat
Explosive	Kill 100 enemies with an unwoven Fireball spell.	+ Shotgun Spray

SWIFT IRREGULAR

After trying dozens of guns, Major Swift insisted all his soldiers were issued with one of these rifles.

ACQUISITION: *Shops.*

Lv5

VALUE	LV0 DMG	LV1 DMG	LV2 DMG	LV3 DMG	LV4 DMG	LV5 DMG
8100	24	30	39	49	74	97

LEGENDARY BONUS	OBJECTIVE	REWARD
Determination	Kill 300 hollow men.	+5 Extra Damage, +80% vs hollow men
Swift Regular	Score 2,000 at the Mourningwood Fort mortar.	+12 Extra Damage
Loyalty	Kill 300 mercenaries.	Earn Guild Seals Faster in Combat

ARKWRIGHT'S FLINTLOCK

Captain Arkwright never missed with this rifle. He accomplished this by never firing it, and yet his neglect seems to have imbued the weapon with almost unerring accuracy.

Lv5

VALUE	LV0 DMG	LV1 DMG	LV2 DMG	LV3 DMG	LV4 DMG	LV5 DMG
8500	24	31	40	50	75	98

LEGENDARY BONUS	OBJECTIVE	REWARD
Socialite	Become friends with 30 villagers.	Earn Guild Seals Faster in Combat
Spendthrift	Spend 10,000 of your personal gold.	Earn Guild Seals Faster in Combat
Revolutionist	Kill 40 nobles.	+15 Extra Damage

THE SHRIEKING PILGRIM

This rifle was fashioned from the thighbone of the revered monk Ethelbert the Hobbled, four years before his death.

Lv5

VALUE	LV0 DMG	LV1 DMG	LV2 DMG	LV3 DMG	LV4 DMG	LV5 DMG
12,200	27	36	47	59	86	111

LEGENDARY BONUS	OBJECTIVE	REWARD
Righteous	Increase your moral standing.	+20% Damage vs Evil Human Enemies
Saintly	Make 5 villagers love you.	Earn Guild Seals Faster in Combat
Sanctify	Kill 150 hollow men.	+ Shotgun Spray

SIMMONS'S SHOTGUN

Lieutenant Simmons carried this shotgun with him at all times, and it saved his life on many occasions. Didn't stop him being torn to shreds by hollow men though.

Lv5

VALUE	LV0 DMG	LV1 DMG	LV2 DMG	LV3 DMG	LV4 DMG	LV5 DMG
12,300	26	35	46	58	85	110

LEGENDARY BONUS	OBJECTIVE	REWARD
Gulliver	Make yourself fatter.	+30% Damage vs Humans
Exhumation	Dig up 30 items.	+ Shotgun Spray
Officer	Score 2,000 at the Mourningwood Fort mortar.	+ 20 Extra Damage

SKORM'S JUSTICE

Though Skorm's few remaining followers are still dedicated to an ancient and outdated religion, they have changed with the times when it comes to weaponry.

Lv5

VALUE	LV0 DMG	LV1 DMG	LV2 DMG	LV3 DMG	LV4 DMG	LV5 DMG
12,600	27	36	47	59	86	111

LEGENDARY BONUS	OBJECTIVE	REWARD
Demon	Decrease your moral standing.	+10 Extra Damage, +30% vs Non-Evil Enemies
Callous	Drag 8 villagers to work.	+15 Extra Damage
Unholy Blast	Kill 3 spouses.	+ Shock Damage

THE EQUALISER

The Ward of the Woods used this rifle to drive away the evil denizens that lived within the forests of Albion.

Lv5

VALUE	LV0 DMG	LV1 DMG	LV2 DMG	LV3 DMG	LV4 DMG	LV5 DMG
12,850	26	35	46	58	85	110

LEGENDARY BONUS	OBJECTIVE	REWARD
Vigilante	Kill 150 mercenaries.	+30% Damage vs Evil Human Enemies
Woodward	Drag 10 criminals to jail.	+ Shotgun Spray
Night Watchman	Kill 200 enemies at night.	+40% Damage to Enemies at Night

THE SANDGOOSE

This incredibly powerful rifle was created by the weaponmaster Sandy Goose. His talents were so sought out that he became a hermit. This is his masterpiece, and all that remains of him.

Lv5

VALUE	LV0 DMG	LV1 DMG	LV2 DMG	LV3 DMG	LV4 DMG	LV5 DMG
16,700	29	41	54	68	97	124

LEGENDARY BONUS	OBJECTIVE	REWARD
Aggressive	Earn Guild Seals from evil expressions.	+1 Gold Per Hit
Adventurous	Complete 20 quests.	+25 Extra Damage
Popularity	Become friends with 30 villagers.	Gain Money with Each Hit

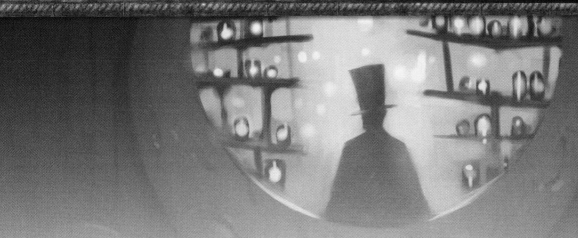

SPELL GAUNTLETS AND MAGIC

Spell gauntlets grant the wearer the power to unleash limitless magic. Each new spell gauntlet is earned by progressing further along the Road to Rule and opening up new spell gauntlet treasure chests. Spell power itself is boosted along the Road to Rule, by opening up treasure chests that unlock new levels of magical aptitude. At first, only one type of gauntlet can be worn at a time, but eventually **spell weaving** enables the use of two types of magic at once.

Slow time in combat by pressing up on ○. By slowing every enemy, your Hero becomes the Mercury of Albion. Attack mercilessly while the effect is active. Slow time lasts longer with higher magic skill.

SINGLE-USE SPELLS: SUMMON CREATURE AND SLOW TIME

There are two arcane spells that are not present in gauntlet form, and can only be accessed with single-use brews. These potions can be found in many places—in shops, in treasure chests, in dig spots, and so on. The spell effects tip the entire battle in your favor, in different ways. Don't hesitate to use them when combat gets overwhelming—slowing or distracting an entire field of adversaries at once is quite a game-changer, and you can find more bottles of each later. Finally, note that these potions become more potent as the Hero's magic skill level increases along the Road to Rule.

Summon creatures in combat by pressing down on ○. Shadow creatures are called forth from the abyss to assail your enemies. The inky apparitions distract just about everyone, allowing you to strike with temporary impunity. This potion is particularly useful to get large enemies out of your hair. With higher magic skill, more powerful creatures are called forth.

CHARGE LEVEL

Spells increase in strength the longer you charge them. Tap **Ⓑ** for a spell at charge level 0 or hold **Ⓑ** for a while longer to charge up before releasing a much stronger blast. The longer you hold down **Ⓑ**, the more powerful the spell. Unlike with melee- or ranged-weapon flourishes, you cannot be interrupted while charging. Charge times can be reduced by opening more magic skill treasure chests along the Road to Rule, and the decrease in charge time is startling, to say the least. The ultimate in magic damage definitely comes from charged-up versions of spells, but at the same time standing still for even five seconds in combat is an eternity. This makes the use of charged-up magic unrealistic at first. But even just upgrading your magic skill twice, to level 2, takes charge level 2 from twelve seconds of charge to *two*! An attack that previously required too much commitment ever to use now has a brief enough charge period to use every time. Considering the overall power and usefulness of magic, no matter how you like to play, getting these charge times down is probably the most significant thing you can do to improve your combat performance.

CHARGE TIME REQUIRED (IN SECONDS) FOR STRONGER SPELLS

ROAD TO RULE LEVEL	LV0	LV1	LV2	LV3	LV4	LV5
Charge Level 0	0	0	0	0	0	0
Charge Level 1	3.5	1	1	1	1	1
Charge Level 2	12	6.7	2	2	2	2
Charge Level 3	27	16.5	8.5	3.5	3.5	3.5
Charge Level 4	55	35	21	12	6.5	6.5

AIMED OR AREA-OF-EFFECT?

Spells can either be aimed at one enemy in particular, or projected outward in a circular blast around the caster. Aimed spells benefit from the focused energy, and deal more damage than area-of-effect spells. Area-of-effect spells have a diminished effect against any single target, but provide excellent crowd control when surrounded by unfriendly, biting things.

AREA-OF-EFFECT SPELL CIRCUMFERENCE

While charging an area-of-effect spell, a ring around your Hero indicates the coverage of the attack. You can use 🕹 to focus the spell on one target without losing the level of charge.

■ *Charge Level 1*

■ *Charge Level 2*

■ *Charge Level 3*

■ *Charge Level 4*

FIREBALL SPELL GAUNTLET

Send forth a ball of trailing flames at your enemies, with a chance of setting them on fire. Combines well with the Blades gauntlet.

ACQUISITION: *Treasure chest along the Road to Rule (cost: 1 Guild Seal)*

This gauntlet is your first, and perhaps most useful. The Fireball spell deals heavy damage and burns the opponent. The damage of the spell and the duration of the burn are determined by magic level. For raw damage, only the Blades spell is superior, but you won't see that one for a while. In the meantime, Fireball is your most damaging magic option. Fireball works well woven with any other spell, but is perhaps most effective when paired with Vortex for crowd control, or Blades for raw magic damage.

FIREBALL SPELL DAMAGE

ROAD TO RULE TREASURE CHEST UNLOCK	LV0	LV1	LV2	LV3	LV4	LV5
Charge Level 0 Aimed	15	18	23	29	50	70
Charge Level 0 Area-of-Effect	10	11.5	14	17	27.5	37.5
Charge Level 1 Aimed	104	68	87	109	189	265
Charge Level 1 Area-of-Effect	54	36	45.5	56	96.5	134.5
Charge Level 2 Aimed	264	286	106	137	246	350
Charge Level 2 Area-of-Effect	140	101	61	76	131	183
Charge Level 3 Aimed	628	473	298	193	357	515
Charge Level 3 Area-of-Effect	304	210	152	100	180	260
Charge Level 4 Aimed	1198	806	733	445	540	770
Charge Level 4 Area-of-Effect	629	408	386	228	270	390

WEAPONS TO WEAR WHILE USING THE UNWOVEN FIREBALL SPELL

WEAPON NAME		LEGENDARY BONUS	OBJECTIVE	REWARD
HAMMER	Trollblight	Trollbane	Kill 150 enemies with an unwoven Fireball spell.	+ Flame Damage
	Dragonbone Hammer	Dragonfire	Kill 150 enemies with an unwoven Fireball spell.	+ Flame Damage
	Hammer of Wilmageddon	Fire Mage	Kill 100 enemies with an unwoven Fireball spell.	+ Flame Damage
RIFLE	Ol' Malice	Explosive	Kill 100 enemies with an unwoven Fireball spell.	+ Shotgun Spray
	Facemelter	Melter	Kill 150 enemies with an unwoven Fireball spell.	+ Flame Damage

SHOCK SPELL GAUNTLET

Shock electrocutes opponents, damaging and momentarily stunning them.

ACQUISITION: *Treasure chest along the Road to Rule (cost: 40 Guild Seals)*

While not as damaging as the Fireball spell, Shock is useful in other ways. Shock may electrocute and stun the enemy, rendering them momentarily helpless. Shock is also highly effective against some of the game's toughest, latest adversaries—minions are weak to this electrical onslaught. Shock works best paired with Fireball or Blades as it fills the same role of low-damage crowd control that Vortex and Force Push do.

SHOCK SPELL DAMAGE

ROAD TO RULE TREASURE CHEST UNLOCK	LV0	LV1	LV2	LV3	LV4	LV5
Charge Level 0 Aimed	10.5	13.2	16	20.3	35	49
Charge Level 0 Area-of-Effect	7	8	9.7	11.9	19.3	26.7
Charge Level 1 Aimed	73	48	61	76	132	187
Charge Level 1 Area-of-Effect	38	25	31	39.9	68.4	97.9
Charge Level 2 Aimed	198	142	84	106	185.9	261
Charge Level 2 Area-of-Effect	101	74	43	55	96	135
Charge Level 3 Aimed	456	356	223	158	271	390
Charge Level 3 Area-of-Effect	224	181	116	80.9	138	201
Charge Level 4 Aimed	573	288	182	18	81	257
Charge Level 4 Area-of-Effect	288	142	93	9	40	128

WEAPONS TO WEAR WHILE USING THE UNWOVEN FIREBALL SPELL

WEAPON NAME		LEGENDARY BONUS	OBJECTIVE	REWARD
SWORD	Thunderblade	Electrocutioner	Kill 200 enemies with an unwoven Shock spell.	+ Chance to Stun Enemy
HAMMER	Hammer of Wilmageddon	Blast	Kill 200 enemies with an unwoven Shock spell.	+ Shock Damage
	Scythe's Warhammer	Stormlord	Kill 200 enemies with an unwoven Shock spell.	+ Shock Damage

ICE STORM SPELL GAUNTLET

Ice Storm summons frozen shards that rain down destruction on your foes.

ACQUISITION: *Treasure chest along the Road to Rule (cost: 40 Guild Seals)*

Ice Storm is what it sounds like—an Ice Storm either around you, or centered on the target. Ice Storm is the only spell that doesn't expressly home in on the enemy, so a little more finesse in use is required than with other spells. Against swarms of threatening but fragile foes, like shadow creatures, Ice Storm can be used like a personal shield. Cast it near you and stay within the storm. Because of how it works, Ice Storm ends up being great against larger enemies—the biggest brutes are a great big target for lots of ice. Non-mobile foes, like marksmen, also make great Ice Storm victims. Interesting combinations are possible with spell weaving, such as Ice Storm and Vortex for a truly brutal maelstrom, or Shock and Ice Storm to electrocute the enemies while pelting them with ice.

ICE STORM SPELL DAMAGE

ROAD TO RULE TREASURE CHEST UNLOCK	LV0	LV1	LV2	LV3	LV4	LV5
Charge Level 0 Aimed	9	12	15	19	33	47
Charge Level 0 Area-of-Effect	9	12	15	19	33	47
Charge Level 1 Aimed	10	12	15	19	34	48
Charge Level 1 Area-of-Effect	10	12	15	19	34	48
Charge Level 2 Aimed	22	16	13	17	29	84
Charge Level 2 Area-of-Effect	22	16	13	17	29	84
Charge Level 3 Aimed	31	30	22	17	30	43
Charge Level 3 Area-of-Effect	31	30	22	17	30	43
Charge Level 4 Aimed	61	79	50	35	32	46
Charge Level 4 Area-of-Effect	61	79	50	35	32	46

VORTEX SPELL GAUNTLET

Vortex creates a windstorm that picks up enemies and hurls them around, preventing them from attacking and potentially knocking them into objects.

ACQUISITION: *Treasure chest along the Road to Rule (cost: 40 Guild Seals)*

The damage of Vortex may be lower than other spells, but that doesn't stop it from being one of the best. The furious gales it creates sweep enemies off their feet, whirling them around in the maelstrom, eventually dumping them onto the turf. Enemies flailing in the air are enemies not attacking you, and they make lovely targets for a firearm. After they land, sprawling, there's a perfect opportunity to go for a downed attack to finish them off—if your dog doesn't beat you to it! As Vortex grants all the crowd control you could want, pair it with Fireball or Blades for some added oomph. Vortex won't work on the sturdiest foes, though.

VORTEX SPELL DAMAGE

ROAD TO RULE TREASURE CHEST UNLOCK	LV0	LV1	LV2	LV3	LV4	LV5
Charge Level 0 Aimed	3.75	4.5	5.75	7.25	12.5	17.5
Charge Level 0 Area-of-Effect	2.5	2.875	3.5	4.25	6.875	9.375
Charge Level 1 Aimed	26	17	22	27	47	66
Charge Level 1 Area-of-Effect	13.5	9	11	14	24	33.5
Charge Level 2 Aimed	70	50	30	38	65	91
Charge Level 2 Area-of-Effect	35	25	15	19	32.5	45.5
Charge Level 3 Aimed	156	125	80	55	94	135
Charge Level 3 Area-of-Effect	78.5	63	40.5	28	47.5	68
Charge Level 4 Aimed	311	217	184	127	148	208
Charge Level 4 Area-of-Effect	156	109	92.5	64	74.5	104

FORCE PUSH SPELL GAUNTLET

Force Push magically propels enemies away from you. Knock them into walls or off ledges for extra damage.

ACQUISITION: *Treasure chest along the Road to Rule (cost: 40 Guild Seals*

FORCE PUSH SPELL DAMAGE

ROAD TO RULE TREASURE CHEST UNLOCK	LV0	LV1	LV2	LV3	LV4	LV5
Charge Level 0 Aimed	3.75	4.5	5.75	7.25	12.5	17.5
Charge Level 0 Area-of-Effect	2.5	2.785	3.5	4.25	6.875	9.375
Charge Level 1 Aimed	26	17	22	27	47	66
Charge Level 1 Area-of-Effect	13.5	9	11	14	24	33.5
Charge Level 2 Aimed	69	50	30	38	65	91
Charge Level 2 Area-of-Effect	34.5	25	15	19	32.5	45.5
Charge Level 3 Aimed	156	125	80	55	94	135
Charge Level 3 Area-of-Effect	78.5	63	40.5	28	47.5	68
Charge Level 4 Aimed	311	217	184	127	148	208
Charge Level 4 Area-of-Effect	156	109	92.5	64	74.5	104.5

Force Push, like Vortex, is weaker than other spells, but makes up for it in effect. Strike enemies with Force Push to knock them back forcibly. If you're looking for a spell to clear crowds from around you, Vortex or Shock are better choices. But in areas with an exposed edge, like a cliff, Force Push can hold its own, scoring easy kills by simply sending enemies plummeting to their death.

BLADES SPELL GAUNTLET

Blades conjures magical swords which seek out and impale enemies.

ACQUISITION: *Treasure chest along the Road to Rule (cost: 40 Guild Seals)*

While Fireball adds a little simmer to go with its damage, the Blades spell is after raw pain. In fact, a fully-charged, aimed Blades cast is the strongest attack in the game! Like Fireball, Blades works well with either Vortex, Shock, or Force Push—one spell supplies the brunt of the damage, the other supplies a useful effect. And, of course, if you're going for raw damage, nothing beats an aimed, charged blast of Fireball from one hand, and Blades from the other! The only drawback to the Blades spell is that it's the least effective spell at actually distracting or deterring foes. It does a lot of damage, sure, but it won't occupy the enemy for long the way spells such as Vortex or Shock do. It will, however, stun some enemies for a short time.

BLADES SPELL DAMAGE

ROAD TO RULE TREASURE CHEST UNLOCK	LV0	LV1	LV2	LV3	LV4	LV5
Charge Level 0 Aimed	15	18	24	30	51	72
Charge Level 0 Area-of-Effect	5	6	8	10	17	24
Charge Level 1 Aimed	105.2	68.5	89	113	195	274
Charge Level 1 Area-of-Effect	26.3	17.125	22.4	28.25	48.75	68.5
Charge Level 2 Aimed	287.6	256	173	204	319	429
Charge Level 2 Area-of-Effect	57.52	40.8	24	30.4	53.2	75.2
Charge Level 3 Aimed	772	636	444	343	508	675
Charge Level 3 Area-of-Effect	108.6	86.5	54.5	37.8	65	92.7
Charge Level 4 Aimed	1526	1108	959	716	811	1064
Charge Level 4 Area-of-Effect	167	115.25	96.75	66.25	78.5	109.9

SWORDS SUMMONED DURING BLADES SPELL (BOTH AIMED AND AREA-OF-EFFECT)

CHARGE LEVEL	NUMBER OF SWORDS		CHARGE LEVEL	NUMBER OF SWORDS
Charge Level 0	3		Charge Level 3	6
Charge Level 1	4		Charge Level 4	8
Charge Level 2	5			

WEAPON TO WEAR WHILE USING THE UNWOVEN BLADES SPELL

WEAPON NAME		LEGENDARY BONUS	OBJECTIVE	REWARD
SWORD	The Channeler	Bladestorm	Kill 100 enemies with an unwoven Blades spell.	+15 Extra Damage

SPELL WEAVING

Spell weaving allows you to wear gauntlets for different spells on each hand. In turn, the spell effects generated are a mix of the two spells. The power and duration of the normal spell effects suffer a penalty (woven spell effects are 70% of unwoven spells in damage and duration), but the overall effect is stronger for the mixing. In addition to the utility offered by spell weaving, there is also an Achievement to unlock by weaving every possible spell combination.

Spell weaving does more than cast the two spells simultaneously—the effects of the spells are combined, with surprising effects.

ACQUISITION: *Treasure chest along the Road to Rule (cost: 50 Guild Seals)*

Once spell weaving is acquired, there's little reason not to use it, the only reason being if you are going for a Legendary weapon bonus that requires unwoven spell usage. Let's say that you're attempting to gain kills with Fireball. If you weave it together with Shock, you run the risk of the Shock part of the woven spell providing the killing damage. This would prevent the kill from counting. However, in the same example, if Fireball provided the killing blow, it would count. Weaving spells for this purpose shouldn't be negated. Just understand that not every woven kill will count toward the Legendary kill requirement.

For the example of the importance of weaving spells, consider Fireball plus Vortex, versus either spell alone. When you cast Fireball alone, enemies take damage, and stagger a bit, but most foes continue bearing down. With Vortex alone, enemies are certainly occupied and you are free to get away or close in, but the damage is low. Combine the two, though, and now you have a damaging spell that also takes an enemy or three out of the picture for several seconds.

Try out various combinations to go for the Achievement, and to see what you like. For our money, no combination outdoes Fireball + Vortex for overall utility!

SPELL WEAVING COMBINATIONS

FIRST HAND	SECOND HAND	FIRST HAND	SECOND HAND	FIRST HAND	SECOND HAND	FIRST HAND	SECOND HAND
Fireball	Fireball	Shock	Shock	Ice Storm	Ice Storm	Vortex	Force Push
Fireball	Shock	Shock	Ice Storm	Ice Storm	Vortex	Vortex	Blades
Fireball	Ice Storm	Shock	Vortex	Ice Storm	Force Push	Force Push	Force Push
Fireball	Vortex	Shock	Force Push	Ice Storm	Blades	Force Push	Blades
Fireball	Force Push	Shock	Blades	Vortex	Vortex	Blades	Blades
Fireball	Blades						

ITEMS AND CLOTHING

A Hero in Albion needs his or her weapons, of course. But apart from instruments of war, there are many other tools available to aid the resistance. From Health potions to food to gifts for potential friends and lovers, and clothing to change appearance, there are many items and trinkets to collect along the way.

ITEM ACQUISITION

Goodies can come to hand in many different ways. For the most part, the items received as rewards from treasure chests, dig spots, and other item-bearing locations are random. The more powerful you are—the more skilled with melee weapons, guns, and magic—the better the loot you obtain. Only a few rewards are fixed.

Treasure Chests: Normal treasure chests are found all over the world, and can simply be opened. Silver treasure chests are in certain locations, and require a specific number of silver keys in your inventory before they can be opened.

Dig Spots: Your dog leads you to all kinds of treasure, but dig spots are the only loot source you can't find without him. Your dog can learn to sniff out more dig spots if you find training books that increase his exploration skill.

Dive Spots: Dive spots may be found while swimming in any body of water. They are indicated by swirling, bubbling water.

Searching Furniture: Bookshelves and other pieces of furniture can be rifled through for money and items. You cannot search furniture inside houses until you've unlocked the Theft ability along the Road to Rule—even if you own the house. Once you can go through drawers, cabinets, and so on, though, homes are a huge potential source of items. Your scruples determine to what extent you take advantage, though, as each incidence of theft causes a -5 ding to Morality. Unless, of course, you own that particular house.

Quest Rewards: Every quest has some sort of reward. At a minimum you'll earn Guild Seals, but many quests also offer monetary compensation and item rewards.

Villager Gifts and Tribute: Townspeople who are taken with your virtue

and charity may approach you with presents. On the other hand, those who regard you as a wrathful tyrant may offer gifts out of fear and fealty. Once you accept the gift, it can be opened in the Hero's Sanctuary.

Xbox LIVE: While playing with friends online on Xbox LIVE you can trade items, or receive gifts. Exchanging items with other players is the only way to complete your collection of certain items, like Legendary weapons or rare trade goods.

Shops, Stalls, and Kiosks: There are traders in every city ready to exchange money for goods. From full-on, brick-and-mortar stores to smaller table stalls and kiosks, items can be bought everywhere, for the right price. Prices can be influenced by sales, by your relationship with store owners and a given town at large, by haggling, and by owning the shop you're perusing. There is another factor for the prices and that is town wealth. Prices are generally higher in Bowerstone Market than they are in Brightwall. Why? The town is wealthier and the populace can afford to spend more on items. You can influence town wealth in various ways. An easy example is that spending money there makes it go up, while crime makes it go down.

WEAPONS TO SPEND ⊙ WITH

WEAPON NAME		LEGENDARY BONUS	OBJECTIVE	REWARD
SWORD	The Merchant's Bodyguard	Big Spender	Spend 8,000 of your personal gold.	+20% Damage in Multiplayer
	Slimquick	Shopping Spree	Spend 8,000 of your personal gold.	Earn Guild Seals Faster in Combat.
	The Channeler	Researcher	Spend 8,000 of your personal gold.	Earn Guild Seals Faster in Combat.
	The Inquisitor	Extravagant	Spend 3000 of your personal gold.	+15 Extra Damage
PISTOL	Reaver Industries Perforator	Retail Therapy	Spend 10,000 of your personal gold.	Earn Guild Seals Faster in Combat.
	Tea Killer Shooter	Accumulator	Spend 10,000 of your personal gold.	Gain Money with Each Hit
RIFLE	Arkwright's Flintlock	Spendthrift	Spend 10,000 of your personal gold.	Earn Guild Seals Faster in Combat

GENERAL STORES

SHOP NAME	LOCATION
Summit Supplies (General Goods)	Dweller Camp
The Werehouse	Silverpines
The Mellow Emporium (General Goods)	Mourningwood
Gifts & Gumf (General Goods)	Bowerstone Market
Ms Elaine Neous's Goods (General Goods)	Bowerstone Old Quarter
Honest Omar's (General Goods)	Aurora

WEAPON SHOPS

SHOP NAME	LOCATION
Brightwall Blades (Weapons)	Brightwall Village
The Iron Hoof (Weapons)	Bowerstone Market
The Armoury (Weapons)	Aurora

POTIONS

Potions can be used during combat to replenish health, and to evoke magic effects that spell gauntlets can't produce.

POTION STORES

SHOP NAME	LOCATION
Brightwall Medicinal Potations (Potions)	Brightwall Village
Peas and Love (Food and Potions)	Mourningwood
The Magic Bottle (Potions)	Bowerstone Market
Potion Emotion (Potions)	Bowerstone Old Quarter
Misca Tonics (Potions)	Aurora

POTIONS

- Health potion
- Slow Time potion
- Summon Creatures potion

CONSUMABLES - DRINKS

Drinks, like potions, can be consumed. Drinks replenish health but may also have side effects, such as adding weight or causing drunkenness.

DRINKS

- Beer
- Fruit Juice
- Spirits
- Wine

WATERING HOLES

SHOP NAME	LOCATION
Brightwall Booze (Drinks)	Brightwall Village
Ye Quill & Quandry (Pub)	Brightwall Village
The Riveter's Rest (Pub)	Bowerstone Industrial
Bowerstone Beverages (Drinks)	Bowerstone Market
The Cock in the Crown (Pub)	Bowerstone Market

CONSUMABLES - FOOD

Like drinks, food items add health, usually along with a side effect. Natural foods tend to decrease weight, while the cuisine of Albion, rich in fat and carbs, adds to these undesirable traits.

FOOD STORES

SHOP NAME	LOCATION
Brightwall Banquets (Food)	Brightwall Village
Hot, Yummy, and Circular (Food)	Bowerstone Industrial
The Old Trout (Food)	Bowerstone Market
Flower Bower (Food)	Bowerstone Market
Num Num Pies (Food)	Bowerstone Market
Eat It! (Food)	Bowerstone Old Quarter
Delectable Delights (Food)	Aurora
Vegetables of Aurora (Food)	Aurora

FOOD

- Apple
- Blueberry Pie
- Carrot
- Celery
- Crunchy Chick
- Dark Sanctum Pie
- Fish
- Lizard on a Stick
- Malanga
- Meat Pie
- Mutton
- Prickly Pear
- Tofu

TRADE ITEMS

Trade items can be purchased from many different shops and stalls. These items tend to be inexpensive and have no use outside of reselling to pawnbrokers. If you have the coin, always err towards buying up available trade items. When you see that a pawnbroker has a huge shortage, you may make your money back two- or threefold.

TRADE GOODS

⇥ Barrel of Coffee	⇥ Box of Lizards	⇥ Crate of Wine
⇥ Box of Crabs	⇥ Box of Odd Fruit	⇥ Sack of Grain
⇥ Box of Fish	⇥ Crate of Tea	⇥ Sack of Potatoes

TRADE GOODS

SHOP NAME	LOCATION
Buy 'n Sell 'n Buy (Trade Items)	Brightwall Village
The Fair Trader (Trade Items)	Bowerstone Industrial
Merchant's Mile (Trade Goods)	Bowerstone Old Quarter

PAWNBROKERS

SHOP NAME	LOCATION
Brightwall Brokerage (Pawnbroker)	Brightwall Village
Bowerstone Broker (Pawnbroker)	Bowerstone Market
Flotsam's Jetsam (Pawnbroker)	Aurora

RARE TRADE ITEMS

Rare trade items are just like trade items, except, as you may have guessed, they are rarer. There are only seven rare trade items, all rare gems, and on a given Gamertag only four manifest themselves. To snag the rest, you must barter with friends online over Xbox LIVE. Keep in mind that a rare gem that isn't native to that world rakes in four times the normal price if sold at a pawnbroker

RARE TRADE ITEMS

| ⇥ Rare Amethyst | ⇥ Rare Diamond | ⇥ Rare Emerald | ⇥ Rare Jet | ⇥ Rare Pearl | ⇥ Rare Ruby | ⇥ Rare Topaz |

MISCELLANEOUS

This modest-but-important category includes the training manuals you use to enhance the abilities of your dog. It also includes a rather important device for socializing. If you've progressed a relationship with a citizen of Albion to the point where you're thinking of getting frisky, you have to make a decision—are you just after bonding and fun, or are you after offspring? If it's the former you prefer, protection is a must!

MISCELLANEOUS

⇥ Condom	⇥ Dog Training: Combat 4
⇥ Dog Training: Charisma 2	⇥ Dog Training: Combat 5
⇥ Dog Training: Charisma 3	⇥ Dog Training: Exploration 2
⇥ Dog Training: Charisma 4	⇥ Dog Training: Exploration 3
⇥ Dog Training: Charisma 5	⇥ Dog Training: Exploration 4
⇥ Dog Training: Combat 2	⇥ Dog Training: Exploration 5
⇥ Dog Training: Combat 3	

DOG TRAINING BOOKSTORES

SHOP NAME	LOCATION
Good Boy (Dog Books)	Brightwall Village
Cultured Mutts (Dog Books)	Bowerstone Old Quarter

GIFTS

Many items exist solely as presents in relationships, whether for making friends, doting on children, or inducing lovers. If you aren't using many gifts, treat them like trade goods and sell when pawnbrokers offer extra money.

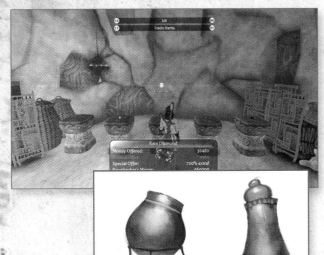

GIFT SHOPS

SHOP NAME	LOCATION
Brightwall Bling (Gifts)	Brightwall Village
Jewell Be Sorry (Gifts)	Bowerstone Market
Gimme, Gimme, Gimme! (Gifts)	Bowerstone Old Quarter
The Curiosity Shop (Gifts)	Aurora

GIFTS

- Amethyst
- Box of Chocolates
- Chessboard
- Diamond
- Emerald
- Flowers
- Goblet
- Hand Mirror
- Jet
- Jewelry
- Pearl
- Perfume
- Porcelain Doll
- Ragdoll
- Ruby
- Silver Bowl
- Teddy Bear
- Topaz
- Toy Bow
- Toy Gun
- Toy Horse
- Toy Sword
- Wedding Ring

FURNITURE

Furniture has decent resale value on its own, but is more valuable when used to make your personal houses more attractive before you try to sell them. Like other items, furniture can be found in a number of places, but most consistently from furniture stores. Who knew? You also gain all the furniture in a house if you purchase it, though of course these pieces remain in that house unless you swap them for pieces of furniture in your inventory.

FURNISHINGS

SHOP NAME	LOCATION
Fabulous Furnishings (Furniture)	Brightwall Village
We've Got Wood (Furniture)	Bowerstone Market

BEDS

- Broken Double Bed
- Worn Double Bed
- Average Double Bed
- Decorative Double Bed
- Luxury Double Bed
- Nightmare Child's Bed
- Restless Night Child's Bed
- Good Night Child's Bed
- Lullaby Child's Bed
- Sweet Dreams Child's Bed

TABLES

- Broken Dining Table
- Worn Dining Table
- Average Dining Table
- Decorative Dining Table
- Luxury Dining Table
- Broken Bedside Table
- Worn Bedside Table
- Average Bedside Table
- Decorative Bedside Table
- Luxury Bedside Table
- Broken Desk Table
- Worn Desk Table
- Average Desk Table
- Decorative Desk Table
- Luxury Desk Table

BOOKCASES

- Broken Bookcase
- Worn Bookcase
- Average Bookcase
- Decorative Bookcase
- Luxury Bookcase

SINKS

- Broken Sink
- Average Sink
- Luxury Sink

STOVES

- Broken Stove
- Average Stove
- Luxury Stove

CLOSETS

- Broken Closet
- Worn Closet
- Average Closet
- Decorative Closet
- Luxury Closet

CUPBOARDS, DRAWERS AND DRESSERS

- Broken Cupboard
- Worn Cupboard
- Average Cupboard
- Decorative Cupboard
- Luxury Cupboard
- Broken Drawers
- Worn Drawers
- Average Drawers
- Decorative Drawers
- Luxury Drawers
- Broken Dresser
- Worn Dresser
- Average Dresser
- Decorative Dresser
- Dresser for Successor

CHAIRS

- Broken Comfy Chair
- Worn Comfy Chair
- Average Comfy Chair
- Decorative Comfy Chair
- Luxury Comfy Chair

RUGS

- Small Worn Rug
- Small Rug
- Small Auroran Rug
- Small Decorative Rug
- Large Round Rug
- Large Auroran Rug
- Large Circular Rug
- Extra Large Worn Rug
- Extra Large Rug
- Extra Large Decorative Rug

SHELVES

- Shelf

AURORAN ITEMS

- Auroran Basket
- Auroran Incense Burner
- Auroran Stool
- Large Auroran Table
- Small Auroran Table

RANDOM ITEMS

- Blackboard
- Grandfather Clock
- Hat Stand
- Telescope
- Toy Box
- Trophy Mount
- Pictures
- Whiskey Keg
- Beer Keg
- Globe
- Iron Maiden
- Torture Rack
- Torture Stocks
- Aged Armour
- Venerable Armour
- Shining Armour
- Ben Finn Portrait
- Elliot Portrait
- Logan Portrait
- Page Portrait
- Sabine Portrait
- Saker Portrait
- Major Swift Portrait
- Theresa Portrait
- Sir Walter Portrait
- Elise Portrait

CLOTHING

It's said that clothes make the man, and this is partially true in Albion; clothes make the man, along with weapons, spells, money, fate, chance, and the assistance of a loyal dog and some good friends. But clothes are definitely involved. Your personal effects and grooming help determine what the people of Albion think of you, and are sometimes used as a disguise.

OUTFITS

The actual garments your Hero wears are broken down by outfit. There are many male- and female-specific outfits, although either gender can wear any outfit. While you can find pieces of many outfits as random loot like any other item, there is also usually a way to buy or otherwise acquire almost every set of clothing.

DYES

PACK	ACQUISITION	GUILD SEAL COST	DESCRIPTION
Dye Pack I	Road to Rule 2: After Music Box	2	Inject some color into your Hero's wardrobe by learning how to dye your clothes or hair red, blue, grey, and green.
Dye Pack II	Road to Rule 4: Sabine Promise	5	Tired of your appearance? Learn how to dye your clothes or hair khaki, purple, orange, and pink.
Dye Pack III	Road to Rule 5: After The Hole	5	Experiment with more colors by learning to dye your clothes or hair white, lime, yellow, and brown.

CLOTHING SHOPS

SHOP NAME	LOCATION
The Raggle Taggle (Clothing)	Dweller Camp
Frou Frou Frocks (Clothing)	Brightwall Village
Bower Threads (Clothing)	Bowerstone Market
Robes Are Us (Clothing)	Aurora

MEN'S PYJAMA SUIT

These handsome PJs are what our dashing Hero wears at the beginning of the game. These clothes can also be purchased at Frou Frou Frocks in Brightwall Village.

PIECE	BASE VALUE	SILLINESS	SCARINESS	ATTRACTIVENESS	TRANSVESTISM (MALE)
Men's Pyjama Bedsocks	70	4.0%	0.0%	-2.0%	0.0%
Men's Pyjama Longjohns	175	10.0%	0.0%	-5.0%	0.0%
Men's Pyjama Nightcap	140	10.0%	0.0%	-5.0%	0.0%
Men's Pyjama Nightshirt	210	12.0%	0.0%	-6.0%	0.0%

WOMEN'S PYJAMA SUIT

Opt to play as a Heroine and these are the duds you'll start out with. Like the men's version, this set can also be purchased at Frou Frou Frocks in Brightwall Village.

PIECE	BASE VALUE	SILLINESS	SCARINESS	ATTRACTIVENESS	TRANSVESTISM (MALE)
Women's Pyjama Bloomers	175	10.0%	0.0%	-5.0%	12.0%
Women's Pyjama Nightcap	140	10.0%	0.0%	-4.0%	10.0%
Women's Pyjama Nightshirt	210	12.0%	0.0%	-6.0%	12.0%
Women's Pyjama Slippers	70	4.0%	0.0%	-2.0%	4.0%

PRACTICAL PRINCE SUIT

As the prince, you decide between this and the Elegant Prince Suit, right at the start. You can't laze about in pyjamas forever, as it turns out. Whichever suit you go for, try them both on before setting out, so both sets count towards your **Fashion Victim** Achievement. The Practical Prince Suit is also available later, at Bower Threads in Bowerstone Market.

PIECE	BASE VALUE	SILLINESS	SCARINESS	ATTRACTIVENESS	TRANSVESTISM (MALE)
Practical Prince Boots	400	0.0%	0.0%	3.0%	0.0%
Practical Prince Gloves	320	0.0%	0.0%	3.0%	0.0%
Practical Prince Jacket	1200	0.0%	0.0%	9.0%	0.0%
Practical Prince Trousers	1000	0.0%	0.0%	8.0%	0.0%

PRACTICAL PRINCESS SUIT

As the princess, you choose between this outfit and the more opulent Elegant Princess Suit. As with the prince, try them both on regardless of which you actually prefer. The Practical Princess Suit can also be purchased later, at Bower Threads in Bowerstone Market

PIECE	BASE VALUE	SILLINESS	SCARINESS	ATTRACTIVENESS	TRANSVESTISM (MALE)
Practical Princess Blouse	1200	0.0%	0.0%	8.0%	12.0%
Practical Princess Boots	400	0.0%	0.0%	3.0%	4.0%
Practical Princess Gloves	320	0.0%	0.0%	3.0%	4.0%
Practical Princess Skirt	1000	0.0%	0.0%	6.0%	12.0%

ELEGANT PRINCE SUIT

For something with a little more grandeur as the prince, opt for this outfit at the start. It can also be purchased later, at Bower Threads in Bowerstone Market.

PIECE	BASE VALUE	SILLINESS	SCARINESS	ATTRACTIVENESS	TRANSVESTISM (MALE)
Elegant Prince Boots	800	0.0%	0.0%	5.0%	0.0%
Elegant Prince Gloves	640	0.0%	0.0%	5.0%	0.0%
Elegant Prince Jacket	2400	0.0%	0.0%	15.0%	0.0%
Elegant Prince Trousers	2000	0.0%	0.0%	12.0%	0.0%

ELEGANT PRINCESS SUIT

The princess's best can be selected over the Practical Princess Suit at the beginning of the game, or picked up later at Bower Threads in Bowerstone Market.

PIECE	BASE VALUE	SILLINESS	SCARINESS	ATTRACTIVENESS	TRANSVESTISM (MALE)
Elegant Princess Bodice	2400	0.0%	0.0%	14.0%	12.0%
Elegant Princess Gloves	640	0.0%	0.0%	5.0%	4.0%
Elegant Princess Hat	1600	0.0%	0.0%	10.0%	10.0%
Elegant Princess Skirt	2000	0.0%	0.0%	12.0%	15.0%
Elegant Princess Slippers	800	0.0%	0.0%	5.0%	4.0%

DWELLER MEN'S SUIT

The Dweller Men's Suit helps the freshly-renegade prince better fit into his more slovenly surroundings. It can be purchased at The Raggle Taggle in Dweller Camp.

PIECE	BASE VALUE	SILLINESS	SCARINESS	ATTRACTIVENESS	TRANSVESTISM (MALE)
Dweller Men's Bandana	75	0.0%	0.0%	-2.0%	0.0%
Dweller Men's Boots	50	0.0%	0.0%	-1.0%	0.0%
Dweller Men's Coat	125	0.0%	0.0%	-4.0%	0.0%
Dweller Men's Gloves	50	0.0%	0.0%	-1.0%	0.0%
Dweller Men's Trousers	100	0.0%	0.0%	-2.0%	0.0%

DWELLER WOMEN'S SUIT

The princess can hardly fit in with the downtrodden wearing her nicest threads. This more humble, and likely far warmer, outfit is available at The Raggle Taggle in Dweller Camp.

PIECE	BASE VALUE	SILLINESS	SCARINESS	ATTRACTIVENESS (MALE)	TRANSVESTISM
Dweller Women's Bandana	75	0.0%	0.0%	-2.0%	5.0%
Dweller Women's Boots	50	0.0%	0.0%	-1.0%	2.0%
Dweller Women's Coat	125	0.0%	0.0%	-4.0%	6.0%
Dweller Women's Gloves	50	0.0%	0.0%	-1.0%	2.0%
Dweller Women's Trousers	100	0.0%	0.0%	-2.0%	4.0%

MEN'S MERCENARY SUIT

No matter which sex you select at the beginning of the game, the Men's Mercenary Suit is acquired through story progression as a means to infiltrate the Mercenary Camp. This outfit can also be purchased at Frou Frou Frocks in Brightwall Village.

PIECE	BASE VALUE	SILLINESS	SCARINESS	ATTRACTIVENESS	TRANSVESTISM (MALE)
Men's Mercenary Boots	100	0.0%	2.5%	-2.0%	0.0%
Men's Mercenary Gloves	80	0.0%	2.5%	-2.0%	0.0%
Men's Mercenary Hat	200	0.0%	2.5%	-5.0%	0.0%
Men's Mercenary Jacket	300	0.0%	5.0%	-6.0%	0.0%
Men's Mercenary Trousers	250	0.0%	5.0%	-5.0%	0.0%

WOMEN'S MERCENARY SUIT

Our female Hero must wear the Men's Mercenary Suit just the same as her male counterpart to progress the story, so the Women's Mercenary Suit is never overtly pointed out. It's tucked away in a corner in Frou Frou Frocks in Brightwall Village, and is much more becoming on the princess.

PIECE	BASE VALUE	SILLINESS	SCARINESS	ATTRACTIVENESS	TRANSVESTISM (MALE)
Women's Mercenary Boots	100	0.0%	2.5%	-2.0%	2.0%
Women's Mercenary Gloves	80	0.0%	2.5%	-2.0%	2.0%
Women's Mercenary Hat	200	0.0%	2.5%	-4.0%	5.0%
Women's Mercenary Jacket	300	0.0%	5.0%	-6.0%	6.0%
Women's Mercenary Shorts	250	0.0%	5.0%	-4.0%	6.0%

MEN'S HIGHWAYMAN SUIT

This firearm-focused outfit, matching the likes of those benevolent but misunderstood criminal legends passed, is available a few different ways. It can be purchased, but not inexpensively, from Brightwall Village. However, if you can hold out long enough, you can also acquire this outfit from the gold door inside the Reliquary.

PIECE	BASE VALUE	SILLINESS	SCARINESS	ATTRACTIVENESS	TRANSVESTISM (MALE)
Men's Highwayman Boots	750	0.0%	0.0%	4.0%	0.0%
Men's Highwayman Coat	4500	0.0%	0.0%	12.0%	0.0%
Men's Highwayman Gloves	600	0.0%	0.0%	4.0%	0.0%
Men's Highwayman Hat	3000	0.0%	0.0%	10.0%	0.0%
Men's Highwayman Trousers	3750	0.0%	0.0%	10.0%	0.0%

WOMEN'S HIGHWAYMAN SUIT

Like its male counterpart, this female outfit is available from Frou Frou Frocks in Brightwall Village. You can also snag it from the gold door within the Reliquary.

PIECE	BASE VALUE	SILLINESS	SCARINESS	ATTRACTIVENESS	TRANSVESTISM (MALE)
Women's Highwayman Boots	750	0.0%	0.0%	4.0%	2.0%
Women's Highwayman Coat	4500	0.0%	0.0%	12.0%	6.0%
Women's Highwayman Gloves	600	0.0%	0.0%	4.0%	2.0%
Women's Highwayman Hat	3000	0.0%	0.0%	8.0%	5.0%
Women's Highwayman Trousers	3750	0.0%	0.0%	10.0%	4.0%

CHICKEN SUIT

The Chicken Suit can be had in one of two ways, both accomplished in Brightwall Village; either complete the **Chicken Chaser** quest for Bernard and Patsy, or simply buy it at Frou Frou Frocks. There's an Achievement in it for you if you don this absurd outfit for important decisions late in the game…

PIECE	BASE VALUE	SILLINESS	SCARINESS	ATTRACTIVENESS	TRANSVESTISM (MALE)
Chicken Body	360	25.0%	0.0%	-12.0%	0.0%
Chicken Feet	120	6.0%	0.0%	-4.0%	0.0%
Chicken Gloves	95	6.0%	0.0%	-5.0%	0.0%
Chicken Head	240	15.0%	0.0%	-10.0%	0.0%

MEN'S WARRIOR SUIT

This is a friendly outfit, isn't it? This intimidating set of armor can be found at Bower Threads in Bowerstone Market. Interestingly, it's actually attractive instead of being horribly frightening.

PIECE	BASE VALUE	SILLINESS	SCARINESS	ATTRACTIVENESS	TRANSVESTISM (MALE)
Men's Warrior Boots	1800	0.0%	0.0%	4.0%	0.0%
Men's Warrior Coat	5400	0.0%	0.0%	12.0%	0.0%
Men's Warrior Gloves	1440	0.0%	0.0%	4.0%	0.0%
Men's Warrior Hat	3600	0.0%	0.0%	10.0%	0.0%
Men's Warrior Trousers	4500	0.0%	0.0%	10.0%	0.0%

WOMEN'S WARRIOR SUIT

The female version of the Warrior Suit is a little more open than the male version, but seems no less effective as a battle vestment. Pick it up at Bower Threads in Bowerstone Market.

PIECE	BASE VALUE	SILLINESS	SCARINESS	ATTRACTIVENESS	TRANSVESTISM (MALE)
Women's Warrior Boots	1800	0.0%	0.0%	4.0%	2.0%
Women's Warrior Coat	5400	0.0%	0.0%	12.0%	6.0%
Women's Warrior Gloves	1440	0.0%	0.0%	4.0%	2.0%
Women's Warrior Helmet	3600	0.0%	0.0%	8.0%	5.0%
Women's Warrior Trousers	4500	0.0%	0.0%	10.0%	4.0%

MEN'S MASQUERADE SUIT

Hide your face, so the world never finds you! This crafty disguise is acquired through storyline progression as the male Hero.

PIECE	BASE VALUE	SILLINESS	SCARINESS	ATTRACTIVENESS	TRANSVESTISM (MALE)
Men's Masquerade Coat	1200	0.0%	0.0%	15.0%	0.0%
Men's Masquerade Gloves	320	0.0%	0.0%	4.0%	0.0%
Men's Masquerade Hat	800	0.0%	0.0%	15.0%	0.0%
Men's Masquerade Mask	600	0.0%	0.0%	4.0%	0.0%
Men's Masquerade Shoes	400	0.0%	0.0%	5.0%	0.0%
Men's Masquerade Trousers	1000	0.0%	0.0%	12.0%	0.0%

WOMEN'S MASQUERADE SUIT

Like the male version of this masked costume, the Women's Masquerade Suit is received through story progression, provided you are playing as the princess.

PIECE	BASE VALUE	SILLINESS	SCARINESS	ATTRACTIVENESS	TRANSVESTISM (MALE)
Women's Masquerade Bodice	1200	0.0%	0.0%	12.0%	12.0%
Women's Masquerade Gloves	200	0.0%	0.0%	5.0%	4.0%
Women's Masquerade Hat	800	0.0%	0.0%	10.0%	10.0%
Women's Masquerade Mask	600	0.0%	0.0%	5.0%	5.0%
Women's Masquerade Shoes	400	0.0%	0.0%	5.0%	4.0%
Women's Masquerade Skirt	1000	0.0%	0.0%	12.0%	15.0%

AURORA MEN'S SUIT

PIECE	BASE VALUE	SILLINESS	SCARINESS	ATTRACTIVENESS	TRANSVESTISM (MALE)
Auroran Men's Bracers	80	0.0%	0.0%	1.0%	0.0%
Auroran Men's Hat	200	0.0%	0.0%	2.0%	0.0%
Auroran Men's Sandals	100	0.0%	0.0%	2.0%	0.0%
Auroran Men's Trousers	250	0.0%	0.0%	2.0%	0.0%
Auroran Men's Waistcoat	300	0.0%	0.0%	4.0%	0.0%

AURORA WOMEN'S SUIT

PIECE	BASE VALUE	SILLINESS	SCARINESS	ATTRACTIVENESS	TRANSVESTISM (MALE)
Auroran Women's Bodice	300	0.0%	0.0%	4.0%	6.0%
Auroran Women's Bracers	80	0.0%	0.0%	1.0%	2.0%
Auroran Women's Hat	200	0.0%	0.0%	2.0%	5.0%
Auroran Women's Skirt	250	0.0%	0.0%	2.0%	5.0%
Auroran Women's Slippers	100	0.0%	0.0%	1.0%	2.0%

MILITARY SUIT

Like the Chicken Suit, the Military Suit is genderless. There's only one set and both Hero and Heroine wear it equally well. Unlike the Chicken Suit, the Military Suit is not a joke. This set is not all found together; the trousers, jacket, and boots are found behind the Mourningwood Demon Door, while the gloves are found in the Reliquary.

PIECE	BASE VALUE	SILLINESS	SCARINESS	ATTRACTIVENESS	TRANSVESTISM (MALE)
Military Boots	250	0.0%	0.0%	2.0%	0.0%
Military Gloves	200	0.0%	0.0%	2.0%	0.0%
Military Jacket	750	0.0%	0.0%	6.0%	0.0%
Military Trousers	625	0.0%	0.0%	5.0%	0.0%

MEN'S MAGIC SUIT

Once Aurora is restored as a city, the Magic Suit can be purchased at the aptly-named Robes Are Us.

PIECE	BASE VALUE	SILLINESS	SCARINESS	ATTRACTIVENESS	TRANSVESTISM (MALE)
Men's Magic Boots	1800	0.0%	0.0%	4.0%	0.0%
Men's Magic Bracers	1440	0.0%	0.0%	4.0%	0.0%
Men's Magic Coat	5400	0.0%	0.0%	12.0%	0.0%
Men's Magic Hat	3600	0.0%	0.0%	10.0%	0.0%
Men's Magic Trousers	4500	0.0%	0.0%	10.0%	0.0%

WOMEN'S MAGIC SUIT

Like the Men's Magic Suit, the female version is available in Aurora later on…provided you help them recover!

PIECE	BASE VALUE	SILLINESS	SCARINESS	ATTRACTIVENESS	TRANSVESTISM (MALE)
Women's Magic Boots	1800	0.0%	0.0%	4.0%	2.0%
Women's Magic Bracers	1440	0.0%	0.0%	4.0%	2.0%
Women's Magic Coat	5400	0.0%	0.0%	12.0%	6.0%
Women's Magic Hat	3600	0.0%	0.0%	8.0%	5.0%
Women's Magic Skirt	4500	0.0%	0.0%	10.0%	4.0%

KING'S SUIT

PIECE	BASE VALUE	SILLINESS	SCARINESS	ATTRACTIVENESS	TRANSVESTISM (MALE)
King's Boots	5000	0.0%	0.0%	6.0%	0.0%
King's Crown	10000	0.0%	0.0%	15.0%	0.0%
King's Gloves	4000	0.0%	0.0%	6.0%	0.0%
King's Jacket	15000	0.0%	0.0%	18.0%	0.0%
King's Trousers	12500	0.0%	0.0%	15.0%	0.0%

QUEEN'S SUIT

PIECE	BASE VALUE	SILLINESS	SCARINESS	ATTRACTIVENESS	TRANSVESTISM (MALE)
Queen's Boots	5000	0.0%	0.0%	6.0%	4.0%
Queen's Crown	10000	0.0%	0.0%	15.0%	6.0%
Queen's Gloves	4000	0.0%	0.0%	6.0%	4.0%
Queen's Jacket	15000	0.0%	0.0%	18.0%	12.0%
Queen's Skirt	12500	0.0%	0.0%	15.0%	15.0%

A ROYAL CONUNDRUM

The **Fashion Victim** Achievement requires that you get almost every article of clothing in the game, no matter which gender you're playing as. This is no big deal for almost every outfit, as you can buy clothes for either sex in every clothing store, and you frequently find pieces of clothing as random rewards from treasure chests, dig spots, and so on. However, there is one outfit that you cannot get on your own, no matter what—the ruling outfit for the gender you aren't playing as! In order to complete your wardrobe and score the Gamer Points, you'll have to hook up with a friend on Xbox LIVE who is playing as whichever gender you aren't, and who has already acquired the ruling outfit in their game. If you already have every other outfit, just convince your friend to let you hold onto their kingly threads for just a second. If either the Queen's or King's Suit was the last bit of fashion you needed, the Achievement unlocks and you're all done with sartorial happenings in Albion! Of course, do return your friend's clothes; they can't get them any other way either!

COOK'S HAT

This is the only outfit that consists only of a single piece, and like the Military Suit and Chicken Suit, it's identical for both genders. You can receive this stylish hat from the cook in Bowerstone Castle later in the game. If you're lucky, you may find it in a chest or dig spot. However, it may be worth your while to befriend a cook in the castle once you're ruling, so that he/she gives you regular gifts. It may take some time, but you may eventually receive this as a gift.

PIECE	BASE VALUE	SILLINESS	SCARINESS	ATTRACTIVENESS	TRANSVESTISM (MALE)
Cook's Hat	400	5.0%	0.0%	1.0%	0.0%

HAIRSTYLES

A full head of hair is the literal capper to your ensemble. Hairstyles are most easily found in some of the stylist salons spread in a few towns across Albion. Just like with outfits, either men or women can rock any hairdo, though perhaps with mixed results in a few cases.

HAIR STYLISTS

SHOP NAME	LOCATION
Mustache Mansions (Stylist)	Brightwall Village
I'll Cut You (Stylist)	Bowerstone Market
Styles of Aurora (Stylist)	Aurora

STYLE	BASE VALUE	SILLINESS	SCARINESS	ATTRACTIVENESS (MALE)	TRANSVESTISM (MALE)	ATTRACTIVENESS (FEMALE)	TRANSVESTISM (FEMALE)
Short Wavy Hairstyle	250	0.0%	0.0%	10.0%	0.0%	10.0%	0.0%
Short Ponytail Hairstyle	250	0.0%	0.0%	7.5%	0.0%	7.5%	0.0%
Short Fringe Hairstyle	250	0.0%	0.0%	5.0%	0.0%	5.0%	0.0%
Warrior Stripe Hairstyle	250	0.0%	5.0%	-5.0%	0.0%	-5.0%	10.0%
Long Thick Hairstyle	250	4.0%	0.0%	4.0%	0.0%	4.0%	0.0%
Bald Dread Hairstyle	250	2.0%	0.0%	-5.0%	0.0%	-5.0%	5.0%
Bob Hairstyle	250	0.0%	0.0%	0.0%	5.0%	8.0%	0.0%
Long Hairstyle	250	0.0%	0.0%	0.0%	10.0%	4.0%	0.0%
Long Bun Hairstyle	250	0.0%	0.0%	0.0%	20.0%	12.0%	0.0%
Short Bun Hairstyle	250	0.0%	0.0%	0.0%	10.0%	10.0%	0.0%
Tied Bun Hairstyle	250	0.0%	0.0%	0.0%	10.0%	4.0%	0.0%
Short Parted Hairstyle	250	0.0%	0.0%	4.0%	0.0%	4.0%	0.0%

FACIAL HAIR

If you'd like, you can adorn your face with one of a few styles of beard. Even female Heroes can do this, though of course this enhances transvestism, which can confuse villagers in large quantities. Like hairstyles, grooming of facial hair is found in stylist salons.

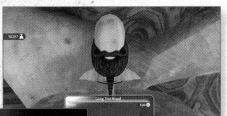

HAIR STYLISTS

SHOP NAME	LOCATION
Mustache Mansions (Stylist)	Brightwall Village
I'll Cut You (Stylist)	Bowerstone Market
Styles of Aurora (Stylist)	Aurora

STYLE	BASE VALUE	SILLINESS	SCARINESS	ATTRACTIVENESS (MALE)	TRANSVESTISM (MALE)	ATTRACTIVENESS (FEMALE)	TRANSVESTISM (FEMALE)
Standard Beard	200	4.0%	0.0%	0.0%	0.0%	0.0%	20.0%
Full Beard	200	0.0%	0.0%	5.0%	0.0%	5.0%	20.0%
Long Tied Beard	200	0.0%	0.0%	10.0%	0.0%	10.0%	20.0%
Mercenary Beard	500	0.0%	3.0%	-2.5%	0.0%	-2.5%	20.0%
Mutton Chops	200	0.0%	0.0%	5.0%	0.0%	5.0%	20.0%
Standard Moustache	200	0.0%	0.0%	7.5%	0.0%	7.5%	20.0%
Moustache and Goatee	200	0.0%	0.0%	5.0%	0.0%	5.0%	20.0%
Sideburns and Beard	200	0.0%	0.0%	10.0%	0.0%	10.0%	20.0%

MAKEUP

Makeup serves as a flipside to the facial hair coin. Both genders can sport it, but makeup tends to get males confused for females (though this is not true of all makeup). Makeup can be bought in shops on occasion, but also in the field wherever treasure is found.

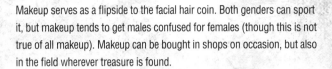

STYLE	BASE VALUE	SILLINESS	SCARINESS	ATTRACTIVENESS (MALE)	TRANSVESTISM (MALE)	ATTRACTIVENESS (FEMALE)	TRANSVESTISM (FEMALE)
Aristocrat Makeup	200	0.0%	0.0%	10.0%	0.0%	10.0%	0.0%
Noble Makeup	200	0.0%	0.0%	0.0%	5.0%	10.0%	0.0%
Enchanting Makeup	200	0.0%	0.0%	0.0%	5.0%	8.0%	0.0%
Eyes of the Beholder Makeup	200	0.0%	0.0%	0.0%	5.0%	8.0%	0.0%
Entertainer Makeup	200	0.0%	0.0%	0.0%	10.0%	4.0%	0.0%
Jewel Makeup	200	0.0%	0.0%	0.0%	10.0%	5.0%	0.0%
Goth Makeup	200	0.0%	1.0%	5.0%	0.0%	5.0%	0.0%
Dweller Makeup	200	0.0%	0.0%	2.5%	0.0%	2.5%	0.0%
Harlequin Makeup	200	0.0%	0.0%	5.0%	0.0%	5.0%	0.0%
Silent Type Makeup	200	0.0%	5.0%	0.0%	0.0%	0.0%	0.0%
World's Oldest Makeup	200	0.0%	0.0%	0.0%	5.0%	6.0%	0.0%
Exotic Makeup	200	0.0%	0.0%	2.0%	0.0%	2.0%	0.0%
Rosy Makeup	200	0.0%	0.0%	0.0%	5.0%	5.0%	0.0%
Mercenary Makeup	200	0.0%	4.0%	-2.0%	0.0%	-2.0%	0.0%
Renegade Makeup	200	0.0%	4.0%	2.0%	0.0%	2.0%	0.0%
Bandit Makeup	200	0.0%	4.0%	-2.0%	0.0%	-2.0%	0.0%
Inkblot Makeup	200	0.0%	8.0%	8.0%	0.0%	8.0%	0.0%
Traditional Makeup	200	0.0%	0.0%	0.0%	5.0%	4.0%	0.0%
Understated Makeup	200	0.0%	0.0%	0.0%	5.0%	5.0%	0.0%

TATTOOS

Tattoos are the final accessory you can use to complete your look. There are tattoo parlors in a few towns, and you can also find many tattoos in the wild. All tattoos add a little bit of attractiveness except the mercenary set of ink, which subtracts attractiveness while adding scariness. Your tattoos glow when charging a flourish or spell, but this may be hidden by clothing covering them. However, certain pieces of clothing also have tattoo-like patterns which glow only when charging flourishes or spells. They're normally invisible otherwise.

TATTOO PARLORS

SHOP NAME	LOCATION
Albion Ink (Tattooist)	Dweller Camp
Organic Ink (Tattooist)	Mourningwood
Tat's the Way to Do It! (Tattooist)	Bowerstone Market
Sketchy Tattoos (Tattooist)	Aurora

TATTOO	BASE VALUE	SILLINESS	SCARINESS	ATTRACTIVENESS (MALE)	TRANSVESTISM (MALE)	ATTRACTIVENESS (FEMALE)	TRANSVESTISM (FEMALE)
Auroran Back Tattoo	150	0.0%	0.0%	2.5%	0.0%	2.5%	0.0%
Auroran Chest Tattoo	150	0.0%	0.0%	2.5%	0.0%	2.5%	0.0%
Auroran Face Tattoo	150	0.0%	0.0%	2.5%	0.0%	2.5%	0.0%
Auroran Left Arm Tattoo	150	0.0%	0.0%	2.5%	0.0%	2.5%	0.0%
Auroran Left Leg Tattoo	150	0.0%	0.0%	2.5%	0.0%	2.5%	0.0%
Auroran Right Arm Tattoo	150	0.0%	0.0%	2.5%	0.0%	2.5%	0.0%
Auroran Right Leg Tattoo	150	0.0%	0.0%	2.5%	0.0%	2.5%	0.0%

TATTOO	BASE VALUE	SILLINESS	SCARINESS	ATTRACTIVENESS (MALE)	TRANSVESTISM (MALE)	ATTRACTIVENESS (FEMALE)	TRANSVESTISM (FEMALE)
Dweller Back Tattoo	150	0.0%	0.0%	2.5%	0.0%	2.5%	0.0%
Dweller Chest Tattoo	150	0.0%	0.0%	2.5%	0.0%	2.5%	0.0%
Dweller Face Tattoo	150	0.0%	0.0%	2.5%	0.0%	2.5%	0.0%
Dweller Left Arm Tattoo	150	0.0%	0.0%	2.5%	0.0%	2.5%	0.0%
Dweller Left Leg Tattoo	150	0.0%	0.0%	2.5%	0.0%	2.5%	0.0%
Dweller Right Arm Tattoo	150	0.0%	0.0%	2.5%	0.0%	2.5%	0.0%
Dweller Right Leg Tattoo	150	0.0%	0.0%	2.5%	0.0%	2.5%	0.0%

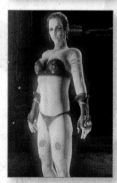

TATTOO	BASE VALUE	SILLINESS	SCARINESS	ATTRACTIVENESS (MALE)	TRANSVESTISM (MALE)	ATTRACTIVENESS (FEMALE)	TRANSVESTISM (FEMALE)
Guild Back Tattoo	150	0.0%	0.0%	2.5%	0.0%	2.5%	0.0%
Guild Chest Tattoo	150	0.0%	0.0%	2.5%	0.0%	2.5%	0.0%
Guild Face Tattoo	150	0.0%	0.0%	2.5%	0.0%	2.5%	0.0%
Guild Left Arm Tattoo	150	0.0%	0.0%	2.5%	0.0%	2.5%	0.0%
Guild Left Leg Tattoo	150	0.0%	0.0%	2.5%	0.0%	2.5%	0.0%
Guild Right Arm Tattoo	150	0.0%	0.0%	2.5%	0.0%	2.5%	0.0%
Guild Right Leg Tattoo	150	0.0%	0.0%	2.5%	0.0%	2.5%	0.0%

TATTOO	BASE VALUE	SILLINESS	SCARINESS	ATTRACTIVENESS (MALE)	TRANSVESTISM (MALE)	ATTRACTIVENESS (FEMALE)	TRANSVESTISM (FEMALE)
Mercenary Back Tattoo	150	0.0%	2.0%	-2.5%	0.0%	-2.5%	0.0%
Mercenary Chest Tattoo	150	0.0%	2.0%	-2.5%	0.0%	-2.5%	0.0%
Mercenary Face Tattoo	150	0.0%	4.0%	-4.0%	0.0%	-4.0%	0.0%
Mercenary Left Arm Tattoo	150	0.0%	2.0%	-2.5%	0.0%	-2.5%	0.0%
Mercenary Left Leg Tattoo	150	0.0%	2.0%	-2.5%	0.0%	-2.5%	0.0%
Mercenary Right Arm Tattoo	500	0.0%	2.0%	-2.5%	0.0%	-2.5%	0.0%
Mercenary Right Leg Tattoo	150	0.0%	2.0%	-2.5%	0.0%	-2.5%	0.0%

TATTOO	BASE VALUE	SILLINESS	SCARINESS	ATTRACTIVENESS (MALE)	TRANSVESTISM (MALE)	ATTRACTIVENESS (FEMALE)	TRANSVESTISM (FEMALE)
Nature Back Tattoo	150	0.0%	0.0%	2.5%	0.0%	2.5%	0.0%
Nature Chest Tattoo	150	0.0%	0.0%	2.5%	0.0%	2.5%	0.0%
Nature Face Tattoo	150	0.0%	0.0%	2.5%	0.0%	2.5%	0.0%
Nature Left Arm Tattoo	150	0.0%	0.0%	2.5%	0.0%	2.5%	0.0%
Nature Left Leg Tattoo	150	0.0%	0.0%	2.5%	0.0%	2.5%	0.0%
Nature Right Arm Tattoo	150	0.0%	0.0%	2.5%	0.0%	2.5%	0.0%
Nature Right Leg Tattoo	150	0.0%	0.0%	2.5%	0.0%	2.5%	0.0%

TATTOO	BASE VALUE	SILLINESS	SCARINESS	ATTRACTIVENESS (MALE)	TRANSVESTISM (MALE)	ATTRACTIVENESS (FEMALE)	TRANSVESTISM (FEMALE)
Old Kingdom Back Tattoo	150	0.0%	0.0%	2.5%	0.0%	2.5%	0.0%
Old Kingdom Chest Tattoo	150	0.0%	0.0%	2.5%	0.0%	2.5%	0.0%
Old Kingdom Face Tattoo	150	0.0%	0.0%	2.5%	0.0%	2.5%	0.0%
Old Kingdom Left Arm Tattoo	150	0.0%	0.0%	2.5%	0.0%	2.5%	0.0%
Old Kingdom Left Leg Tattoo	150	0.0%	0.0%	2.5%	0.0%	2.5%	0.0%
Old Kingdom Right Arm Tattoo	150	0.0%	0.0%	2.5%	0.0%	2.5%	0.0%
Old Kingdom Right Leg Tattoo	150	0.0%	0.0%	2.5%	0.0%	2.5%	0.0%

TATTOO	BASE VALUE	SILLINESS	SCARINESS	ATTRACTIVENESS (MALE)	TRANSVESTISM (MALE)	ATTRACTIVENESS (FEMALE)	TRANSVESTISM (FEMALE)
Royal Back Tattoo	150	0.0%	0.0%	2.5%	0.0%	2.5%	0.0%
Royal Chest Tattoo	150	0.0%	0.0%	2.5%	0.0%	2.5%	0.0%
Royal Face Tattoo	150	0.0%	0.0%	2.5%	0.0%	2.5%	0.0%
Royal Left Arm Tattoo	150	0.0%	0.0%	2.5%	0.0%	2.5%	0.0%
Royal Left Leg Tattoo	150	0.0%	0.0%	2.5%	0.0%	2.5%	0.0%
Royal Right Arm Tattoo	150	0.0%	0.0%	2.5%	0.0%	2.5%	0.0%
Royal Right Leg Tattoo	150	0.0%	0.0%	2.5%	0.0%	2.5%	0.0%

TATTOO	BASE VALUE	SILLINESS	SCARINESS	ATTRACTIVENESS (MALE)	TRANSVESTISM (MALE)	ATTRACTIVENESS (FEMALE)	TRANSVESTISM (FEMALE)
Scythe Back Tattoo	150	0.0%	0.0%	2.5%	0.0%	2.5%	0.0%
Scythe Chest Tattoo	150	0.0%	0.0%	2.5%	0.0%	2.5%	0.0%
Scythe Face Tattoo	150	0.0%	0.0%	2.5%	0.0%	2.5%	0.0%
Scythe Left Arm Tattoo	150	0.0%	0.0%	2.5%	0.0%	2.5%	0.0%
Scythe Left Leg Tattoo	150	0.0%	0.0%	2.5%	0.0%	2.5%	0.0%
Scythe Right Arm Tattoo	150	0.0%	0.0%	2.5%	0.0%	2.5%	0.0%
Scythe Right Leg Tattoo	150	0.0%	0.0%	2.5%	0.0%	2.5%	0.0%

TATTOO*	BASE VALUE	SILLINESS	SCARINESS	ATTRACTIVENESS (MALE)	TRANSVESTISM (MALE)	ATTRACTIVENESS (FEMALE)	TRANSVESTISM (FEMALE)
Balance Back Tattoo	150	0.0%	0.0%	2.5%	0.0%	2.5%	0.0%
Balance Chest Tattoo	150	0.0%	0.0%	2.5%	0.0%	2.5%	0.0%
Balance Left Arm Tattoo	150	0.0%	0.0%	2.5%	0.0%	2.5%	0.0%
Balance Left Leg Tattoo	150	0.0%	0.0%	2.5%	0.0%	2.5%	0.0%
Balance Right Arm Tattoo	150	0.0%	0.0%	2.5%	0.0%	2.5%	0.0%
Balance Right Leg Tattoo	150	0.0%	0.0%	2.5%	0.0%	2.5%	0.0%

Special tattoo available from retailer code.

TATTOO*	BASE VALUE	SILLINESS	SCARINESS	ATTRACTIVENESS (MALE)	TRANSVESTISM (MALE)	ATTRACTIVENESS (FEMALE)	TRANSVESTISM (FEMALE)
Dragonbreath Back Tattoo	150	0.0%	0.0%	2.5%	0.0%	2.5%	0.0%
Dragonbreath Chest Tattoo	150	0.0%	0.0%	2.5%	0.0%	2.5%	0.0%
Dragonbreath Left Arm Tattoo	150	0.0%	0.0%	2.5%	0.0%	2.5%	0.0%
Dragonbreath Left Leg Tattoo	150	0.0%	0.0%	2.5%	0.0%	2.5%	0.0%
Dragonbreath Right Arm Tattoo	150	0.0%	0.0%	2.5%	0.0%	2.5%	0.0%
Dragonbreath Right Leg Tattoo	150	0.0%	0.0%	2.5%	0.0%	2.5%	0.0%

Special tattoo available from retailer code.

TATTOO*	BASE VALUE	SILLINESS	SCARINESS	ATTRACTIVENESS (MALE)	TRANSVESTISM (MALE)	ATTRACTIVENESS (FEMALE)	TRANSVESTISM (FEMALE)
Crystal Back Tattoo	150	0.0%	0.0%	2.5%	0.0%	2.5%	0.0%
Crystal Chest Tattoo	150	0.0%	0.0%	2.5%	0.0%	2.5%	0.0%
Crystal Left Arm Tattoo	150	0.0%	0.0%	2.5%	0.0%	2.5%	0.0%
Crystal Left Leg Tattoo	150	0.0%	0.0%	2.5%	0.0%	2.5%	0.0%
Crystal Right Arm Tattoo	150	0.0%	0.0%	2.5%	0.0%	2.5%	0.0%
Crystal Right Leg Tattoo	150	0.0%	0.0%	2.5%	0.0%	2.5%	0.0%

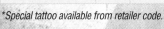

Special tattoo available from retailer code.

TATTOO*	BASE VALUE	SILLINESS	SCARINESS	ATTRACTIVENESS (MALE)	TRANSVESTISM (MALE)	ATTRACTIVENESS (FEMALE)	TRANSVESTISM (FEMALE)
Swirlwing Back Tattoo	150	0.0%	0.0%	2.5%	0.0%	2.5%	0.0%
Swirlwing Chest Tattoo	150	0.0%	0.0%	2.5%	0.0%	2.5%	0.0%
Swirlwing Face Tattoo	150	0.0%	0.0%	2.5%	0.0%	2.5%	0.0%
Swirlwing Left Arm Tattoo	150	0.0%	0.0%	2.5%	0.0%	2.5%	0.0%
Swirlwing Left Leg Tattoo	150	0.0%	0.0%	2.5%	0.0%	2.5%	0.0%
Swirlwing Right Arm Tattoo	150	0.0%	0.0%	2.5%	0.0%	2.5%	0.0%
Swirlwing Right Leg Tattoo	150	0.0%	0.0%	2.5%	0.0%	2.5%	0.0%

*Special tattoo available from retailer code.

TATTOO*	BASE VALUE	SILLINESS	SCARINESS	ATTRACTIVENESS (MALE)	TRANSVESTISM (MALE)	ATTRACTIVENESS (FEMALE)	TRANSVESTISM (FEMALE)
Industrial Back Tattoo	150	0.0%	0.0%	2.5%	0.0%	2.5%	0.0%
Industrial Chest Tattoo	150	0.0%	0.0%	2.5%	0.0%	2.5%	0.0%
Industrial Left Arm Tattoo	150	0.0%	0.0%	2.5%	0.0%	2.5%	0.0%
Industrial Left Leg Tattoo	150	0.0%	0.0%	2.5%	0.0%	2.5%	0.0%
Industrial Right Arm Tattoo	150	0.0%	0.0%	2.5%	0.0%	2.5%	0.0%
Industrial Right Leg Tattoo	150	0.0%	0.0%	2.5%	0.0%	2.5%	0.0%

*Special tattoo available from retailer code.

TATTOO*	BASE VALUE	SILLINESS	SCARINESS	ATTRACTIVENESS (MALE)	TRANSVESTISM (MALE)	ATTRACTIVENESS (FEMALE)	TRANSVESTISM (FEMALE)
Clockwork Back Tattoo	150	0.0%	0.0%	2.5%	0.0%	2.5%	0.0%
Clockwork Chest Tattoo	150	0.0%	0.0%	2.5%	0.0%	2.5%	0.0%
Clockwork Face Tattoo	150	0.0%	0.0%	2.5%	0.0%	2.5%	0.0%
Clockwork Left Arm Tattoo	150	0.0%	0.0%	2.5%	0.0%	2.5%	0.0%
Clockwork Left Leg Tattoo	150	0.0%	0.0%	2.5%	0.0%	2.5%	0.0%
Clockwork Right Arm Tattoo	150	0.0%	0.0%	2.5%	0.0%	2.5%	0.0%
Clockwork Right Leg Tattoo	150	0.0%	0.0%	2.5%	0.0%	2.5%	0.0%

*Special tattoo available from code in BradyGames Collector's Edition Fable III Strategy Guide.

ENEMIES OF ALBION

Enemies numerous and vile await you at every step of your journey toward the liberation of Albion. Some enemies, like bats and wolves, are simply beasts who follow their natural instincts to hunt and attack. You can't blame them, but then you also can't reason with them, either. Others, such as Logan's royal guards, are humans just like you, though, unfortunately, they've fallen into misguided servitude at the feet of a madman. Some people also choose to become opportunistic mercenaries, living in the wilderness and preying on the law-abiding masses. Still other foes are animated by little-understood spiritual forces, or are humanoid monsters seeking to be people, or are strange beings that hail from exotic lands across the sea. The only certainty with regards to these adversaries is that they will all meet their ends before your steel, your guns, and your spells.

You almost never fight only one adversary at a time. Learn to manage your position! Don't allow yourself to be surrounded—unless you're doing so on purpose, to unleash a hellacious weapon flourish or charged, area-of-effect spell.

Aside from the largest foes, like enemy leaders and balverines, most enemies can be knocked down with spells—like Vortex. From here, either your dog can finish them off, or you can stand astride them and press the X button for a killing blow while they're floored.

As is discussed in other sections of this guide, your primary stats are increased through combat. You'll receive some experience toward a given stat simply by dealing damage; experience doesn't just come from kills. But, of course, you receive a premium on experience for scoring a killing blow with a given type of attack. The strength stat is increased by using swords and hammers, while stature is augmented by using guns. Magical aura is improved, in case you haven't guessed, by using magic. As each stat increases so too will the damage of the attack type tied to that stat. But, again, while you don't have to kill with a given attack for experience, you must at least deal damage, so you can't simply stand somewhere safe and cast magic or whiff a particular type of attack over and over to increase your power. Increasing these stats also has a couple side effects: higher strength makes you more muscular, higher stature makes you taller, and higher magical aura causes you to glow while charging up flourishes and spells. Strength, stature, and magical aura are also the primary factors driving your hidden Hero Level. (Hero Level is also increased as you open more chests, thus unlocking or enhancing abilities, along the mystical Road to Rule.) You can't know your Hero Level for sure, but its function is critical; the higher your Hero Level, the fiercer the foes you'll meet. Of course, having an elevated Hero Level in the first place also means you'll be well-prepared to take on these tougher adversaries.

To maximize your damage output, focus on opening treasure chests within the Road to Rule that augment the combat skills you use most often, and have thus leveled up the most.

Towns are usually safe havens from hostile elements. The countryside, however, certainly is not. You'll run into groups of enemies just about everywhere. Which enemies you run into is random to a certain extent, though there are certain factors at play. Naturally, you'll find more hollow men underground, near graveyards, and at night, while mercenaries tend

Killing enemy leaders greatly weakens the group. However, if you'd like to farm experience (or bonuses on Legendary weapons) and let the leaders live, and kill their reappearing minions for as long as you like.

to roam wooded areas near roads, or congregate near the Mistpeak Mercenary Camp. (What a surprise, huh?) Beyond this, the actual makeup of the enemy forces you meet is driven by your Hero Level. At lower levels, you tend to run into disorganized groups which mainly consist of easily-dispatched lackeys. At higher Hero Levels, however, stronger enemies show up as well, and sometimes even enemy leaders take the field against you. They are much tougher than their toadies, and can often summon more servants to send after you at will. Once you start running into these tougher baddies, you should make it your mission to focus on them first. Taking out the leader not only prevents him or her from summoning more underlings, but it also utterly demoralizes the forces remaining, causing them to flee, or fight with diminished passion

Finally, be careful if you opt to just run past groups of enemies. They give chase, and just because you've triggered one group of enemies, that does not preclude triggering more. A careless run may result in dozens of foes of all kinds bearing down on you. The silver lining here is that different types of enemies may also fight each other in addition to you! Keep this in mind if you ever run from a group of, say, balverines and end up smack-dab in the middle of a mercenary ambush. Allow the groups to merge, then get out of the way, and you may find they do all the hard work for you.

ENEMY CATEGORIES

Foes are broken down into different categories based on their alignment, size, location, and general characteristics. These categories are important for unlocking bonuses on Legendary weapons. Several weapons require that you kill evil enemies for progress toward a bonus, for example. In this case, you'd have the option to kill hollow men, mercenaries, hobbes, balverines, and shadows for credit.

ENEMY CATEGORIES

EVIL ENEMIES
- Hollow Men
- Mercenaries
- Hobbes
- Balverines
- Shadows

UGLY ENEMIES
- Hollow Men
- Hobbes
- Balverines

LARGE ENEMIES
- Mercenary Commanders
- Hollow Men Summoners
- Balverines
- Balverine Sires
- Sentinels

AURORAN ENEMIES
- Sand Furies
- Shadows
- Minions
- Sentinels

HUMANOID ENEMIES
- Hobbes
- Mercenaries
- Soldiers

SHORTER ENEMIES
- Hobbes
- Minions

BATS AND CROWS

After a sheltered life within the walls of Bowerstone Castle, your first brush with the unfriendly elements of Albion occurs in the Catacombs beneath the castle. Here, swarms of bats will encircle and harangue you, along with your compatriots Walter and Jasper. Your newly-acquired Fireball spell gauntlet

proves more than adequate for dispatching the flying vermin without much fuss. Later on, as you encounter other swarms of flying creatures in other areas, the tune won't change much. There might be more of them as you increase in strength, but no matter; charge up a powerful area-of-effect spell to take out huge swaths of them at a time. Neither type of flying foe poses a serious threat.

POTENTIAL BAT AND CROW SPAWNS PER HERO LEVEL

HERO LEVEL	POTENTIAL FAMILIES		HERO LEVEL	POTENTIAL FAMILIES	
1	10x Bat	10x Crow	6	37x Bat	37x Crow
2	10x Bat	10x Crow	7	50x Bat	50x Crow
3	15x Bat	15x Crow	8	50x Bat	50x Crow
4	20x Bat	20x Crow	9	50x Bat	50x Crow
5	27x Bat	27x Crow	10	50x Bat	50x Crow

WOLVES

Like bats and crows, wolves are simply wildlife that doesn't coexist well with humans. Unlike your trusty, domesticated, four-legged companion, these feral canines are completely wild, and all you represent to them is a meal. They are a dangerous nuisance, but still just a nuisance; if you have trouble with wolves, that does not bode well for the

challenges the rest of the game has in store. A liberal application of your favorite type of attack is often enough to silence the yelping, snapping packs.

POTENTIAL WOLF SPAWNS PER HERO LEVEL

HERO LEVEL	POTENTIAL FAMILIES		
1	2x Wolf	-	-
2	5x Wolf	-	-
3	2x Wolf Elite, 4x Wolf	3x Wolf Elite, 1x Wolf	-
4	3x Wolf Elite, 8x Wolf	4x Wolf Elite, 4x Wolf	5x Wolf Elite
5	10x Wolf Elite	-	-
6	10x Wolf Elite	-	-
7	10x Wolf Elite	-	-
8	10x Wolf Elite	-	-
9	10x Wolf Elite	-	-
10	10x Wolf Elite	-	-

WEAPONS TO USE AGAINST WOLVES AND BALVERINES

	WEAPON NAME	LEGENDARY BONUS	OBJECTIVE	REWARD
SWORD	Wolfsbane	Lupinator	Kill 50 wolves or balverines.	+40% Damage vs Wolves and Balverines
HAMMER	Lunarium Pounder	Hunter	Kill 100 wolves or balverines.	+40% Damage vs Wolves and Balverines

WEAPONS THAT CAN DO EXTRA DAMAGE AGAINST NON-EVIL ENEMIES

WEAPON NAME		LEGENDARY BONUS	OBJECTIVE	REWARD
SWORD	Shardborne	Unholy	Decrease your moral standing.	+5 Extra Damage, +30% vs Non-Evil Enemies
PISTOL	Reaver Industries Perforator	Fiend	Decrease your moral standing.	+7 Extra Damage, +30% vs Non-Evil Enemies
RIFLE	Skorm's Justice	Demon	Decrease your moral standing.	+10 Extra Damage, +30% vs Non-Evil Enemies

WEAPONS THAT CAN HAVE DAMAGE BONUSES AGAINST HOLLOW MEN

WEAPON NAME		LEGENDARY BONUS	OBJECTIVE	REWARD
PISTOL	The Bonesmasher	Cleric	Kill 300 hollow men.	+7 Extra Damage, +80% vs Hollow Men
RIFLE	Swift Irregular	Determination	Kill 300 hollow men.	+5 Extra Damage, +80% vs Hollow Men

HOLLOW MEN

The first foes you'll face besides aerial pests are hollow men. These ancient bags of bones are reanimated and not too happy about it. As you might expect, though, being a dusty, creaking compendium of old fossils and armor is not the greatest prospect for durability, and most hollow men can be bashed apart without much effort. Sturdier, elite hollow men begin to show up later, boasting thicker armor and stronger weaponry. Hollow men capable of summoning can make your life miserable with a steady stream of lesser bone soldiers, so focus on these enemies if possible to avoid getting overrun.

POTENTIAL HOLLOW MEN SPAWNS PER HERO LEVEL

HERO LEVEL	POTENTIAL FAMILIES			
1	6x Melee, 2x Ranged	7x Melee, 1x Ranged	8x Melee	-
2	6x Melee, 2x Ranged	7x Melee, 1x Ranged	8x Melee	-
3	6x Melee, 2x Ranged	7x Melee, 1x Ranged	8x Melee	-
4	6x Melee, 4x Ranged, 2x Spellcaster	8x Melee, 1x Ranged, 2x Spellcaster	1x Summoner, 2x Melee	1x Summoner, 2x Ranged
5	1x Elite, 7x Melee, 4x Ranged, 2x Spellcaster	1x Elite, 9x Melee, 2x Ranged, 2x Spellcaster	1x Summoner, 10x Melee	1x Summoner, 6x Melee, 4x Ranged
6	2x Elite, 8x Melee, 4x Ranged, 3x Spellcaster	2x Elite, 10x Melee, 2x Ranged, 3x Spellcaster	1x Summoner 1x Elite, 12x Melee	1x Summoner, 1x Elite, 8x Melee, 4x Ranged
7	1x Spellcaster Elite, 1x Summoner Elite, 5x Elite, 4x Ranged, 2x Spell	1x Spellcaster Elite, 1x Summoner Elite, 5x Elite, 2x Melee, 2x Ranged, 2x Summoner	1x Spellcaster Elite, 1x Summoner Elite, 5x Elite, 4x Melee, 2x Summoner	-
8	2x Spellcaster Elite, 1x Summoner Elite, 6x Melee, 4x Ranged	2x Spellcaster Elite, 1x Summoner Elite, 7x Melee, 2x Ranged	2x Spellcaster Elite, 1x Summoner Elite, 8x Melee	-
9	3x Spellcaster Elite, 1x Summoner, 1x Summoner Elite, 2x Elite, 4x Ranged	3x Spellcaster Elite, 1x Summoner, 1x Summoner Elite, 4x Elite	-	-
10	3x Spellcaster Elite, 2x Summoner Elite, 2x Elite, 4x Ranged	3x Spellcaster Elite, 2x Summoner Elite, 4x Elite	-	-

WEAPONS FOR KILLING HOLLOW MEN

WEAPON NAME		LEGENDARY BONUS	OBJECTIVE	REWARD
SWORD	Avo's Lamentation	Holy Blast	Kill 200 hollow men.	+ Shock Damage
HAMMER	Hammer of Wilmageddon	Bonebreaker	Kill 150 hollow men.	+15 Extra Damage
PISTOL	The Bonesmasher	Cleric	Kill 300 hollow men.	+7 Extra Damage, +80% vs Hollow Men
RIFLE	Swift Irregular	Determination	Kill 300 hollow men.	+5 Extra Damage, +80% vs Hollow Men
RIFLE	The Shrieking Pilgrim	Sanctify	Kill 150 hollow men.	+ Shotgun Spray

MERCENARIES

Rebels aren't so bad. As the main character of the game, *you* are a rebel, after all! It has been said that willingness to dissent is a sign of a healthy political system. A mercenary is something different than a rebel, though. While rebels transgress against the state for a purported greater good, a mercenary has no ultimate cause except himself, and answers to no ideologies save money and survival. In Albion, mercenaries are based (insofar as they have a power structure at all) out of the Mercenary Camp at Mistpeak, but they can be found hiding in wait for passers-by throughout the land. They frequently spring an ambush, surrounding travelers and unleashing their assault. Mercenary groups do not eventually have summoners who spawn lesser helpers like some other enemy types, but instead they have mercenary leaders. These commanders are huge, hulking brutes with flaming fists for close-quarters combat, and firebombs for attacks from range. When a leader stomps after you while other mercenaries are also engaged, you'll be well-served to exercise great caution and dispatch him as quickly as possible. The Summon Creatures and Slow Time potions are invaluable in these instances, as are carefully-timed rolls to avoid their firebombs from afar. Few foes in Albion can inflict pain on you more carefully than a mercenary commander if you aren't careful.

POTENTIAL MERCENARY SPAWNS PER HERO LEVEL

HERO LEVEL	POTENTIAL FAMILIES				
1	4x Melee	3x Melee, 1x Ranged	2x Melee, 2x Ranged	-	-
2	4x Melee	3x Melee, 1x Ranged	2x Melee, 2x Ranged	-	-
3	5x Melee	3x Melee, 2x Ranged	3x Melee, 2x Ranged	-	-
4	2x Melee, 3x Ranged, 1x Melee Elite	3x Melee, 2x Ranged, 1x Melee Elite	1x Leader, 1x Melee Elite, 2x Melee	2x Melee Elite, 2x Melee	-
5	1x Leader, 2x Melee, 3x Ranged , 2x Melee Elite	1x Leader, 3x Melee, 2x Ranged, 2x Melee Elite	1x Leader, 2x Melee, 3x Ranged, 2x Melee Elite	1x Leader, 3x Elite	2x Melee Elite, 2x Elite
6	2x Leader, 2x Melee, 3x Ranged, 2x Elite	2x Leader, 3x Melee, 2x Ranged, 2x Elite	2x Leader, 4x Melee, 2x Elite	1x Leader, 1x Leader Elite, 2x Elite	1x Melee Elite, 3x Elite
7	1x Leader Elite, 4x Elite, 1x Melee, 3x Ranged	1x Leader Elite, 4x Elite, 3x Melee, 1x Ranged	1x Leader Elite, 4x Elite, 4x Ranged	1x Leader, 1x Leader Elite, 1x Elite, 1x Super Elite Melee	4x Elite
8	1x Leader Elite, 3x Elite, 1x Super Elite	2x Leader Elite, 1x Super Elite, 1x Super Elite Melee	5x Elite	-	-
9	1x Leader Elite, 2x Super Elite, 4x Elite	2x Leader Elite, 2x Super Elite Melee	-	-	-
10	1x Leader Elite, 2x Super Elite, 4x Elite	2x Leader Elite, 2x Super Elite Melee	-	-	-

WEAPONS TO USE WHILE KILLING MERCENARIES

WEAPON NAME		LEGENDARY BONUS	OBJECTIVE	REWARD
SWORD	The Merchant's Bodyguard	Profiteer	Kill 400 mercenaries.	+10 Extra Damage
RIFLE	Swift Irregular	Loyalty	Kill 300 mercenaries.	Earn Guild Seals Faster in Combat
RIFLE	The Equaliser	Vigilante	Kill 150 mercenaries.	+30% Damage vs Evil Human Enemies

WEAPONS TO USE WHEN KILLING HUMANS

	WEAPON NAME	LEGENDARY BONUS	OBJECTIVE	REWARD
SWORD	The Splade	Stabber	Kill 300 human enemies.	+10% Chance of Knockback vs Human Enemies
	Really Sharp Pair of Scissors	Artist	Kill 400 human enemies.	Gain Health With Each Hit

WEAPONS THAT CAN BOOST DAMAGE AGAINST EVIL ENEMIES

	WEAPON NAME	LEGENDARY BONUS	OBJECTIVE	REWARD
SWORD	Avo's Lamentation	Righteous	Increase your moral standing.	+20% Damage vs Evil Enemies
HAMMER	Aurora's Shield	Policeman	Drag 10 criminals to jail.	+30% Damage vs Evil Human Enemies
RIFLE	The Equaliser	Vigilante	Kill 150 mercenaries.	+30% Damage vs Evil Human Enemies
	The Shrieking Pilgrim	Righteous	Increase your moral standing.	+20% Damage vs Evil Human Enemies

WEAPON TO USE AGAINST EVIL ENEMIES

	WEAPON NAME	LEGENDARY BONUS	OBJECTIVE	REWARD
HAMMER	Scythe's Warhammer	Avenger	Kill 300 evil enemies.	+21 Extra Damage
PISTOL	Holy Vengeance	Avenger	Kill 200 evil enemies.	+ Shotgun Spray

HOBBES

These strange, squat creatures are humanoid, but they are not human. Fighting them has many similarities to fighting people, though. Initially, hobbe warriors attack with either melee or ranged weapons, just like mercenaries or guards. Eventually, however, you'll run into skilled hobbes casters who can either use magic, peppering you with fierce spell attacks from far away, or who can use their arcane powers to summon skeletal hobbes forth from the very earth. These boney hobbes, which are to hobbes what hollow men are to humans, occasionally show up as a brittle attack force all their own.

POTENTIAL HOBBES SPAWNS PER HERO LEVEL

HERO LEVEL	POTENTIAL FAMILIES				
1	3x Hobbe, 3x Sniper	5x Hobbe, 1x Sniper	3x Hobbe, 3x Sniper	4x Ambusher	1x Easy Elite, 2x Hobbe, 1x Sniper
2	3x Hobbe, 3x Sniper	5x Hobbe, 1x Sniper	3x Hobbe, 3x Sniper	4x Ambusher	1x Easy Elite, 2x Hobbe, 1x Sniper
3	3x Hobbe, 3x Sniper	5x Hobbe, 1x Sniper	3x Hobbe, 3x Sniper	4x Ambusher	1x Easy Elite, 2x Hobbe, 1x Sniper
4	1x Spellcaster, 2x Hobbe, 3x Sniper, 1x Easy Elite	1x Spellcaster, 4x Hobbe, 1x Sniper, 1x Easy Elite	1x Spellcaster, 2x Hobbe, 3x Sniper, 1x Easy Elite	1x Ambusher Elite, 4x Ambusher	3x Easy Elite, 1x Sniper Easy Elite
5	2x Spellcaster, 2x Easy Elite, 2x Hobbe, 1x Sniper Elite	2x Spellcaster, 2x Hobbe, 1x Elite, 2 Easy Elite	2x Spellcaster, 2x Hobbe, 1x Sniper Elite, 2x Elite	3x Ambusher Elite, 4x Ambusher	2x Easy Elite, 2x Elite
6	2x Elite, 2x Sniper Elite, 1x Spellcaster Elite, 1x Easy Elite	3x Elite, 1 Sniper Elite, 1x Spellcaster Elite, 1x Easy Elite	2x Elite, 2x Sniper Elite, 1x Spellcaster Elite, 1x Easy Elite	5x Ambusher Elite, 6x Ambusher	3x Elite, 1x Elite Sniper

POTENTIAL FAMILIES (continued)

HERO LEVEL	POTENTIAL FAMILIES				
7	1x Hobbe Boss, 2x Elite, 2x Sniper Elite, 1x Spellcaster Elite	1x Hobbe Boss, 3x Elite, 1x Sniper Elite, 1x Spellcaster Elite	1x Hobbe Boss, 2x Elite, 2x Sniper Elite, 1x Spellcaster Elite	1x Hobbe Boss, 2x Elite, 1x Elite Sniper	-
8	1x Hobbe Boss, 3x Elite, 3x Sniper Elite, 2x Spellcaster Elite	1x Hobbe Boss, 5x Elite, 1x Sniper Elite, 2x Spellcaster Elite	1x Hobbe Boss, 4x Elite, 2x Sniper Elite, 2x Spellcaster Elite	2x Hobbe Boss, 2x Elite	-
9	1x Hobbe Boss, 3x Elite, 3x Sniper Elite, 2x Spellcaster Elite	1x Hobbe Boss, 5x Elite, 1x Sniper Elite, 2x Spellcaster Elite	1x Hobbe Boss, 4x Elite, 2x Sniper Elite, 2x Spellcaster Elite	2x Hobbe Boss, 2x Elite	-
10	1x Hobbe Boss, 3x Elite, 3x Sniper Elite, 2x Spellcaster Elite	1x Hobbe Boss, 5x Elite, 1x Sniper Elite, 2x Spellcaster Elite	1x Hobbe Boss, 4x Elite, 2x Sniper Elite, 2x Spellcaster Elite	2x Hobbe Boss, 2x Elite	-

POTENTIAL SKELETAL HOBBES SPAWNS PER HERO LEVEL

HERO LEVEL	POTENTIAL FAMILIES	
1	10x Hobbe Skeleton	1x Spellcaster, 6x Hobbe Skeleton
2	10x Hobbe Skeleton	1x Spellcaster, 6x Hobbe Skeleton
3	10x Hobbe Skeleton	1x Spellcaster, 6x Hobbe Skeleton
4	10x Hobbe Skeleton	1x Spellcaster, 6x Hobbe Skeleton
5	20x Hobbe Skeleton	2x Spellcaster, 11x Hobbe Skeleton
6	4x Skeleton Elite, 12x Hobbe Skeleton	2x Spellcaster, 1x Spellcaster Elite, 10x Hobbe Skeleton, 2x Skeleton Elite
7	8x Skeleton Elite, 10x Hobbe Skeleton	2x Spellcaster Elite, 6x Skeleton Elite
8	20x Skeleton Elite	3x Spellcaster Elite, 2x Skeleton Elite
9	20x Skeleton Elite	3x Spellcaster Elite, 2x Skeleton Elite
10	20x Skeleton Elite	3x Spellcaster Elite, 2x Skeleton Elite

WEAPONS TO USE WHEN KILLING UGLY CREATURES

	WEAPON NAME	LEGENDARY BONUS	OBJECTIVE	REWARD
SWORD	Slimquick	Perfection	Kill 150 ugly creatures.	+12 Extra Damage
	The Casanova	Perfectionist	Kill 200 ugly enemies.	+12 Extra Damage

WEAPONS TO USE AGAINST SHORT ENEMIES

	WEAPON NAME	LEGENDARY BONUS	OBJECTIVE	REWARD
HAMMER	Mallett's Mallet	Bleurgh!	Kill 200 short enemies.	+15 Extra Damage
PISTOL	Gnomewrecker	Shortist	Kill 200 short enemies.	+30% Damage vs Short Enemies

WEAPONS THAT CAN DO EXTRA DAMAGE TO SHORT ENEMIES

	WEAPON NAME	LEGENDARY BONUS	OBJECTIVE	REWARD
PISTOL	Gnomewrecker	Shortist	Kill 200 short enemies.	+30% Damage vs Short Enemies

SAND FURIES

You first encounter these strange whirling dervishes while infiltrating Reaver's Manor in a masquerade outfit. Apparently Reaver has something of a collection of rare wildlife from all regions. Sand furies normally make their home in the deserts surrounding Aurora, and that is where you'll encounter them next. Furies attack quickly and mercilessly, and are capable of taking evasive action that is just as fast. They are so fast that you may find melee attacks less useful than usual, as sand furies often vacate the area you're attacking before you finish a swing. Keep moving, and focus on using firearms and spells to strike regardless of how rapidly sand furies move.

POTENTIAL SAND FURY SPAWNS PER HERO LEVEL

HERO LEVEL	POTENTIAL FAMILIES	HERO LEVEL	POTENTIAL FAMILIES
1	4x Sand Fury	6	4x Sand Fury
2	4x Sand Fury	7	1x Elite, 3x Sand Fury
3	4x Sand Fury	8	2x Elite, 3x Sand Fury
4	4x Sand Fury	9	4x Elite, 2x Sand Fury
5	4x Sand Fury	10	6x Elite

WEAPONS TO USE AGAINST ENEMIES NEAR AURORA

	WEAPON NAME	LEGENDARY BONUS	OBJECTIVE	REWARD
SWORD	Souldrinker	Shadow Drain	Kill 100 enemies found near Aurora.	30% Damage vs Human Enemies
HAMMER	Aurora's Shield	Protector	Kill 30 enemies found near Aurora.	+40% Damage vs Enemies Found Near Aurora
	Tannar's Glory	Defender	Kill 30 enemies found near Aurora.	+30% Damage vs Enemies Found Near Aurora
PISTOL	Desert Fury	Fury	Kill 30 enemies found near Aurora.	+30% Damage vs Enemies Found Near Aurora
RIFLE	The Marksman 500	Auroran Champion	Kill 100 enemies found near Aurora.	+30% Damage vs Enemies Found Near Aurora

WEAPONS THAT CAN DEAL EXTRA DAMAGE TO ENEMIES NEAR AURORA

	WEAPON NAME	LEGENDARY BONUS	OBJECTIVE	REWARD
HAMMER	Aurora's Shield	Protector	Kill 30 enemies found near Aurora.	+40% Damage vs Enemies Found Near Aurora
	Tannar's Glory	Defender	Kill 30 enemies found near Aurora.	+30% Damage vs Enemies Found Near Aurora
PISTOL	Desert Fury	Fury	Kill 30 enemies found near Aurora.	+30% Damage vs Enemies Found Near Aurora
RIFLE	The Marksman 500	Auroran Champion	Kill 100 enemies found near Aurora.	+30% Damage vs Enemies Found Near Aurora

BALVERINES

Like sand furies, these fearsome lupine monsters fight at Reaver's beck and call. You can also find them in Silverpines. Eventually, you'll find balverines in any wilderness where you once found only wolves, such as in Mistpeak Valley or around Millfields. Balverines share another similarity with sand furies in that they are incredibly fast, but they are far more dangerous as they combine blazing speed with the power of a mercenary commander. Balverines can slash over and over, with follow-up attacks strung together so seamlessly that you sometimes won't be able to get out of their flurries. They're also capable of lunging suddenly from a surprising distance.

Being overrun by balverines is perhaps the game's fastest path to suffering a knockout. Use extreme discretion; single or coupled balverines are more susceptible to melee strikes than sand furies, but any more than two balverines in front of you, and wading in with a melee weapon becomes awfully foolish. The normal solution to large groups of enemies—liberal application of Vortex—doesn't work on balverines unless you have unlocked several chests augmenting magic along the Road to Rule. Additionally, if you ever see a balverine jump straight up and out of the screen, roll away immediately! Remain in the same spot, and they will fall directly behind you with a brutal strike.

POTENTIAL BALVERINE SPAWNS PER HERO LEVEL

HERO LEVEL	POTENTIAL FAMILIES	
1	1x Balverine, 4x Wolf Elite	2x Balverine
2	1x Balverine, 4x Wolf Elite	2x Balverine
3	1x Balverine, 4x Wolf Elite	2x Balverine
4	1x Balverine, 4x Wolf Elite	2x Balverine
5	1x Balverine, 4x Wolf Elite	2x Balverine
6	2x Balverine, 4x Wolf Elite	3x Balverine
7	1x Blooded, 1x Balverine, 4x Wolf Elite	1x Blooded, 2x Balverine
8	2x Blooded, 1x Balverine, 4x Wolf Elite	2x Blooded, 2x Balverine
9	1x Sire, 2x Blooded, 4x Wolf Elite	1x Sire, 2x Blooded, 1x Balverine
10	1x Sire, 3x Blooded, 2x Balverine	

WEAPONS TO USE AGAINST WOLVES AND BALVERINES

	WEAPON NAME	LEGENDARY BONUS	OBJECTIVE	REWARD
SWORD	Wolfsbane	Lupinator	Kill 50 wolves or balverines.	+40% Damage vs Wolves and Balverines
HAMMER	Lunarium Pounder	Hunter	Kill 100 wolves or balverines.	+40% Damage vs Wolves and Balverines

WEAPONS THAT CAN DO EXTRA DAMAGE TO LARGE ENEMIES

	WEAPON NAME	LEGENDARY BONUS	OBJECTIVE	REWARD
HAMMER	Trollblight	Giantbane	Kill 10 large enemies with flourishes.	+80% Damage vs Large Enemies

ROYAL GUARDS

Logan's guards are stationed throughout the kingdom as police, essentially, and won't normally be aggressive toward you. If you engage in minor criminal activity and resist arrest, or if you engage in heavy criminal activity such as murder, this changes in a flash. Every guard in a town will swarm you to stop your transgressions. Of course, soldiers also treat you as the enemy during events that make it obvious you are a member of the rebellion. While it's a pity to put down good men who are merely serving a bad one, diplomacy is not an option.

POTENTIAL ROYAL GUARD SPAWNS PER HERO LEVEL

HERO LEVEL	POTENTIAL FAMILIES	HERO LEVEL	POTENTIAL FAMILIES
1	4x Soldier	6	5x Soldier, 1x Pistolier
2	4x Soldier	7	1x Elite, 4x Soldier, 1x Pistolier
3	4x Soldier	8	2x Elite, 3x Soldier, 1x Pistolier, 1x Grenadier
4	4x Soldier	9	4x Elite, 2x Soldier, 1x Pistolier, 1x Grenadier
5	4x Soldier	10	5x Elite, 2x Grenadier

WEAPONS THAT CAN HAVE DAMAGE BONUSES VERSUS HUMANS

WEAPON NAME		LEGENDARY BONUS	OBJECTIVE	REWARD
SWORD	The Splade	Stabber	Kill 300 human enemies.	+10% Chance of Knockback vs Human Enemies
	Beadle's Cutlass	Braggadocio	Complete 30 quests.	+30% Damage vs Human Enemies
	Souldrinker	Shadow Drain	Kill 100 enemies found near Aurora.	30% Damage vs Human Enemies
	Really Sharp Pair of Scissors	Surgeon	Kill 80 human enemies with flourishes.	+30% Damage vs Human Enemies
HAMMER	Dragonbone Hammer	Headsmacker	Kill 100 human enemies with flourishes.	Extra Knockdown vs Human Enemies
	Sorrow's Fist	Lovestruck	Kill 5 villagers who love you.	Extra Knockdown vs Human Enemies
	Jack's Hammer	Blademaster	Kill 50 villagers or soldiers with flourishes.	+30% Damage to Humans
RIFLE	The Marksman 500	Flourisher	Kill 50 human enemies with flourishes.	Extra Knockdown vs Human Enemies
	Simmon's Shotgun	Gulliver	Make yourself fatter.	+30% Damage vs Humans

WEAPON FOR KILLING VILLAGERS AND SOLDIERS

WEAPON NAME		LEGENDARY BONUS	OBJECTIVE	REWARD
SWORD	The Inquisitor	Bloodsucker	Kill 300 villagers or soldiers.	Gain Health Per Hit
HAMMER	Jack's Hammer	Murderer	Kill 100 villagers or soldiers.	+20 Extra Damage
PISTOL	Bloodcraver	Blood Drainer	Kill 300 villagers or soldiers.	Gain Health With Each Hit

MINIONS

In the faraway land of Aurora, among ancient and sprawling ruins, you'll encounter strange statues animated by dark forces. These are called minions, and they are similar to most melee-type combatants. Perhaps as a consequence of essentially being suits of metal armor given life by darkness, minions are particularly susceptible to the Shock spell, which incapacitates them. These beings are also easier to bash apart with swords and hammers than their clanking steel frames would seem to suggest.

WEAPONS THAT CAN ADD DAMAGE VERSUS DARK MINIONS AND SENTINELS

WEAPON NAME		LEGENDARY BONUS	OBJECTIVE	REWARD
HAMMER	Jack's Hammer	Shade	Kill 400 shadow creatures.	+30% Damage to Dark Minions and Sentinels

SHADOW FORCES

While King Logan's methods are unquestionably flawed, his reasoning specious, and his aims obtuse, he may be aware of something that the public at large is not. An ominous force may be forming that is so strong that it threatens the entire world, Albion included. An inky black legion, hell-bent on utter negation, and on the undoing of civilization itself is rising. The shadow swarm will first be stumbled upon in the appropriately-titled Shadelight Cavern, where swarms of smoky, fluid shadows rise up from the floor and take shape as horrifying, murderous, murmuring harbingers of chaos. What each distinct shadow lacks in fortitude, the whole mess of them makes up for in numbers, and it will be impossible to avoid being surrounded by the charcoal-tinted multitude.

Your weapons will decimate each shadow easily enough, but you will also want to rely on spells like Ice Storm to provide some extra cover. Ice Storm doesn't expressly home in on particular enemies, but that can actually work to your advantage. Unleash an area-of-effect Ice Storm and take refuge in the center of the maelstrom, letting the hail beat back the oncoming horde. However, it's not just shadows with which you'll have to contend. The darkness can also manifest as a far graver, more powerful attacker in the form of sentinels. These angels of death come cloaked, wielding scythes and casting powerful, wide-ranging magic. Give yourself a fighting chance by using your best weaponry and spells, and possibly by fighting shadows with shadows. Remember that the Summon Creatures potion grants you a powerful advantage by distracting nearly all enemies.

POTENTIAL SHADOW FORCE SPAWNS PER HERO LEVEL

HERO LEVEL	POTENTIAL FAMILIES			
1	2x Melee, 2x Ranged	4x Melee	1x Melee, 3x Ranged	1x Sentinel Easy
2	2x Melee, 2x Ranged	4x Melee	1x Melee, 3x Ranged	1x Sentinel Easy
3	2x Melee, 2x Ranged	4x Melee	1x Melee, 3x Ranged	1x Sentinel Easy
4	2x Melee, 2x Ranged	4x Melee	1x Melee, 3x Ranged	1x Sentinel Easy
5	2x Melee, 2x Ranged	4x Melee	1x Melee, 3x Ranged	1x Sentinel Easy
6	2x Melee, 2x Ranged	4x Melee	1x Melee, 3x Ranged	1x Sentinel Easy
7	3x Melee, 3x Ranged, 4x Shadow Mercenary	5x Melee, 1x Ranged, 4x Shadow Mercenary	1x Melee, 5x Ranged, 4x Shadow Mercenary	1x Sentinel Easy, 1x Melee, 1x Ranged
8	1x Sentinel	1x Sentinel Easy, 3x Melee, 2x Ranged	1x Sentinel Easy, 5x Melee	1x Sentinel Easy, 5x Ranged
9	1x Sentinel, 2x Melee, 2x Ranged	1x Sentinel, 4x Melee	1x Sentinel, 4x Ranged	-
10	1x Sentinel, 4x Melee, 4x Ranged	1x Sentinel, 8x Melee	1x Sentinel, 8x Ranged	-

WEAPON TO USE AGAINST SHADOW FORCES

WEAPON NAME		LEGENDARY BONUS	OBJECTIVE	REWARD
HAMMER	Jack's Hammer	Shade	Kill 400 shadow creatures.	+30% Damage to Dark Minions and Sentinels

WEAPONS THAT CAN ADD DAMAGE VERSUS DARK MINIONS AND SENTINELS

WEAPON NAME		LEGENDARY BONUS	OBJECTIVE	REWARD
HAMMER	Jack's Hammer	Shade	Kill 400 shadow creatures.	+30% Damage to Dark Minions and Sentinels

ACHIEVEMENTS & AVATAR AWARDS

Fable III is packed with 50 Achievements with a cumulative Gamer Score of 1000, as well as a number of unlockable

Avatar Awards that allow you to dress your Xbox Avatar with the latest in Albion fashion. The following pages contain

proven tactics for unlocking every Achievement and Avatar Award in the game. We've done our best to avoid spoiling any of the

story, but consider yourself warned. We strongly encourage you to get at least a couple of hours with the game before reading this

section. You won't miss out on any Achievements and you'll get to immerse yourself in the story without risk of spoilers.

SPOILER WARNING! SPOILER WARNING! SPOILER WARNING!

ACHIEVEMENTS

STORY PROGRESSION

7 Achievements with a cumulative Gamer Score of 280.

These seven Achievements are unlocked as you progress through the story. Descriptions and tips on how to unlock them are omitted to avoid the risk of spoilers. Follow along with "The Road to Rule" portion of this book and complete the main story to unlock them. Each of these Achievements is tied to unavoidable moments in the story. You cannot complete the game without unlocking each and every one of these Achievements.

ACHIEVEMENT ICON	ACHIEVEMENT NAME	GAMER POINTS
	The Guild Seal	10 pts
	And So It Begins	20 pts
	Swift Justice	20 pts
	The Resistance	50 pts

ACHIEVEMENT ICON	ACHIEVEMENT NAME	GAMER POINTS
	Distant Friends	20 pts
	The Ruler of Albion	80 pts
	For Albion!	80 pts

SIDE QUESTS AND STORY BONUSES

8 Achievements with a cumulative Gamer Score of 80.

 TRAGICAL-COMICAL-HISTORICAL   10 pts

Help the celebrated thespians Lambert and Pinch put on the world's greatest play.

Accept the quest **The Missing Play** at Brightwall Village and head to the rear of the Brightwall Academy to find the missing play. The spirit of the playwright pulls you into the book where you then  have to perform three plays in order to win your freedom. Put on each of the costumes when prompted and follow the on-screen instructions to impress the playwright and win your freedom—and a copy of the play. Give the play to the two thespians outside the Brightwall Academy to see it performed and unlock this Achievement. Detailed tactics for **The Missing Play** are found on page 70.

 GHOST BROTHERS   10 pts

Make sure Max and Sam get home in time for tea.

You can unlock this Achievement while earning Guild Seals to impress Page during the Bowerstone Resistance chapter. Accept and complete the quest  **Bored to Death** in Mourningwood to retrieve the ever-powerful Normanomicon for the brothers Sam and Max. Leave Mourningwood and return later when the **Gone But Not Forgotten** quest is available. Complete this quest to set things right with the brothers and their overbearing mother—and to unlock this Achievement, of course. Complete tactics for **Bored to Death** and **Gone But Not Forgotten** are found on pages 97 and 98, respectively.

SAVE THE PRINCESS! — 10 pts

Rescue the princess from the evil Baron.

Accept the quest **The Game** in Bowerstone Market and speak with the guys in robes inside the last house on the left, on the road leading to Bowerstone Old Quarter. These three men are what you might call role-playing fans. They've constructed an elaborate table-top board for their game and even wrote their own story for it. Now all they need is a Hero to act it out. Accept the orb to be shrunk into the size of a common miniature game piece and make your way through the brief story to save the princess and unlock this Achievement. Detailed tactics for **The Game** are found on page 102.

THE DARK SANCTUM — 10 pts

Reinstate an ancient, evil temple.

Reinstating the Dark Sanctum requires completion of multiple quests, beginning with the **Peace, Love, and Homicide** quest first available during the "Bowerstone Resistance" chapter. Complete the aforementioned quest, leave Mourningwood, then return to gain access beyond the fiery barrier sealing off the Dark Sanctum area. Enter the area beyond the barrier and speak to Lesley about the **Excavation** quest. Return later and enter the Dark Sanctum area to continue the thread of quests. Accept and complete **Awakening** and **Leverage** to finally open the Dark Sanctum and unlock this Achievement. Complete coverage of all four of these quests can be found in the "Bowerstone Resistance" chapter, beginning on page 89.

ISLAND PARADISE — 10 pts

Establish the island of Driftwood.

Driftwood is a coastal area located beyond the woods of Millfields. It is not readily available when you first begin exploring Albion. In order to access it you must first complete the **Restoration** quest in Millfields to have a bridge built. Return later and cross the bridge to the old gypsy camp and continue north to discover Driftwood. Once you've discovered Driftwood, accept and complete the **Pest Control** and **Gift Wood for Driftwood** quests. Leave the area to unlock the Achievement.

KNIGHT JUMPS CHESTY — 10 pts

Defeat Chesty at his own game.

Chesty, that lovable sadistic chest from *Fable II*, makes a return in *Fable III* and he wants to play chess. Visit the Sunset House area at night (if it's not night, simply leave and return) and approach the four ghostly statues in the cupola on the left of the lawn. Approach one of the statues and press the A button to interact with the statue four times, then move to the right and do the same for each of the other three statues. Interact with each of the four statues four times to cycle through their various poses to make the house atop the hill magically transform from a ghostly residence to a real thing of bricks and mortar.

Enter the Sunset House mansion, read the letter, and sleep in the bed to be transported to a life-sized chessboard in the garden. Speak to Chesty to initiate the chess game. Don't worry if you don't know how to play chess, as Chesty is going to cheat anyway. Play along until he suddenly lobs a bomb at your pieces and switches the rules; he much prefers to see you battle his chess pieces. Defeat each of the four waves of enemies to survive the game and unlock the Achievement.

KABOOM! — 10 pts

Score 2000 on the Mourningwood Fort mortar game.

Return to Mourningwood after meeting Page in the Sewers and purchase Mourningwood Fort for roughly 45,000 gold. Once purchased, head up onto the upper walkway and interact with the mortar to initiate the **Mortar and Mourning** mini-game. Jammy reappears from beyond the grave and you have 200 seconds to kill as many hollow men as possible. Each hollow man is worth 10 points and you need to score 2000 points to win the top prize—a legendary weapon! Focus your attention on large groups of hollow men, preferably while they are still spawning to ensure a direct hit before they split up. It only takes three seconds to ready another shot so keep firing at all times. Pan back and forth in sweeping semi-circular motions and keep firing! It's better to fire on a single hollow man than to pass over it and fire no shot at all. This plays exactly like the scene during "The Hollow Legion" part of the story. You are free to play the mini-game as many times as you'd like. After all, it's your fort!

TOUGH LOVE | 10 pts

Save the maximum amount of Albion citizens.

Unlocking this Achievement requires you to save all 6.5 million Albion citizens during the Weight of the World portion of the story. This requires accumulating over 6.5 million gold in the treasury, as there is a 1:1 ratio of gold to citizens saved. There are a number of ways to go about accumulating the gold, but you can extend the amount of time you need to accomplish this by delaying your return to the throne room come time to pass rulings. Spend that extra time accumulating vast quantities of gold by spending time in other Heroes' worlds and by owning all of the expensive shops in Albion (see the "Real Estate Magnate" chapter of this book for details). Another quick way to increase your gold reserves is to unlock the Demon Door in Sunset House after becoming Ruler of Albion; the chest behind that Demon Door contains 1,000,000 gold. Taking work as a blacksmith, pie maker, or lute player is also a great way to earn gold quickly. Each of these techniques increases your personal wealth which, by using the ledger in either the Sanctuary or the Treasury room, can be transferred to the Treasury. Of course, the easiest way to save all of the citizens is to reduce the amount of gold you need to add to the treasury in the first place. You can do this by making the hard, unpopular decisions that don't cost the kingdom any gold leading up to the invasion. You may have to break some promises, but doing so may save a lot of lives.

COMBAT

11 ACHIEVEMENTS WITH A CUMULATIVE GAMER SCORE OF 240.

 TOTAL WARRIOR | 10 pts

Kill enemies with melee, ranged, and spell attacks.

Jasper calls you back to the Sanctuary early on during your quest to present to you several of the Hero weapons your parent—and former Hero—had left behind. Weapons come in three styles: melee, ranged, and spell. Kill an enemy using either the sword or hammer to get the melee kill; the rifle or pistol to earn the ranged kill; and any of the magic gauntlets to earn the required spell attack. You receive your first gauntlet during a visit to the Road to Rule. Kill at least one enemy with each weapon type to unlock this Achievement.

 SPELLWEAVER | 5 pts

Combine two gauntlets to cast a "woven" spell.

This is an Achievement that takes a little time to get, but only because the Spell Weaving ability is reserved for those who persist in their journey along the Road to Rule. You visit the Road to Rule many times, but this ability is not available until after surviving an unexpected journey through a certain hobbe-infested cave. Spend your Guild Seals to unlock the Spell Weaving ability then return to the Sanctuary and select a combination of two different gauntlets. Cast them both simultaneously with this powerful new ability to unlock the Achievement.

 PULL! | 10 pts

Send an enemy flying into the air and kill him while he's airborne.

There are many ways to knock an enemy into the air, depending on the power of your attack and relative strength, size, and vulnerability of the enemy. The easiest way, however, is to catch an enemy inside a powerful Vortex spell then open fire on him with your pistol or rifle as he flies around the room in circles. It's also possible to knock enemies into the air with a melee attack or even a powerful rifle shot. Fire again with your ranged weapon to kill him while he's airborne to unlock the Achievement.

ARCHMAGE | 20 pts

Cast all 15 possible spell combinations.

This Achievement is all about getting you to experiment with each of the different spell weaving combinations. Follow along with the main story through the gathering of allies and become the ruler of Albion. This unlocks all of the segments of the Road to Rule needed to purchase the Spell Weaving ability and each of the Gauntlets: Fireball, Shock, Vortex, Ice Storm, Force Push, and Blades. Now visit the weapon room in the Sanctuary and equip one of the 15 combinations of Gauntlets, exit the Sanctuary and cast the spell, then return and swap them for another set. Follow the suggested pattern in the list below to ensure you attempt each of the 15 combinations.

Fireball + Shock, Vortex, Ice Storm, Force Push, and Blades.
Shock + Vortex, Ice Storm, Force Push, and Blades.
Vortex + Ice Storm, Force Push, and Blades.
Ice Storm + Force Push and Blades
Force Push + Blades

GUNNING FOR GLORY | 20 pts

Kill 500 enemies using firearms.

This Achievement is unlocked by making use of your pistols and rifles in combat. 500 enemies may sound like a lot, but even with a well-balanced battle plan that incorporates all three disciplines, you can still unlock this Achievement by the time you leave Reaver's masquerade party. A great way to rack up ranged kills is to equip the Bonesmasher pistol and use it exclusively during your time in Mourningwood and whenever you travel to The Reliquary. The Bonesmasher is devastating against hollow men and these locations are filled with them.

 ## IF IT BLEEDS, WE CAN KILL IT | 20 pts

Kill 500 enemies using melee weapons.

As with the **Gunning for Glory** Achievement, this one can also be unlocked before you even leave Reaver's masquerade party without any special focus on melee attacks. One way to accumulating a wealth of melee kills is to use a powerful hammer such as Scythe's Warhammer or Trollblight and use it to deal the fatal blow to numerous enemies after weakening them with area-of-effect attacks. Cast a low level magic attack to soften up the enemies then rush in and finish them off with the melee weapon.

 ## WIZARD'S REVENGE | 20 pts

Kill 500 enemies using magic.

Magical attacks make it possible to inflict damage on large numbers of enemies simultaneously. The ability to weave two different spells together for added damage increases the chance of delivering mass casualties to enemies. Using charged area-of-effect attacks against lesser enemies is a great way to increase your kill count. The Vortex spell is particularly useful in that it can smash enemies against walls and other objects. Force Push is great for narrow ledges, as you can gain kills by pushing enemies off.

 ## SUPER HERO | 50 pts

Fully upgrade your Melee, Ranged, and Magic abilities on the Road to Rule.

You begin the game with what amounts to Level 0 melee, ranged, and magic abilities. Unlock this Achievement by purchasing all five upgrades for each, at the total cost of a whopping 900 Guild Seals! There are countless ways to earn Guild Seals, but completing as many side-quests as you can, using weapons with an improved ability to generate Guild Seals in combat, and interacting with villagers is a great way to gain them. The following table provides a breakdown for when each new attack upgrade can be purchased along the Road to Rule. All three attack styles can be upgraded at the same point along the Road to Rule.

LEVEL UPGRADE	GUILD SEALS	STORY POINT
1	20	After finding the Music Box.
2	40	Following the battle with Saker.
3	60	Defeat the hollow men at Mourningwood Fort.
4	80	Make a promise to Page.
5	100	Following your first decision as Ruler.

 ## YOU CAN'T BRING ME DOWN | 50 pts

Complete Fable III without being knocked out in combat.

Do you have what it takes to survive the entire story and see the credits roll without getting knocked out even once? That's what you must do to unlock this Achievement. Fortunately, it's not as difficult as it sounds. There are a few things you can do to make your eternal survival that much more likely. For starters, always carry at least four Health Potions and don't hesitate to use them as soon as the edges of the screen start to turn red. The more Health Potions you carry, the more prudent you can be while consuming them. Another tactic to keep yourself alive is to try to remain as far away from enemies as possible. Most do not have powerful ranged attacks and you can often get the jump on them by using your ranged weaponry and targeted magic attacks. Along those same lines, always look for barrels to shoot—one well-aimed bullet can defeat multiple enemies! Lastly, take your time and be as thorough as possible. The more side-quests you complete and Guild Seals you earn, the sooner you can fully upgrade your attacks and the stronger you'll be. The game naturally advances in difficulty as the Hero gains experience, but you can keep ahead of the curve by fully upgrading your melee, ranged, and magic attack abilities at every first opportunity.

MY WEAPON'S BETTER THAN YOURS | 25 pts

Complete 3 unique upgrades on one of the legendary weapons found around Albion.

Finding a new legendary weapon is always an exciting moment, especially given the random system that governs what weapon you get—you just never know! Whenever you get a new legendary weapon, immediately press the Start button, then left on the D-Pad to go to the weapon room. Find the weapon on its respective rack and inspect the upgrade requirements to find a weapon that suits your playing style best. Each weapon can receive three unique upgrades, but the requirements for these upgrades vary quite substantially from one to the next (see the "Weapons of Yore" chapter for details). The one thing each legendary weapon has in common is that earning all three upgrades tends to be time consuming. Though the never-ending sandbox that exists after the story is completed makes it possible to play forever, we recommend committing to upgrading one or two weapons during the "Bowerstone Resistance" portion of the story. This gives you plenty of time to not only earn all three upgrades, but hopefully have the fully-upgraded weapon in time to use it against the game's toughest foes!

BARREL OF LAUGHS | 10 pts

Kill 30 enemies with explosive barrels.

Many of the areas in which you'll be fighting contain red explosive barrels. These barrels are often positioned in close proximity to walls of sandbags and other enemy defenses. Target these barrels with your rifle or pistol when enemies are nearby to detonate the barrel and instantly kill the nearby enemies. You can often kill two or more enemies with a single barrel explosion by timing your shots well. There are more than enough barrels to accumulate the required 30 kills, but there are a few areas where you can really pad your stats. Look for barrels in the following areas: The Hole, Mercenary Camp, and Bowerstone Old Quarter (Battle for Albion).

BEING SOCIAL

12 Achievements with a cumulative Gamer Score of 145.

HE'S A WOMAN. SHE'S A MAN. | 5 pts

Wear a full set of clothing intended for the opposite sex.

This Achievement simply requires that you dress in a complete outfit designed for the opposite sex. The easiest way to accomplish this is to accept the quest **The Missing Play** in Brightwall Village. You have to don three separate costumes during this quest: a woman's outfit, a chicken suit, and a man's outfit. You unlock this Achievement whether you're playing as a prince or princess. Of course, you could also just purchase an outfit designed for the other sex from one of the many clothing shops in Albion. Purchase the outfit then return to the Sanctuary's dressing room and put on the entire outfit to unlock the Achievement.

HAND IN HAND | 5 pts

Hold hands with someone.

One of the new mechanics in *Fable III* is the act of holding hands with another person. You must hold a character's hand to lead (or drag) them with you where you are going. You are introduced to this new feature in the early moments of the game, during the Life in the Castle portion of the story. This is the first Achievement you unlock.

CORONATION CHICKEN | 10 pts

Perform a royal judgment while dressed as a chicken.

You have plenty of opportunities to stop by the Sanctuary and slip into the Chicken Suit (acquired during the **Chicken Chaser** quest in the Leaders and Followers portion of the story) on your way to the throne room. There are five scheduled days that you'll have to sit on the throne and rule on various matters. Wear the Chicken Suit to the throne room and rule on any issue to unlock the Achievement.

DYE HIPPIE, DYE 5 pts

Dye each part of an outfit you're wearing a different color and have long hair.

Purchase a dye pack that has five different colors (or two smaller dye packs) along the Road to Rule and head to the clothing room in the Sanctuary to turn each article in your outfit a different color. Dye the pieces of clothing marked as head, upper body main, hands, lower body main, and feet. Now you only need to find the long hairstyle. Hairstyles are most often found in dig spots and unlocked chests. Another way to receive hairstyles is to befriend Stylists and receive them as a gift. This is particularly common after you become Ruler (provided you are well liked). The long hair cut is the default hairstyle for female players. Men can purchase the long thick hairstyle from the stylist in Brightwall Village.

LUTE HERO TOUR 10 pts

Play in each town as a 5-star lute player.

The first step in unlocking this Achievement is to become a Level 5 lute player. This is done by unlocking each of the lute playing upgrades on the Road to Rule. You begin life as a Level 1 lute player, but must spend a total of 100 Guild Seals unlocking the lute playing skill upgrades. You needn't purchase all four chests in order; you can purchase just the Level 5 upgrade for 100 Guild Seals if you so desire. The Level 5 lute upgrade becomes available on the Road to Rule immediately after meeting Page in the Sewers. Once you have the appropriate skill level, all you have to do is play one bar of music without missing a note in each of four different towns: Aurora, Brightwall Village, Bowerstone Market, and Dweller Camp.

TOUCHED BY A HERO 10 pts

Use touch expressions to interact with 20 different people.

Albion is a living, breathing land inhabited by over six million people. Though you won't see all of them, you will encounter countless villagers during your travels. Stop and interact with any of them by pressing the A button then perform an expression that touches the other villager—dance and pat-a-cake are two common ones. That's all it takes to get credit towards this Achievement. Perform either of these actions with 20 different people to unlock this bonus.

POPULARITY CONTEST 15 pts

Make 20 friends.

There are two ways to go about unlocking this Achievement. Those wanting to unlock the maximum number of Achievements as quickly as possible can make friends the old-fashioned way: perform expressions to get a person to like you, then complete the quest they offer to earn their friendship. You can do this early in the game and earn quite a few Guild Seals in the process.

REMODELING 10 pts

Remodel 5 different houses by changing the furniture.

The first step to unlocking this Achievement is to own five properties, either houses or caravans. You can accomplish this via the map table by selecting a settlement and using the magnifying glass to inspect a property for purchase. Now you need to visit each property in person to decorate it. The easiest way to do this is to fast travel directly to one of your properties, go inside, and press Up on the D-Pad to have Jasper auto-decorate the house by changing the rugs, wall decorations, and furniture with items from your inventory. You must have at least one valid item in your inventory to get credit for remodeling the house. Furniture items are often found in dig spots, unlocked chests, and received as gifts. You can also purchase high-dollar pieces of furniture at shops throughout Albion. Adding nice furniture and accessories to a home increases its value and the amount of rent you collect.

MAGNATE PERSONALITY — 50 pts

Build a property empire worth 2,000,000 gold.

This Achievement is going to take some time to unlock, so it's best to get a jump on it early on. The goal is to accumulate a collection of properties (wagons, houses, stalls, shops, and pubs) worth a total of 2,000,000 gold. The value of the homes and shops in your possession goes up over time as life improves for the villagers and your efforts raise the quality of life in the town so it pays to buy early on while prices are low. The value of the properties also increases as you improve the decorations and furnishings within the houses and wagons. These increases in value do affect your total property empire, but not enough to truly reduce the number of properties you must purchase. Purchase a few stalls early on to begin generating revenue while you're out questing. This gives you enough money to purchase the more lucrative stores and pubs sooner rather than later. Buying and renting out houses is also a good source of rent, but you have to invest some of that money back into the house in the form of maintenance otherwise your tenants will move out. Pawnbrokers and taverns are your top revenue sources—and also among the most expensive buildings to own. Save up for one or two early on then use the proceeds to purchase valuable houses to push yourself over the threshold and unlock the Achievement.

CRIME SPREE — 10 pts

Get a 15,000 gold bounty placed on your head.

Even if you live life in Albion as a sort of sociopathic warmongering barbarian, striking down anything or anyone that's even mildly displeasing, you still might not reach the lofty heights of a bounty past 15,000 gold. That's fine, though—you don't need to walk a dark path at all. You just need to save your game, then travel to a heavily populated area. Something like Brightwall Village is ideal. OK, ready? Draw a weapon, turn off safety, and start killing everyone indiscriminately. When you thin out a given area, move elsewhere in the same city. By the time you've cycled through previously-depopulated areas, new townspeople will be milling about. Of course, this kind of activity doesn't go unnoticed, and guards inevitably attempt to stop your spree. Resist arrest and take them out, too. After about 10 to 20 minutes of outright slaughter, your bounty should be high enough to nab this Achievement. Afterward, simply reload your last saved game. Unless wanton mayhem was your goal anyway, of course, in which case carry on, then.

HENRY VIII — 10 pts

As ruler of Albion, get married 6 times and kill 2 of your spouses.

This is a straightforward Achievement to unlock and though you need not be married to six different people simultaneously, it does add some good entertainment, especially if you have them live next to one another! Purchase five (plus the castle) houses or caravans and kick out any tenants that may be living in them. Acquire a half dozen pieces of jewelry so you have gifts to give and find six villagers who are of a compatible sexuality and who are already friends with you. Being friends isn't necessary, but it does save you from having to befriend them first. Seduce each of these potential spouses with positive expressions, then ask them to marry you. Select a house and assign your spouse to it. Now pick two of your spouses and kill them. Don't forget to turn the safety off.

ADOPT OR DIE — 5 pts

Adopt a child.

Visit the orphanage and select a child to adopt. There's a small fee involved, but this is a way for even single, unwed Rulers to start a family. Assign the child to your spouse's home or select an unoccupied house you own to place the child. A nanny is hired at the rate of 25 gold per cycle if no spouse is present.

TREASURE AND COLLECTIBLES

8 Achievements with a cumulative Gamer Score of 215.

BRIGHTWALL BOOK CLUB — 30 pts

Collect all 30 rare books for the Brightwall Academy.

Accept the **The Pen is Mightier…** quest in Brightwall Village after meeting Page in the Sewers to learn about the rare books scattered across Albion. These books are often difficult to find, given their size and tendency to be located off the beaten path. Consult the maps in the "Albion Atlas" portion of this book for the locations of all 30 books. For every five books you return to the Brightwall Academy, Samuel offers you a special quest to find one of five rare books. These books are linked to specific quests that must be accepted in order to find the given book—these books do not exist in the world outside of these quests. The following table lists the number of books found in each area.

BOOKS BY AREA

AREA NAME	DISCOVERABLE BOOKS	QUEST-ONLY BOOKS	AREA NAME	DISCOVERABLE BOOKS	QUEST-ONLY BOOKS
Aurora City	2	-	Millfields	1	-
Bowerstone Castle	1	-	Mistpeak Valley	1	-
Bowerstone Industrial	1	-	Mourningwood	1	1
Bowerstone Market	2	-	Ossuary	1	-
Bowerstone Old Quarter	1	1	Reaver's Manor	1	-
Brightwall Village	3	-	Reliquary	2	1
Cesspools	1	-	Sandfall Palace	1	-
Chillbreath Caverns	1	1	Shifting Sands	-	1
Dankwater Cavern	1	-	Silverpines	1	-
Driftwood	1	-	Sunset House	1	-
Dweller Camp	1	-			

I AM THE KEYMASTER — 30 pts

Collect all 50 Silver Keys and 4 Gold Keys.

It wouldn't be *Fable* without 50 Silver Keys to collect, but now there are 4 Gold Keys as well! These are scattered across Albion (and Aurora) and require some thorough searching in order to find them. You absolutely must venture away from the glowing trail if you are to ever find even half of the keys! Fortunately, you have two helpful resources at your disposal. For starters, the map table inside the Sanctuary (and war room in the Castle) can be used to see how many keys are in a given area. Move the magnifying glass over a settlement to view a table of collectibles. The numbers listed here also account for any sub-areas that may be within that settlement too. For example, the data on the map table for Mistpeak Valley also includes collectibles found within Chillbreath Caverns and The Hole. Use this information to narrow your search then turn to the "Albion Atlas" portion of this book for detailed descriptions of where all 54 keys are, including complete guides to each of the four Gold Keys. Unlike Silver Keys, Gold Keys can typically only be found after solving an elaborate puzzle.

FLOWER POWER — 30 pts

Collect all 30 Auroran flowers.

Return to the City of Aurora after retrieving the Desert Star diamond and accept the **Temple's Treasure** quest. This quest requires you to find 30 Auroran Flower Blooms, five of six different colors: Red, Green, Orange, Purple, Blue, and Yellow. The 30 flowers are scattered throughout the areas of Aurora City, Shifting Sands, Sandfall Palace, The Veiled Path, and The Enigma. The flowers are not quite as difficult to find as many of the other collectibles and your dog does an excellent job of sniffing many of them out, so long as his exploration level is 3 or higher. Each and every flower has been marked on the appropriate maps in this book. The following table details the breakdown of which flowers are located in each area.

AURORAN FLOWER BLOOM DISTRIBUTION

AREA	GREEN	RED	BLUE	PURPLE	ORANGE	YELLOW
City of Aurora	1	0	1	1	1	1
Shifting Sands	0	0	1	2	2	2
Sandfall Palace	2	2	1	0	0	0
The Veiled Path	1	2	2	2	2	2
The Enigma	1	1	0	0	0	0

GNOME INVASION — 30 pts

Destroy all 50 gnomes.

Return to Brightwall Village after defeating Saker at the Mercenary Camp and accept the **Gnomes are Great!** quest. Retrieve the gargoyle statue for Brian, leave the area, then return and accept the **Gnomes are Evil!** quest. This quest requires that you search all over Albion (and Aurora) for 50 missing gnomes. You'll locate the first gnome as part of the quest's introduction—enter Brian's house and shoot the gnome on the wall. Finding the other 49 won't be nearly as easy. Fortunately, the gnomes are extremely mean and love nothing more than to hurl insulting and hurtful commentary at you whenever you are near. Keep your ears open for the sound of a gnome's mockery, then immediately search the nearby area. Move in the direction of the sound, hold the Left Bumper to pan around in first-person view, then shoot the gnome once you locate it. Once shot, the gnome automatically returns to Brian in Brightwall Village. As with the keys, you can consult the map table in the Sanctuary to track how many gnomes are still unaccounted for in each settlement. These settlements also include the sub-areas within them. We've marked each and every gnome location on the maps in the "Albion Atlas" portion of the guide and also include screenshots and descriptions for finding every one of them. Find all 50 to gain some rather special prizes, as well as this impressive Achievement.

DIGGER — 15 pts

Dig up 50 items.

Every area in the game contains a number of invisible dig spots. Listen for your dog's bark and follow him to a nearby dig spot. Wait for him to start digging, then press the A button to use your shovel (automatically equipped) and dig up whatever is there. Each dig spot is linked to a particular exploration level. Find and purchase dog training books that improve your dog's exploration rating to locate higher level dig spots. Your dog can detect all dig spots at and below his current exploration level so improving the exploration rating significantly increases the number of dig spots your dog detects. That said, you can still unlock this Achievement without increasing the dog's exploration level so long as you venture off the beaten path and don't pass up any digging opportunities. Consult the maps in the "Albion Atlas" for every dig spot location and its corresponding dig level.

Collect all 50 legendary weapons. They won't all appear in your world, so trade with other Heroes!

Apart from the 4 Hero weapons acquired more or less immediately, there are 51 Legendary weapons to collect as well. Since only 30 of them can be found on any one given playthrough, you'll have to get by with a little help from your friends to snag them all. You see, everyone's distinct world has a slightly different mix of available weaponry. This is actually based on your save game, so you can create a new save game to collect different weapons. Stock up on the weapons you can find in your world, before heading online to barter with other players. The following table provides a checklist of all 51 Legendary Weapons.

LEGENDARY WEAPONS CHECKLIST

SWORDS	HAMMERS	PISTOLS	RIFLES
Avo's Lamentation	Aurora's Shield	The Barnumificator	Arkwright's Flintlock
Beadle's Cutlass	Dragonbone Hammer	Bloodcraver	Defender of the Faith
The Casanova	Faerie Hammer of the Moon King	The Bonesmasher	The Equaliser
The Love Sword	Hammer of Wilmageddon	Briar's Blaster	Facemelter
The Merchant's Bodyguard	Jack's Hammer	Chickenbane	The Hero's Companion
Mr Stabby	Lunarium Pounder	Desert Fury	Marksman 500
Really Sharp Pair of Scissors	Mallett's Mallet	Dragonstomper .48	Ol' Malice
Slimquick	Scythe's Warhammer	Gnomewrecker	The Sandgoose
Souldrinker	Sorrow's Fist	Holy Vengeance	Scattershot
The Splade	Tannar's Glory	The Ice Maiden	The Shrieking Pilgrim
The Swinging Sword	The Tenderiser	Mirian's Mutilator	Simmons's Shotgun
Thunderblade	Trollblight	Reaver Industries Perforator	Skorm's Justice
	The TYPO	Tee Killer Shooter	Swift Irregular

FASHION VICTIM | 20 pts

Collect every item of clothing.

This Achievement is pretty straightforward—nab all the clothes. There are 25 outfits in the game. You receive most of the outfits for the gender you pick by playing through the game normally, but this Achievement requires *every* piece of clothing—so whether or not you're interested in cross-dressing, you still have to stock for it. The military suit for the gender you select comes from appeasing a Demon Door. The rest of the outfits are found in a variety of places. Some are available in shops, from tailors. The rest are discovered in random gifts, treasure chests, dig spots, and furniture.

It's possible to find every outfit on your own except one—the ruling suit for whichever gender you're not playing as. In order to snag the Achievement, you'll have to get a player over Xbox LIVE to let you hold their royal vestments, via gift or trade. If that was the only suit you're missing, the Achievement should unlock. Then, you can give your online friend back their kingly clothes—there's only one set per playthrough, after all!

OUTFIT CHECKLIST

- Men's Pyjama Suit
- Women's Pyjama Suit
- Elegant Prince Suit
- Elegant Princess Suit
- Practical Prince Suit
- Practical Princess Suit
- Dweller Men's Suit
- Dweller Women's Suit
- Men's Mercenary Suit
- Women's Mercenary Suit
- Chicken Suit
- Men's Masquerade Suit
- Women's Masquerade Suit
- Men's Highwayman Suit
- Women's Highwayman Suit
- Men's Warrior Suit
- Women's Warrior Suit
- Men's Magic Suit
- Women's Magic Suit
- Cook's Hat
- Military Suit
- King's Suit
- Queen's Suit

CHEST GRANDMASTER | 40 pts

Unlock all of the chests on the Road to Rule.

This is an Achievement that you can unlock during the Weight of the World portion of the story if you are *extremely* thorough. Otherwise you need to invest additional time in the endgame portion to get the requisite Guild Seals. Acquiring the wealth of Guild Seals needed to purchase every upgrade and ability along the Road to Rule requires you to complete most, if not all, of the side-quests that present themselves during the course of the game. You can gain additional Guild Seals by interacting with villagers, befriending them, and performing expressions for them. It's also important to not shy away from combat. You can earn a lot of Guild Seals in combat (especially with a weapon that generates additional Guild Seals during combat) and "farming" Mourningwood, Mistpeak Valley, and Shifting Sands for additional Guild Seals is a great way to earn extras. Visit the Road to Rule any time you desire by stepping into the light within the main room of the Sanctuary. Remember to travel back to the beginning of the Road to Rule to make sure you didn't miss any early chests.

XBOX LIVE PLAY

4 ACHIEVEMENTS WITH A CUMULATIVE GAMER SCORE OF 40.

LONG DISTANCE RELATIONSHIP | 10 pts

Get married to another Xbox LIVE player.

Join another player's game on Xbox LIVE (see user's manual for details) and ask him/her to marry you (you must have a family home you can move to). You can also unlock this Achievement by being the one who is proposed to, so long as you agree to marry the other player (don't worry, you can divorce them anytime you want). You are free to marry a player of either sex—the residents of Albion enjoy life in a progressive society.

CROSS-DIMENSIONAL CONCEPTION | 10 pts

Have a child with another Xbox LIVE player.

Follow the tips for **Long Distance Relationship** to marry another player on Xbox LIVE then join your spouse near a bed and agree to have unprotected sex. Unlike the marriage Achievement, this one does require players of the opposite sex. Though you can adopt a child from the Bowerstone Shelter and Orphanage, doing so does not unlock this Achievement.

ONLINE MERGER | 10 pts

Enter into a business partnership with another Xbox LIVE player.

To get this achievement, you must enter a business partnership with another Xbox LIVE player. This can be done by having another player join your game or join their game. Once in game, interact with the player and press the left bumper to propose a business partnership. Once both players accept the partnership, the achievement unlocks for both players. Business partnerships allow the client to buy property in the Host's world and you also share gold (just like marriage) so you have to be careful with whom you make a business partnership with.

WE CAN BE HEROES | 10 pts

Earn 1,000 gold in Henchman wages in another Hero's world.

Join another player in their world over Xbox LIVE and accumulate over 1,000 gold before leaving. This can be done in any number of ways, but the easiest way is to take up a job as a lute player, blacksmith, or pie maker. You can also earn gold by finding chests, completing quests, or by purchasing a shop or rental property. Lastly, you earn a wealth of gold for every five minutes you spend in another Hero's world so just sit tight and watch the money roll in!

AVATAR AWARDS

Unlocking specific Achievements tied to the main story also earns you special props and articles of clothing for your Xbox Avatar. Complete the main story to unlock each of these special *Fable III* Avatar Awards!

ACHIEVEMENT	AVATAR AWARD	SEX	TYPE	ICON
Swift Justice	Royal Trousers	Male/Female	Clothing	
The Resistance	Royal Shirt	Male/Female	Clothing	
And So it Begins	Royal Boots	Male/Female	Clothing	
The Ruler of Albion	Crown	Unisex	Hat	

OFFICIAL STRATEGY GUIDE

Written by Doug Walsh & Joe Epstein

DK/BradyGames, a division of Penguin Group (USA) Inc.
800 East 96th Street, 3rd Floor
Indianapolis, IN 46240

ISBN-10: 0-7440-1224-4

ISBN-13: 978-0-7440-1224-8

UPC Code: 7-52073-01224-3

Printing Code: The rightmost double-digit number is the year of the book's printing; the rightmost single-digit number is the number of the book's printing. For example, 10-1 shows that the first printing of the book occurred in 2010.

13 12 11 10 4 3 2 1

Printed in the USA.

BRADYGAMES STAFF

Global Strategy Guide Publisher **MIKE DEGLER**

Editor-In-Chief **H. LEIGH DAVIS**

Operations Manager **STACEY BEHELER**

Digital & Trade Category Publisher **BRIAN SALIBA**

CREDITS

Title Managers **CHRISTIAN SUMNER • TIM COX**

Lead Designer **CAROL STAMILE**

Designers **TIM AMRHEIN • AREVA • JULIE CLARK**

Map Illustrations **ARGOSY PUBLISHING**

DOUG WALSH'S ACKNOWLEDGEMENT

This long-awaited return to Albion was quite the pleasure thanks to the excellent team I had around me. It's always great to work with Joe Epstein, my co-author, and this project was no exception. The crew at BradyGames did another fantastic job crafting our text into a polished collectible product. Special thanks to our project editor Christian Sumner, designers Carol Stamile and Areva Ragle for the great work. I'd also like to thank Leigh Davis of BradyGames for assigning me this project. The Fable series is one of my favorites and getting to write the guidebooks for the two latest installments is something I'm really proud of. Lastly, I want to thank Chris James and Kevin Erickson of Microsoft Game Studios for their outstanding assistance and support throughout this project. It truly was a pleasure to work with both of you! Thank you all so much!

JOE EPSTEIN'S ACKNOWLEDGEMENT

To begin, I've been playing Peter Molyneux's games since Populous. The great designers, like Fumito Ueda with Ico and its spiritual successors, or Will Wright with the Sim series, or Sid Meier and Civilization or Gabe Newell's teams at Valve (and on, and on! I have to stop this list somewhere!), always try a little harder, always make you think. Mr. Molyneux and Lionhead are no different. Since their maiden voyage with Black and White they've continued a tradition of turning genre conventions on their head and producing unique, memorable content. Fable III manages to impart the difficulties of being a leader like few games have, and few games have even bothered to try. I hope you enjoy playing Fable III as much as we enjoyed working on this guide, and I hope this guide adds to that enjoyment.

Unfortunately, these books don't write themselves. Well, I suppose that's actually good, as the opportunity gives a lot of people work. Just a couple names are listed as authors, but that doesn't begin to describe the team that assembles these things, which are always fivefold more work than you'd guess. Thanks to Chris James, Kevin Erickson, and everyone at Microsoft Game Studios for their invaluable assistance throughout the project. Thanks to Leigh Davis for the opportunities and guidance, and to Christian Sumner for the editorial vision and leniency (thanks for having a baby mid-project! If only every editor could do that, makes things much easier!). Thanks to Carole Stamile and Areva Ragle for the pretty pictures under duress. Thanks to Doug Walsh — We've written, I don't know, a half-dozen or so books together at this point, and it's always a pleasure. In addition to being my most frequent guide writing partner, he and his wife Kristen have done as much as anyone to help me integrate into the Pacific northwest, as an expatriate of sunny south Texas. That's quite a gear change, so: Thanks, y'all. And thanks to Mia Vo, who keeps me sane, and who gives me entirely too little crap about staying up all night for weeks toiling on vidyagame books. Sorry, babe! And sorry to anyone I'm forgetting. I owe you...um...a copy of the Fable III guide? (BradyGames: please send copies of the Fable III guide!) Finally, congratulations to my sister Katie Raubs né Epstein! So happy to see you happy, sis! Perhaps as a gift for your nuptials you and Rusty would like some Fable III guides...?

BRADYGAMES ACKNOWLEDGEMENT

Fable has become one of those properties that I can't wait to begin working on. My thoughts race as soon as I hear that another Fable title is on the schedule. Granted, as a gamer I can't wait to dig into the game and 100% it. However, as an editor, I have the unique position of being able to meet and work with some truly amazing folks. Without exception, everyone at Microsoft and Lionhead fall into that category. There was quite a team involved on this project and I'd like to thank them all. Thanks to Andrea Roberts, Patrick Perkins, Mark Smart, Jeremie Texier, John McCormack, JC Taylor, Jerome Hagen, and Mike Green. Chris James and Kevin Erikson worked tirelessly to bring this guide to light. Rich Bryant, the masterful wordsmith, pitched in and truly made this book something special. Jennifer Clixby, Mike McCarthy, and Emrah Elmasli were instrumental in creating, gathering, and providing the beautiful art in the guide. Of course, thanks much to Gareth Sutcliffe, the New Zealander with the plan, who came in with an open mind and was on-board from the get-go.